Somebody Scream!

Somebody SCREAM!

Rap Music's Rise to Prominence in the Aftershock of Black Power

MARCUS REEVES

Faber and Faber, Inc.

An affiliate of Farrar, Straus and Giroux

New York

Faber and Faber, Inc.
An affiliate of Farrar, Straus and Giroux
18 West 18th Street, New York 10011

Library of Congress Cataloging-in-Publication Data
Reeves, Marcus, 1969–
    Somebody scream! : rap music's rise to prominence in the aftershock of black
power / by Marcus Reeves.— 1st ed.
        p.   cm.
    Includes bibliographical references (p.   ) and index.
    ISBN-13: 978-0-571-21140-1 (hardcover : alk. paper)
    ISBN-10: 0-571-21140-2 (hardcover : alk. paper)
    1. Rap (Music)—History and criticism.   I. Title.

ML3531.R44 2008
782.42164909—dc22

                                                        2007036129

Designed by Jonathan D. Lippincott

www.fsgbooks.com

10   9   8   7   6   5   4   3   2   1

To my wife, Ronke Idowu Reeves, the love and sun of my life, whose love, wisdom, and patience contributed immensely to this work

And to the memory of my mother, Jean Reeves

Contents

Introduction

Rap music and black power. People have been making
the link between the two for years. But to anyone who has witnessed
the evolution of commercial rap music since the release of "Rapper's
Delight" and "King Tim III" in 1979, an in-depth exploration of rap's
rise in the aftershock of black power would have been appropriate
twenty years ago. That's when rap and black nationalism were being
merged, purposely, by rap artists like Rakim and the group Public Enemy. But rap had only been on the national airwaves for close to a
decade, and we would soon discover that that was just one of many developments within a music—rap, the poetry, and hip-hop music, its big
beat accompaniment—born of urban decay in the South Bronx. (The
catalyst for the community-based cultural movement rap sprang from,
hip-hop, was a response, author Jeff Chang would later write, "to the
politics of abandonment and containment.") Rap was still testing its
artistic, philosophical, and commercial boundaries, figuring out the
limits between *honestly* "representin' " its core audience and chasing the
almighty dollar. Time for such observations wouldn't come until after
rap had reached the new millennium, a few years after it had hit its
commercial apex, solidifying itself as a bankable art—a part of a bankable hip-hop culture—and as the popular voice of America's black,
brown, and white underclass. (Those huddled masses yearning to
breathe free and, one day, be rich enough to drive off in a Bentley.)

As rap had generated that much heat, it was natural that the genesis for this book began during a summer heat wave. It was a 90-plus-
degree day in August 2001, two weeks before 9/11, and I sat in
Brooklyn's Jay Street subway station. Staring at the newsstand kiosk, I
was struck by the covers of *The Source* and *Vibe*. They sat next to each
other in the neon-lit display window, and both covers sported an image

of rap's hardcore king, DMX, the heir apparent to Tupac Shakur. At first I was amused by the realization that, although one magazine displayed a photo and the other a colorfully expressionistic painting, the two rival publications in essence had the same cover. Then I found myself escaping the discomfort of the oppressive heat by thinking deeply about how folks—especially black and brown people—loved DMX. And I don't mean just his music or his showmanship, but DMX *the man*, and what he represented: an authentic, rebellious, avenging spirit articulating the angst, anger, joys, trials, struggles, cold-blooded ruthlessness, and brash confidence of his environment. Or, as many hip-hop heads (thug and non-thug) call it, "the streets."

The previous night, I had been watching MTV's celebrity-insider show *Diary*, featuring the MC. Aside from the usual footage of the artist cracking jokes and having fun (and conflicts) with his entourage, the most revealing segment was DMX's show at Howard University in Washington, D.C. The fervor with which people responded to him, young black women crying as if he were a thug Jesus Christ and young black men intensely mouthing his lyrics—absorbing his hardcore persona as if he had *the answer*—showed DMX was a mouth for a voiceless segment of society. More a leader, so to speak, than a mere pop star. Granted, I'd already been aware of X's allure, having interviewed him shortly before the release of his 1998 CD *It's Dark and Hell Is Hot.* But the sight of DMX casting his spell over that audience stuck in my head and, when I saw the magazine covers, turned over in my mind until the thoughts avalanched into a larger, broader idea. (Having such moments had become a habit since I'd begun my journalism career in the early 1990s, writing about hip-hop culture and politics for magazines like *The Source* and *The College Entertainment Revue*.)

Sitting in that heat, I began mentally charting rap music's rise to prominence through its icons. I also began mapping the evolution of the MC's role, from nuevo entertainer to cultural/racial spokesperson and sociopolitical lightning rod for black America after the demise of the black power movement. That struggle, having been a part of black popular culture until the mid-1970s, was black America's final collective push toward progress, self-determination, and self-expression, especially for its urban underclass denizens. (Thus my concept for periodically referring in this book to black America, heading into the days after that revolution, as post–black power America.) It was toward the end of black power that hip-hop culture—breaking, graffiti, DJing, and rap music—formed in the South Bronx, reshaping African-American culture for a new, emerging generation, a post–black power generation. And within the void left by the struggle's end, particularly the disappearance of grassroots advocacy on behalf of the young and the poor, rap music and the MC—especially the hardcore rap star—emerged in the early 1980s as the chief articulator of black urban life. This book developed with my understanding that, as Amiri Baraka (né LeRoi Jones) wrote in *Blues People*, "each phase of the Negro's music [is] issued directly from the dictates of his social and psychological environment."

And in the years following the struggle for black empowerment, that musical expression, as many acknowledge, was the poetry of rap recited to the beat of hip-hop music. It was the vehicle providing hope and a future for so many MCs like DMX, an ex-con and former stickup kid, to rap their inner thoughts and, inevitably, use those words to affirm the struggles of their fans. The only difference, though, between now and when I was, ahem, younger (having the same catharsis from the Furious Five and Run-D.M.C. and Public Enemy) was now rap music was a major force within American pop culture. It had become a billion-dollar business, outselling country music. Lauryn Hill had swept the Grammy Awards with five wins in 1999, and the headline "HIP-HOP NATION" graced the cover of *Time* magazine. Meanwhile on MTV, the hardcore MC was in video rotation as much as his/her rock music counterpart, and 75 percent of all rap music was being purchased by white consumers. For all intents and purposes, rap music had arrived. But it had also grown rougher since I was younger, as MC after MC, encouraged by the fact that black thugness was rap's biggest appeal to a pop (read: white) audience, marketed and sold their gangland music and backgrounds—fabricated or not—as "real hip-hop." (More than poetic and verbal dexterity, which was the case in my day.) Despite how much a mainstream juggernaut rap music and its thug fascination had become, the music was still the unmitigated voice of young black and brown folks, talking loud and telling their story.

The map of that journey I'd taken in my head solidified into this book, covering hip-hop culture and rap music's emergence from the death of black power, moving from New York–based art form to commercial music revolution to unifying expression for a post–black power generation and, eventually, the world. At its crux, this journey is an observation—in the old style of "New Journalism," you might say—of the hardcore MC's ascent out of rap music's commercialization, becoming the prototypical "man/woman of the people." The signposts for this historical metamorphosis over thirty years are the icons of the music, the poets who epitomized, revolutionized, and transformed their particular era—in other words, the artists who were at the forefront of the various movements within rap music, and whose artistry, image, and music most embodied the social, political, and economic moments that called them to success. Comprised of my personal accounts as a music journalist—having interviewed several of the artists—and as a fan and member of the post–black power generation—having observed and been impacted by the same events that shaped the culture, the music, and the people—the essays in this book are as much a personal journey as they are a professional one. I no longer have the love or connection to rap music I once had; every hip-hop fan has a moment when, for them, the music kicked the bucket. But I do, as a writer whose career (and adolescence) was inspired by hip-hop, have a deep need to keep folks' eyes on the music's legacy. (Especially at a time when the average cash-focused rap artist doesn't give a shit about history or culture or integrity.)

Now that the music is firmly embedded in American popular culture, the purpose of this book is to put rap's journey into a sociohistorical perspective, one that looks beyond the controversies currently engulfing the genre—the foul language, violence, misogynistic lyrics, the corporate manipulation—to critically examine rap and its pioneers holistically. It's a story that couldn't be written without including the tale of a black generation whose story the music told. It's the revision of their dreams that made the music speak, and it was their perseverance, by any means necessary, that keeps rap music relevant and evolving. So despite what views folks may have about the direction, or lack thereof, of rap or rappers, this book will help readers see the genre for what it is: a hard-rock vessel carrying the hopes, anger, disappointments, attitude, and history of post–black power America.

Somebody Scream!

ONE

Generation Remixed
Post-nationalism and the Black Culture Shuffle

Hip-hop emerged because nothing had changed since the '60s.
—Sonia Sanchez

A final goal should be to prevent the long-range growth of militant black nationalist organizations especially among the youth.
—FBI Counterintelligence Program memo

Whoa! What's that?" I asked Uncle William. In the spring of 1975, a business card with a black panther on it caught my six-year-old eyes. It was exposed through the cardholder of my uncle's wallet as he searched for the usual dollar penance one pays a young nephew upon an occasional visit. After I'd gotten the money, I asked to hold the wallet and immediately extracted the card for a look. Next to the panther, seemingly about to jump from the matte paper and pounce, were the boldfaced words "Black Panther Party." I thought it was a gang (it sounded like one) because I vaguely remembered adults mentioning something about Black Panthers in quick, hushed tones. When I asked my uncle who the Panthers were, his brown bearded face broke into a mischievous smile. "Why don't you go ask your mother?" he said. Instantly, I whirled around and ran into the kitchen, card in hand.

"What's the Black Panthers?" I greeted my mother, holding the card up to her face. Once she'd gotten a look at what I was holding and understood what she was being asked—to explain the aftermath of the black power movement—the expression on her face morphed into shock and anger. It was as if I'd discovered something I wasn't supposed to, some deep, beaten-down secret freshly buried in a grave.

"Who gave you that?" she scolded, snatching the card out of my hand. After I explained that I had gotten it from William and inquired, again, who the Panthers were (from her response, I could see these dudes were *bad*, and from that moment my interest was piqued), my mother looked at me and twisted her mouth. "Don't worry about who they are. They were a bunch of damn bank robbers!" she responded before storming out of the kitchen and into my room where my uncle was sitting, laughing to himself. I could hear her yelling at him, "Don't start telling that boy about that Panther mess!"

Obviously, I couldn't understand my mother's dismay over a business card or a question about the Panthers, nor was I going to find out why she was so upset. So, shrugging off the curiosity, I proceeded to the living room to join millions of post–black power babies (later to be known as the Hip-Hop Generation) in watching and absorbing the phenomenon of *Soul Train*, the hippest trip in America. (Later in life, I learned that my mother responded as she did partly because of how close Panther *super-baaaadness* had been to our family. Four years earlier, my cousin's father, Iverson Burnett—a former Black Panther—had been a defendant in the trial of the Panther 21, a group of Panthers arrested and charged with conspiracy to blow up buildings in New York.) But the main reason for my mother's response—like that of so many black folks who'd lived through the civil rights and black power heyday and were trying to move on—was merely a sign of the times. It was more of a disconnect between black baby boomers' now fractured quest for the promised land (many had gone in with placards and guns and came out with jobs) and the post–black power generation's journey toward finding its voice to speak its story in a revised black America.

By the early to mid-1970s, the black social, cultural, and political landscape was changing once again. From 1955 to 1965, the political thrust was the civil rights movement, galvanizing and organizing its grassroots constituency, primarily in the South, to fight Jim Crow segregation, discrimination, and racial oppression. Integration was the mandate. Two of the struggle's most notable victories—the passage of the Civil Rights and Voting Rights acts—provided black America unprecedented access to social and political power, giving blacks equal access under the law. When fatigue and the fiery impatience of youth set in, the idea of using this legislation to take political control of black communities and put it in black hands spawned the movement's nationalist twin: black power. The name of this revolution was made popular at a park in Greenwood, Mississippi, on June 16, 1966, when Stokely Carmichael, fed up with nonviolent tactics and the less-than-enthusiastic enforcement of civil rights, angrily introduced "black power" as the slogan for a new political direction. He'd given a name to the nationalist sentiment growing among young African Americans who were inspired by the anticolonialist revolutions taking place in Africa and Asia. From 1966 to the mid-1970s, the black power movement, as an offshoot of the civil rights struggle, organized its grassroots constituency (primarily in the urban ghettos of the North) around the idea of cultivating black empowerment through black unity. It was about establishing a racial and cultural identity as a means of obtaining (and maintaining) political, social, and economic power, of realizing and developing, as the writer Komozi Woodard would later call it, a "nation within a nation." While the struggles of black power may not have produced such idealistic results, they did create the national swell of racial pride, political optimism, and cultural commerce that turned black urban creativity into both a strike for freedom and a wet dream of black capitalism—all of this culminating in a Saturday television dance program.

As African slaves had traveled the Underground Railroad in preparation for liberation from bondage of the body and spirit, the children of post–black power were prepared psychologically for their sociocultural movement, in part, aboard the vehicle of *Soul Train*. The brainchild of a Chicago DJ, Don Cornelius, it began as a local television teen dance show in 1970 on Chicago's WCIU and went into national syndication a year later. That same year, the show moved to a new studio in Los Angeles. With sponsorship from Sears and Johnson Products (the Chicago-based, black-owned black-hair-care company), *Soul Train* was, as the writer Greg Tate wrote in the *Chicago Tribune*, a product of a "timely upswing of black power politics, soul music, and insurgent black entrepreneurship." The prominence and popularity of black nationalism transformed black culture into "soul" culture, the word "soul" not only celebrating the spiritual resilience of black people (soul music, soul food, and soul brothers) but becoming the signifier in the commodification of *real* black culture (soul music, soul food, and soul brothers and sisters dancing on *Soul Train*). As blackness crossed over (white boys wore 'fros, too), soul culture turned black culture—with all its pride and funkiness—into American popular culture. *Soul Train* emerged alongside such media moments as the blaxploitation film revolution, *The Flip Wilson Show* and *Fat Albert and the Cosby Kids* on television, and the trickling crossover of soul music.

Soul Train was definitely a black *American Bandstand*, but more than a mere dance show, it was a phenomenon. No longer were black music, fashion, and dance limited to developing regionally. *Soul Train*, for the first time in history, provided a national stage for black urban youth culture, displaying the funkiest cultural by-products the ghettos of black America had to offer. Along with soul-music guests and wild, gawdy fashions (the platform shoes, bell-bottoms, micro/mini skirts, afros and afro-puffs), especially in the early to mid-1970s, one of the show's most prominent attractions was its dancing. That's because within all that bobbing, jerking, hopping, and gyrating was a celebration, the movements reflecting a sense of liberation from TV's former programming mandate of dehumanizing black people or ignoring them (the youth, in particular) altogether. Now with the whole country watching and enjoying (and copying) those dance moves—especially in easing down the "Soul Train Line"—while looking great, the show echoed the affirmation of black creativity and humanity expressed in Sly and the Family Stone's cry of "Thank you for lettin' me be myself again." One scene in particular exemplified the freedom *Soul Train* allowed young black folks: As guest James Brown and his band performed "Super Bad," female *Soul Train* dancer Damita Jo Freeman, in an afro-puff, hot pants, and leather go-go boots, jumped onstage. After dancing a hot routine in front of James, which included locking and the robot (as if showing J.B. that girls could bust a few moves, too), the sista threw up her fist to give the musical guest and audience a black power salute. (You think that would have been allowed on *American Bandstand*?)

A vehicle for setting trends, *Soul Train* became the first media outlet showcasing an emerging street dance movement, one that would expand America's dance lexicon and give the generation of post–black power its first taste of an approaching cultural influence and destiny. The first dance style was "locking," that animated dance of jerking the body into different poses in which every move coming off the lock is exaggerated with style. "In locking," explained Fred "Rerun" Berry, locking pioneer and former star of the television show *What's Happening!!*, "you don't just point, you twirl your wrist and point. You don't just look, you pop your neck and look. When you walk, you dip and walk." Locking was as much a symbol of post–black power pride and confidence as the Lindy Hop, before the Tuskegee Airmen, was a defiance of America's refusal to let black people achieve the aeronautic greatness of Charles Lindbergh.

Originally it was called the Campbellock. Don Campbell, a Watts teenager who stumbled upon his creation while trying to learn another dance, invented locking in 1969. Campbell and his outrageously dressed dance crew, the Campbellockers, became the first celebrities of *Soul Train*, setting a fashion standard for would-be street hoofers (those knee-high striped socks and oversized applejack hats) and bringing the dance to a national audience. Alumni from the group would garner their own celebrity, such as Fred Berry, who became a major television star; Adolfo "Shabba-Doo" Quinones, who went on to star in the 1984 classic hip-hop film *Breakin'*; and singer/choreographer Toni Basil, the only female (and the only white) member of the Lockers. She would go on to sing the 1980s hit song "Mickey," and choreograph its video, which became a classic in its own right.

"Popping" and "boogaloo" were the other dance styles, developed in the mid-1970s by Fresno, California, teens Poppin' Pete, his brother Boogaloo Sam, and their dance crew (also named the Electric Boogaloo). They built their moves off the inspiration they had gotten from watching the Lockers on television. Instead of perpetually throwing the body into a stop-start motion, like locking, popping and the boogaloo (borrowing from locking's hydraulic movements and the controlled fluid execution of mime) emphasized propelling the body through simultaneous movement in the joints. In popping, a dancer continuously snaps his limbs into various positions to the beat of the music, while a person doing the boogaloo uses flowing movements and foot gliding (like moonwalking) to keep time with the rhythm. The Electric Boogaloo team also became stars of the *Soul Train* stage, further turning street dance into a profession. In fact, the group is credited with teaching Michael Jackson, who popularized the dance on a broader scale on shows like his family's short-lived 1976 variety show, *The Jacksons*, to perfect his own "moonwalk" into pop history.

Through the vehicle of *Soul Train*, post–black power America finally gained a mass-media outlet putting common black people and their style on display. Not actors. Not comedians. Not a scripted sitcom or variety show or protesters on the evening news angrily demanding "Power to the People." Just afro-wearing youngsters bumping, locking, and popping *their* bodies to *their* music—funk music—that expressed *their* feelings, being beamed to millions of American homes. The moves of those *Soul Train* hoofers in the early days were like a victory dance, overcoming America's denial of black humanity to prove to the country that "yeah, black really *is* beautiful." But it meant even more for the youngsters of black America who watched the show. For them, the dance moves and the black pride leaping from their television screens greatly informed their future reconfiguration of black popular culture. It was an inspiration that was wholly needed because, although the struggle for black power opened corporate doors for such displays of fashion and self-pride, in the street—where the collective bodies of black folks struggled in advocacy of *the people*—the black power movement and its spirit were crumbling.

Specifically, its grassroots muscle, the organizations, had either diminished in size and impact or vanished into history. The Black Panther Party for Self-Defense. The Nation of Islam. The US Organization. The Black Liberation Army. The Student Nonviolent Coordinating Committee (SNCC). The Republic of New Africa. The Conservative Vice Lords and numerous others: intellectual offspring of black power's modern-day patron saint, Malcolm X, and the high priest of the civil rights movement, Martin Luther King, Jr. These groups were the community-based fuel for the modern black nationalist revolution, raising a new black consciousness out of the old Negro one. Where the civil rights movement had organized against America's legalized segregation and discrimination, wishing to get equal access and treatment legislated, the black power movement was about building and controlling institutions and resources vital to black communities, and about fighting de facto racism. Promoting self-realization, learning, and reclaiming a stolen identity (Africans in

America)—connecting with one's African roots—put the black nationalist struggle on a world stage, making it a part of a larger global Pan-Africanist quest for freedom.

Giving voice to this sentiment—rapping the struggle, so to speak—were leaders of black power. Malcolm X. Huey P. Newton. Stokely Carmichael. Elijah Muhammad. Maulana Karenga. Imamu Amiri Baraka. And H. Rap Brown. Brown, who became SNCC's head after Stokely Carmichael in 1967, was known for his pro-black Afro-poetics, angrily advocating violence as a means of responding to America's racial repression. "I say violence is necessary," he famously declared at a rally in Washington, D.C. "It is as American as cherry pie." Named for his deft skills at "rapping"—running down one's pedigree within a rhyming performance poetry—Brown's black power legacy, more than his organizing, was his verbal ability for speaking to the urgency of a black revolution. Through his name, the term "rap," also a black slang word for talking, was further exposed to ears outside of black urban centers (read: white) at the height of the nationalist movement. But organizational leaders weren't the only ones rapping the movement's rhetoric.

Maverick black entertainers also articulated the ideas of black power through the poetry of rap within American popular culture. Like boxing great Muhammad Ali, who, while stunning the country by joining the Nation of Islam and declaring himself a Black Muslim, taunted opponents and incensed white America with his boastful rhymes. Or the Last Poets, the New York–based poetry group who fused spoken word poetry and African rhythms with the message of black pride, nationhood, and activism. Or, most notably of all, James Brown, the Godfather of Soul and innovator of funk music, who popularized the idea of this new racial identity with the 1968 hit song "Say It Loud (I'm Black and I'm Proud)." Brown's rhythmic innovation, deepening the polyrhythms of soul music into a groove theory we now know as funk, became the new musical expression for this black consciousness. And Brown, known as "Soul Brother Number One" and "Brother Rapp," became the voice of the people, speaking the concerns of folks who congregated in churches as well as on street corners. Brown and numerous other figures informed the lyrical and contextual voice, the vanguard cultural and musical expression, of the generation after civil rights and black power. Only it was the ghosts of their inspiration that did so. That's because at the dawning of post–black power America, the voices and the vanguard organizations that inspired them were no longer on the scene. Systematically, most of the remnants of the black power struggle—the leaders, the language, the grassroots fire, the music, even the fashion—had been buried like the secret I discovered in my uncle's wallet.

A major part of the destruction was government sanctioned, courtesy of the FBI's Counterintelligence Program (COINTELPRO). Initiated by FBI head J. Edgar Hoover in 1956 during the early days of the civil rights movement, the program had as its primary purpose the surveillance and disruption of groups deemed subversive, such as communists and socialists, and hate groups like the Ku Klux Klan. But as the fight for civil rights gained momentum (and national attention), much of COINTELPRO began to focus on tailing, disrupting, and attempting to discredit the movement's leadership, namely Martin Luther King, Jr. (who Hoover thought was being influenced by communists). As impatience with the quest for civil rights gave way to cries of nationalism, Hoover expanded the objectives of COINTELPRO on August 25, 1967, to include the growing black power movement. (Hoover's disdain for progressive black power actually went as far back as 1922, when he destroyed the nationalist leader Marcus Garvey and his organization, the Universal Negro Improvement Association.)

With fears of a black revolution rekindled, Hoover concentrated his efforts on two of the most influential groups of the black nationalist movement: the Nation of Islam (NOI) and the Black Panther Party for Self-Defense (BPP). Founded in the 1930s, the NOI advocated *religious nationalism*, declaring that white people were devils and that blacks should separate from whites and build their own nation as Black Muslims. The NOI set the standard for black power's recruitment, fishing for its members and leadership among the urban ghettos and black lower class. Unlike the civil rights movement, whose key figures came from the middle class, the NOI pulled its leaders from the lower rungs of black society: prisons, pool halls, and drug dens. Through the dynamic speeches and celebrity of its national spokesman, Malcolm X, an ex-con and an ex-junkie, the NOI inspired the youth of the civil rights era to begin forming a modern black nationalist movement.

Following Malcolm's assassination in 1965, the Black Panther Party, formed in 1966, became the most famous by-product of his call for self-defense. Influenced by the organizational structure and recruitment philosophy of the NOI, the BPP also aimed at organizing young blacks who were on the lower rungs of black society (gang members, convicts, and street-corner hustlers). Taking up arms, the BPP organized around the concept of *revolutionary nationalism*, the idea that a community should govern, feed, and protect itself against any threatening force (i.e., the police). The romantic image of the Panthers, with black-beret-covered afros, black leather blazers, and rifles in their hands, bravely standing up against the cops, motivated ghetto (and middle-class) black youth across the country to join the black liberation struggle. The impact of the Panthers also scared Hoover into labeling them "the greatest threat to the internal security of the United States."

With a growing number of black power organizations being created in the late 1960s, COINTELPRO's aim was to stop any coalition from forming between black nationalist groups. For these so-called hate groups the goal of COINTELPRO was to "prevent the rise of a 'black messiah' who could unify, and electrify, the militant black nationalist movement." Covert opposition was increased. Phones were tapped. Groups and their leadership were under constant surveillance. Divisions between groups were fostered and exacerbated. Violence between opposing groups was covertly encouraged. Propaganda aimed against organizations and their leadership was secretly coordinated with "friendly" media outlets. Constant police harassment was facilitated with help from local police departments across the country. Much of that harassment resulted in false imprisonment of activists and the murder of numerous black power figures such as that of Chicago Black Panther leader Fred Hampton in 1969. The end result was the deterioration of vanguard organizations, many of which were constantly mired in turmoil, battling the police, other organizations, their own members, or numerous court cases. Much of the movement became weighed down in chaos—paranoia, infighting, violence, numerous celebrated trials, and plenty of causes célèbres. Free Huey! Free

Angela Davis! Free the Soledad Brothers! The Chicago 8! The New York 21! By the time the covert actions of COINTELPRO were exposed by the Senate's Church Committee in 1975, the damage to and deterioration of a movement had begun.

At the same time, black power politics and black political leadership experienced a steady mainstreaming. Passage of the 1965 Voting Rights Act, along with a significant population shift in major cities (white flight left many of them predominantly black and brown), caused a historic shift in America's political landscape. Elections in 1970 saw a record twelve African Americans elected to Congress. Over the next four years, cities nationwide elected America's first generation of black mayors. There was Kenneth Gibson in Newark, New Jersey, thanks to community organizing by the poet Amiri Baraka and the organization Citizens for a United Newark. Maynard H. Jackson won Atlanta, aided by a grassroots campaign advocating equality on behalf of the city's black majority. Gary, Indiana, elected Richard Hatcher, and Walter Washington became the mayor of Washington, D.C. (both called "Black Power Mayors"). Black political struggle seemed finally to produce some black political leverage (or at least folks with some political clout). And with black political leadership overwhelmingly pledging its loyalty to the Democratic Party, it seemed the black liberation movement now had a political party to protect its interests. "You don't need the bullet when you got the ballot," rapped funk pioneer George Clinton, on Parliament's 1975 hit, "Chocolate City," celebrating the black urban population boom and asking the inhabitants, "Are you up for the down stroke?"

Replacing radical black power leadership, black politicians were the new power brokers of black America, expected to deliver the goods of equal access and empowerment. Despite resistance from the white business establishment and white political opposition, parts of this mandate were fulfilled. Through enforcement of affirmative action policies, African Americans were given a fair chance at education, business-building, and job opportunities. The proportion of young blacks in college increased from 10 percent in 1965 to 18 percent in 1971. And while 48 percent of black families lived below the poverty line in 1959, that number had dropped to 27.8 percent in 1974. The writer Peter Shapiro noted in his book *Turn the Beat Around* that "from 1965 to 1969, the percentage of blacks making less than $3,000 decreased, while the percentage of blacks earning over $10,000 increased to 28 percent." Given a way of entering the professional workforce, numerous blacks joined the ranks of the middle class, giving rise to what *Black Enterprise* magazine, founded during these progressive years, dubbed the "black professional class."

These developments translated into promise only for those who could take advantage, which was hardly comparable to the whole of black America after black power. Other than welfare assistance and numerous poverty programs (thanks to President Lyndon Johnson's Great Society initiatives), not much in the way of economic progress trickled down to African Americans living in urban ghettos. The writer Tom Wolfe put it bluntly while observing Oakland's poverty program in his 1970 essay "Mau-Mauing the Flak Catchers": "The bureaucrats at City Hall . . . talked 'ghetto' all the time, but they didn't know any more about what was going on . . . than they did about Zanzibar." While the government offered Band-Aid remedies like welfare and poverty programs, they did very little (almost nothing) to fight the invisible hand of institutional racism that made lives worse. And so by the mid-1970s most cities, which had been devastated by riots and afterward by governmental neglect, were becoming major concrete pockets of poverty, left behind not only by a society hightailing it for the suburbs but by manufacturing jobs fleeing major cities as well.

This combination of white flight and corporate divestment would, according to a 1971 report by the National Urban Coalition, render the majority of these urban centers "black, brown, and totally bankrupt" by the end of the decade. By 1975, over 12 percent of African-American adults and almost 40 percent of work-age youth were unemployed—hardly a triumphant picture in the aftershock of a struggle for black pride and political empowerment. Although economic opportunities opened by the civil rights and black power struggles created avenues of advancement for blacks, they also drained working-class black communities of their middle and professional classes (most of which also fled to the suburbs).

The diminishing voice of the people and the devastating economic shifts of American cities came to define the sociocultural needs of the generation that succeeded groups like the Panthers and the NOI. The children of the 1970s (and even their young counterparts in the '80s) were the ones expected to reap the benefits available to them in a changing society. But how could they, while trying to survive in America's ghettos and left with little or no resources (community-based or otherwise) to do so? They were expected to forge and build black America's future, but with no guidance or grassroots leadership or organizational component to constructively thrust them forward, they lived in an environment that had become comparable to the one in *Lord of the Flies* where children stranded on an island with no adult guidance create a new, brutal social order of their own. While parents were out working, many attempting to capture gains from the struggle, these "latch-key kids," as they were referred to by the press, were left to fend for and supervise themselves. Existing in postindustrial urban centers that were becoming increasingly poor and violent, the youth set out on their own quest for power. Street power. Neighborhood power. So, in between the descent of the black revolution and the development of a new black America, there was the resurgence and growing problem of street gangs.

Nationwide, gangs have always existed in one form or another in urban communities—white, black, Latino, and so on—especially in major urban centers. Harlem. Chicago. Los Angeles. In low-income communities with no resources to nurture their young, gangs were (and still are) simply expressions of a youthful need for power, organization, protection, and, in the absence of a solid familial structure, family. At the height of the black power struggle, though, there were signs of that wayward energy merging with the consciousness of the movement. In 1967, the Vice Lords, one of Chicago's largest gangs, were incorporated and turned into a pro-black community development organization after their leader, Bobby Gore, was moved by a Martin Luther King, Jr., speech. Two years later, the Black P. Stone Nation (also called the Blackstone Rangers), a confederation of Chicago street youths, moved to form an alliance with the Black Panther Party, which was attempting to politicize street gangs (though the plan was thwarted by COINTELPRO). In fact, numerous members of the Panthers, including the head of its Los Angeles chapter, Bunchy Carter, were former gang members who had been recruited from the ranks of their gangs. The Young Lords Organization, a Puerto Rican gang in Chicago's Lincoln Park, was also inspired by the Black Panther Party to restructure itself into an organization fighting police brutality, racism, and the urban renewal that displaced poor Latinos out of their community. The

Young Lords Party in New York, another "brown power" organization, while struggling for Puerto Rican independence and justice, also worked to reprogram the gang energy growing in the Bronx. Even the Los Angeles Crips gang, founded in 1969, was inspired by the Black Panther Party. According to Crip lore, its founders, initially sporting black leather blazers like the Panthers, used the word "Crip" as an acronym for "Community Revolution in Progress," forming the gang as a way to unify and protect local youth.

But in the wake of black (and brown) power's demise, and the economic devastation that blighted American cities from the early 1970s through the '80s, this youthful energy was once again left to develop to destructive ends. No place exemplified this more than New York City, where by 1973 there were an estimated 315 gangs with membership reaching 19,503. The genesis of the resurgence occurred in the Bronx, a borough devastated by the effects of urban renewal and deindustrialization. In 1948, urban planner Robert Moses began clearing a massive path through the borough to make way for the construction of the Cross-Bronx Expressway. The project uprooted small, tight-knit communities and initiated a great white exodus out of the borough. Through the 1950s and '60s, middle-class Jews, Italians, Germans, and Irish fled the heart of the Bronx for the suburbs of Westchester County or, once it was opened in 1968, the promise of ownership in the newly built Co-op City, located at the northeastern end of the borough. Business and factories also relocated. By the end of the 1960s, replacing the Bronx's white middle-class population was a population of poor black, Afro-Caribbean, and Latino families, especially in the South Bronx, where 600,000 manufacturing jobs had been lost over the last two decades. Low-income housing was abundant in this area, but the mass influx of low-income families panicked the otherwise reputable landlords, who hastily sold off their property to professional slumlords. The new landlords, who refused to keep up the basic maintenance of these properties, found destroying their buildings for the insurance money more profitable than keeping them. So, in the early 1970s, the South Bronx, as well as other parts of the borough, was eviscerated by arson scams, leaving the area so filled with burned-out apartment buildings and trash-strewn lots that it resembled, as has been said so many times, a war-torn planet.

The population upheaval of the South Bronx, with black and

brown kids being terrorized by bands of white youths whose families remained in the area, initiated a surge in New York gang culture in the early 1970s. Blacks and Latinos formed makeshift street families to protect themselves, not only from the white gangs but also from other black and brown gangs. The Black Spades, one of New York's largest street gangs, were predominately black. The Savage Skulls, another of the city's largest gangs, were primarily Hispanic. In between these two groups sat a massive roster of other street organizations (black, white, and Hispanic) helping to carve the Bronx into territories and turfs. The Savage Nomads. The Seven Immortals. The Ghetto Brothers. The Golden Guineas. While the activities of these gangs consisted primarily in robbing the elderly and beating up non-gang-affiliated youths and rival groups, their wrathful violence against drug dealers and junkies, in the early days of the gang surge, made them appear to be equally an asset to the communities they terrorized. "There are no junkies on Hoe Street in the South Bronx," wrote *Amsterdam News* reporter Howard Blum about one street gang. "The Royal Charmers ordered all junkies and dealers to leave." The antidrug stance of the gangs may have made their reemergence seem like the "best single thing" to happen to New York City, as *New York Post* columnist Pete Hamill wrote, especially given the reduction of services (sanitation, health, transportation, education, and police) to the inner city. But these gangs were less interested in leading or sustaining their community's fight against a growing drug problem than they were in the brutal flexing of a collective muscle. And so from 1970 to 1973, with each passing summer the strength of the Bronx's gang culture (and its violence and self-destruction) grew.

Then out of the gang violence and destruction and quests for power came the rumblings of an urban cultural movement in the Bronx, an alternative way for ghetto youth to say (as Jesse Jackson put it) "I am somebody." First graffiti, the aerosol art form growing from names of gangs painted on walls to the "tags" of individuals spray painted big, bold, and stylish. On buildings. On buses and trains. These youths could capture fame through this illegal art, constructing identities that were larger than the overcrowded and crumbling environment around them. The painter Catherine Mackey described it best on her 2005 painting *Red Wall (Recombinant)*: "Graffiti is an index of the intersection of public and private, a way of inscribing an architectural, monumental structure with the immediate concerns of an individual."

Then came the music, developed by the Jamaican-born DJ Kool Herc, who reconfigured the break beats of funk music records so that the huge, intricate rhythms were continuous. Herc's beat sensation satisfied a population that desired a return to the funk of black music, which was slowly disappearing with the approaching tide of disco. James Brown's "In the Jungle" and "Soul Power." Jimmy Castor's "It's Just Begun." At Herc's parties also came the development of a new dance, breaking, its acrobatic style inspired by the moves of James Brown and developed by street dancing celebs like the Nigga Twins, who attended Herc's parties and skillfully used their bodies, according to Herc, as a way of "expressing how the music sounded." By the early to mid-1980s, breaking would inspire black and Latino youth nationwide to become part of a street dance movement, their enthusiasm for this rhythmic dance revolution informed by the popping and locking they had seen on *Soul Train*. Then came rap music, the musical poetry of this generation.

In 1974, the waning spirit of black power would come to be anchored within this cultural movement by way of Afrika Bambaataa, a DJ and former gang member. As a member of the Black Spades, Bambaataa was radicalized by the teachings of the Nation of Islam and the Black Panther Party. Inspired by their ideals of racial unity and consciousness, Bambaataa redirected his life away from gangs and organized the components of this burgeoning cultural movement (breaking, graffiti, rapping, and DJing) under the banner of the Zulu Nation, envisioning this new street movement as a "revolutionary youth culture." By way of this radical street development—soon to be dubbed "hip-hop"—Bambaataa offered the youth of his community a new identity and an alternative to the destructive life of street gangs the same way his nationalist predecessors had.

The components of hip-hop may have initially come together within the "jams" (or parties) thrown by Herc, but it was Bambaataa who incorporated the spirit of black power (and the 1960s ideals of peace) into hip-hop, consciously organizing the movement under the tenets of cultural and racial pride and self-awareness, as well as peace, music, creativity, and fun. Bambaataa's political awareness was opened by the sounds of socially conscious funk, tunes like "Stand!" by Sly and the Family Stone and James Brown's "Say It Loud (I'm Black and I'm Proud)." In the book *Yes Yes Y'All: The Experience Music Project Oral History of Hip-Hop's First Decade*, former gang member Lucky Strike remembers being told about the Zulu Nation by one of its members after attending the funeral of another gang member: "What he talked to me about in the Zulu Nation was about finding yourself, who you are . . . They were teaching me things about my culture that I never knew and things I never learned in school." Although hip-hop was, by no means, a political movement, it was through the unifying efforts of Bambaataa, as well as jams thrown by other DJs such as Grandmaster Flash, that hip-hop grew and expanded, helping socially reshape the identities of its urban followers. Hip-hop turned politically abandoned and socially outcast black and brown youths into celebrities and cultural power brokers, this notion especially holding true for the rapper or MC.

Their art was street poetry, braggadocio rhymes recited over break beats to excite, enthrall, and entertain hip-hop's faithful. Much of their metered speech and tall tales were rooted in black oral traditions of African griots (storytellers and history holders), in toasts (black epical, rhyming poetry), in the fiery, rhythmic cadence of black Baptist preachers, in the oral acrobatic put-downs of the "dozens." Not surprisingly, though, it was from the mouths of the civil rights/black power era that rappers drew most of their poetic technique, inspired by the rapping virtuosity of figures like Muhammad Ali, James Brown, H. Rap Brown, George Clinton, and the Last Poets. Before they shook up the world, rappers simply rocked the party, giving a voice to the DJ's set and dazzling the crowd with verbal derring-do. From hip-hop's ghetto, stars grew. Chief Rocker Busy Bee. Grandmaster Flash & the Furious Five. Cold Crush Brothers. The Fantastic Five. Funky 4 + 1. Sequence. Lisa Lee. Treacherous Three. These artists laid the foundation for the musical voice of post–black power America: its youth, nationwide, prepared for the music's arrival by the rapping (and popping and locking) voices of black history. The mainstreaming of black music and leadership by the late 1970s was leaving the generation after black power without voice or representation in the world of art, culture, and politics. Luckily, the impact of rap music and the MC eventually reached beyond the borders of New York City by decade's end, redefining the idea of a black cultural revolution and offering a voice to the power and pain of youth in the new sociopolitical fun house of black America.

TWO

The New Afro-Urban Movement
Rap Redefines the Voice of America's Chocolate Cities

I'm the Grandmaster with the three MCs
That shock the house for the young ladies . . .
—"Rapper's Delight," 1979

Please, no one call this radio station. Our telephone lines are locked. We will play the record again." The words were fresh in Sugarhill Gang's Big Bank Hank's memory as he told VH1 *Classic Soul* about the time when his group's seminal record, "Rapper's Delight," premiered on 92 WKTU and detonated a national music movement. As it has often been noted, the story of commercial rap music begins with the release of "Rapper's Delight" in October 1979. The song's eruption onto the American musical landscape was akin to a blast of dynamite—a musical upheaval on wax. Once radio put it on the street, the damn thing was everywhere. Shortly after its release, the song sold fifty thousand copies a day, eventually going double platinum, reaching number four on *Billboard*'s pop singles chart and number forty-six on the R&B chart. In Canada, it was number one. In Europe, Israel, and South Africa, it went to the Top 5. So many copies of "Rapper's Delight" were sold that in 1980 the National Association of Recording Merchandisers named it "Black Single of the Year." Finally, the musical genie developed on the streets and in the playgrounds of New York City was out of its five-borough magic lamp.

But by no means was "Rapper's Delight" the first rap record (another story etched into hip-hop history). Two months prior, the Fatback Band released "King Tim III (Personality Jock)," featuring the party-rocking rhymes of the New York rapper King Tim (Tim Washington). Only Fatback's label, Spring Records, wasn't willing to take the promotional risk of being the first label to push rap, instead making "King Tim III" the B-side of a cut called "You're My Candy Sweet." That song went nowhere, while "King Tim III" became a club favorite in the Northeast, reaching number twenty-six on the R&B chart. But by the time the label recognized the tune's potential, finally putting it out as an A-side single, they'd missed the boat. "Rapper's Delight" had become the musical phenomenon.

The Sugarhill Gang's version of rap, performed over a thumping replay of the bass line from Chic's hit "Good Times," succeeded at bottling the feel of hip-hop music (the rhymes, the style, and the attitude) into a fifteen-minute record. Much of that was achieved because a third of the song—the rhymes recited by Big Bank Hank—was written by the rap pioneer and Cold Crush Brothers' member Grandmaster Caz. Though the Gang wasn't officially involved in hip-hop's burgeoning New York scene, the New Jersey trio succeeded at filling "Rapper's Delight" with all the entertaining artistry of the hip-hop MC. There were the highly stylized raps, the rhythm of their words comparable to the infectious music. They told stories ("I was coming home late one dark afternoon, reporter stopped me for an interview"). They were funny ("Have you ever went over a friend's house to eat, and the food just ain't no good?"). But most important (and jarring for those outside New York City), they unabashedly spoke with the youthful language—and attitude—of the black urban ghettos.

Although the song's novelty reached all audiences ("to the black, to the white, the red and the brown, the purple and yellow"), its style struck a significant chord with the post–black power generation—a group, as Nelson George described them in his book *The Death of Rhythm & Blues*, for whom "the optimistic agitation of the 1960s was not even a memory." "Rapper's Delight," with all its tall talk and party-centric lyrics, wasn't an overt political statement, but at a time when black popular music and black politics were in flux, the song's profundity came from its mere presentation: three boastful young black men assaulting the airwaves with rhymes and the language of street folk, talking about getting "some spank" (sex) and driving off in a "def Ojay" (a nice Cadillac). Simply put, it was unashamedly black and accessible: anyone could recite the rhymes—no prodigious singing required—and those who were skilled enough at learning them were endowed with the power of the MC while reciting the rap for classmates, friends, or family members.

But it was ironic—and symbolic—that "Rapper's Delight" arrived at the decade's end. Not only did it introduce America and the world to rap music, giving young black America a taste of its sociocultural destiny, it also gave black culture a sampling of its future reconfiguration. Music fueled by urban poets who spoke straight from the heart to life's immediate needs and wants. This development was significant given the changing sociopolitical tide America was flowing in. A year prior to the release of "Rapper's Delight," white conservative backlash against the gains of the civil rights movement struck a significant blow with the U.S. Supreme Court ruling in the *Bakke* decision. The Court ruled that the University of California's special admissions programs favoring minorities—programs which hindered Allan B. Bakke, who was white, from being admitted to medical school—were unconstitutional and a form of "reverse discrimination." According to cultural critics and scholars, this outcome would mark the end of civil rights progress and a reversal of federal support for the cause of black empowerment. Even figures of the black power struggle were still locked in personal battles with government-sanctioned tyranny.

A month after the Sugarhill Gang's debut, Assata Shakur (née JoAnne Chesimard), a member of the Black Panthers and the Black Liberation Army, escaped from a New Jersey prison where she'd been serving a life sentence for the 1973 killing of a New Jersey state trooper. After her guilty verdict, many questioned the validity of her conviction, citing "flimsy" evidence and the fact that during the Church Committee hearings in 1975, it was revealed that Shakur was a major target of the FBI's COINTELPRO operations. News of Shakur's well-planned escape—her picture splashed all over the evening news—introduced Shakur to black and brown youth and would make her 1987 biography, *Assata*, a popular read during rap music's future political phase.

The streetcentric sensation of "Rapper's Delight" also arrived when post–black power America's geography had become overwhelmingly urban and a priority shift had arisen within black popular culture. By 1980, 11.2 percent of the U.S. population was African American. And among the 26,495,070 black people in the United States, about 85 percent (22,595,061) were considered urban dwellers. Cities with the largest black populations were Washington, D.C. (70 percent), Atlanta

(67 percent), Detroit (65 percent), New Orleans (55 percent), and Memphis (40 percent). Just as the development of rhythm and blues in the 1940s was an outgrowth of the northern migration of southern blacks to urban industrial centers, rap music's emergence grew out of black America's almost total urbanization in deindustrialized chocolate cities.

Rap music's commercial allure within post–black power America also rose out of a growing chasm: the fracturing of black communities following integration along class, age, and political lines. For black popular culture and indeed the masses of black America, the late 1970s were about escapism. Following the social justice movements of the 1960s and '70s, black America—as well as the rest of the country—was battle weary, jaded by unfulfilled promises, but ready to snatch its piece of the dream. The struggle opened doors for blacks to better employment opportunities, expanding the black middle class (those who would move on up . . . and out of the black urban ghettos). As well, it opened the eyes of the big music companies to the power of the black dollar and the revenue-generating power of African-American music. Thus black music—formerly driven by regional marketing and independent labels—steadily found its way into corporate boardrooms, becoming a huge commodity of the major labels.

By the late 1970s, this union had been accelerated by the discofication of black music. Fueled by the overwhelming success of PIR (Philadelphia International Records) earlier in the decade, the sound of producers Kenny Gamble and Leon Huff—an infectious, dance-inducing mixture of lush strings, big brass, and high-hat heat—would, as James Brown's trombonist Fred Wesley later commented, "put a bow tie on the funk." Bold, hard-driving rhythms evolved into hypnotic dance tracks. Lyrics of social awareness (PIR music included) morphed into melodic commands to dance, dream, and "do it" all night. Dissatisfied Americans assembling to protest gave way to thrill-seekers gathering in hi-fi discotheques. And black music became a hot commodity in the form of disco, its lyrics and rhythm laced with a palpable (even ethnic) ambiguity, helping people dance and escape their concerns. Even the cry of "burn, baby, burn," a popular chant during many a 1960s urban rebellion, was co-opted by the times, becoming the chorus for the 1977 dance hit "Disco Inferno." But more important, and more than ever, within the halls of the corporate structure, the rhythm of black music was marketed to selling records that appealed not only to black audiences but to a majority white one. In its quest for lucrative mainstream dollars and a wider (read: whiter) audience, black music and black popular culture were headed for "crossover" fever.

Even black radio, in its quest for adequate mainstream ad dollars, began erasing any ethnic or racial association with its call letters (New York's WBLS—Black Liberation Station—being the most widely cited for attempting to deracialize), going, instead, under the label "urban." In *The Death of Rhythm & Blues*, Nelson George explains: "Coming out of black FM radio and disco, urban was supposedly a multicolored programming style tuned to the rhythms of America's crossfertilized big cities . . . but more often, urban was black radio in disguise." Along with Earth, Wind & Fire, George Benson, and Ashford and Simpson, stations also played the hottest records from white artists (Rolling Stones, Rod Stewart, Queen) who, in a phenomenon of reverse crossover (ha!), were getting play on black airwaves. The gods of rock, too, were being seduced by the sound of the discotheques.

So it was amid disco fever, a growing corporate presence in black music, and the disappearance of black music's bold, funky voice that "Rapper's Delight" was able to usher in a new era of music. Commercially, it was under the radar, while musically it stayed in step with rhythms popular on America's dance floors. The song's live sampling of "Good Times" wasn't just Sugarhill Gang staying within hip-hop music's practice of reconfiguring prerecorded music, but a wise pop music move. "Good Times" was one of the most popular grooves, a major dance hit selling nine million copies. Musically, "Rapper's Delight" walked the fine line of mass appeal while lyrically and unflinchingly "representin' " the language and attitude of a young black urbanized audience whose voice was slowly disappearing from commercial black music as well as mainstream black politics. Ironically, rap music's anti-disco feel provided this generation with its own form of escapism— from the overwhelming homogenization of black music. Not that hip-hop music was born an ultraconscious concept. It, too, sprang from an escapist mind-set of black America after the 1960s, from the partycentric desires of the "me" generation, with the cash-is-king ethos of the 1980s soon to fan the flames. Only instead of escaping from massive social discontent, or into the crossover mentality, the pioneers of hip-hop music and their New York followers fled the inescapable pangs of ghetto life, the decay of their environment, their lack of worth in society, and the growing disco-fication of black dance music. The rhythmic congregations of Herc and Bambaataa and Grandmaster Flash all wanted to party, just not to disco. They wanted a return to the funk, hardcore funk—music that, by now, was considered "too black" for commercial black radio. That same desire—for funky music with a youthful street edge—helped rap spread within black America.

It also spawned another rap hit with Kurtis Blow's "The Breaks" in 1980. As "Rapper's Delight" had been, "The Breaks" was an instant commercial success, and the second rap single to certify gold. Outside the growing independent kingdom of Sugar Hill Records, Kurtis Blow became the first rap artist to sign with a major label (Mercury) and embark on a national tour. His 1980 self-titled LP became rap music's first album.

Most notably, Blow pushed rap into the commercial realm by constructing his rhymes to the formula of popular music. "The Breaks" was the first commercial rap song to have a chorus ("These are the breaks!") and a bridge. And whereas "Rapper's Delight" was just three MCs rappin' and "rockin' the house," "The Breaks" became the first rap song built around a concept or a hook—the word "break" being a popular word within black communities of the Northeast, especially New York's hip-hop community. From the idea of the "breaking point," numerous creations of hip-hop culture were labeled: the break beat; break dance; b-boy—break boy or Bronx boy; b-girl; break down. Blow's record, as a way of "breaking down" the word, was a slightly humorous, funk-laden look at the various breaks one gets in life ("Breaks in love. Breaks in war. But we got the breaks to get you on the floor!"). But, again, like its Sugarhill predecessor, "The Breaks," while working within the confines of pop culture, garnered its biggest appeal among the youth of black America because it dealt in a concept—music, language, and vocal style—that came straight from their environment. And although Blow's debut album was primarily constructed with an eye toward the pop world that shuffled crooning love songs like "All I Want in This World (Is to Find That Girl)" and arena rock remakes ("Takin' Care of Business") in between his hip-hop raps, it, too, had exceptional moments of bottling the hip-hop experience for its audience ("Rappin' Blow, Pt. 2"). It was even the first rap album to deal with harsh urban realities. The song "Hard Times," a sociopolitical rap, predated the musical revolution caused by Grandmaster Flash & the Furious Five's "The Message" by two years. Although "Hard Times"—a rap on the ills of the world—never received much, if any, airplay, its creation was a prophetic glance, given the political forecast for African Americans.

The ideals of the nation's capital were shifting toward conservative leadership. But before Reagan officially arrived at the White House, a racial explosion occurred in Miami-Dade County, the first major rebellion since the 1960s rocked the country. Following the acquittal of four white police officers in the beating death of Arthur McDuffie, a black insurance salesman, black Miami ignited into the worst riot since the Newark rebellion of 1967. While the acquittal set off the violence, the root of the explosion was diagnosed by many as the poverty and despair of Miami's growing black underclass. "Whatever the spark," wrote David F. Pike in *U.S. News & World Report*, "the basic tinder would be the economic frustration . . . For many Blacks, the hopes raised after the riots in the 1960s—for better jobs, schools, housing and social services—have been dashed." Although numerous blacks advanced to the middle class, there were still large numbers of African Americans at the bottom of society's economic escalator. There, black unemployment reached 13.5 percent, and black teen unemployment reached 80 percent. Where the riots took place, four out of every ten black adults were unemployed. Compounded by the country's double-digit inflation, if lack of finances wasn't enough to make the lives of those rioting harder, the shifting political landscape made sure it got worse.

By the 1980 presidential race between Jimmy Carter and Ronald Reagan, federal politics had become a confusing and disheartening game. Without question, the black vote was vital to Carter (taking advantage of the Voting Rights Act, massive voter registration drives helped). But many felt promises of his current administration weren't being kept. Job training and public assistance programs (programs that greatly benefited the black lower class), though maintained during the Carter administration, were in danger of cuts during his final days in the White House. And for the upcoming vote, much of black America felt between a rock and a guillotine, a sentiment James Baldwin expressed in his essay "Notes on the House of Bondage": "No black citizen . . . supposes that either Carter or Reagan . . . has any concern for them at all," he wrote, "except as voters . . . or dupes . . . and while one hates to say that black citizens are right, one certainly can't say they are wrong." The disappointment, ironically, was enough to make civil rights activists Ralph Abernathy and Hosea Williams shift their endorsement from Carter to Reagan, a candidate whose first stop along the campaign trail was Philadelphia, Mississippi, where civil rights activists James Cheney, Mickey Schwerner, and Michael Goodman were killed by the KKK in 1964. The hope of a Reagan victory lay in the shift of southern allegiance from the Democratic to the Republican Party that had begun in 1968 with the South's support for the "law and order" president Richard Nixon. One of Reagan's promises to his white southern audience was restoring "states' rights" (read: segregation). And with an unofficial boycott of the election by blacks who felt, as Baldwin wrote, that they couldn't support either candidate, Reagan and the new conservative age were ushered in by a landslide.

At the same time, the phenomenal success of "Rapper's Delight" and "The Breaks" ushered in a cultural revolution; rap's commercial viability allowed the pioneers of this new street poetry onto the airwaves for national exposure, though their success wasn't due to the support of the major labels or their Negro executives in charge of "black music" departments (many of whom saw no future in "ghetto music"). The adventurous spirit of the black independent labels, primarily through the talent synergy of two companies—Harlem's Enjoy Records and New Jersey's Sugar Hill Records—brought rap to the masses. Of the two labels, the little R&B label in New Jersey ultimately became rap music's first industry powerhouse. As the story goes: Sugar Hill's co-owner Sylvia Robinson, a former R&B singer, got the idea to put hip-hop on wax after hearing the DJ Love Bug Starski rap at her birthday party at the legendary hip-hop club Harlem World. She was unable to procure Starski's services for Sugar Hill, so with the aid of her son Joey Robinson she set out to create the first commercial rap group— hip-hop's first boy band, so to speak. And the Sugarhill Gang was born. With the financial and marketing power created by the success of "Rapper's Delight," Sugar Hill Records was able to increase its roster with the pioneers of rap and fill its hit list with this new sound of the streets. Most of this came with the acquisition of talent from Enjoy Records, a label that didn't have the marketing or promotional muscle or the production quality of Sugar Hill. From Enjoy, Sugar Hill Records acquired groups like the Funky 4 + 1. Following their hit "That's the Joint" in 1980, the foursome plus one moresome was the first rap act to perform on *Saturday Night Live* thanks to Debbie Harry, the lead singer of the rock group Blondie. Before she performed her hit "Rapture" (rap's first song by a white artist), she let the Funky 4 rap and rock the house. Next, the Treacherous Three, a group that introduced the concept of "speed rap" or fast rapping, made the exodus from Enjoy and garnered the hit "Feel the Heart Beat" in 1981. But of all the groups to cross over to Sugar Hill, the biggest and most influential was Grandmaster Flash & the Furious Five. Prior to becoming stars on wax, they were hip-hop's original supergroup, their leader, DJ Grandmaster Flash, being a critical part of the pioneering trinity of hip-hop music (Herc, Bam, and Flash). He introduced hip-hop DJing techniques like "cutting" (repeating a phrase or rhythm of a record with a quick, well-timed mix) and "backspinning" or "back cueing" (turning the record counterclockwise), and so the group came with a built-in fan base (at least in New York) who had partied at Flash's jams. The group also made rap music history with their member Cowboy being credited as hip-hop's first rap artist. On Enjoy the group scored a moderate hit with 1980's "Super-rappin'." But on Sugar Hill Records, the group reached a wider radio audience that same year with the song "Freedom." Beyond any rap record released since "Rapper's Delight," "Freedom," with its display of Flash's DJ derring-do and the Furious Five's mic skills, shined as *the* first complete embodiment of the hip-hop throwdown—the energy, creativity, even the excitement of a jam—that had been recorded. That's because the real star of hip-hop music, the DJ, led this high-octane boast-fest-on-wax. The song—done over a turntable mix (not a live band's version) of "Get Up and Dance" by the group Freedom—showcased the true essence of the hip-hop DJ and his skillful band of MCs. The dazzling rhymes of the Furious Five unleashed the full-tilt, back-n-forth energy of the hip-hop MC, unfiltered and true. And while other groups scrapped their DJs, the Furious Five constantly kept listeners attuned to the proficiency of their maestro ("Grandmaster / Cuts faster . . . than any known, strong to the bone / Full-grown / He's a one of a kind and Flash is gonna rock your mind!"). For the first time, non-hip-hoppers heard a hip-hop DJ ply his trade, manipulating a record on a rap song. With "Freedom," listeners outside of New York's hip-hop network heard and somewhat experienced the techniques of hip-hop DJing accompanied by the kinetic freestyle of real show-stopping rap artists. As the new stars of Sugar Hill, Grandmaster Flash

& the Furious Five went on to become one of the most lucrative rap groups during the early commercial years of rap. But most important, Sugar Hill became the solid home base needed for the consistent production, marketing, promotion, and distribution of quality rap records and innovative rap artists.

As disco was for the older constituents of black America (and those seeking the opulence the music alluded to), rap music's growing hit list appealed primarily to its urban-dwelling youth. For them, the MCs spoke the unfiltered language of their world, doing so as residents of the inner city who, in their new public role, steadily garnered the power of affirmation for a group constantly reminded of their outsider status in mainstream society.

With the mantra of rugged individualism (going for self through the doors of opportunity) taking over where community organizing and political protest had reigned supreme, rap artists emerged as this development's most potent icons. At their core, hip-hop culture and rap music are about rugged individualism, and the MC is all about the "I" and the "me," using the airwaves to promote the most crucial and important aspect of this music: himself. *He* is the biggest. *She* is the baaadest. *They* rock the party. And though many weren't financially well-off, MCs had all the wealth in the world (albeit fictional) on the mic. But it was also the rapper's constant referencing of himself—that personal and personable touch—that made rap and rap artists appealing to the young black (and brown) audiences. While disco records sang mostly about escapism, MCs constantly communicated the realization (and the mythologizing) of the self directly to their audience. Moreover, they expressed the social perspective, cultural voice, and self-worth of their audience ("you're the one, you're the one, you're the one, you're the one!" as the Furious Five shouted to listeners on "Freedom"). Simply put, as the antithesis of disco, rap music and rap artists were tangible and real, which made them empowering for their audiences. Moreover, through the hyperbole of rap, MCs became larger-than-real-life characters, building their own ghetto-hero mythology with words and music ("I'm slick / I'm cool / I'm solid gold / They call me . . . the Kid Creole!"). The combination of self-referencing and self-mythologizing was crucial to building the status (to almost a worshipful state) of the MC with his/ her audience. So in the early days of commercial rap, in the midst of an evolving political, cultural, and social dance floor, rap artists were transforming into heroes of the airwaves, the poet laureates for a new era of funk, even as they took up an age-old mantle.

For MCs—with all their tall talk and bravado—were on their way to becoming reincarnations of Stagger Lee or the Bad Nigga Hero, the bandit archetype of black folklore who emerged in the late nineteenth century and was widely immortalized in song. His violent temperament and refusal to live within the laws of society were matched only by this hero's gift of hyperbole. While the early MCs weren't necessarily bad men—not just yet—they were viewed as fearless, speaking their minds and creating music from the unadulterated language and perspective of black urban America, successfully existing outside of mainstream popular culture or the black popular culture (radio, music, and politics), bent on smoothing out its ethnic edginess. In the context of a mainstream black cultural and political leadership too concerned with crossover appeal, rap artists emerged as the confident, strong black voices of the black urban aesthetic. When it seemed the Bad Niggas had all but disappeared—leaving very few in music or politics to speak for the street and its people—rap artists filled the void, commanding the airwaves with their own ghettocentric ideology. At the dawn of Ronald Reagan's vision for America, some Bad Niggadom pumped loud over a boom box—even if it was simply the self-affirming words of young black men boastfully rapping on the mic—formed a great breeze of change. Something—anything—needed to be said.

Once Reagan took office in January 1981, the conservative backlash against the legislative gains and programs of the civil rights era was set in motion. If the *Bakke* decision marked the death of black political progress, Reagan was definitely its grim reaper. Anyone unsure about the new president's stance on the civil rights or any past progressive movement for equality only needed to witness his pardoning of former FBI deputy director W. Mark Felt and Edward S. Miller, former head of Squad 47, a COINTELPRO unit in the FBI's New York field office. In 1980, both were convicted of "conspiring to violate the constitutional rights of Americans," their crimes being in the context of the Counter-intelligence Program. Three months after taking office, Reagan pardoned Felt and Miller, stating their crimes occurred during an especially turbulent and divisive period in American history. According to Reagan, it was time to "end the terrorism that was threatening our nation," referring to the protests and anti–Vietnam War activities of the not-too-distant past. This same sentiment or consideration was never extended to the freedom fighters (political prisoners) falsely jailed because of COINTELPRO.

But one thing was definite: Reagan was vigilant about putting the turbulent past—black progress and all—behind him and the country. Shortly after his inauguration, the U.S. Department of Justice announced it would no longer demand employers maintain affirmative action programs or hire according to racial quotas. Moreover, the Department of Labor announced an easing of antidiscrimination rules affecting contracts involved in federal jobs. And because Arthur S. Flemming, the chairman of the U.S. Commission on Civil Rights, supported affirmative action, voting rights legislation, and busing to desegregate schools, Reagan fired him as commission chairman and appointed black conservative Clarence Pendleton, Jr. Another of the first areas to feel Reagan's wrath was education. After student aid programs were cut, black student enrollment in colleges and universities plummeted in the early 1980s.

Under Reagan, Lyndon B. Johnson's vision of a Great Society turned into a war on the impoverished. Programs designed to aid the poor were on the chopping block. And since blacks made up 30 to 40 percent of the enrollment in social programs (while constituting 11 percent of the U.S. population), these cuts affected them more than others. After Reagan significantly pared spending on Aid to Families with Dependent Children, 408,000 families lost their benefits over the next six years. Social welfare programs such as food stamps were reduced. Employment and job training programs were slashed. Budgets for health care services were decreased. Grants to fund local antipoverty agencies shrank significantly. By the end of Reagan's eight-year tenure in the White House, the black poverty rate had risen to 33 percent while the white poverty rate had fallen to 10.5 percent. It is needless to say who benefited more from the Reagan years. During all of this misfortune, compounded by a recession, the national unemployment rate rose to a six-year high with black unemployment reaching a staggering 22 percent.

In the Reagan era, with its budget cuts and demonization of the black poor, black urban America experienced an increase in poverty and crime, and a looming drug problem with the emergence of crack cocaine. Even though civil rights and labor leaders attempted to ad-

dress the legislative hostility coming from Capitol Hill by galvanizing 300,000 people to protest the Reagan administration's assault on
civil rights programs (the same way the 1963 March on Washington
protested Jim Crow), black popular music, for the most part, didn't address or acknowledge the problem. Even rap, the fledgling sound of the
urban grassroots, didn't initially confront the issues facing the masses
of black people (apart from their need to hear their joys, language, and
attitude on the radio), mainly because during the early days of commercial rap it was primarily party music fresh from its Bronx birthing
grounds. The confident voice of rappers, at the outset of the Reagan
era, only addressed their status as the high priests of block parties, their
boastful spirit at best a symbol of black social boldness. Otherwise,
they were purveyors of escapism, rhyming themselves and their audience out of the ghetto's demoralizing misery. Only unlike disco, which
was associated with homosexuality and hedonism, rap celebrated and
affirmed the black machismo aesthetics of the urban ghetto. Within the
confines of the park jams, block parties, and hip-hop clubs, the job of
the MC and the DJ was to be innovative at entertaining a crowd with
verbal badness, keeping hip-hop's faithful dancing and amazed.

And commercial rap music would continue to do so until 1982, when
DJ Afrika Bambaataa, who had injected the spirit of peace, unity, and
Afrocentricity into hip-hop culture just eight years prior, entered rap
music's commercial space and revolutionized its possibilities. Signed to
the fledgling independent label Tommy Boy, Bam teamed with the rap
group the Jazzy 5 to garner his first underground hit, "Jazzy Sensation,"
a remake of Gwen McCrae's disco classic "Funky Sensation." Later that
year Bam, with another new group, Soul Sonic Force, collaborated with
seminal hip-hop producer Arthur Baker to release the groundbreaking
rap song "Planet Rock." Just as "Rapper's Delight" had been before,
"Planet Rock" was an undeniable force that drastically increased rap
music's impact, reaching number four on *Billboard*'s R&B chart. Atop
Baker's reworking of Kraftwerk's 1977 new wave dance hit "Trans-
Europe Express," the cut single-handedly pushed rap music into the age
of computerized music, beginning the "electrofunk" period of rap. Totally synthesized and electronically programmed, the rhythm was accentuated with a towering drumbeat. Live bands were replaced with

technology, which now took the sound of hip-hop—and dance music in general—to new rhythmic heights. Beats were faster, livelier, and more atmospheric—another reminder (along with the emergence of home computers and the video game explosion) that the future was at hand. With the heavily synthesized sound of Europe's new wave rock influencing the electro-funk era, "Planet Rock" was the first rap record to bridge the gap between hip-hop and rock music, emblematic of an era of hip-hop in 1980–81 when the pioneers of the movement were brought together with Manhattan's downtown art/punk scene (thanks, in large part, to Brooklyn artist/bohemian Fab Five Freddy). This wasn't surprising, considering Bam was instrumental in bringing together hip-hop and punk rock audiences at Manhattan clubs like Negril, Danceteria, and the Roxy. In fact, during the early 1980s, evidence of hip-hop's influence on the rock world became pronounced as rock acts began introducing the sounds and attitude of rap and hip-hop into their music. English punk rockers the Clash, whose music was already infused with world-beat rhythms, incorporated rap into their hard-rock sound with "Radio Clash" in 1981. That same year, punk princess Debbie Harry and her group, Blondie, released their hit "Rapture."

Bam, through the Soul Sonic Force, also pioneered the packaging of the new age hip-hop music hero. The Soul Sonic Force was the first commercial rap group conceptualized as a band, with a uniform sound, a uniform look, and its own credo. Everyone before was a loose cadre of MCs whose costumes ranged from street clothes to Mob-style suits to leather outfits accentuated with punk rock accessories, but Bam and Soul Sonic wore set costumes. From their eclectic outfits (a spaced-out seventeenth-century aristocrat, a Battlestar Viking), it was obvious Bam and Soul Sonic were reincarnations of George Clinton's Parliament-Funkadelic. That black funk/rock band, with its kooky cosmic outfits and mantra of "free your mind . . . your ass will follow," transformed funk from a genre into the musical movement of the 1970s. Taking their cues from Clinton's Dr. Funkenstein, Bam and Soul Sonic went about pushing hip-hop culture and rap music into the collective consciousness of the generation after black power, touting this new black music as a tool for social change and mind expansion. In doing so, Bam and Soul Sonic became the first act to approach rap and hip-hop music cerebrally as rap music's new conscious avant-garde, thrusting a new generational spirit into the genre.

The formulaic party banter of the hip-hop MC was reshaped into collective cosmic chants urging listeners to enter the space age of black urban culture—the futuristic world of the Zulu Nation, "body rockin' " music, and consciousness-expanding concepts. The crowd responding to Soul Sonic's call-n-response shouts of "Planet Rock! It's the sure shot!" sounded as if they were at an intergalactic party, the place where you wanted to be. And listeners were invited to join this galaxy of the hip-hop party. "We are the future!" Bam declared on Soul Sonic's next hit, "Looking for the Perfect Beat," a song about people seeking their own (musical) life path. For those unwilling to acknowledge the power or even the existence of hip-hop's force and its growing audience, Bam smugly responded, "You are the past!"

They would cultivate this burgeoning hip-hop consciousness more on their third hit, "Renegades of Funk," in late 1983. Where "Planet Rock" invited the world into hip-hop's solar system, "Renegades of Funk" connected listeners and their embrace of this revolutionary sound and culture to the mavericks of world history. "Since the prehistoric ages," they shouted at the song's beginning, "and the days of ancient Greece. On down to the Middle Ages. Planet Earth kept going through changes." Acknowledging history's renegades such as Sitting Bull, Thomas Paine, Dr. Martin Luther King, Jr., and Malcolm X, Bam and Soul Sonic then put their listeners and their musical voice into the historical fray. "Now renegades are the people with their own philosophy. They change the course of history; everyday people like you and me. Now renegades are the people with their own philosophy. They change the course of history; everyday people like you and me." But Bam and Soul Sonic weren't just pioneering rap's commercial possibilities, they were expanding rap's artistic and intellectual importance, handing it to listeners as (to quote George Clinton) the "new type thang." After all, hip-hop music was the reincarnation of funk, a black musical revolution for the latter part of the twentieth century and beyond.

But even while Bam and Soul Sonic elevated rap's vocabulary, it was still constructed as an escapist vehicle. MCs were still about rocking the mic while the world around their audience was crumbling. By 1982, the party in the streets was coming to an end and the winter of black discontent was setting in—unemployment, crime, growing poverty, and inequality—while commercial rap, for the most part, did nil to acknowledge this picture, almost rendering itself irrelevant with the changing times . . . until shortly after the release of "Planet Rock," when Sugar Hill Records released Grandmaster Flash & the Furious Five's "The Message."

A blunt, unflinching commentary on the state of black urban America, "The Message" instantaneously changed the nature of rap music from egocentric party music to a powerful sociopolitical vehicle for speaking the realities of black America. The MC expanded his role from dance floor mouthpiece to prophet of the streets, the musical messenger of the generation after black power. "Don't push me 'cause I'm close to the edge," the song's intensely pensive chorus cautioned its listeners. "I'm tryin' not to lose my head . . . It's like a jungle sometimes; it makes me wonder how I keep from going under." Not many hits of the day discussed the underside of the ghetto the way "The Message" did, detailing the violence and frustration of poverty so vividly that listeners could see and smell it. "Broken glass everywhere," Melle Mel rapped, "people pissin' on the stairs. You know they just don't care." Unlike its commercial rap predecessors, "The Message," with its mid-tempo synth-beat, was a song to be *heard* more than one for dancing. The meticulously descriptive writing of MC Melle Mel and his Furious Five cohorts put listeners, nationwide, in the heated, harsh reality—the smells and the noise—of America's urban hardlands. Within the world of "The Message," bill collectors were constantly calling, children were disillusioned with education, and men could get knifed in the heart at any given moment. Even in their own cautionary message, the Furious Five weren't immune to the whims of the city, as the song ends with the group being racially profiled and arrested by the police. When one member tries to explain that they are Grandmaster Flash & the Furious Five, the frustrated officer blurts out, "What is that? A gang?" as he shoves them into the police car before the song ends. With "The Message," the creative and contextual bar for rap music was raised.

Despite eschewing the up-tempo rhythms common in early commercial hip-hop music, the song was a smash, reaching number four on *Billboard*'s R&B chart and eventually going platinum. Both *The Village Voice* and *Rolling Stone* honored "The Message" as "Single of the Year." Music writer Kurt Loder, commenting on the record, wrote that it was "the most detailed and devastating report from underclass America since Bob Dylan decried the lonesome death of Hattie Carroll—or, perhaps more to the point, since Marvin Gaye took a look around and wondered what's going on." Finally, rap music had morphed into an entity bigger than its hip-hop stomping ground. Now, it was officially the mouthpiece of the streets outside of its New York origins, with Grandmaster Flash & the Furious Five as the town criers. The artistic, cultural, and social possibilities of rap music were finally realized, establishing its relevance in black popular culture by giving its black urban audience a vehicle to speak their pain and frustration along with their hedonistic needs and self-mythology. Now all that was needed were heroes to take rap even further, to put the genre and the voice of a post–black power America on the global stage. What was needed, quite frankly, were superstars.

THREE

Black Pop in a B-Boy Stance
Run-D.M.C.

The sound of their beats alone, compared to what had come be-fore . . . were the audio equivalent of low-kiloton-yield bunker busting.

—Harry Allen

The spring of 1983 was cracked by the thunderous rhythm of change—more like a huge-ass drumbeat with enough force to shake the sun . . . *Boom Bap Bap Bap Bap Bap Bap Bap Bap* . . .

The opening bombast of "Sucker M.C.'s (Krush-Groove 1)" was the perfect metaphor for the arrival of Run-D.M.C.: simple but sudden and overpowering, an instant blast of freshness that was, in a word, *street*. Single-handedly, the song and its performers introduced the boom boxes of black America to a new era of rap. Like many a hip-hop classic, Run-D.M.C.'s breakthrough moment came as the B-side to a commercial offering for radio airplay. Where the Furious Five's "The Message" elevated MCs as poets who could report the grim realities of black urban America, Run-D.M.C. debuted as street-corner prophets decrying the world's problems. On the song "It's Like That," D.M.C. yelled, "Wars goin' on across the sea! Street soldiers killing the elderly/ What ever happened to unity?" Setting the trio apart from their predecessors wasn't just their forceful delivery, or their global outlook, or even their name (which stood apart from the usual names of rap groups like the Treacherous Three or the Fantastic Five), but the brooding, extremely pared-down drum tracks they rhymed over. Their big beats, produced by both drums and drum machines, came closer to hip-hop's early break beat sound than any record before it. But while

"It's Like That" used its tall, plodding rhythm to transmit Run-D.M.C.'s global message (and went to number fifteen on *Billboard*'s R&B chart), "Sucker M.C.'s" utilized a sonically gigantic beat to usher in the new age (some would even say the new school) of hardcore rap, one drawing its style and focus from the merciless, competitive nature of the MC battle.

Instead of advertising a rap artist's abilities to move crowds, this strand of rap concentrated on downing the competition, dazzling listeners by articulating how other MCs couldn't measure up to one's rhyme skills or ghetto brawn. Compared with "Rapper's Delight" or "Freedom" or "Planet Rock," "Sucker M.C.'s" was more akin to a lyrical fight. And just as aggressive as its rhymes was its beat. Loud, raw, and sonically huge, nothing about its rhythm was constructed for crossover appeal—no disco-fied re-creations or pop melody overtures or dance-centric grooves. With the release of "Sucker M.C.'s," the earliest b-boy sound—the uncompromised funk and competitive nature of hip-hop music—finally arrived. And instantly, the standards for proving one's own worth in rap, distinguishing oneself from the crowd of other rappers, were reset by Run-D.M.C.

There were still the delusions of an MC's wealth ("Champagne, caviar, and bubble bath," rhymed Run, "ya see, that's the life that I lead). Only instead of devastating listeners with the dynamics of keeping the party alive, they primarily focused on "dissin' " (disrespecting) their competitors, the sucker MCs. " 'Cause, it takes a lot to entertain," rapped D.M.C. "And sucker MCs can be a pain." The song's confrontational theme worked twofold: giving rap's growing core audience the honest, raw, and competitive energy of hip-hop culture, and instantly establishing Run-D.M.C. outside the ranks of rap's original rhyme masters (the Bronx gatekeepers of the culture, so to speak). Coming from Queens—a borough not even considered on the early New York hip-hop map—Run-D.M.C. weren't about gaining the respect of their uptown predecessors (an insurmountable task if you weren't a part of the Bronx scene). They snatched it by strengthening the relationship between the rapper and his/her urban audience with a new style of honesty. Besides dishing insults ("You don't even know ya English, ya verb or noun") and MC grandstands ("I dress to kill, I love to style"), Run-D.M.C. were the first rap artists to begin opening the real files of their lives—as opposed to the fictional ones rappers usually made up—

through their raps. For Run, it was how his rap career came to be ("Two years ago, a friend of mine . . ."). For D.M.C., it was his educational background ("I'm D.M.C. in the place to be / I go to St. John's University"), his complexion ("I'm light-skinned!"), where he was from ("I live in Queens"), and his favorite soul food ("And I love eating chicken and collard greens"). So, upon hearing the duo, listeners didn't just know how bad these Negroes were, they had an understanding of *who* these bad Negroes were.

Though nothing was more jarring than seeing them. For viewers getting an initial look at Run-D.M.C. in 1983 during their television debut on the video show *New York Hot Tracks*, all perceptions of these newjack badasses were confirmed. Standing in their signature b-boy stance staring defiantly at the camera, Run and D (sans their DJ, Jam Master Jay) *were* the hardest and the coolest and the realest Negroes in music. The moment instantly turned them into the minimalist heroes of hip-hop culture and rap music. Like their music, their look was bare-bones and forceful. The duo's wardrobe was the hip-hop uniform, gear straight from the street corner: shell-toe Adidas sneakers, Adidas sweat suits, black godfather hats, and a facial expression that said, "I'm fresh, damn it!" They were the complete antithesis of established commercial rap stars like the Furious Five and the Soul Sonic Force, who wore costumes on par with Parliament-Funkadelic or the punk/S&M set. Among their contemporaries, Run-D.M.C. posed themselves as outsiders in an outsider art form, shunned by the old-schoolers for their pared-down look. "Man, y'all come just like y'all come off the street," they were berated by members of the punk-clad rap group Fearless Four. However, considering that whenever young black males who looked or dressed like Run and D were on television they were usually on the evening news being led on a perp walk, their image spoke volumes to a young black audience. Even with their culture gaining momentum, hip-hop's faithful could never really escape society's brutal misperception of (or reaction to) them, as had been proven eight months prior to Run-D.M.C.'s arrival, when graffiti artist Michael Stewart died from a beating given to him by transit police officers.

The twenty-five-year-old Brooklyn man had been arrested for "tagging" (writing his graffiti alias) on a Manhattan subway station wall. After white officers used "excessive restraining techniques" to subdue and apprehend Stewart, he lapsed into a coma and died thirteen days later, causing black leaders and activists to cry racism and police brutality, believing the excessive force used on the young black man by the white officers to be racially motivated. All six officers charged in the case were eventually acquitted, but the case became one of many to spark the burgeoning social consciousness (for now a subconsciousness) of the post–black power generation.

More than a shock to the rap establishment, Run-D.M.C.'s arrival was a cultural coup, giving voice and representation to urban black youth of the Reagan era. The early 1980s were a startling picture of contrast in black America. While a disproportionate number of lower-income black families felt the effects of the conservative backlash, America's political power base attempted to make poverty, racial injustice, despair, and black youth (like Michael Stewart) invisible. Or their despair was dressed up to appear less of an eyesore, like the way New York City dealt with the leagues of abandoned buildings along the Cross-Bronx Expressway in 1983. Instead of fixing the buildings, the city simply decorated their boarded-up windows with a poor man's trompe l'oeil: vinyl decals depicting shutters, potted plants, venetian blinds, and window shades—a weak gesture on the part of a neighborhood improvement program to enhance the image of New York's dilapidated areas. But on a federal level, with program cuts, rising unemployment, and growing crime rates, the black urban poor saw their lives getting worse.

On the other hand, in mainstream media black progress seemed more apparent than ever. Hollywood's top box-office draw was comedian Eddie Murphy. Mr. T, a former bodyguard, was on his way to becoming America's superhero with the debut of the television show *The A-Team*. In Chicago, a city that erupted into racial unrest when Martin Luther King, Jr., marched against racism there in 1966, Harold Washington became the city's first black mayor. And in October 1983, the Reverend Jesse Jackson announced he'd run to become America's first black president. In the realm of popular music, numerous black artists—from Lionel Richie to Kool & the Gang to Billy Ocean to Chaka Khan—were making the exodus from soulful R&B and funk to the racially homogenized sound of pop, the defining moment being the release (and gradual explosion) of Michael Jackson's record-breaking LP *Thriller*. The biggest-selling pop album in music history, *Thriller* broke down every barrier in pop music imaginable, from desegregating

MTV to finally making an African-American artist the center of adoration for the world. If civil rights were being challenged (and eradicated) on Capitol Hill, their outcome and rewards were still shining on television and Top 40 radio, and even in mainstream politics. Even Dr. King enjoyed a little crossover in 1983: with the stroke of Reagan's pen, the celebration of Martin Luther King, Jr.'s birthday became a federal holiday.

But Run-D.M.C.'s rise, their lives and their fame, squarely reflected the social duality of this black progress. Unlike hip-hop's pioneers, who grew themselves and their creation out of the crumbling landscape of the Bronx, Run, D, and their DJ, Jam Master Jay, came from the Hollis section of Queens, New York. A former semi-suburb, the area was 70 percent white when Run's parents (Daniel Sr. and Evelyn Simmons) moved to the neighborhood in 1964, fourteen days before their youngest son, Run (Joseph Simmons), was born. That same year Congress—under heavy pressure from President Lyndon B. Johnson—passed the Civil Rights Act. Daniel Sr., an attendance supervisor for Queens School District 29, was also a civil rights activist, attending the historic 1963 March on Washington, after leading a protest against discrimination at a Queens construction site. His social awareness was the family legacy. "I think I passed on that kind of controlled anger at social injustice to all my sons," he would later tell Run-D.M.C.'s biographer and former publicist, Bill Adler. But by the time Run turned ten, according to Daniel Sr., white flight had turned Hollis from an integrated neighborhood to all black. Along with white residents, businesses (supermarkets, butchers, bakers) left, and city services disappeared or were drastically cut. Even with the arrival of drugs and New York City's growing gang problem in the early to mid-1970s, the Hollis that Run-D.M.C. grew up in wasn't a slum but "a ghetto in the suburbs."

It was the kind of deterioration that caused Byford and Bannah McDaniels, the parents of D.M.C. (Darryl McDaniels), to send their son to Catholic school, attempting to protect him from the whims of the public school system and the lure of the streets. "And since kindergarten, I acquired the knowledge," D barked on "Sucker M.C.'s." "And after twelfth grade I went straight to college." This was also the Hollis that a ten-year-old Jam Master Jay (Jason Mizell) moved to from Brooklyn in 1975, his parents, Jesse and Connie Mizell, wishing to provide a better environment for their children. Despite the improvements his parents wanted for their offspring, Jay learned immediately that Brooklyn's street rules also applied to Hollis's manicured blocks.

In this transformed neighborhood, the three formed a friendship around their love of hip-hop culture and rap music, especially the hard stuff, which would inform their own musical futures. "The Funky 4 was the aggressive niggas I wanted to be," explained D.M.C. The success of Run-D.M.C.'s brand of hardcore resulted from the visionary management of Run's older brother Russell, who saw rap music as, to borrow from Berry Gordy's Motown prophecy, the music of young America. The world, of course, came to know Russell Simmons as cofounder and CEO of Def Jam Records, becoming the godfather of the rap music industry, marketing hardcore rap music to the streets as well as to white America. The early work of his Rush Management was behind Kurtis Blow's groundbreaking career; the push Russell gave to Run-D.M.C. wasn't propelled by his marketing savvy alone, but by the revolution taking place within both black and American popular culture.

The year Run-D.M.C. debuted, hip-hop was making its debut before the American public. Now rap wasn't the only creative expression taking hold in the ghettos of post–black power America. The art of break dancing had been slowly gaining national exposure, featured on such television programs as ABC's *That's Incredible!* But a cameo of b-boy pioneers the Rock Steady Crew in the hit 1983 film *Flashdance* turned breaking into a national street dance revolution, inspiring urban youth to put aside negative street antics, pick up a piece of cardboard, and spin their way to neighborhood celebrity. Suburban white kids also picked up on the craze, further spreading the sensation of hip-hop culture outside the movement's core urban audience. Moreover, the documentary *Style Wars* about New York City's graffiti art movement aired on PBS, exposing the art—its heroes, its techniques, and its history—to youth starving for a creative outlet. Most notably, though, the release of the film *Wild Style*, an ultra-indie flick featuring the pioneers of hip-hop culture—from graf artist Lee Quinones to DJ Grandmaster Flash to the Cold Crush Brothers—helped assemble the whole movement together for viewers to witness in its entirety. At a time when public schools were cutting or obliterating arts programs across the country, hip-hop became the alternative, emerging, according to one hip-hop pioneer, as the greatest social program of the twentieth century.

At last, like the black boomers before them, the generation after black power found its own sociocultural voice, a revolution it could pour its creative juices into. To the public, hip-hop—its art, its fashion, and its attitude—may have seemed a passing fad. But to the post–black power generation, hip-hop was—more than a racial stance—*the* answer to the question of social identity and value. (Class, in the post–black power/civil rights era, became just as big a factor in one's place in society as race.) As the first group of blacks devoid of Jim Crow memories, this new generation of black America was supposedly the beneficiary of civil rights victories (no matter how limited or invisible those gains might have seemed). For them, the struggle had passed into the romanticized annals of history, but in place of the movement that had vanished, hip-hop culture and rap music arrived to offer what was missing in the wake of its dissolution: pride, direction, and a sense of self-worth and self-determination. As a product of the fertile minds of urban youth—the woefully underprivileged and culturally deprived—hip-hop was unabashedly street and proud. "[T]he subsequent rise of hip-hop music," observed writer Norman Kelley in his book *The Head Negro in Charge Syndrome*, "shows that black youth have always been ready to receive the word of engagement if given guidance and groomed for future leadership positions." Within this revolution brewing in black culture, Run-D.M.C., in all their *super-baadness*, became the representatives of these underrepresented denizens of America, thrusting the MC—now the hardcore MC—into the role of sociocultural leader.

Run-D.M.C.'s self-titled debut album, released in March 1984, affirmed that impact, becoming the first rap album to go gold. In *The Village Voice*, music critic Robert Christgau proclaimed the LP was "easily the canniest and most formally sustained rap album ever." Even the album's cover was an announcement of change in black popular music and culture. In a stark, grainy black-and-white photo, Run and D, dressed in their trademark godfather hats and sweat suits, stand confidently against a brick wall. D leans forward, sternly staring into the camera, while at his side Run glares defiantly, pointing straight at you as if signifying to his partner whom they are going to take over or "take out." The cover's minimalist quality was greatly reminiscent of the Ramones' 1976 self-titled debut eight years earlier. Where the anti–corporate rock posturing of the four leather-clad misfits (also from Queens) worked to reinvigorate rock music with punk, the stone-faced urban realism of Run-D.M.C. prepared to sharpen rap's focus and image on the hardcore.

The rear of the *Run-D.M.C.* LP jacket continued the deft display of the crew's style. Atop a picture of Run and D posing against an alleyway wall are photos of Jay (the architect of the crew's street look) and of the crew, sporting black leather outfits (their blazers reminiscent of the Panthers) and posturing in the crew's official pose, dubbed the "b-boy stance." Their arms are folded with one hand cupping the opposite elbow, their feet pointing at a right angle, and a look of indifference is on their faces. This stance was originally struck by stickup kids as a way of sizing up and intimidating victims until Run-D.M.C. appropriated the pose with "Sucker M.C.'s" as a signifier of hip-hop confidence and machismo. "I cold chill at a party in a b-boy stance," declared Run. "And rock on the mic and make the girls wanna dance."

But just as hard and defiant and revolutionary as the look of *Run-D.M.C.* was their music—all original and nothing sampled. Though many critics later discounted their debut as an album of singles (lacking the cohesive feel of a *real* album), the LP was, without a doubt, hip-hop's first attempt at a profoundly cohesive statement, one reflecting the dual consciousness (self-assured *and* socially insightful) of its post–black power constituency. At one end of this dual consciousness was the cocksure (and innovative) blast of hardcore battle raps, Run-D.M.C. following up "Sucker M.C.'s" with their sonic declarations of dominance atop gigantic beats. The ode to their turntablist "Jam-Master Jay" recognized his skills while simultaneously proclaiming Run and D's own reconfiguration of the game (and their old-school multi-member competition). "The good news is that there is a crew," announced D.M.C., signifying to naysayers like the Furious Five, "Not five. Not four. Not three. Just two. Two MCs who are claiming the fame"; and the rhyme for the hometown posse, "Hollis Crew (Krush-Groove 2)," put the duo's Hollis enclave at the center of rap music's new universe with a song that jumped out of boom boxes like a street-centric circus barker.

At the opposite end was the crew's eye on society, a multifaceted look at an increasingly complex environment, one Run-D.M.C. wouldn't just talk *about* but directly *to*. Their remake of Kurtis Blow's "Hard Times," more than a reflection on problems facing black urban

America (unemployment, sociopolitical obstacles, poverty), was a hip-hop-style pep talk—"Hard times is spreading just like the flu / Watch out, homeboy, don't let it catch you / (PaPaPa)Prices go up, don't let ya pocket go down / When ya got short money you're stuck on the ground . . . Turn around"—while the woeful optimism of "Wake Up," borrowing thematically from Dr. Martin Luther King's "I Have a Dream" speech, found Run feeling elated due to a promising vision of peace he had while sleeping. On the topic of race relations, Run dreamed: "Everyone was treated on an equal basis / No matter what colors, religions, or races." With regard to world conflict, he rapped: "There were no guns (no what?), no tanks (no what?), atomic bombs / And to be frank, homeboy, there were no arms / Just people working hand-in-hand / There was a feeling of peace all across the land." The world had even worked "to fight starvation."

Nevertheless, as in King's day, Run soon discovered upon waking up that, alas, it *was* all only a dream. But at a moment when black poppular music and culture were too preoccupied with crossover appeal to notice or comment on a troubled world, Run-D.M.C. was positioned as the crucial voice on the horizon. After attending the duo's show at the New York club Danceteria, reviewer Richard Grabel of England's *New Musical Express* said of their message: "They've got the headlines and the street news flashing like a very quick teletype in every line. No banners waving, no big deal emphasis on it, but these raps tell true tales about all kinds of crises, economic, social and personal."

Between the sonic commentary and the atomic boasts, though, was the groundbreaking sound and fury of "Rock Box," a hardcore rap blending the rebellious spirit of hip-hop and the hard-driving guitars of rock. The brainchild of bass guitarist/producer Larry Smith and Russell Simmons, "Rock Box" was rap music's first true moment at crossing rap (and its attitude) over without compromising its street image and sound. Larry's beat, accompanied by the heavy metal guitar of Eddie Martinez, was up to b-boy standards, while Run-D.M.C.'s rhymes were just as dis-ful, boastful, and attitudinal as they'd ever been. The two boldly defended their streetcentric uniform, now their signature look and most profound statement. "Your Calvin Klein's no friend of mine," Run declared. "Don't want nobody's name on my behind / Lee on my leg, sneakers on my feet / D by my side and Jay with the beat." Defying the crossover mandate of their commercial predeces-

sors ("No curls, no braids. Peasy head, and still get paid"), Run-D.M.C.
redefined the boundaries and ideals of rap music's tread into the mainstream with "Rock Box."

The song's melding of rap and hard guitar rock was the perfect match based on a simple premise. As Russell saw it: "Rap is black outlaw music and rock is white outlaw music. Two opposites together as one." And once again, the results were the genius of perfect timing as "Rock Box" became the first rap video played on MTV, a monumental task considering that only the year before, Michael Jackson became the first black artist to get played on the racially exclusive network. This breakthrough at last gave Run-D.M.C. and rap music access to a crucial mainstream marketing tool. "A million people wouldn't know us if it weren't for MTV," D.M.C. later reflected in an interview with *The Source* magazine. Being the first rap group to break down the racial barricades of pop marketing and media, Run-D.M.C. saw its value (in relation to hip-hop and its young constituency) entered another stratosphere. Frank Rodriguez wrote: "In today's pop landscape of megastars with sequined gloves and perfectly coiffed limeys with arty but empty ditties, Run-D.M.C.'s message and sound have an aural punch that is more than interesting: it is vital."

On the screen and the airwaves, Run-D.M.C. were the mouthpiece for a voiceless post–black power generation. Moreover, they became so just as black mainstream politics received a symbolic push from Jesse Jackson's run for the U.S. presidency. Jackson was seen as the de facto political heir to Martin Luther King, Jr., but his historic attempt to run for the White House came twelve years after congresswoman Shirley Chisholm became the first black candidate to run for the presidency. Prior to his presidential bid, Jackson and his Chicago-based Operation PUSH, in an effort to defeat Ronald Reagan, began a massive get-out-the-vote campaign to register new black voters. These drives, as described by one report, "had the feeling of [church] revivals," an atmosphere which gave Jesse such a possession of the political Holy Spirit that he announced his candidacy. Looking back, though, one could see it as part of a thought-out power move: the year before announcing his intentions, Jackson had turned himself into a serious candidate.

The civil rights leader widened his profile, proving his diplomatic skills and effectiveness at implementing foreign policy by negotiating the release of U.S. Navy lieutenant Robert O. Goodman from a Syrian prison. (Goodman had been shot down and captured during a December 1983 airstrike over Lebanon.) Jackson's bid, however, was deemed controversial when he teamed with Nation of Islam leader, Louis Farrakhan. In the late 1970s, Farrakhan became head of the militant black Muslim organization, resurrecting the group after it (and its black nationalist mythology) was disbanded in 1975 following the death of Elijah Muhammad. The pairing of two political heirs was viewed as a (momentary) reconciliation of ideology between the civil rights and the black power movements. Where the civil rights movement valued integration as the means of black sociopolitical progress, the proponents of NOI nationalism preached black unity as the answer to advancement. Jackson, for his part, presented a black united front. Farrakhan, whose Fruit of Islam provided security for Jackson, broke Elijah Muhammad's rule of not participating in American politics by allowing (and encouraging) NOI members to register and vote in the upcoming election. The inclusive spirit of Jackson's bid looked promising, his campaign aimed at appealing to a "rainbow coalition" of voters—mainly minorities, poor whites, gays, and so on—left out of Reagan's agenda. But Jackson's ignorance (and arrogance) within this black united front ultimately derailed his presidential dreams. His infamous reference to Jews as "Hymies" and New York as "Hymietown"— Jackson's moment of talkin' "black talk" reported by *Washington Post* reporter Milton Coleman—destroyed his white support base and, inevitably, his run for the White House. The leader's costly mistake was ripe for parody as Eddie Murphy lampooned Jackson on *Saturday Night Live* with a soul ditty called "Don't Let Me Down (Hymietown)."

Without a truly viable opponent to capture the minority vote, Reagan handily won a second term and the Republican reign continued. But while Jesse's comet came and went, the sociocultural power of Run-D.M.C. persisted with the release of their sophomore LP, *King of Rock*, in 1985. Now the monarchs of hip-hop music and culture, Run-D.M.C. were *the* ambassadors of their post–black power constituency. Nonetheless, *King of Rock*, which incorporated still more rock elements, was crafted to build off the marketing momentum created by "Rock Box," increasing Run-D.M.C.'s audience, their empire, their influence, and their musical terrain, all without "alienating their core audience of black teens." The album's title song aided this mission, brashly delivering the message that American popular music and culture had another perspective—a young, black, and uncompromising perspective—to consider. The song's video played a huge role in breaking the news, its premiere on MTV creating a buzz that was the hiphop equivalent of Michael Jackson's video for "Thriller."

In the clip, Run and D enter a building only to be stopped by a white guard (played by comic actor Calvert DeForest) who informs them, "Hey, this is a rock 'n' roll museum! You guys don't belong in here," and laughs in their faces. In response to DeForest's put-down and hearty guffaw, D.M.C. thunderously declares: "I'm the King of Rock, there is none higher / Sucker MCs should call me sire / To burn my kingdom you must use fire / I won't stop rockin' till I retire." And, accompanied by Larry Smith's hardcore drumming and Eddie Martinez's guitar, Run and D defiantly enter the museum and American music history with the force of a category five hurricane. Once inside, they proceed to defile and disregard the museum's honorees, stepping on a sequined glove with their shell-toe Adidas ("It's not Michael Jackson and this is not *Thriller*"). They break a pair of rhinestone glasses (supposedly belonging to Elton John). They even slam one of their fedoras on a bust of the Fab Four ("There's three of us, but we're not the Beatles"). After their tour of the museum, thumbing their noses at rock's legends, Run and D pimp confidently out the building's front door, having successfully pushed their way into history as their names and album title are left behind, painted in red on the wall of the museum's hallway entrance. Their two-pronged message was clear: Run-D.M.C. was taking rap to a wider arena and reclaiming the throne of a genre invented by African Americans but now considered "white music." The song and video helped *King of Rock* become the second platinum-selling rap album in history (the first was by the Brooklyn duo Whodini), garnering praise and respect not just from its core black audience but from mainstream rock media. "These guys are no mere pretenders to the throne," a writer for *Rolling Stone* commented.

Though considered among the more subpar of all their albums, *King of Rock* was a daring step for Run-D.M.C., not only expanding their audience but broadening rap's musical scope. Although a forced-sounding meld of rap and its Jamaican musical cousin, the otherwise inventive "Roots, Rap, Reggae," a collaboration with dance hall and reggae legend Yellowman, set the groundwork for future (and more successful) mixing of the two genres. Most of the tracks on the album, though, were rock-inflected continuations of the first record, with another dedication to Jay ("Jam-Master Jammin' ") or über-hard-rock boasts 'n' disses ("King of Rock" and "Daryll and Joe [Krush-Groove 3]") as well as their message songs. Only this time, their social gaze went deeper than global reportage and pep talks, delving into the psychological pitfalls of urban life. The song "You're Blind," written for the most part by Tony Rome, was more than commentary. It was an exploration of the criminal psychosis befalling many a ghetto dweller, driven to a life of crime and fast money by hopelessness and impatience. "Tenement buildings and skycrapers," Run and D begin, "are polluted and often invaded / With troubled hearts and weakened minds / Living their lives and hoping to find / The golden key to prosperity / Never have a grip on reality." Their commentary also extended to the fantasy-become-reality of the rap star. With their growing profile, Run-D.M.C. had to contend with the pressures of celebrity, which they expressed on the song "Can You Rock It Like This," written by hardcore rap newcomer—and soon to be trailblazing idol—LL Cool J. A rock-punched exposé of the insanity and soul-draining life of an entertainer, the song boasts: "I got jet-set women who offer me favors / My face is a thousand lipstick flavors!" Whereas a rapper's wealth and fame and illusions of rocking the nation were a mere fantasy-on-wax six years earlier, Run and D were offering a peek into the new reality of the emerging rap superstar.

The success of *King of Rock* helped Run-D.M.C. take rap music and hip-hop culture to commercial spaces (and heights) it had never experienced or imagined. The year of their second LP, Run-D.M.C. garnered more monumental firsts. On August 3, 1985, they performed on Dick Clark's *American Bandstand*—the first rap act to do so. Two months earlier, they captured global attention as the only hip-hop act performing for the benefit rock concert Live Aid (their short performance beamed to a worldwide television audience of 1.5 billion people). The duo also added to the growing arsenal of hip-hop films with the release of their movie *Krush Groove*. The semi-biographical film (based on Russell Simmons's creation of Rush Management and Def Jam Records) marked a milestone in hip-hop-centered cinema, being the first movie built around the stardom of the MC. Whereas prior movies featured graffiti artists (*Wild Style*) and b-boys (*Breakin'*) as the centerpiece, *Krush Groove* was a serious acknowledgment of the burgeoning force and financial might of rap artists and rap music.

A year prior to *Krush Groove*'s release, *The Wall Street Journal* ran a front-page story about rap music "moving mainstream," and how Russell Simmons, who now represented seventeen rap acts, was its mogul. The acknowledgment of Wall Street got *Krush Groove* to the big screen the same way nationalist chic pushed Hollywood to bankroll blaxploitation after the independent phenomenon of *Sweet Sweetback's Baadasssss Song*. Ten years after the demise of such 1970s black action heroes as those in *The Mack*, *Shaft*, and *Foxy Brown*, the generation after black power was given a moment to see and cheer its black urban badasses (even though they were only rocking the mic instead of "The Man") in American cineplexes.

And Run-D.M.C. wasn't the only act being plugged by *Krush Groove*. The film launched LL Cool J on the hardcore rap scene. His brief cameo in the film, playing a hungry, street-hardened MC, dressed in the tough wardrobe of urban street corners and angrily rapping, "I can't live without my radio!" showed that younger MCs were adopting (and adding to) the Run-D.M.C. standard. The release of LL's gold-selling debut, *Radio*, in 1985 not only marked the launch of Def Jam Records as a major institution nurturing the growth of a rap music industry; the album also infused hardcore rap with an even larger amount of machismo and aggressive energy, as the youthful ego and verbal abilities of LL were massive. "My story is rough," he declared on "I Can't Live Without My Radio." "My neighborhood is tough / But I still sport gold, and I'm out to crush." As the "hip-hop gangster," LL approached hardcore rap with less social awareness, displaying more of a street-fortified attitude and focusing mostly on rugged hedonism and thuggish bravado—a trend that, along with LL's intricate and innovative lyricism, eventually anchored a hold in hip-hop music.

But LL's growing appeal only affirmed the impact of Run-D.M.C., who, a month before the release of *Krush Groove*, finished headlining the second annual Fresh Fest. Started in 1984, this tour, too, was an indicator of hip-hop's escalating economic sway. Fresh Fest was rap's first major tour, elevating the genre from clubs to sponsored (Swatch) arena shows. The first tour grossed $3.5 million. Featuring rap acts like Who-

dini and the Fat Boys as well as the Dynamic Breakers and other pop-
pers and lockers, the Fresh Fest took rap music and hip-hop culture to
arenas in fifty-five cities across the country. As the second year's main
draw, Run and D were finally able to perform at major venues in their
home state, such as Nassau Coliseum, where one reporter was so
moved by the number of fans in attendance that he tagged Fresh Fest
"The Woodstock of Hip-Hop." The sophomore tour would eventually
gross over $7 million.

But whereas the explosion of Run-D.M.C. and Fresh Fest at the
coliseum exemplified the growing cultural and economic power of hip-
hop, nouveau nationalist figures like Louis Farrakhan were attempting
to rejuvenate the economic power of black America during part two of
the Reagan regime. A month after Fresh Fest, the Nation of Islam leader
held a historic rally at New York's Madison Square Garden, ending a
fourteen-city speaking tour promoting (along with the NOI's doctrine
of black pride, self-reliance, and entrepreneurship) his new black economic program, POWER (People Organized and Working for Economic Rebirth). In the October 12, 1985, issue of *The Economist*, a
reporter writing about the rally spoke of the economic condition Farrakhan was trying to remedy. "Since 1980 black families have lost
ground in the amount of money they have to spend," read the piece,
"both in absolute terms and compared with other American families.
One-third of all blacks, and more than half of all black children, live
below the poverty line . . . Black joblessness is more than twice that of
whites . . . and about half the people in prison are black." Although the
reporter cited an increase in black-owned businesses from 1977 to
1982, the caveat was that only 165,765 people (primarily the business
owners themselves) worked for black businesses. POWER, while a half-
baked attempt at what some critics called "bean-pie capitalism," was
Farrakhan's answer to the socioeconomic devolution of post–black
power America, recycling black dollars and creating work for African
Americans. To the twenty-five thousand in attendance, he unveiled his
economic initiative, a plan to manufacture and distribute a line of
soaps, toothpastes, deodorants, and hair care products called Clean N'
Fresh. (Reportedly, the program was being financed by a $5 million
loan from either Syria or Libya.) Farrakhan sold the POWER project as
a means of growing black America's economic self-sufficiency by controlling, selling, and profiting from products black people used daily. "I

feel strong," chanted Farrakhan laughingly, referring to the planned line's deodorant, "because under my arms I got POWER." But, ultimately, POWER failed, petering out (and eventually disappearing) in just a few short years, having never fully caught on with its primary market.

Meanwhile in Philadelphia, mainstream black political power was incinerating its nationalist brother when, on May 13, 1985, Wilson Goode, Philly's first black mayor, ordered police to firebomb the headquarters of the cultural nationalist organization MOVE. Founded in the early 1970s, the back-to-nature, Afrocentric group had had a tumultuous relationship with Philadelphia police following a 1978 shoot-out that left one officer, James Ramp, dead and nine MOVE members serving life sentences for his murder. The 1985 showdown between MOVE and the police was initiated by complaints from neighborhood residents about MOVE members carrying weapons, the stench of feces around their headquarters, and the blaring antigovernment messages coming from the building via loudspeakers (in an attempt to free its nine incarcerated members). A visit from police to serve arrest warrants was met with gunfire, setting off a ninety-minute gunfight. Via the evening news, America then witnessed the overstated operation to expel MOVE after Mayor Goode ordered police helicopters to bomb the building. Viewers watched in disbelief as the maneuver incinerated not only the organization's home but the entire block (sixty-one houses, of which sixty belonged to innocent neighbors). Of eleven MOVE members burned in the mayor's commando raid, five were children. The horrific event was enough to cause African Americans to question the value of black life even in the hands of black political leadership. Unbeknownst to African Americans witnessing the inferno, though, the fire of Philadelphia (a nationally televised black-on-black crime) would prove a powerful metaphor for the devastating narcotics inferno approaching the borders of post–black power America. It had also been quite prophetically announced and decried two years earlier by Grandmaster Flash & the Furious Five on their second pop hit, "White Lines (Don't Don't Do It)," which warned against the allure of cocaine and all of its derivatives.

In the year leading up to the release of Run-D.M.C.'s 1986 album, *Raising Hell*, the industry of crack cocaine rose in conjunction with climbing black unemployment, growing poverty rates, federal program cuts, and the deindustrialization of urban centers nationwide. Crack, the "fast food" of the cocaine world—easy to make, easier to get hooked on, and available in the abundance needed to maintain a high that lasted only fifteen minutes at a clip—instantly turned young, enterprising black folk into sidewalk Blake Carringtons and Al Capones, while culling addicts from all walks of life (particularly women and single mothers). The unfortunate effect on urban black youth culture, as Nelson George observed in *Buppies, B-Boys, Baps & Bohos,* was that it made it "increasingly nihilistic and materialistic." While the 1960s liberation struggle had provided a legacy of black pride and legislation, it failed to effectively build an economic plan to leverage real black economic power. For that shortcoming, the "slingin' " of crack rock became the driving force for an underground urban economy. And its big-wheeling industry leaders (the new street legends and, unfortunately, heroes) emerged with respect that rivaled the greatest hip-hop star, offering youth an alternative means (other than hip-hop culture) of attaining ghetto celebrity.

The rumblings of this shift could also be heard in the evolving sound of hardcore rap, which, like the swelling nihilism and violence in black ghettos across America, had grown rougher. The growing popularity of samplers, used in conjunction with electronic drum machines, pushed the decibels of hip-hop beats (sometimes slower and more menacing) even higher, with their layered production becoming increasingly complicated. Matching the volume (and complexity) of these rhythms were the rap styles, which, in response to the labyrinthine beats, evolved in meter, form, and pacing—twisting ghetto-fed wit within traditional brags and boasts. Along with the rising competition for rap's commercial space, artists—now sporting the fashions of the local drug kingpin (thick gold chains, suede sweat suits, and Dapper Dan outfits covered in the emblems of Gucci or Fendi)—escalated their display of attitude and ego and aggression, all of it inspired by Run-D.M.C.

LL's *Radio* led the charge with hits like "Dangerous" and "Rock the Bells," dishing insults to sucker MCs and androgynous black pop stars alike. ("So all you Jheri curl suckers wearing high-heeled boots / Like ballerinas what I mean is you're a fruit-loop troop.") Then other artists contributed to the remix of hardcore rap's soundtrack. Slick Rick and the human beatbox Doug E. Fresh added material flash and storytelling pizzazz with 1985's "The Show" backed with "La Di Da Di." Philadelphia's Schoolly D (a former member of Philly's Park Side Killers gang) projected hedonistic gangsterdom on the songs "Gucci Time" and "P.S.K. What Does It Mean?" the next year. Former Queens hustler Kool G Rap mixed lyrical fury with rabid pimp-tude on "I'm Fly" backed with "It's a Demo" in 1986. While on the philosophical end, former Long Island stickup-kid-turned-ghetto-Islamic-sage Rakim merged stone-faced seriousness with the wisdom of the Black Muslims on the song "Eric B. Is President" backed with "My Melody."

The creative pressure from rap's new crop of hardcore talent pushed Run-D.M.C. to produce their magnum opus, *Raising Hell*. They'd already anchored hip-hop's commercial voice within the world of pop. But with *Raising Hell*, Run-D.M.C. wanted to craft an album displaying the undeniable artistic and cultural might of rap music and hip-hop culture. They wanted to thrust *Raising Hell* into the creative pantheon of great American albums, proving, once and for all, that this post–black power expression known as hip-hop music was just as viable as other great American musical genres (blues, jazz, rock, etc.). And as co-producers of the album (a hat they hadn't worn for the first two LPs), Run, D, and Jay did so, solidifying their legacy as the "Beatles of Rap" and driving the creative soul child of their generation to triumph over those who wouldn't take this music or its message seriously.

For anyone (including forgetful hip-hoppers) who doubted their protracted status as pioneers and cultural leaders, Run-D.M.C. reassured them with the release of *Raising Hell* in the spring of 1986. The album's first single, "My Adidas," while paying homage to the crew's favorite footwear, celebrated their trailblazing accomplishments using their "kicks" (slang for sneakers) as a metaphor for achievement. "My Adidas walked through concert doors," loudly claimed D.M.C. "And roamed all over coliseum floors / I stepped onstage at Live Aid. All the people gave and the poor got paid / And out of speakers I did speak. I wore my sneakers but I'm not a sneak / My Adidas touched the sand of a foreign land. With mic in hand I cold took command." That shell-toe Adidas had fallen out of fashion with core hip-hop devotees by the song's release was irrelevant. The sentiment, overall, worked as an in-your-face retrospective, looking back at how far rap music—the sound of young black urban America—had come with the help of the boys from Hollis. The single also garnered Run-D.M.C. another feather for their Stetsons: as the first rap artists to get a sneaker endorsement deal. Indeed, they'd taken the "beat from the street and put it on TV." But more than rejoicing over Run-D.M.C.'s power moves, "My Adidas" was also laced with an even larger congratulatory subtext. In trumpeting their own journey, Run-D.M.C. also honored the accomplishments of hip-hop's faithful. Finally, their sociocultural voice was becoming a part of the American social lexicon. The Hollis duo, through their rubber-soled metaphor, attached the travails of their fans—many of whom had worn the sneakers—to their own journeys and triumphs. (After all, it was through their support that Run-D.M.C. could now "chill in Cali.") And "My Adidas" provided a genuine moment for hip-hoppers, joyously rapping along with the song, to indirectly cheer and celebrate themselves.

Raising Hell ultimately established rap music as an honorable art form, becoming, as Public Enemy's Chuck D later wrote in *Rolling Stone*, "the first true rap album, a complete work of art." Whereas *King of Rock* lacked a clear musical delineation between rock and hip-hop, *Raising Hell* carved an exceptional path between the two, giving listeners a noteworthy interpretation of the hip-hop music experience even more than their debut LP had. And as Run-D.M.C.'s rap/rock formula expanded the racial makeup of the genre's fan base, that audience came to include an increasing number of nonurban and white youths as well. Predictably, the melding of genres propelled *Raising Hell* into phenom status. An example of the melding was when Def Jam's Rick Rubin created the genius pairing of Run-D.M.C. with the rock band Aerosmith on a remake of the band's hit "Walk This Way." The union not only revived Aerosmith's career (a profound statement about rap's commercial power) but also catapulted *Raising Hell* to rap's first multiplatinum-selling album (three million) in under a year. For this feat, Run-D.M.C. were also the first hip-hop artists to grace the cover of *Rolling Stone*.

Raising Hell exposed hip-hop's growing flock (especially young whites) to the ego-heavy intricacies and streetcentric creativity of hardcore rap. Reacting to pressure to stay locked into the aesthetics of their core audience, Run-D.M.C. wove samples of hip-hop's traditional break beat sound into their tracks. The cut "Peter Piper," Run and D's nursery-rhyme-inspired dedication to Jay's turntable skills, included a scratch 'n' cut tasting of Bob James's 1975 pop-jazz remake of "Take Me to the Mardi Gras," the song considered a break beat classic. "Hit It

Run," featuring D.M.C.'s über-hard-rock rhyme skills and Jay's quick-wrists abilities, surprisingly showcased Run's skill as a human beatbox (the process of orally creating drum sounds, pioneered by Doug E. Fresh and the Fat Boys' human percussionist, Darren "Buff" Robinson). Moreover, the lanky rhythms of the cut "Is It Live" were electronically laced with the obscure sounds of go-go, a funk offshoot born in Washington, D.C.

On *Raising Hell*, though, Run-D.M.C.'s beats weren't the only thing showcasing the duo's evolution. To keep up with the ballooning roughness of underground rap—now fueled by the growth of mix shows like Mr. Magic's *Rap Attack* on New York's WBLS—Run and D juiced up their lyrical edge, pushing the ruggedness of their content. Anonymous sucker MCs weren't just dissed, they were downright threatened, as on "Is It Live" where Run commands: "When I write don't bite, and I might check. And if I find yo' behind, I'll break your neck." Even women weren't spared from this new power trip, as Run also rhymed: "Cool chief rapper / I see a girl I tap her / Then I take her on the floor: she don't dance, I slap her." Likewise, the language was stretched profanely in an effort to make a point; for instance, when asserting his dominance over other rap artists, D.M.C. declared on "Hit It Run": "I once was lost but now I'm found / Tell your bunch I'm boss—I run this town / I leave all suckers in the dust / Those dumb motherfuckers can't mess with us!" (Not that Run-D.M.C. didn't cuss; at live shows, Run always declared it was his "fuckin' house.") So to their expanded record-buying audience, especially those white kids whose parents heard their children listening to (and enraptured by) these black prophets of post–black power America, Run-D.M.C. were *the* new Bad Niggas of American music and culture.

Their social gaze also evolved with *Raising Hell*, concentrating on the changing social and economic dynamics of post–black power America. The song "Dumb Girl," a cautionary rhyme about a loose girl caught up in the fast life, spoke to the growing allure of materialism and escapism, in this instance tripping up young women—getting high ("Always sinning never winning 'cause you're last in the race / You getting high and tell a lie and think that makes you the ace") and dating men for their wealth ("You like his money / You'll be his honey / It's the truth . . . you're a great big dummy"). But the album's most radical and socially explosive message was, without a doubt, "Proud to Be Black." Run-D.M.C.'s declaration of racial pride in the vein of James Brown's "Say It Loud (I'm Black and I'm Proud)." The cut was an audacious expression of black awareness about history and racial ignorance over an explosive drum track. "You know I'm proud to be black, y'all," Run shouted to listeners, "and that's a fact, y'all / And if you try to take what's mine I'll take it back, y'all," while D, sounding exasperated, opined: "God damn! I'm tired my man. Don't worry about what color I am / Because I'll show you how ill this man can act / It could never be fiction 'cause it is all fact." The song never made it onto radio, but "Proud to Be Black" articulated a welling racial awareness growing among the post–black power generation. This consciousness wasn't just fueled by the hostility from a Republican White House, but from growing racial unrest once again making its way into the news, including the infamous incident in which, several months after the release of *Raising Hell*, three black males were attacked by a gang of white youths in the Howard Beach section of Queens, New York. The end result was the death of twenty-three-year-old Michael Griffin, hit by a car while fleeing across a highway to escape the bat-wielding mob. The attack was one of several racially charged episodes—including the deaths of Michael Stewart and Eleanor Bumpurs, an elderly black woman who was shot by a white police officer—fomenting black power's return within rap music and its core black audience. Run-D.M.C.'s audacious display on "Proud to Be Black" only hinted at the development.

Shortly after releasing their magnum opus, though, Run-D.M.C. would also learn the price of becoming cultural icons (especially ones who rouse the spirit and imagination of black urban youth). As stars of rap's second-largest national tour and the focus of the mainstream media's budding fascination with hip-hop, Run-D.M.C. were now *the* face of black urban music and youth culture. Unfortunately, their position—along with their dress, language, and attitude—also made them visible targets, easily used as scapegoats for the ill conditions and behavior of their young black followers. This was especially the case with the violent mishaps following a few of their concerts during the early leg of the *Raising Hell* Tour: first, after a show at Pittsburgh's Civic Arena, when kids went on a vandalism spree, breaking store windows and damaging nine city buses. After the tear, twenty-five youths were arrested. Then, following their concert at New York's Madison Square Garden, *The New York Times* reported the arrest of eighteen people after the show for harassing and robbing pedestrians.

Reporter Don Thomas of the Brooklyn-based black weekly paper *Big Red* criticized the group directly, saying he was offended by the profanity and other foul language used onstage. To which Run responded, "The curses are like punctuation marks in our raps. They are the commas, periods, and question marks." But the most infamous stop on the *Raising Hell* Tour was their performance at the Long Beach Arena in California on August 17, 1986, at which a two-hour gang fight within the arena instantly brought the concert to a halt. In the melee, five people were stabbed, and one was shot; four were arrested, and forty-five fans needed hospitalization. Even though police took two hours to arrive (the reason the violence was able to escalate), and in spite of an already overwhelming gang problem in the black communities of Long Beach and South Central Los Angeles, the focal point of the incident— the supposed cause of this mini riot—became rap music and Run-D.M.C. Those who had no idea of what rap or hip-hop culture or Run-D.M.C. stood for made the loudest case against the music. Tipper Gore, wife of future vice president Al Gore and founding member of the antirock lobbying group Parents' Music Resource Center, commented irately in *USA Today*: "Angry, disillusioned, unloved kids unite behind heavy metal and rap music, and the music says it's okay to beat people up." To which Russell Simmons appropriately responded, "Instead of attacking rap, Mrs. Gore should spend some time investigating the sources of the anger and disillusionment she sees in America's youth." No longer was rap's energy for just expressing the lives and worldview of a new black generation; now it needed to protect that generation from outside forces ready to stymie them.

Nevertheless, even though Gore's sister Jennifer Norwood, upon listening to *Raising Hell*, admitted she found "nothing in the lyrics that [was] really explicit or would incite kids to violence," not much could dispel the ominous cloud over rap music and Run-D.M.C. Despite the fact that following the Long Beach debacle, there were no incidents reported in other cities hosting the tour, such as West Palm Beach, Florida, and Greenville, South Carolina, the mishap instilled a rabid fear of hip-hop culture in authorities. Even break dancing, which had become a sensation by 1985, was labeled a nuisance in shopping malls and on street corners nationwide. In the city of Providence, Rhode Island, the license for the tour's date at the Civic Center was revoked. Most of those against rap concerts spoke of concern for violence, property damage, and the congregating of unruly patrons. But Rick Rubin, in a piece he wrote for *The Village Voice*, hit at the core of the fear. "The problems that people have with rap concerts," he wrote, "have to do with society's own troubles with black youth, not with a lyric from a Run-D.M.C. record . . . Music is not the problem. Racism is." Though the charges leveled against Run-D.M.C. and rap music came from a refashioned racism and the now-disguised pistol of racial fear, in hindsight the fiery violence of the Long Beach concert symbolized a brutish nihilism and self-destruction growing within the youth of post–black power America, a vicious disregard for life that would later take the life of Jam Master Jay, who was senselessly murdered in his Hollis, Queens, recording studio in 2002.

Having catapulted rap into America's mainstream, inadvertently inventing (as writer Harry Allen later acknowledged in *The Village Voice*) "the modern hip-hop music business," Run-D.M.C. emerged from hip-hop's struggle for respect as post–black power icons. Whereas black megastars of 1980s pop such as Michael Jackson and Prince entered America's playlist by embracing the sounds (and look) of ethnic ambiguity, Run-D.M.C. uncompromisingly elbowed their way into America's culture club by boldly defining themselves within the parameters of racial, cultural, class, and stone-faced social *badness*, laying a foundation for future black pop stars—from R. Kelly to Usher—to be themselves. Unfortunately, they also became victims of rap's rapidly evolving styles and tastes, their reign ending by the release of their 1988 lackluster LP, *Tougher Than Leather*. But Run-D.M.C. will always be credited with doing for rap what Marlon Brando did for acting: turning it into a raw, magnificent art for its audience. Hardcore rap artists will forever be indebted, and pay homage, to the bravery and ingenuity of Run-D.M.C. They gave rap music its first taste of real power by infusing commercial hip-hop with the honest spirit and look of the streets. And in doing so, Run-D.M.C. were a watershed moment in the rise of black popular culture.

They became a continuum of the historical black folk hero, the Bad

Nigga Hero, installing the character as *the* archetype of rap music. Run-D.M.C. embodied for the generation after black power the same sentiment the mythical Bad Nigga embodied for nineteenth- and early-twentieth-century blacks. For them, as Lawrence W. Levine wrote in his book *Black Culture and Black Consciousness*, the bad black bandit expressed a "profound anger festering and smoldering among the oppressed" who felt that "within the circumstances in which they operate, to assert any power at all is a triumph."

So with Run-D.M.C., the MC—especially the hardcore MC—officially crystallized into the supreme heroic figure, the holy social outlaw, of black America following black power. Once again, the mythical Bad Nigga who had manifested himself in such outspoken figures as James Brown, Muhammad Ali, and Huey P. Newton was now flesh. Coincidentally, this would unfold twenty-seven years after singer Lloyd Price pushed the folktale of the baddest nigga, "Stagger Lee," to the top of the pop charts. Both Run-D.M.C. and Stag wore Stetson hats, and both became larger-than-life figures of the sacred corners of black urban life. Run-D.M.C. was the Bad Nigga myth brought to life through the séance of hip-hop culture. Whereas black history has had its share of Bad Nigga Hero reincarnations (Marcus Garvey, Angela Davis, H. Rap Brown, Martin Luther King, Jr., Malcolm X), figures who, without concern, fought invisibility through the voice of the people, in the age of hip-hop Run-D.M.C. slammed down their fists on the head of black invisibility by taking a stand and putting Stagger Lee into the mix.

FOUR

Stumbling Through Black Power Revisited
Public Enemy

*The whole black nation has to be put together as a black army . . .
We're going to walk on this racist power structure. And we're going to say to the whole damn government, "Stick 'em up, motherfucker! This is a hold up. We come for what's ours."*

—**Bobby Seale**

The head of Public Enemy, Chuck D, is tired. He's
weary from holding things together, from being the voice of reason,
from being considered *the* voice at all—it's just another name for
"leader." And leading gets tiring. Sitting in the back of a trailer, Chuck
takes a break from shooting the video for 1998's "He Got Game," the title track for P.E.'s comeback. Chuck sighs, assessing all the labor that
has gone into the resurrection thus far. "This project, here," he says,
washing his cupped palms over his face, "has been an internal and external hell." Outside, the winter winds whip and sting on perhaps this
coldest day of the season.

All the steps leading to this day turn over in Chuck's mind: the call
from director Spike Lee, the reuniting of Public Enemy, putting the
music together for the album. No: the soundtrack. Yes. Definitely a
soundtrack. A Spike Lee Joint, the film *He Got Game* has reassembled
this hip-hop supergroup, a rap outfit many thought, years ago, would
lead its young black listeners to action. Along with pumping a movie,
the soundtrack was supposed to prop Public Enemy back up, to make
Chuck D relevant again and inject some intellect into hip-hop's sugar-
coated world of premillennial party 'n' bullshit. While Spike's mission
for the movie is to comment on basketball's exploitation of black play-

ers, Chuck's mission is to use the sports theme as a metaphorical comment on the straying of hip-hop music and the values of its young black audience. "Proud to be called a bunches a bitches and niggas," Chuck shouts on "Is Your God a Dog," condemning the self-hate and degradation grown rampant in the youth of post–black power America. This return of Public Enemy was to give the young 'uns a sense of history, an awakening, a challenge to the status quo.

Only Spike Lee Joints tend to have an X-ray effect on Public Enemy at moments (or, in this case, providing the moments) when the true, internal workings (with all the contradictions and dysfunction) of this righteously pro-black group get exposed. Like right after they recorded "Fight the Power" for Spike's racially combustible film *Do the Right Thing* in 1989, and Professor Griff, P.E.'s "minister of information" and head of the Security of the First World (S1W), made his anti-Semitic statement to a *Washington Times* reporter. Then came the aftershock— the protests and the firing and the breakup and the first resurrection and the reinstatement and the album *Fear of a Black Planet*. Now it's the set of a Spike Lee production that's providing an honest look at Public Enemy's skeleton and the frayed edges of its united front.

There's Professor Griff waiting to be called up to the set to shoot his scene for the video. But the time seems like it's never coming. "I've been waiting around since six-thirty this morning," he says, slightly agitated. It's now three in the afternoon. And, though Griff looks cool, his agitation grows as he periodically walks between the trailer and the lobby of the SoHo complex where the shoot is taking place two or three flights up. He knows the delay (or denial) is the price for his indiscretion nine years earlier. "I paid for it, and am still paying for it," he quips. He also knows that none of this would go down if Chuck took a stronger stance on his behalf. "I told Chuck," he says, "you can lead and the group will follow your lead. Then lead. I'm a trooper, man."

There's also the tension between Griff and P.E.'s clown prince of irony, Flavor Flav, who arrives at the complex's lobby an hour later with his baby's mother and three of his children in tow. For the past two weeks, according to Griff, Flavor Flav has promised that if Griff is in the video, he's out. Their rift? A ten-year-old feud of the yin and yang, between Griff's rigid discipline and Flavor Flav's celebrity ego. Both are in the lobby, separated by a crowd of production assistants and fans and label execs. They say nothing to each other. But that's of no concern to those on hand who liven when Flavor arrives and instantly makes his way around the space greeting folks, hugging some, joking with others, but brightening the entire room with the humorous electricity of his skinny frame and boyish charm. With his well-publicized bouts with the law and drugs (and as a member of Public Enemy) he seems more like the quintessential manchild in the promised land.

This is just the tip of what Chuck has to hold together (has been holding together), although he's convinced that it will miraculously work itself out. Because, after all, "you're talking about individuals," believes Chuck. Grown men assembled for the purpose of making rap music and raising awareness. But to be still looked upon as *the leader* continues to boggle and aggravate him. "Why I got to be the spokesperson when there's internal disorder?" he asks no one in particular. Then he remembers a promise he made to himself eight years prior, the promise he made to himself following the racial brouhaha that engulfed P.E. at its apex. "I made up my mind in 1990," he says, "that if I was gonna lead the ship, I'm gonna lead it because the bottom line is if I don't steer the ship, it won't run. And every year, I've steered the ship."

Only the musical voyage Public Enemy is currently on is destined for failure (at least commercially), no matter how much mental fire Chuck puts into his rhymes, no matter how much he uses the metaphor of basketball to speak to the materialism and self-degradation and self-destruction currently running amok in rap music. He can expose the new messianic complex of black America—for the Negro making major NBA (and hip-hop) dollars—on "What You Need Is Jesus." He can question the façade of power black folks present in the NBA (and hip-hop) on "He Got Game." It will all fail. Because no matter how much he breaks down the racial power dynamic of music and sport ("When the Feds come and doom your party / Cracker in the back. Don't you know we it's Illuminati?") and assures listeners that "ain't nothin' changed, P.E. be the same crew. Resurrection in the game here to save you," Public Enemy's not going to save anybody. Not because of internal tension or external pressures or the music being weak. But because P.E. (the median age of its members at the time was thirty-eight) has resurfaced into commercial rap's cold reality of old-school rapper made irrelevant by new-school taste in heroes. Like basketball, rap music is a young person's sport. And at the moment it's a Puff Daddy game, with commercial hip-hop music once again mixing material obsession and pop danceability into its gangsta attitude. Moreover, new, younger, and hungrier MCs like Nas, Master P, Mase, and the ghosts of Tupac Shakur and the Notorious B.I.G.—hardcore voices no doubt influenced by the consciousness-raising rhymes of P.E.—are saving the day. *He Got Game* doesn't even go gold.

This moment of failure—being overshadowed by the fog of young hip-hoppers obsessed with dancing, money, and being badasses—is ironic for Public Enemy. It was they who had begun an eclipse within a similar scenario in commercial rap music with the not-so-noticed release of their debut album, *Yo! Bum Rush the Show*, in 1987. The revolution of Public Enemy was the mortar of what is considered rap music's golden age, an era between the years 1987 and 1993 of tremendous creative and commercial growth following the reign of Run-D.M.C. With P.E.'s pioneering achievements occupying the space of the commercial mainstream, rap music had taken Run-D.M.C.'s hardcore baby in a funkier direction, technologically enhancing the rhythms and expanding the word power and verbal dexterity of the MC beyond imagination.

Producing hip-hop music was no longer a matter of a backup band re-creating popular dance licks or a DJ cutting records back and forth or programming a drum machine. Hip-hop production was now a technological stew of turntables, beat machines, and the latest addition to the music-making process, the sampler. "A sampler is basically a sonic copy machine," wrote Harry Allen in a 1988 *Village Voice* piece, "though a much better, more flexible copy machine." Allowing DJs and producers to record several seconds of sound or music, the machine then looped the sample to play on forever or, if loaded into a sampler drum machine, to be played percussively or hooked into a keyboard and played in a scale. Queens-born DJ/producer Marley Marl pioneered hip-hop's use of samplers. (Not that hip-hop wasn't sampling already; the turntable wizardry used since the beginning to create hip-hop music was a form of looping.) But with the digital aid of samplers, hip-hop production evolved into a complex layering of human expression, technology, and music/social history. Rap's beat had become a veritable sound collage of prerecorded music enhanced with the ultra boom of computer-enhanced drum kicks (a far cry from Run-D.M.C.'s *boom bap*). And by incorporating snippets of original music, commercial hip-hop, while reinvigorating its sound, also reintroduced the forgotten rhythms of great soul and funk music to the youth of post–black power America, such as the infectious funk of James Brown and his backup band the J.B.'s, whose innovative grooves, prideful grunts, and shouts ("Heeeeeey!") punctuated many a hip-hop beat during this era and whose racially conscious rhythms subtly informed the changing ebb and flow of rap.

By the latter half of the 1980s, a cultural shift had reshuffled the playground of hip-hop culture. Breaking, which had been exploited to no end by film, television, and "marketing overkill," faded into obscurity, giving way to trendy dances like the Wop, the Biz Markie, the Cabbage, and a host of others. Graffiti, no longer the ghetto darling of art galleries, and finally removed from New York's subway system (the introduction of "graffiti-free" trains being the nail in the coffin in 1989), was pushed back underground, pouring "onto streets and highways and freight trains, initiating a new wave of police crackdowns." And the role of the DJ—the maestro's ghetto celebrity ceding to the commercial fame of the rap artist—had expanded to record producer. But rap music, as the movement's premier commodity, had become the public face of hip-hop culture and attitude.

And during their golden era, MCs were elevating the art of rhyme, utilizing the layered intricacy of sampled rhythms to enhance the meter of their poetry, approaching the delivery of their words like musicians and poets. With labyrinthine flows and off-rhyming techniques, this new breed of MC laced his/her lyrics with complex wordplay, titillating the ear and imagination of listeners much the way bebop pioneers intensified the riffs, solos, and chord changes of their swinging forefathers. Accompanying this development in writing was a budding self-consciousness among rap artists: tinting this beat-rhyme renaissance with an awareness of rap's potential impact not only as urban-style entertainment but as consciousness-raising poetry for a generation. "No tricks in '86, it's time to build," rapped Rakim on the Marley Marl–produced "Eric B. Is President," which ushered in this new development. The Bronx artist KRS-One (Knowledge Reigns Supreme Over Nearly Everyone), hip-hop music's teacher and vocal head of Boogie Down Productions, declared rap a literary force on songs like "Poetry" and defended hip-hop from revisionist history on "South Bronx."

There was also the introduction of hardcore abstract poetics by the quartet Ultramagnetic MC's on "Ego Trippin'." The Jungle Brothers, hip-hop's MCs on urban safari, blended black sexual machismo with a hint of Afro-consciousness on "Jimbrowski" and "Behind the Bush." And Brooklyn rhyme virtuoso Big Daddy Kane (King Asiatic Nobody's Equal) debuted rap's might with the metaphor on his duet with the original clown prince of rap, Biz Markie, on "Just Rhymin' with Biz." However, while this burgeoning realization and creative energy unfolded, the primary focus of the music remained what it had been during the late 1980s: destroying rival MCs, rocking the party, and looking "dope" from neck to toe.

Not much of rap reflected or responded to the tumultuous events or developments brewing in the wider realm of black America and beyond. The conservative steamroller that was the Reagan administration was going seven years strong, though it was a year away from ending. In a 1987 television interview, Supreme Court justice Thurgood Marshall rated Reagan the worst president in terms of his record on civil rights. A thriving crack industry, which by now employed a growing number of young blacks (especially males), fed a swelling epidemic of crack addiction and an accompanying increase in crime and violence affecting urban black communities across the country. The increasing incidence of racial violence toward blacks (Michael Stewart, Howard Beach, Eleanor Bumpurs, the Tawana Brawley rape case), while filling the news headlines, was jarring the racial awareness of young African Americans. A growing anti-apartheid movement against the white racist government of South Africa had taken hold on American college and university campuses. Parallels between South Africa's apartheid system and America's former Jim Crow segregation ignited a renewed nationalist spirit among black college students nationwide. (The struggle of black South Africans inspired their American Negro brethren the same way Africa's anticolonialist movement in the early 1960s had fed the Pan-Africanist scope of the black power movement.)

These issues of the 1980s fueled late night conversations between Chuck D and his friends Bill Stephney, Harry Allen, and Hank Shocklee. Being fans of rap, they wondered if this genre could be used as a political tool to wake up black folks to these topics. This was when the components of Public Enemy came together in the early 1980s at Long

Island's Adelphi University, where Chuck D (born Carlton Ridenhour in 1960) majored in graphic design. As the story goes, Public Enemy began at and around the school's WBAU radio station. Carlton formed a coalition with local DJ Hank Shocklee, designing flyers for Hank's parties, which led to the two getting a hip-hop mix show at the station in the early 1980s through which they were credited with introducing listeners to the likes of Run-D.M.C. and LL Cool J. From there Carlton Ridenhour transformed into Chuck D, commandeering the mic with a booming voice while Hank handled the turntable mixes. Soon afterward, the show included P.E.'s future DJ, Terminator X, and neighborhood musician/MC/hypeman/all-around cutup Flavor Flav.

But it was when Def Jam's Rick Rubin (a fellow Long Islander) heard a tape of the crew's show, specifically Chuck's rhymes over the Shocklee-produced track "Public Enemy No. 1," Chuck's voice towering and authoritative, that P.E. began to take shape. Rick wanted to sign Chuck, but Chuck refused, thinking—since he was a bit past his mid-twenties—he was too old to be rapping. Then he witnessed the media's crucifixion of Run-D.M.C. and rap music following the Long Beach debacle. "That's when I decided to get involved in this," Chuck later told a *Los Angeles Times* reporter, "and go toe to toe with the media." Rick's offer got Chuck thinking about forming a team that his group could lead, just the way Bambaataa had envisioned a revolutionary movement in rap music, a Black Panther–like revolution to inspire and maybe protect hip-hop culture. He would be the voice, the "messenger." Flavor Flav, representing the unfocused energy of "niggas" in the street, would be MC sidekick and comic foil. Terminator X would DJ. Hank, his brother Keith Shocklee, and his friend Eric Sadler would form the crew's production team, the Bomb Squad. And completing this organization—giving this collective its militant look—would be Professor Griff, a martial arts expert and Nation of Islam member who provided security for Hank's parties. Taking a cue from the Panthers, Chuck installed Griff as the group's minister of information and head of P.E.'s security/backup dance squad, the S1Ws. It was upon Def Jam's acceptance of this vision that Chuck accepted Rick's offer (one he persistently made over several months), though selling Public Enemy's image and music to the masses would be a slow burn.

Initially, the multitude of rap's faithful didn't know what to make of this hardcore anomaly: Chuck D, an obviously older MC (in hip-hop years), his forceful, commanding voice much like a sports commentator; the impatient, frenetic movements of a skinny, dark-chocolate-colored Flavor Flav—donning a baseball cap and a huge clock around his neck—maniacally backing up Chuck's lyrical assault; the S1Ws (huh?), this paramilitary-dressed foursome sporting berets like the Panthers, holding fake Uzi machine guns in the background, and executing martial arts moves and precision march drills. To those witnessing the crew initially, it was apparent that Public Enemy was taking rap's concept of "two turntables and a microphone" to another level, albeit one they weren't sure they were ready for. "It didn't turn out the way we wanted it," Professor Griff explained some years later, "because, in the beginning, no black people would listen." Although P.E. didn't get prime-time airplay on black radio stations at the outset, they did win some spins on rap music mix shows in the tristate area. But radio DJs primarily played instrumental cuts from *Yo!* like "M.P.E.," beats without Chuck's lyrics. Yet even that proved a hard platform to win, as WBLS's Mr. Magic, so repulsed by their first single, "Public Enemy No. 1," broke the record into pieces on the air and declared to his audience, "No more music by the suckers!"

Commercially, *Yo! Bum Rush the Show* didn't fare much better, failing to rise above the fray of hardcore rap albums (such as Boogie Down Productions' *Criminal Minded*) that were already reinvigorating rap music. For northeastern hip-hoppers, though, the gold-selling album, particularly the single "Public Enemy No. 1," delivered the basic essentials: phat sampled rhythms and tons of hard-rock MC bravado—enough to garner P.E. minimal notice among hardcore rap's budding cadre of new-schoolers. "Well, I'm all in—put it up on the board," Chuck introduced himself and crew on "Public Enemy No. 1." "Another rapper shot down from the mouth that roared." As a voice of rap's new age, Chuck armed *Yo!* with the required über-rap machismo, offering tracks like a souped-up ode to his automobile ("You're Gonna Get Yours"), a celebration of the weapon-like power of his mind ("Miuzi Weighs a Ton"), and a dis to class-conscious, status-seeking black women ("Sophisticated Bitch").

But what made P.E. exceptional to the circle of hip-hop heads and critics who were taking notice was Chuck's poetic (almost literary) approach to socially aware hardcore rap, imparting chunks of racial consciousness within his sociopolitical wisdom—lyrics that went beyond ghetto reportage on poverty and crime into the arena of downright speaking up and speaking out against the powers that be—throughout his music. In between bragging about his ride, Chuck laced "You're Gonna Get Yours" with his maverick thoughts on the U.S. government ("Put me on a kick but—line up, time's up. This government needs a tune up") and on the police ("No cop gotta right to call me a punk / Take this ticket—go to hell and stick it"). Within the metaphorically boastful track "Timebomb," Chuck took aim at economic racism ("The one who makes the money is white, not black") and South Africa's oppressive regime ("I'm a MC protector—U.S. defector / South African government wrecker"). Songs like "Rightstarter (Message to a Black Man)"—the title inspired by Elijah Muhammad's book *Message to the Blackman in America*—pumped *Yo!*'s primary focus of inciting a "mind revolution" within the post–black power generation. "Give you pride that you may not find," Chuck rhymed to his young black constituency, "if you're blind about your past then I'll point behind. Kings, Queens, warriors, lovers. People proud—sisters and brothers." As a substantial number of black youths were in college, entering college, or finishing high school, P.E.'s debut ushered in an era of growing racial awareness within black America, awareness brought on by the outward hostility the U.S. government (as well as some white citizens) showed toward black progress. For this generation, whose ideas of black pride and black empowerment hadn't yet formed, Public Enemy were set to resuscitate the ideals of a bygone black power era. The need for this nationalist revival was invoked by Public Enemy's logo—designed by Chuck—of a b-boy's silhouette with folded arms in the crosshairs of a rifle's scope, signaling that black youth were in danger (but didn't know it) and that Public Enemy, rap's connection to the buried black nationalist thoughts and notions of yore, had arrived to awaken them.

What ultimately made folks listen, though, was P.E.'s release of the single "Rebel Without a Pause." As with all monumental rap songs, the song's appeal was undeniably its beat. Starting with the sampled voice of Jesse Jackson ("Brothers and Sisters, I don't know what this world is coming to!"), the cut exploded into a looped combination of James Brown's "Funky Drummer" and the J.B.'s' "The Grunt." The song's piercing saxophone sample sounded as if it had the same purpose as Gabriel's trumpet in the Bible: to signal the Resurrection. While the beat ordered a march to the dance floor, Chuck forcefully rapped an unconventional rebelliousness, the boom of his voice loud and proud and bold as if he were hip-hop's Malcolm X, lyrically invoking the forgotten names of black power ("Supporter of Chesimard!"). "I guess you know—you guess I'm just a radical," declared Chuck. "Not on sabbatical—yes to make it critical / The only part of your body should be parting to / Panther power on the hour from the rebel to you."

Equally powerful was P.E.'s follow-up song, "Bring the Noise," a pro-black defense of rap music against a hostile mainstream media, this time beginning with the sampled voice of Malcolm X declaring, "Too black, too strong." Featured on the soundtrack for the 1987 film *Less Than Zero*, the song officially introduced Public Enemy to the public at large (as well as the hip-hop community), being the first P.E. single, ironically, to get prime-time airplay. For this unveiling, however, listeners heard a fully realized Public Enemy, a group finally displaying its musical and political voice. Chuck, in his fearless defense of rap's integrity and ingenuity, now fashioned himself the crucified black messenger of rap, using his platform to galvanize the post–black power generation around unorthodox black leadership (namely Louis Farrakhan) and the new struggle to fight racial suppression. "Now they got me in a cell," explained Chuck on "Bring the Noise," "'cause my records, they sell / 'Cause a brother like me said, 'Well, Farrakhan's a prophet, and I think you ought to listen to . . . What you ought to do' / Follow for now, power of the people, say, 'Make a miracle, D, pump the lyrical' / Black is back, all in, we're gonna win." "Bring the Noise" and "Rebel Without a Pause" showcased P.E.'s new signature sound, a tornado of samples coloring their music with a profound sense of urgency. The deep, ominously throbbing rhythms of *Yo!* were replaced by increased beats-per-minute topped with a barrage of samples, from the world of black music to unnerving sounds like a blaring siren to the reconfigured words of black leaders past and present. If a new consciousness was developing in the revolutionary halls of rap, Public Enemy had become the vanguard shaping it.

Their second LP, *It Takes a Nation of Millions to Hold Us Back*, released in 1988, sounded the definitive change in guard—from rap kingship to black leadership. This seismic shift could be heard during

Run-D.M.C.'s *Tougher Than Leather* tour, for which Public Enemy was the opening act. The substance of P.E.'s showmanship caused some to question the importance of Run-D.M.C. during the last year of their reign. "Run-D.M.C. . . . enjoyed unprecedented popularity . . . at the time," wrote a *Chicago Tribune* reporter about their performance during the tour. But Public Enemy's "rage-filled performances" made the pioneers of rap's hardcore look and sound and focus seem "irrelevant." The commercial (and critical) disappointment of *Tougher Than Leather* marked Run-D.M.C.'s fall from the spotlight, while *Nation of Millions* was P.E.'s push to the commercial (and creative) forefront of a new movement in hip-hop, the million-selling album becoming a soundtrack for the sociopolitical dynamics taking shape within America at the time. Chuck D, as hip-hop's new Bob Dylan, bestowed on rap the higher purpose of awakening the black masses. (Public Enemy's mission, Chuck often said, was to create five thousand new black leaders for the black community.) As the crew soon discovered, for those suffering and desperate for a Moses to lead them, well, anywhere, a popular rap group might do. Coincidentally, *Nation of Millions* accompanied an electrifying renaissance in black consciousness and leadership, voices answering black folks' need for some kind of response to the aftermath of the decade-long conservative backlash.

During his final year in office, President Reagan threw one more egg at the 1960s, vetoing a civil rights enforcement bill that would have strengthened federal laws prohibiting discrimination, saying the bill allowed "unwarranted" government interference in the affairs of business and religion. Although Congress overrode Reagan's decision—some speculated the override marked a decline in Reagan's influence—the upcoming election had yet to prove that America was now less interested in a Republican agenda.

Jesse Jackson made a second historic attempt at the White House despite the mishaps and controversies of his 1984 campaign. In his bid for the Democratic nomination, Jackson, who over the years fashioned himself a rapper of sorts ("Up with hope, down with dope" and "from the outhouse to the White House" were among his signature lines), made an even bigger impact than in the 1984 contest, winning 7 million votes during the primaries (up from 3.5 million in 1984). In addition to receiving 92 percent of the black vote, he gained 12 percent of the white vote. Out of the fifty-four primary contests, he came in first or second in forty-six (five of the states he won were, ironically, in the Deep South). Moreover, he added two million more black voters to the rolls through his voter registration campaign (a million more than he had registered in 1984). Overall, he officially became the second (and third) *serious* black presidential candidate in American history. Although he eventually lost the nomination to Michael Dukakis, Jackson left an indelible mark on the Democratic convention with his "Keep Hope Alive" speech (another famous rap). Along with increasing his profile as broker of African-American issues within the Democratic Party, Jackson, that coming December, initiated a monumental change in the ever-evolving issue of black identity. Before a group of black leaders in Chicago, he proposed blacks adopt the term "African American" as their ethnic description, a name connecting them to the motherland, their place of origin. Though the proposal sparked major debate in post–black power America, the term began gaining in popularity the following year when 26 percent of blacks surveyed said they preferred the term "African-American." No longer were folks married to skin color as the sole identity of black people—an idea made popular in the 1960s by Elijah Muhammad, his spokesman Malcolm X, and the Nation of Islam.

The NOI's term for racial identity may have been on the way down, but the organization was experiencing an upswing of interest in the late 1980s thanks to the popularity of Louis Farrakhan. As his POWER tour in 1985 reintroduced post–black power America to the Nation's program of black unity and economic development, Farrakhan's ability to fearlessly articulate the frustrations and anger of black America elevated his profile among the usual suspects of black leadership (Jesse and the like). The black poverty rate, according to a 1987 study by the Census Bureau, rose to 33 percent (while the white poverty rate fell to 10.5 percent), and folks were looking for a militant response to "We shall overcome" rhetoric. Although mainstream civil rights leadership shunned Farrakhan because of his caustic racial theology and reported anti-Semitic statements, in 1988 his message of black pride, unity, and self-sufficiency gained an audience outside the Nation's usual demographic of the black impoverished and disaffected. Farrakhan began appealing to the black middle class (also frustrated by Reaganomics), particularly the youth, by making appearances at churches. On the college lecture circuit Farrakhan became the hottest ticket. A huge factor in his popularity boost among black students was Chuck's endorsement on the song "Bring the Noise." Farrakhan's nonconformist stance fed a nationalist resurgence growing among black college students, especially those at predominantly white colleges and universities, where incidents of racial intolerance were on the rise. Farrakhan's Nation also reestablished its relevance within the besieged ghettos of post–black power America through its daring antidrug initiative, Dope Busters, in which the Muslims closed down crack houses and patrolled dangerous streets in cities like Washington, D.C. (by now considered America's murder capital). At the same time, black scholar Molefi Asante published *The Afrocentric Idea*, inspiring blacks to put their African history and roots at the center of their lives.

Meanwhile, in New York City, a militant grassroots leadership was developing, giving voice to the black rage seething over the racial violence there. The Reverend Al Sharpton, a preacher and former promoter for James Brown, emerged from the bloodshed of Howard Beach to become *the* prominent figure in this racial brouhaha. Along with fiery lawyers C. Vernon Mason and Alton Maddox, Sharpton, community leader Sonny Carson, and former student activist Lisa Williamson began mobilizing blacks at the community level, organizing marches and protests against racial injustice, all to the chants of "No justice, no peace!"

Within the reawakening, *Nation of Millions* catapulted Public Enemy to the head of this revival of blackness. Run-D.M.C. may have revolutionized the culture, the rap industry, and a generation, but they were ineffective and ill prepared to counteract the negative ink thrown at them and rap music (Rick and Russ did most of the responding). To hear Chuck tell it, P.E.'s ascension was a profound post–Run-D.M.C. plot to arm rap (and its hordes) with the mental weaponry to respond intelligently to racist attacks.

Yo! set the bait, unnerving critics with black nationalist–tinged raps stirred with rhymes about guns, bourgeois "bitches," and fly rides ("I set traps for [the media]," Chuck explained to a *Los Angeles Times* reporter). The scribes bit; following a Public Enemy set marred by violence, writer Steve Hochman wrote, "One must wonder just how much the group's confrontational approach—and speeches and lyrics that draw on the philosophies of Malcolm X and Louis Farrakhan . . . contributed to the tension." And *Nation of Millions* delivered a resounding smack to the skull of rap's adversaries. If the media (or Capitol Hill) wanted to cast *any* ill light on P.E. or rap music, Chuck D was prepared to return fire. In defense of P.E.'s militant image and hardcore pro-black message, Chuck boldly responded to his critics on the LP's single "Don't Believe the Hype." "They claim that I'm a criminal," Chuck blasted. "By now I wonder how / Some people never know / The enemy could be their friend, guardian / I'm not a hooligan / I rock the party and / Clear all the madness, I'm not a racist / Preach to teach to all."

Becoming rap's next million seller and 1988's most controversial album (another hip-hop first), *It Takes a Nation of Millions to Hold Us Back* arrived, immediately, as one of the genre's best and most significant albums. Whereas *Raising Hell* had elevated rap music's artistic profile and commercial value two years prior, P.E.'s masterpiece pushed rap as both art and sociopolitical statement. Now, along with rocking the crowd and titillating the ear, rap added black nation building to its repertoire, sonically resurrecting the spirit of black power for the youth of black America.

The Bomb Squad expanded the vocabulary and technique of sampling, masterfully building tapestries of furious beats, squeals, sirens, turntable scratches, and the digitally reconfigured voices of black America's political past. So while backing Public Enemy's rhymes, the beats thrust their message into the context of American history, presenting Chuck as a successor to the black heroic voices of the past. For example, on "Terminator X to the Edge of Panic," samples taken from a recorded Farrakhan speech backed up Chuck's wrathful words to black radio DJs (particularly WBLS's Mr. Magic, who initially refused to support his music). "Black people's minds are being controlled," screamed Farrakhan, "and you are the aides of black music!"

As the conduit through which the ideas of black power now flowed to the airwaves, Public Enemy seemed to fit perfectly into the shoes of youth leaders. The "us" in the title of their album was a reference not just to P.E. but to the generation they were attempting to wake up and speak on behalf of. Chuck, hyped by the frenetic encouragement of Flav and protected by the S1W army, fashioned himself a truth-telling prophet railing against the nonprogressive forces of racism and black subservience (because Uncle Toms are sucker MCs, too). Over the stark, haunting rhythm of "Black Steel in the Hour of Chaos," Chuck spun the tale of being arrested for refusing the draft—in response to America's racism—and staging a valiant prison break. On the one hand, Chuck's rhyme spoke the fantasy of black macho heroics in the face of the *real* enemy, while on the other, his yarn of bravery could be interpreted as a blaxploitationesque revision of Muhammad Ali's famous 1967 refusal to fight in the Vietnam War. "No Vietcong ever called me nigger," were the poetic boxer's famous words during his battle against the draft board and the U.S. government. Chuck's reasoning was in the same vein as he rapped, "Here is a land that never gave a damn." On the riotously crafted "Louder Than a Bomb," P.E.'s chief continued building on the weaponry metaphor, comparing his politically charged raps to a bomb and portraying himself as the outspoken, persecuted MC. "Your CIA, you see I ain't kiddin'," he warned. "Both King and X they got rid of both . . . And not the braggin' or boastin' and plus / It ain't no secret why they're tappin' my phone, although / I can't keep it a secret / So I decided to kick it." And whereas "Rebel Without a Pause" introduced P.E.'s fiery cause to a wider, uninitiated fellowship, "Prophets of Rage" loudly reiterated the mission for a post–black power generation who now understood Chuck's message. "You find we're the quotable; you emulate," Chuck noticed. "Brothers and sisters, that's beautiful / Follow a path of positivity you go . . ."

Nation of Millions also addressed issues (imagined or otherwise) within the black community. Some topics, like the love black women have for the white world of soap operas, explored on "She Watch Channel Zero?!," may have glaringly displayed Chuck's flawed sexist perspective, much the way "Sophisticated Bitch" had. But other issues, like the nihilism and self-destructive attitudes of black males, humorously explored by Flavor Flav on "Cold Lampin' with Flavor," showed P.E. had a silly side. On the most pertinent issue of the time, the explosion of crack, Chuck unleashed a literary wrath in "Night of the Living Baseheads," a brutal critique on the soul-robbing effects the crack trade had on the community. And Chuck's defense of rap music's artistic and cultural integrity was equally as forthright. Accompanying the genre-praising anthem "Bring the Noise" was his defense of sampling on the panicked-sounding "Caught, Can We Get a Witness?" The music-making technique had already begun to cause debates and concern over copyright infringement. As in the controversy over music downloading that came years later, many musicians thought sampling was thievery. Artsy rocker Frank Zappa inserted a "no sampling" clause into the copyright infringement notice on all his music; James Brown had already legally come after Eric B. and Rakim for "I Know You Got Soul" (the matter was eventually settled out of court). Black music artists, like songwriter James Mtume (a former member of Maulana Karenga's cultural nationalist US Organization), were particularly critical of hip-hop's reliance on sampled music. In response, Chuck rapped a biting rebuttal, defending himself while telling disapproving artists (particularly the black ones) what he thought of their work. "You singers are spineless," he commented, "as you sing your senseless songs to the mindless / Your general subject love is minimal; it's sex for profit / *Scream* that I sample / Example, [Uncle] Tom you ran to the federal / Court." Whereas musicians viewed sampling as thievery and regression, hip-hop producers like the Bomb Squad saw it as a revolutionary avenue for creating sound art. "We use samples like an artist would use paint," Hank Shocklee explained. Its proponents believed the popularity of sampling had revived interest in artists whose music had long faded from the airwaves, a point made by Brooklyn-based rap band Stetsasonic on their 1988 hit "Talkin' All That Jazz," where they rapped: "Tell the truth, James Brown was old / 'Til Eric and Rak came out with 'I Got Soul' / Rap brings back old R&B, and if we would not / People could have forgot."

Most notably, rap introduced the revolutionary rhythms of James Brown to a new generation just as the singer was on his way to prison to serve three years of a six-year term for illegal possession of a weapon and fleeing police. All of the Godfather's troubles stemmed from a violent outburst on September 24, 1988, during which, reportedly high on PCP, disheveled, enraged, and armed with a shotgun, Brown burst into an office next to his business and accused its occupants of using his bathroom. When cops arrived, Soul Brother Number One led them on a high-speed chase that ended with officers firing on Brown's truck. The six-year sentence Brown received for the incident—in which he had only possessed a gun and run from police—made some question the factor race played in the harsh punishment. "Compare Brown's case to the separate but unequal treatment accorded Jerry Lee Lewis and maybe you'll just be stunned," wrote *Playboy* writer Dave Marsh in 1990. Marsh juxtaposed Brown's persecution with Lewis's lack thereof for "shooting up quiet streets" in Memphis, "wounding a band member," spousal abuse, and his "long-standing addiction to alcohol." Black music artists, in particular, had already picked up on the unequal treatment of Brown. This was especially the case among rap artists who revered Brown's contribution to black culture and empowerment politics. They were indebted to him for laying the musical, social, and artistic foundation of their own movement. So "Free James Brown!" became a minor cause célèbre expressed on T-shirts worn by rap artists and fans alike.

But as the funky dynamo was headed to confinement, Public Enemy assumed Brown's former command as political lightning rod and mouthpiece of black frustration. The racial consciousness developing within rap was now under Public Enemy's charge. With the platinum success of *Nation of Millions*, blackness became the commercial mandate for the hardcore rap set. Boogie Down Productions' follow-up to their *Criminal Minded* album was the philosophy-filled gold seller *By All Means Necessary*. The album title was a nod to Malcolm X's famous phrase, and the photo it was paired with displayed KRS-One reenacting Malcolm's well-documented peek out of a window holding an automatic weapon in his hand. Moving away from the crime themes of BDP's first LP, KRS's choice was in large part a response to the violent murder of his BDP collaborator/DJ, Scott La Rock (hip-hop artists were by no means immune to the escalating problem of black-on-black crime). And Rakim, who had given listeners a taste of his beliefs as a Five Percenter (a black Muslim sect founded as an offshoot of the NOI) on *Paid in Full*, was now exhibiting them full throttle on 1988's *Follow the Leader*. Even newcomer Big Daddy Kane laced his boastful debut, *Long Live the Kane*, with praise of the black man's homeland on "Word to the Mother(Land)." Being a prophet in rap was becoming profitable as the expression of black pride now signified street cred for the hardcore MC.

Despite being one of the bestselling rap groups of 1988, Public Enemy, not compromising their message for the crossover, heralded the idea of rap as black music speaking on behalf of black people. Their unconventional position came as rap made tremendous strides in the music marketplace. On August 6, 1988, MTV debuted *Yo! MTV Raps*, the network's thirty-minute block showcasing the latest rap videos. Hosted by Fab Five Freddy, the show (which received the highest ratings of any on the network) became instrumental in establishing interest in hardcore rap and hip-hop culture among suburban white youth, giving rap artists like Public Enemy direct access to a wider audience. That same month David Mays and Jon Shecter, two white Harvard students, started a one-page hip-hop music newsletter called *The Source*. In three years, the newsletter would expand into a full-fledged glossy and the leading hip-hop magazine, not only as a premier document of the culture but as a platform for a new generation of journalists and scribes of color. Also in 1988, the Grammys finally extended honors to hip-hop, giving the new Best Rap Performance award to DJ Jazzy Jeff and the Fresh Prince (Will Smith) for the crossover rap hit "Parents Just Don't Understand." (The milestone wouldn't come without controversy, though, as the honorees, along with Salt-N-Pepa, Kid 'n Play, and Public Enemy, boycotted the ceremony because the rap award presentation wouldn't be televised. During the press conference announcing the boycott, Chuck, with an ice-cold swagger, scolded the music academy in the name of the hip-hop nation, saying: "The Grammys should give more of a fuck about the people. Then the people will give more of a fuck about the Grammy. 'Cause, where I'm at right now, we don't give a fuck about a goddamn Grammy.")

Public Enemy had become the political vanguard not only to rap fans but to the rank-and-file artists of commercial rap as well. "What [P.E.] are doing is trying to uplift the black youth," recognized Will Smith. "I agree with them . . . and what they are saying needs to be heard." Despite their goals of fame and fortune, rap artists weren't too far removed from the hardships faced by the youth they were rapping to. In being dubbed the "Black Panthers of rap," aligning themselves with controversial black leadership, and setting themselves apart from humor-oriented rappers like the Fresh Prince and Biz Markie or corporate ruffians like LL Cool J and Run-D.M.C., Public Enemy represented a boldness that MCs across the board could support and find strength in. "Every generation needs a Chuck D," commented scholar Cornel West in an interview, "because his heart is tied to the pain of the people." And, apparently, Public Enemy's presence offered hope not only to hip-hoppers but also to black boomers wishing for the return of a black revolution. Bill Stephney, who by now worked with Def Jam, discovered this when the city of Philadelphia threw a parade for Public Enemy. "What struck me," said Stephney, "we saw these guys . . . in their mid-forties. They had all run back . . . into their apartments and homes and two-story brick houses . . . and gotten all their Panther shit out. Got the berets, got the black leather jackets, got their camouflages out and everything . . . You're seeing these graying, forty-something black men, tears in their eyes, throwing the black power salute like the revolution has come back."

But if *Nation of Millions* signaled the reawakening of post–black power America, the days preceding P.E.'s third album, *Fear of a Black Planet*, marked the zenith of the movement's return. At the center was P.E.'s fiery baptism at the hands of the media during the racially hot summer of 1989. Director Spike Lee prepared to release his most polarizing work, *Do the Right Thing*, a film set in Brooklyn's Bedford-Stuyvesant, exploring the growing racial tension in New York City (*New York* magazine, interpreting the film as inflammatory, predicted it would spark race riots). Public Enemy was hired to produce, write, and perform the film's theme song, which resulted in hip-hop's official pro-black anthem, "Fight the Power." But just as preparation for the song and its video—a filmed youth march against racial violence with P.E. at the helm—was set to push Chuck and his comrades further into the role of "leader," the infamous Griff interview pushed the group to the center of the summer's racial heat. On May 9, 1989, while Public Enemy was in Washington, D.C., Professor Griff was interviewed by David Mills, a reporter for *The Washington Times*. When pressed to explain why he refused to wear gold because of Israel's support of South Africa's racist government, Griff said that since Jews help the apartheid regime (a place where the gold probably came from) Jews have a "tight grip" on black South Africans. The dialogue ended with Griff stating that Jews were responsible for "the majority of wickedness that goes on across the globe."

The comment went relatively unnoticed after *The Washington Times* ran the story on May 22. The explosive fallout began a month later following a reprint of Griff's comments in *The Village Voice*. Jewish groups like the militant Jewish Defense Organization began protesting against P.E. The mainstream media began shining an anti-Semitic light on the group, helping to strain black-Jewish relations as folks began to take sides in the debacle. Pressure from Def Jam, from its parent company, CBS, even from within the group (namely Bill Stephney and Hank Shocklee) put Chuck in the awkward position of having to single-handedly address the matter without jeopardizing P.E.'s credibility. There was no way of appeasing all parties, though, and the mission of Public Enemy was what was most in jeopardy. So since Griff was the source of the controversy, without fully denouncing the infamous comment, Chuck apologized to the offended and reluctantly fired Griff.

For black fans of Public Enemy, Chuck's apology and dismissal of Griff were a devastating blow of defeat: further proof that whites—in this case, Jews—were still pulling the strings. But most crushing was that P.E., despite all of its nationalistic rhetoric, seemed to be caving to the pressure, selling out one of its own for speaking his mind. No one understood that Griff's venomous statement to Mills, as would be discovered later, was a result of his feeling underappreciated by the group (that he was no more than a glorified road manager and bodyguard), just one of the many tensions and rifts growing in Public Enemy. Many fans missed the point that Griff's statement was another kind of racism. All they saw were P.E.'s ideals of black unity and self-determination being held to the fire and melting like ice cream. "Here's the sad part," Armond White wrote in Brooklyn's *City Sun*, "the fiery beauty of Public Enemy was that it refused to pander to 'brotherhood' sentimentalists. P.E. made the uplifting of black people seem connected to all human struggles. Now, in apology, Chuck . . . isn't good for anything except recording mindless, pointless confections . . . This is the first tough fight Public Enemy has had to face and they've crumbled like chalk." Chuck looked even weaker when, in response to the mounting criticism after firing Griff, he briefly disbanded Public Enemy—so much for one-upping Run-D.M.C.'s handling of Long Beach. But the Griff storm, while straining and weakening P.E.'s inner sanctum, helped expose a vacuum of black leadership within black America, so much so that African Americans would mistake a rap group (cultural icons) for *real* political leadership. "I remember around the period of '88 and '89," reminisced Bill Stephney, "there was this mass of different people who really wanted P.E. to solve all the problems of black youth . . . And, to a large extent, it would get overwhelming . . . There were too many expectations of P.E. to transcend being a music group and somehow provide the critical political leadership that is needed in our community."

Public Enemy may not have officially been political leaders, but they were undoubtedly prophetic with Chuck opening "Fight the Power" with the words "1989 the number! Another summer! Sound of the 'Funky Drummer,' " as if announcing the explosive atmosphere of the season. The summer of 1989 was one of the most racially volatile (and violent) summers witnessed by the generation after black power. Once again, New York experienced the death of an African American at the hands of a white mob, this time in Bensonhurst, a predominantly Italian section of Brooklyn. On August 23, Yusef Hawkins, a sixteen-year-old from Bedford-Stuyvesant, went to the neighborhood with three friends to look at a used car. Just before reaching the home of the car owner, they were stopped by a mob of white youths armed with bats, golf clubs, and at least one gun, inquiring, "What are you niggers doing here?" Prior to the confrontation, the group of white males had been taunted by a white female saying her black and Hispanic boyfriends were coming into the neighborhood to party with her (obviously a taboo in the community). Whether they were mistaken for the girl's friends or not, Yusef and his friends were confronted by the mob. After threats of a beating were yelled out, one teen shot Yusef Hawkins four times in the chest. He died shortly thereafter. The murder set off a series of demonstrations marshaled by a new militant leadership. Al Sharpton led marches through the neighborhood where Hawkins was killed; and for a September 1 Day of Outrage demonstration, Sonny Carson, his son's hip-hop group, X Clan, and the group's Blackwatch Movement marched ten thousand protesters through downtown Brooklyn toward the Brooklyn Bridge, where a violent standoff with the police ended the protest. Hawkins's death brought New York's racial heat to an inferno, but more notably, his murder became a glaring example of an epidemic of racial intolerance growing among teens and young adults across the country. According to *The New York Times*, figures from the Justice Department showed that between 1986 and 1987 racial incidents classified as "school related" were up 50 percent. And in 1988, college campuses where racial incidents were increasing or had the potential to increase rose from 48 to 77. Some experts speculated that Reagan's challenge to affirmative action sat at the root, making it easier for racists to express their attitudes. Others said it was a matter of competition for jobs as urban white youths (like their black neighbors) were affected by the loss of industrial jobs, which were vanishing from urban centers. Janet Caldwell, a program associate at the Atlanta-based Center for Democratic Renewal, speculated that "young people are out of touch with history" and "don't have a connection to the civil rights movement, and they don't have that kind of ideal."

But it would be that sense of history—though with no youth-centered outlet to constructively handle matters—that contributed to the summer ending with a riot. It didn't involve impoverished blacks in a depressed ghetto, though, but the fed-up members of black America's talented tenth vacationing in a beach town. The annual Greekfest, a Labor Day weekend gathering of black college students in Virginia Beach, erupted into a rebellion against excessive police action. Prior to the upheaval, students were already made to feel unwelcome as many of the town's shop owners either refused to let black students into their stores, closed up shop for the weekend, or overcharged their young black customers. Tensions came to a boil around 2:00 a.m. after police began forcefully clearing out students who were milling about the beachfront. A five-hour melee of rock throwing and looting ensued, causing $1.4 million worth of damage to over a hundred shops along the beach. Ironically, several months after the violence, Virginia elected its first black governor, L. Douglas Wilder. While many a news outlet, as well as the town's mayor and business owners, cast the students as lawless troublemakers, their cause would find a voice with P.E., who countered the negative accounts on their next album.

On August 1, a month before the undergrad rebellion at Virginia Beach, Chuck announced the reuniting of Public Enemy, and Griff was reinstated, though with the new title of Supreme Allied Chief of Community Relations. In other words, while Griff would act as a community liaison, he would give no more interviews. Chuck later ignited P.E.'s return with a jet-fueled response to the Griff controversy (and the explosive summer) on "Welcome to the Terrordome." Cloaked in a furious, sweltering rhythm, Chuck lashed out: "I got so much trouble on my mind / Refuse to lose." He articulated the pain of the summer's most poignant murder ("First nothing's worse than a mother's pain /

Of a son slain in Bensonhurst") and beach riot ("The Greek weekend speech I speak / From a lesson learned in Virginia [Beach]"). But most notably, Chuck gave an especially caustic response to the Jewish leaders protesting P.E. following the Griff matter, chiding: "Crucifixion ain't no fiction / So-called chosen frozen / Apology made to whoever pleases / Still they got me like Jesus." Those lyrics and others like "told a Rab get off the rag" once again caused a furor in the Jewish community, particularly in New York and especially in Brooklyn, where tensions between blacks and Jews were growing.

Nevertheless, the uproar didn't slow the momentum of a reunited P.E. as their third release, *Fear of a Black Planet*, was the first to enter *Billboard*'s Top 10, going platinum. Now at the artistic center of hip-hop's pro-black revolution and, subsequently, the political reawakening of black America, Chuck turned P.E.'s attention to confronting issues of organizing and empowerment. *Fear of a Black Planet* was as much a musical assault on America's racism as it was a call to blacks to effectively react to it. The album's title track explored the roots of white fear of African Americans, focusing primarily on racist concerns over the effect growing miscegenation would have on the white gene pool ("White man, black woman, black baby. Black man, white woman, black baby"). The song "Burn Hollywood Burn" decried Tinseltown's perpetuation of black stereotypes in movies (Chuck's message was emboldened by Spike Lee's groundbreaking revival of black independent filmmaking). The record industry's exploitation of black recording artists (whose creativity had built the industry) was also condemned on "Who Stole the Soul?" with Chuck charging: "Ain't no different than in South Africa / Over here they'll go after ya to steal your soul / Like over there they stole our gold." Chuck even balanced his ever-sexist critique of black women (this time it was "Pollywanacraka") with a defense of black womanhood on "Revolutionary Generation." Not the least, his call for a black response to the issues rang loud on the cuts "Fight the Power," "Power to the People," and, most notably, "Brothers Gonna Work It Out."

The call to arms within *Fear* was especially relevant as Reagan's Republican vision continued through the administration of President George Bush, who, a year after being elected, vetoed the Civil Rights Act of

1990. Like the "Great Communicator," he claimed in a congressional record that it would "introduce the destructive force of quotas." Bush was keeping in step with white conservative voters, although he did eventually approve the act a year later. Despite such grim opposition in Washington, a song like "Brothers Gonna Work It Out" reverberated with a promising development abroad, as global pressure building against South Africa's apartheid government spurred President F. W. de Klerk to lift the ban on the vanguard anti-apartheid organization, the African National Congress (ANC). Shortly afterward, on February 11, 1990, Nelson Mandela, ANC leader and the movement's most celebrated and revered figure, was released from prison after serving nearly twenty-seven years of a life sentence for treason. Unlike the numerous black leaders who died in the pursuit of freedom, Mandela lived to see victory in his forty-eight-year fight for justice, as the walls of apartheid were soon dismantled. In gratitude to the Americans who supported him, Mandela visited the United States. His twelve-day stay in New York included a ticker-tape parade, a rally at Yankee Stadium, and an Afrocentric homecoming in Bed-Stuy. While his presence was celebrated by all of New York's multiculti citizenry, Mandela's visit was particularly emotional for its black denizens who felt they shared in the Pan-Africanist win for the motherland. For the post–black power generation, black consciousness was now in full effect with many a hip-hop youth, as leather African medallions made popular by rappers like P.E. replaced thick gold chains as the ultimate fashion statement.

And in hip-hop music, P.E.'s million seller sat at the front of a full-blown black pride resurgence within rap, the genre's roster of top acts now filled primarily with groups spouting one form of black nationalism or other. From Trenton, New Jersey, the Poor Righteous Teachers flexed their *Holy Intellect* through the religious nationalist teachings of the Five Percenters. The Oakland, California, rapper Paris espoused the revolutionary nationalism of the Panthers with *The Devil Made Me Do It*. And in the vein of Maulana Karenga's US Organization, the X Clan touted the Africa-on-my-mind sentiment of cultural nationalism with their debut, *To the East, Blackwards*.

But with blackness at such a premium one could just as easily question the substance of such a movement, especially with its heroic figures being popular music artists. Even though their involvement helped spread and popularize the message, note that the overwhelming popularity of a cause eventually swells to a trend. And nationalism, under America's hypercapitalistic spell, has been easily whittled down to symbols, merchandised, and used as cover by opportunists. This was especially the case among the flattop haircut, kente cloth, and African-medallion-sporting members of the hip-hop nation—who were no different from the Afro-and-dashiki-wearing set of the movement's past. With the renewed racial awareness of black America, the clothes and rhetoric might have changed, but true consciousness-raising was in short supply. Drug dealers wore "Black by Popular Demand" T-shirts while riding in their BMWs, blasting tapes of Louis Farrakhan—all bought with the deflated souls of black folks. And in many a black neighborhood, Afrocentric medallions could be purchased at the liquor store along with the poison of your choice. Just as black nationalism—strained through symbols and merchandising—declared blackness was once again *in*, the consciousness struggle became less about fighting for power than it was (to quote a phrase popular on T-shirts at the time) about being simply a "black thang."

In response, Public Enemy's 1991 release, *Apocalypse 91 . . . The Enemy Strikes Black*, turned its critical eye on the black community, examining the deep-rooted problems of black America, especially urban black America. On the single "Can't Truss It," over a marching, trumpet-laced rhythm, Chuck explored the origins of black America's internal strife, setting it at the foot of the American slave trade, which, as he notably pointed out, was aided by the lack of unity among Africans ("King and chief probably had a big beef, because of that now I grit my teeth"). But even more, hip-hop's prophet of rage took aim at modern-day obstacles (the ones with black faces) in the way of progress. Chuck attacked the black crack peddlers, especially ones draped in symbols of Afrocentricity, with "Nighttrain," a stinging indictment of the drug dealer as race traitor, adding: " 'Cause he ridin' the train you think he's down for the cause / 'Cause his face lookin' just like yours." Similar accusations were thrown at black radio execs on "How to Kill a Radio Consultant," which blasted black radio stations for still not giving rap significant daytime airplay (despite a third of the black albums charted in *Billboard* being by rap artists).

Equal attention was paid to destructive habits within the hip-hop nation, such as the overwhelming support given (in money and healthy livers) to the malt liquor industry (not to mention the numerous rappers such as former N.W.A member Ice Cube who were offering their celebrity and talent to peddle such black-targeted brands as St. Ides), to which Chuck responded with a resounding denouncement on "1 Million Bottlebags." And the lack of respect and financial reciprocation given to black communities by companies like Nike, whom black folks loyally gave their money to, a matter Chuck angrily focused on with "Shut Em Down." To African Americans' casual use of the word "nigger," especially as a term of endearment, Flav added his own disapproval on the song "I Don't Wanna Be Called Yo Niga."

But while P.E.'s assessment of post–black power America was bold and necessary, it was also ironic, as the same problems plaguing black folks also manifested themselves within the group, the first incident being Flav's arrest on February 9, 1991, for physically assaulting his longtime girlfriend. Flav discussed the matter on *Apocalypse* ("A Letter to the New York Post"), though only as a self-righteous harangue on the coverage of the incident by white newspapers, not as a denial of the charges. The song ends with Chuck defending his partner and continuing Flav's rail against the media. For many critics, Chuck appeared just as contradictory as Flav, having blasted all the ills of black folks except the one his own partner was guilty of: violence against women. Chuck's choice to focus P.E.'s social gaze on the problems of blacks made *Apocalypse*, while reaching number four on the pop chart and going platinum, less appealing to hip-hop's hardcore nation. Some also saw P.E. as selling out with their rock remake of "Bring tha Noize" featuring the heavy metal band Anthrax (how dare P.E. collaborate with white folks?!). Not many saw this as the usual rap/rock hybridity fostered by Def Jam's founders (beginning with Run-D.M.C. and Aerosmith) because, as *the* pro-black political voice of young black America's sociocultural revolution, Public Enemy was held to a stricter standard. And many felt their decision to chastise black people was ill-timed: the August before they released *Apocalypse*, Crown Heights, Brooklyn, erupted into a riot following the accidental hit-and-run killing of a seven-year-old black boy by a Jewish driver. Violence broke out amid false rumors that a private Jewish ambulance service had refused to treat the child, the uproar further exacerbating the relations between blacks and Jews. While injustice visited both sides (a Hasidic student was killed in retaliation), P.E.'s critique of the black community (no matter how relevant or true) was not appreciated amid what was viewed, especially by blacks, as protracted racial strife.

The constant rule in American popular culture continued: The sway once held by a revolutionary hero eventually wanes and is transferred to the new voice of rebellion. So, too, did it slip away from Public Enemy and onto a grimier phalanx of MCs (now coming from the West Coast), fashioning rap's social commentary with the nihilistic realism of the streets. What would become known as gangsta rap took P.E.'s by-any-means-necessary attitude toward getting ahead, discarded the political analysis and the nationalistic rants, and put the crack-era neurosis of post–black power America on full display.

By the time P.E. released their fifth studio album, 1994's *Muse Sick-N-Hour Mess Age*, the formula had become the dominant (albeit dysfunctional) face of rap music, completely overtaking Public Enemy in more ways than one. Rap's growing preoccupation with guns, drugs, and trouble, while seen as a disappointing and exaggerated development (given its former political state), was now emanating from P.E.'s house, their family starting to resemble many a black household with one of its members on the pipe and in trouble with the law. In November 1993, Flavor Flav checked into the Betty Ford clinic seeking treatment for an addiction to crack—this after being arrested for the attempted murder of a neighbor whom Flav had shot at after accusing him of fooling around with his girlfriend. (The charges were later dropped.) The arrest further damaged P.E.'s staunch political image, and Flav's well-publicized crack problem turned their antidrug position (and the crew, in general) into a joke. Chuck, who by now had grown extremely weary of his label as leader, took a hands-off position in the matter, letting his partner work out his own problems, only addressing black people's overblown disappointment at a P.E. member's fall from grace. "We exist in a time," he explained in a 1994 interview with *The Source* magazine, "where we're waiting for leadership out of rappers, singers, dancers, ball players, part-time actors and comedians." It was as if Chuck were responding à la Charles Barkley's infamous 1993 Nike commercial ("I am not a role model"). But Chuck, unlike basketball's bad boy, did recognize the growing influence rap had on the youth of black America.

The thought was abundantly clear on the cover for *Mess Age*. A skeleton, clenching a spliff between teeth made of bullets and sporting an Afrocentric hat, sits before a table with malt liquor, a law book, and marijuana on it. As the skeleton's right hand secures a set of earphones on its skull, the left hand holds a gun to its temple, preparing for suicide. Behind him sits a glee-filled white guy and a KKK member looking on. To hip-hop's prophet, the explosion of gangsta rap and the gangsta lifestyle was hip-hop's black audience playing right into the demise America planned for them. "Talkin' that drive-by shit, everybody talkin' that gangsta shit," exclaimed Chuck on the song "So Whatcha Gone Do Now?" "Slaves to the rhythm of the master / Buck boom buck, another neighborhood disaster /A gun is a gun . . . But an organized side keep a sellout nigga on the run." On *Mess Age*, P.E.'s mouthpiece expanded his musical role to that of moralist, now waging a fight of "right versus wrong, good versus evil, God versus the devil," telling African Americans to stop using drugs and alcohol ("Give It Up" and "Live and Undrugged") while driving home the message that gangstadom being sold in rap was only fueling the destruction of post–black power America.

As usual Chuck made it a point to call out the *real gangstas* of America. Condemnation was handed out for white America's disregard for the planet and the environment ("Bedlam 13:13"), white exploitation of blacks ("White Heaven / Black Hell"), and the conquering of Africa and the lands of Native Americans ("Thin Line Between Law & Rape"). But, unfortunately, the nationalist stance and anti-gangsta rap touted on *Mess Age* proved futile in rap's new world order, garnering gold sales only on the dying momentum of P.E.'s former glory. Besides, their comments on hardcore rap's gun play sounded ironic given that the formula for such pop music success could be traced, in large part, to them. "A strong case could be made," wrote Nelson George in a review of the album for *The Village Voice*, "that brandishing of guns on stage by the S1Ws and the rhetoric of early tracks like 'My Uzi Weighs a Ton' laid the groundwork for a gun crazy mentality that sold millions of copies." As George pointed out: "Once the genie of gun mania is unleashed, as the Black Panthers found out years ago, it's hard to squeeze automatic weapons back into their carrying case."

In the end, though, Public Enemy accomplished Chuck's vision of pushing rap beyond just music to make urban throngs yell "yes y'all," into a tool capable of awakening the social consciousness and racial awareness of its core black audience, shouting their plight to the world. Although P.E. weren't literal political activists (or leaders) per se, their activism existed where a music group could be most effective: in the art. With their performance and their formation, Public Enemy, for their part, turned political activism, as far as hip-hop music was concerned, into a performance art, turning hardcore rap into the black steel folks needed *whenever* they were caught in that ever-present hour of chaos.

FIVE

Niggas Selling Attitude
N.W.A

Niggers are scared of revolution
But niggers shouldn't be scared of revolution
Because revolution is nothing but change
And all niggers do is change.
                    —The Last Poets, "Niggers Are Scared of Revolution"

Before a scheduled appearance at a Chicago record store, rapper Ice Cube told writer Cheo Hodari Coker how he learned he had become a part of an impending rap rebellion—not a rebellion in rhyme style or politics or necessarily one in blackness (at least not in the noble and romantic sense of black nationalism), but a hip-hop up-rising of America's black Frankenstein: *niggas*. It was in 1987, when he was informed by his partners Dr. Dre and Eric Wright about the new name for a rap supergroup (a collective of Los Angeles rappers, DJs, and producers) for which he'd been the chief songwriter. "One day Dre and Eric picked me up in the van," Cube explained, "and they was like, 'You know what we gonna call the group?' " Cube, having no clue, in-quired. "Niggaz With Attitude," replied Dre and Eric in unison. The name gave Cube an instant shock, but the feeling was matched with intrigue as Cube was conscious of his own internal response upon hearing the name. "Ain't nobody gonna put that out," he shot back incredulously at the suggestion. But Dre had that bump figured out. "We'll break it down to N.W.A," he responded, "and [we'll] wait 'til people ask."

"Sounded like a plan," Cube said, finishing his recollection.

Indeed, what N.W.A planned was the shock and awe of hip-hop's faithful with a fresh brand of reality rap. One that gave listeners an unfiltered, humorous, almost cinematically exaggerated view of black urban life—all from the perspective of niggas, the ultimate ghetto dwellers. If Public Enemy fought white fears and black stereotypes with black pride, N.W.A's defense was to embrace the fears and myths, flipping them into a source of strength and power. The word "nigger," in their hands, was now turned into *nigga*, a term of endearment and a moniker for super black *badass*ness instead of a racist word to dehumanize black people. If black men were white folks' (and some bourgeois black folks') bogeymen, then, Boo!—with a sneer, a middle finger, and a bullet. The results of such an idea would go beyond what N.W.A (or anyone) imagined.

In the end, N.W.A's contribution did for rap music what Melvin Van Peebles did for black American cinema with his groundbreaking 1971 film, *Sweet Sweetback's Baadasssss Song*: open a whole new movement (and industry) within the medium and create a heroic archetype that revolutionized American popular culture. Both did so by embracing and enhancing America's myth of the black male as violent black stud. Whereas Peebles politicized the figure—pitting him against racist white cops—to give black audiences a taste of cinematic control in the age of black power, N.W.A injected the myth with steroids, turning rap's golden age on its ear. As a result, N.W.A's creation inadvertently gave post–black power America a new brand of hardcore hero, the gangstafied or gangsta rapper, and spawned the rap subgenre of gangsta rap. The explosion of this phenomenon came from the desires of post–black power youth (outside New York's creative stronghold) to have their 'hoods' perspective represented and respected in rap's growing commercial space.

Public Enemy preached racial unity, upliftment, and enlightenment, but their message primarily sprang from dilemmas shaping an East Coast—specifically a New York—point of view. There were the racial tensions and violence igniting the five boroughs; the media's antagonism toward New York's rap elite and their music; the devastating effects of crack. Rap's overall renaissance, with rhyme dynamos like Rakim, KRS-One, and Big Daddy Kane leading the pack, overwhelmingly reflected a New York aesthetic of style, language, and culture. Rap music, by and large, was still being governed by old rules: to move the crowd, skills and verbal dexterity were the yardstick by which top griots were measured, not the force and impact of what they said. But on the West Coast, a different set of circumstances shaped the environment of a black Los Angeles that developed around the members of N.W.A.

Gang culture in New York evolved into the competitive spirit of hip-hop. In Los Angeles's black communities—from Compton to Watts and the rest of South Central—gang culture, which had developed from the ashes of black power organizations like the Panthers, grew into a religion, one in which the faithful were "as contemptuous of opposing belief systems as Christians are of Islam," as Nelson George described it in *The Village Voice*. And for South Central, the two opposing faiths among post–black power youth meant the Crips and the Bloods. What turned gangs from expressions of a youthful desire for power and protection (according to Athens Park Bloods member Cle "Bone" Sloan, gang violence began to slow down in the late 1970s) into a black L.A. institution in the 1980s was partly the same circumstances that made the South Bronx a cauldron of gang activity in the early 1970s: the deindustrialization of the city and the disenfranchisement of its youth. As Jeff Chang wrote in *Can't Stop Won't Stop: A History of the Hip-Hop Generation*, a huge part of this came when manufacturing plants for Firestone, Goodyear, and General Motors closed their doors in South Central Los Angeles. Throughout the 1980s, 131 plants shut down, "eliminating unionized manufacturing jobs" and "leaving 124,000 people unemployed in the center city." Not only did this devastate the hopes and finances of the black working class; it snatched prospective work from black youth who might have banked their futures (and a transition out of gangbanging) on those jobs. So with not many prospects for work, and a lot of time to kill, banging became *the* full-time gig.

In black Los Angeles, crack found a ready-made organizational structure of gang sets and territories in which to thrive. Now the lure for banging wasn't just obtaining community muscle but lucrative employment that promised more than a living wage. The gang rivalries/violence that began slowing at the end of the 1970s revved up with the onset of drug wars, resurfacing like a whirling plague by the mid-1980s. But instead of knives and pistols, the bounty of drug-produced funds afforded bangers advanced automatic weaponry (Uzi submachine guns and AK-47 assault rifles), setting off a Cold War–like arms race that turned the streets of South Central—as with drug-devastated black communities nationwide—bloody, paranoid, and cynical. This dynamic, combined with a heavy-handed and racist police force that had a propensity for brutalizing folks of color in the name of the law, made South Central in serious need of self-expression.

Out of the social tumult, the region's own hip-hop music identity began taking shape in the mid-1980s, developing just south of Watts in the ghetto suburbs of Compton. First was the local sensation caused by a mixtape of raps by Compton DJ Toddy Tee, who twisted hits by East Coast rap artists into streetcentric rhymes reflective of a South Central reality: after reworking the beat for Rappin' Duke's self-titled smash into "Batterram," a rap about the new military-armored vehicles used by the LAPD to smash in doors of suspected crack houses, Toddy Tee became a minor celebrity. The success of the song would have Toddy Tee in a professional studio by the end of 1985 recutting "Batterram," this time "with a major-label budget." Another homegrown inspiration for South Central was L.A. rapper Ice-T. Motivated by the release of "Rapper's Delight," he'd been rhyming and putting out rap songs independently since the pioneering days of L.A.'s hip-hop scene in the early 1980s. But the local success of "Batterram" filled Ice-T with the desire to write about the new streets of South Central. He was especially inspired by the emergence of rap artist Schoolly D, an ultra-laid-back-sounding MC out of Philadelphia who was pioneering gangsta rap on national airwaves. In 1985, Schoolly had independently released two thick, reverb-heavy, ominous-sounding hits, "Gucci Time" and "P.S.K.," humorously reflecting the flashy and violent sides of his life in Philly. His impact on Ice-T resulted in the 1986 cut "6 'N the Mornin'," about a criminal-minded antihero whose home gets raided by the LAPD. With a rhyme style (and beat) closely resembling Schoolly D's, Ice-T became the first West Coast rap artist to get national distribution (Sire Records) for hip-hop's introduction to L.A.'s gangsta rap aesthetic.

But the real breakthrough came in the formation of Niggaz With Attitude, a legendary culmination of ideas from neighbors on the same Compton block. Each was at his own crossroads in 1985. There was the disillusionment of the drug hustler Eric Wright, later to be known as Eazy-E. The son of a grade-school teacher mom and a postal worker dad, he'd been the product of a traditional middle-class family and upbringing, though it hadn't kept him from the lure of the streets. Hanging with the local hard-rocks to do dirt ("steal cars and all kinds of shit," he later told a reporter for *The Source*), Eric eventually dropped out of high school his sophomore year, graduating instead to the lucrative business of dealing crack. Around this time, legendary cocaine dealer "Freeway" Ricky Ross was turning South Central into a crack capital with his cheap wholesale coke—first as powder, then as a form called "ready rock"—just as Eric entered high school in the early 1980s.

But by the age of twenty-two, Eric had begun to realize the limitations of such an occupation, the end results always being jail or death. Besides, America was ratcheting up its War on Drugs, the most prominent weapon coming the following year. In 1986, Reagan would sign his omnibus drug bill, allocating $97 million to build new prisons along with $425 million for drug education and treatment. The most consequential aspect of the bill was its creation of mandatory minimum penalties for drug offenses. So selling five grams of crack, for instance, led to a mandatory five-year prison term for offenders. As drugs overwhelmingly affected poor black and Latino communities, the creation of this law increased the racial disparities in America's prison population, sending more black men to prison (overwhelmingly on drug offenses) than there were enrolling in college. So Eric looked for a transition out of the drug trade and a way to launder his illegal funds into a legal life. If all else failed, he reportedly told a friend, he could get a postal job like his father. But seeing the rising popularity of rap music, he wanted to try his hand at another profitable hustle: the music business. He decided to start a record label, though he knew nothing about the business and had never been involved in any aspect of hip-hop culture.

Dr. Dre (born Andre Young) was looking to make rugged and raunchy hip-hop music that people wouldn't believe they were hearing. Since 1982, he'd been obsessively building his record collection while holding two jobs as a DJ, one for the R&B group the World Class Wreckin' Cru, a Prince-inspired outfit that produced keyboard-laden music. Like the Purple Wonder, they sported androgynous costumes and makeup (photos of a lip-gloss-wearing Dre, dressed in his white sequined doctor uniform, would haunt him in years to come). The group acquired regional success with a 1984 hit, "Surgery," independently produced by the Cru's lead vocalist/manager, Alonzo Williams. (They had a national hit with "Turn Off the Lights" in 1988.) While the gig offered Dre exposure and local celebrity, the Wreckin' Cru's sound and look were soft, and none of the money made from the music was his (most all of it went to Alonzo). Moreover, none of his work with the group showcased *his* own talents, *his* work, at least not like what he did on the weekends.

On those nights, he DJed at the club Eve After Dark or at Compton's Skateland roller rink. There Dre, accompanied by his fellow disgruntled Wreckin' Cru member DJ Yella (Antoine Carraby), could rock the audience his own way, playing beats he'd spent all week producing at home for the crowd. He could also use the spaces to feature the off-color rhyme talents of sixteen-year-old rapper Ice Cube (O'Shea Jackson, who lived a few doors down from Dre's family) and his rap group CIA (Criminals In Action). Dre had been mentoring Ice Cube, a prolific rhyme writer since grade school, and producing music for his group on the side. To entertain and excite skating rink audiences, Dre urged Ice Cube and his crew to write and perform sexually explicit versions of popular rap tunes, giving them a South Central edge. So Run-D.M.C.'s "My Adidas" became "My Penis." And the audience loved it, especially Eric Wright, who frequented the shows and was looking to Dre as a producer for his planned label, Ruthless Records. This happened after Eric bailed Dre out of jail following an arrest for unpaid traffic tickets. Once Alonzo refused to spring him (having done so numerous times), Eric sensed an opportunity and stepped in with cash and an offer the DJ couldn't refuse. A deal was struck and both had what they were looking for. Dre had money (Eric's) to make the music he wanted, and Eric possessed the production talent he needed to get his venture off the ground.

This formidable combination of money and talent didn't begin to gel until the middle of 1986, though. Dre, looking to sign a New York rap group called HBO, approached Eric and another local moneyman, Laylaw, about financing the record. He had Ice Cube write a song for them called "Boyz-N-the-Hood," a rap laced with excessive violence and South Central details. He planned to record the song at Alonzo's studio. But when HBO heard the lyrics, they refused to record, complaining the song was on "some West Coast shit." Then they walked out. With no rap group to record and plenty of paid studio time being wasted, Dre suggested Eric try his hand at rapping the song. Eric, looking only to manage and never having rapped a day in his life, refused. Dre persisted, since there was no one else to perform, and Eric reluctantly agreed. After two days of recording, as the story's often been told, Eric Wright was reborn into rapper Eazy-E, and an unexpected hit was completed.

The song "Boyz-N-the-Hood" rapped the violent day-in-the-life tale of a Compton badass. Atop a thick, ominously slow drum track sprinkled with menacing keyboard work, Eazy, with a rap style closely resembling Schoolly D's, took listeners on a nihilistic journey through his 'hood during which he was forced to draw his gun on a rival gang-banger, beat a crackhead for breaking into his car, slap the father of a girl he wanted to screw, and attempt to bail a neighborhood car thief out of jail. "Boyz" was as raw and authentically street sounding as its predecessors, but what set it apart was Eazy's delivery: the evil, almost Munchkin-like sound of his voice—spewing the rhymes as if they were threats issued by a bloodthirsty, hypersexed kid—gave "Boyz" a humorously dark quality.

After Eazy secured a distribution deal with Macola records, a label that manufactured and distributed records by independent artists for a relatively cheap fee, "Boyz-N-the-Hood" was released in September 1987. Its promotion, the story goes, was a strong grassroots effort combining Eazy's street marketing (hiring gangbangers and local kids to give copies to record stores and leaders of neighborhood cliques) along with Dre and Yella's juice at the radio station KDAY. By the end of the year, "Boyz" and its gang of collaborators were the hottest things in Los Angeles. To take his project even further, Eazy paid Alonzo Williams $750 to introduce him to Jerry Heller, a fifty-something white manager who had worked with rock acts like Pink Floyd and Elton John.

Eazy's initial idea of a super talent collective began to develop. Dre and Yella provided the beats and DJing expertise. A local rapper named Arabian Prince (Mik Lezan) was recruited to write and perform (though he'd leave the fold a short time afterward), while Cube primarily wrote the lyrics. Cube left Compton shortly following the release of "Boyz" to study architectural drafting in Arizona at the Phoenix Institute of Technology. "The rap game wasn't looking too solid at that time," explained Cube. "So I decided to go ahead and go to school." As replacements Eazy enlisted the rhyme-writing talents of MC Ren (Lorenzo Patterson), who lived a few doors from Eazy, and a Texas rapper by the name of the D.O.C. (Trey Curry).

While away at school, Cube had no idea of the impact his song was making: that it was selling thousands of copies, independently, each week; that after the song hit, Eazy thought up a radically innovative (yet racially acidic) title—Niggaz With Attitude—to call his new circle of talent; that due to the success of "Boyz," after numerous rejections from major labels, Jerry Heller secured Ruthless Records and its roster—Eazy and N.W.A—a deal with Priority Records. The backing from a larger, more established label helped "Boyz" go on to sell 300,000 copies. Within their recording deal, N.W.A and Ruthless were given complete freedom to record the kind of music they wanted. Only after Cube returned home from school did he learn he had become a major player in an approaching Nigga revolution. Even Macola records smelled the breeze of change with "Boyz," as it hastily compiled a bunch of demos and rough recordings from artists who recorded under the Ruthless banner and released the LP *N.W.A and the Posse* in 1987. The album didn't amount to huge sales, with only three of the songs performed by the artists who would become Niggaz With Attitude, but its release began building the group's name and reputation.

Laying the groundwork for N.W.A's commercial arrival, though, was the 1988 release of Eazy's solo debut, *Eazy-Duz-It*. One part traditional hip-hop brag-fest and two parts inauguration for a revolutionary mantra, this LP acted as a preliminary showcase not just for the crew's musical talent but also for their urban avant-garde approach to rap music. Writing the album was a three-pronged effort involving Ren's elaborate storytelling and acrobatic verbiage, D.O.C.'s syllabically punchy boasts, and the masterfully insightful (and sadistically humorous) first-person narratives of Ice Cube, whose risqué writing was inspired by comedians Richard Pryor and Rudy Ray Moore. "We knew the value of language," Cube explained to the *Los Angeles Times* in 2002. "We weren't that sophisticated, but we knew the power it had." The beats were a tag-team display of Yella's comical scratches (cutting words and phrases together on the turntables) and Dre's exceptionally funky loops.

The end result was the holistic realization of the character Eazy-E, rap's diminutive reincarnation of Stagger Lee: a violent, megasexual black urban menace with a sense of humor (and justice) that was darker than several midnights. Alongside hip-hop's other gangsta heroes, Eazy was the well-crafted extreme: extremely vicious, extremely callous, but extremely funny. Moreover, within hip-hop's golden era of hardcore (rap's jaded ruggedness fueled partly by the crack explosion), he became, for South Central, an underground symbol of the growing nihilism and cynicism among young African Americans. Proof of this was in the response: *Eazy-Duz-It* went gold with much support from L.A.'s hip-hop underground but little radio or video promotion. The ultimate evidence, though, was the anticipation the LP created for the arrival of N.W.A, which happened on January 25, 1989, with their debut album, *Straight Outta Compton.*

Whereas Public Enemy infused rap with racial/cultural pride and black political awareness, N.W.A's first offering kicked such notions in the teeth. Instead of stoic nationalism or stiff-faced consciousness or cries of unity, *Straight Outta Compton* totally rapped the opposite. N.W.A's philosophy was progress "by any means necessary," and their ideas of advancement were selfish and brutal, straight from the front lines of South Central's embattled black ghettos. Being a gun-toting gangsta represented strength. Crime (even against your own kind) was the way to get ahead. Any scandalous or unfriendly woman was a "bitch." "Smoking" (shooting) someone who wronged or threatened you earned you respect. And *all* black folks, whether friend, foe, or family, were referred to as *niggas.* As an insult, a term of endearment, or a mere response ("Nigga, please"), the word became a source of power for N.W.A, the same way it had been for Richard Pryor or the Last Poets twenty-some-odd years earlier. That's because they chose to speak to the conditions of the black urban masses from inside the harsh reality (poverty, crime, violence, poor education) that turned many black folks, for better or worse, into niggas. And, as N.W.A understood, one way of surviving the drowning effects of oppression was to find strength within it.

So while Chuck D (and Rakim) cultivated the racial self-awareness and spirituality bubbling within rap music, N.W.A began refining a ghetto-real consciousness (a nigga power concept) growing within hip-hop's ranks. "You are now about to witness the strength of street knowledge," Dre warned listeners at the start of the album. On *Straight Outta Compton,* N.W.A fused gangstafied antiheroism with black humor and social commentary, rhyming about more than just antics from badass hoodlums. They stretched the theatrical force of rap music to thrust listeners into the rampant nihilism, violence, and hostility of their Compton hometown. Hearing the album, wrote Cheo Hodari

Coker in *The Vibe History of Hip Hop*, "was akin to being wired into a sensory camera . . . You could smell the room, sense the bullets whizzing by your head, and feel your adrenaline pump as the police raced you around the block." This effect stemmed not just from N.W.A's powerful rhyme writing but from how authentic they came across. These guys—especially their chief writer, Ice Cube—sounded like *real* gangstas, ones who would step out of the record and annihilate you without a second thought. "Straight outta Compton, a crazy motherfucker named Ice Cube," barked the rapper on the title track, "from the gang called Niggaz With Attitude / When I'm called off / I got a sawed-off / Squeeze the trigger and bodies are hauled off." Indeed, N.W.A, with all their passion for "malt liquor, bitches and ultraviolence," were a gang-on-wax. Six years after Run-D.M.C. transformed commercial rap, introducing an authentic urban look and attitude to America, N.W.A took their hardcore baby even further, injecting a hardened street mentality that was as ruthless as anything rap or the streets had ever witnessed. Their menacing antics, outlook, and image may have been overstated for shock value and entertainment, but these exaggerations showcased the inadvertent results of post–black power America being given the cold shoulder. With no reinvestment, deindustrialized urban centers like South Central L.A. were now overrun by an underground economy (crime) and the dog-eat-dog mantra of individualism. And for post–black power youth "weaned on racism and Reaganism," a generation facing "downward mobility" because of poor education and poor communities, N.W.A were about to become the embodiment of a "fuck the world" doctrine. At a time when the line between rap and political leadership was blurring, N.W.A began obscuring the link between rap and the gritty reality of the streets.

"Here's a little something about a nigga like me," Ice Cube introduced himself on the cut "Gangsta Gangsta," "never should have been let out the penitentiary." As the quintessential ghetto hard rock, Cube offered a gruesomely 3-D perspective on a gangsta's morbid pastime ("Takin' a life or two / That's what the hell I do / You don't like how I'm livin', well, fuck you!") as well as his life's motivation ("To a kid lookin' up to me, life ain't nothing but bitches and money"). On the ode to a favorite malt liquor, "8 Ball," Eazy continued vividly spinning tales of his brutal adventures through the 'hood (this time, while high on Olde English 800). But the mood for the LP's menacing feel was set by the title track, a souped-up posse cut with Cube, Ren, and Eazy introducing their criminally maniacal characters over Dre's forward-stomping drum/guitar loop, the three MCs replacing rap's usual emphasis on wit and wordplay with one-upmanship displays of raw, Compton-grown gangstaness. "See, 'cause I'm the motherfuckin' villain," exclaimed Ren, "the definition is clear, you're the witness of a killin' that's taking place without a clue / And once you're on the scope your ass is through!"

Just as coldhearted as their threats of violence was N.W.A's street-corner philosophy on women, which narrowly bounced between images of them as whores and gold diggers. Thoughts on the opposite sex were dispensed by Cube, dishing candid advice to men about avoiding materialistic women on "I Ain't Tha 1." And as a nebulous definition of the negative term "bitch" used for the ladies on "A Bitch Iz a Bitch," Cube's description sounded a bit like Chuck D's rant two years earlier with "Sophisticated Bitch." Since its start, rap always possessed a misogynistic view of women, but N.W.A's view came through as acidly so, summed up in the words of Eazy on the title track when discussing a girl who got shot: "Fuck her! You think I give a damn about a bitch, I ain't a sucker."

But there was also a hard-to-see profundity within *Straight Outta Compton*'s caricature portraits of gangsta life, a subtext of social consciousness speaking through the ridiculously exaggerated and fantastical snapshots of an urban black monster with nothing to lose but looking to gain everything. For instance, over the sparse, glaring rhythm of "Dopeman," Cube describes, in candid detail, the life of a crack dealer and the soul-robbing power he has over the community. "Young brutha gettin' over by slangin' 'caine," Cube explains. The dealer's life is painted in glamorous strokes of material wealth ("Gold around his neck—a 14K habit"), raw greed, and female adoration. But within this illusion of control and influence, Cube also explored the destruction caused by crack (addiction, women prostituting themselves for drugs), though, ironically, not to condemn the pusher's occupation but to criticize folks for supporting his product. "If you smoke 'caine, you a stupid motherfucker," Cube decried. "Known around the 'hood as the schoolyard clucker / Doin' that crack with all the money you got / On your hands and knees searching for a piece of rock." Driving home the point, Eazy emerged toward the end of the song as the Dopeman, taunting crack addicts to "keep smokin' that rock, and my pocket's getting bigger." Picking at the irony of ghetto absurdity, N.W.A's shtick was more profound in its street reporting and covert commentary than it was in merely telling a story. Even after his shotgun-toting rampage on "Gangsta Gangsta," Cube ends up back in jail "dressed in the county blues," indirectly letting listeners know that that's where gangstas usually wind up.

The forceful ghetto rhetoric and innovative funk of *Straight Outta Compton* were what sent the album gold in six weeks. They were also what scared off radio, which wouldn't even consider playing messages as raw as N.W.A's. Regardless, it was this same emotional chord the group struck that turned their debut from a growing buzz to a national phenomenon. Most notable was the right-wing furor caused by the crew's fierce harangue against police brutality on "Fuck tha Police." "Fuck the police, coming straight from the underground," Cube shouted, leading the charge. "A young nigga got it bad 'cause I'm brown / And not the other color. So police think / They have the authority to kill a minority." Taking a page from the Black Panthers, N.W.A's lyrical response to this abuse of power was to return the favor with deadly force. "A young nigga on the warpath," Cube warned. "And when I'm finished, it's gonna be a bloodbath of cops dying in L.A. / Yo, Dre, I got something to say." The song's vitriolic lyrics, while boldly expressing resentment many blacks felt toward abusive police, set off an uproar within the nation's law enforcement. On August 1, 1989, the FBI's assistant director of public affairs, Milt Ahlerich, sent a letter to Priority Records saying the track encouraged "violence against and disrespect for the law enforcement officer." After the song's lyrics were faxed to various police departments, cops across the country protested, refusing to provide security for N.W.A concerts in certain cities. There was even alleged harassment as federal agents in Cincinnati, subjecting the group to drug searches, asked if they were "L.A. gang members using their tour as a front to expand their crack-selling operation." And at a Detroit concert, where the audience constantly chanted "Fuck the police!" during the show, police rushed the stage as N.W.A began performing the song.

In turn, the caustic response of law enforcement and conservatives fueled voices in defense of N.W.A's First Amendment rights. The ACLU and industry leaders were rallied for protests by publicist Phyllis Pollack and music journalist Dave Marsh through their organization

Music in Action. Congressman Don Edwards, head of the House's Subcommittee on Civil and Constitutional Rights, spoke out against Ahlerich's letter, saying: "The FBI should stay out of the business of censorship." N.W.A's impact was even felt at MTV, which banned the title track's video two months after the release of *Straight Outta Compton*. Fab Five Freddy, host of the network's *Yo! MTV Raps*, defied MTV's top brass and devoted an entire show to N.W.A, letting its members lead his cameras on a tour through the streets of Compton while millions of youthful viewers, especially suburban white kids, came along for the ride.

"That's how we sold two million," Bryan Turner, owner of Priority Records, told writer Jeff Chang. "White kids in the Valley picked it up and they decided they wanted to live vicariously through this music. Kids were just waiting for it." For rap hopefuls outside New York's stronghold—namely in the South, Midwest, and on the West Coast—the phenomenal success of *Straight Outta Compton* torched the commercial barriers keeping their versions of hip-hop music from being heard. N.W.A's debut debunked New York as hip-hop's center and democratized the aesthetics of rap, inspiring others with their formula for becoming a rap sensation. Now you didn't have to have the verbal dexterity of Rakim or Kool G Rap to reach stardom. Just tap into the uncharted hunger for hip-hop in your own region with rhymes of your gangsta exploits (drug sales and busting caps). And Compton, as the new symbol of urban decay, became the prototypical rap 'hood for these upstarts to match. But with one-third of post–black power America living below the poverty level and 45 percent of black children living in poverty, gangstafied rap was as much a verbal response to demoralizing social and economic conditions as it was an innovative way to sell records.

Public Enemy may have harvested the racial sensibilities of post–black power youth, but N.W.A tapped a bubbling reservoir of cynicism growing among them. They were the first generation to grow up without Jim Crow–style racism. Only now they were feeling the self-destructive effects of Jimmy's invisible stand-in: institutionalized racism. Instead of Klansmen keeping America's racial order intact, there was overzealous law enforcement policing black neighborhoods. Economic segregation formerly upheld by law was now simply the disappearance of jobs from black urban centers, the underfunding of education, and the cutting of youth programs. The threat of lynching was replaced by the fear of being senselessly murdered at the hands of another black man. And instead of outright enslavement there was the overwhelming imprisonment of African Americans, especially those snagged by the lure of the drug trade who were handed long prison terms under America's new drug policies. By 1990, there were 610,000 black males (one in four) between the ages of twenty and twenty-nine either locked up, on probation, or on parole. But only 436,000 blacks of the same age were enrolled in college. Yet where was the massive, *updated* fight for the rights of the post–black power generation? In particular, where was the leadership of the former movement?

That several of these civil rights and black power figures were caught in the same struggles and escapist traps as the youth also fueled the cynicism rumbling within post–black power America. For instance, drugs were at the destructive center of very public falls for two prominent men of black politics (as if they were the ones Dr. Dre was referring to on the song "Express Yourself" when he rhymed: "Some say, 'No to drugs,' and take a stand. But after the show they go looking for the dopeman"). The first was Huey P. Newton, co-founder of the Black Panther Party. On August 22, 1989, he was murdered by a small-time drug dealer looking to advance his position within the Black Guerrilla Family, a black power organization turned drug-distribution gang that had been around since the late 1960s. The dealer, twenty-five-year-old Tyrone Robinson, shot the former Panther to death after Newton, addicted to crack, argued with him over drugs. Reports later revealed that Newton's death brought an unfortunate end to the miserable last days of a black power hero, reduced to using the legend of his revolutionary past ("I'm Huey P. motherfuckin' Newton!" he'd yell at young dealers) to score free crack. But the destructive trail of rock cocaine also extended to the lips of mainstream black political leadership.

The whole country watched the videotaped drug bust of Washington, D.C.'s mayor, Marion Barry, on January 18, 1990. The sting was the finale of an investigation by the FBI and D.C. police into allegations of Barry's drug use. Ironically, before the mayor's arrest he had led the city's war against crack. Murky black-and-white footage showed the married Barry in a room at the Vista Hotel with Rasheeda Moore, a former mistress who set him up for the bust, making sexual advances and taking two long puffs from a crack pipe. It was the taped inhale that brought FBI agents bursting through several doors in the room to arrest Barry, whose crude response reverberated throughout the country. "The bitch set me up," Barry repeatedly muttered to himself. "That goddamn bitch . . . Tricked me." With all the furor over N.W.A, it was obvious that the life and language of black Americans (regardless of class or status or political affiliation) wasn't *too* far removed from the one portrayed on *Straight Outta Compton*.

It was with N.W.A that the media, attempting to describe their brand of music and focus, officially titled the new hip-hop subgenre gangsta rap. Once again, the target of the hardcore rapper was changing, shifting from the annihilation of sucker MCs (pioneered by Run-D.M.C.) and racists, along with their black cronies (the bull's-eye of P.E.), to the citizens of post–black power America. Be they fellow thug, hardworking parent, a female on the street, a friend who wronged you in the slightest way, or a racist cop: no one was above getting their ass whupped or their "cap peeled" if they stood in the way of financial progress or social pleasure. The age of crack turned urban black communities into cauldrons of selfishness, paranoia, and violence, and N.W.A turned those sentiments into a fresh musical movement.

Their ranks, too, would start to unravel due to the same selfishness, paranoia, and violence plaguing post–black power America. The first to unhinge was Ice Cube, who felt he was being unfairly compensated. From the $650,000 grossed on their tour, he had received only $23,000 while their manager, Jerry Heller, took home $150,000. *Eazy-Duz-It* and *Straight Outta Compton* sold a combined three million units, but despite having written the majority of the songs, Cube received only $32,700 for his work. Having never officially signed on as a member of N.W.A, Cube left the group, zapping his bandmates of their key writer/performer. Heading to New York to work on his solo debut with Public Enemy's Bomb Squad, Cube sharpened his political chops under the tutelage of Chuck D and released a gangsta rap masterpiece of his own, *AmeriKKKa's Most Wanted*, in February 1990.

Despite the split, N.W.A continued to carve their piece of music history. They released their second LP, *Efil4zaggin* (*Niggaz4life* spelled backward) in May 1991 and, with no airplay, debuted at number two on the pop chart. This feat was due in large part to *Billboard*'s tracking of record sales with the new data-tracking system SoundScan, which electronically tabulated album sales via a bar code–reading system. In the past, the magazine based its charts on what a network of retail reporters *said* was number one, reports that may have undercounted top-selling rap records. Now there was no denying hip-hop's commercial success when the first charts based on SoundScan were released: *Niggaz4life* had gone platinum in just two weeks, proving that the power of hardcore rap, the voice of post–black power America, reached farther than the chocolate cities of the United States, out to young hearts in the vanilla suburbs. N.W.A was proof that a nigga revolution of music and culture had indeed arrived. At least, that was the case on *Niggaz4life*.

Facing criticism (especially from image-conscious blacks) over their name and material, the Compton foursome now wielded the title "nigga" as a flag of *real* blackness, an honest representation of the Afro masses trapped in the urban sphere of crime, violence, poverty, and ignorance. Moreover, within this redefined idea of niggadom, N.W.A fashioned themselves the ruthless heroes. "Why do I call myself a 'nigga,' you ask me," Ren rhymed on the song "Niggaz 4 Life." "Well it's because mother-fuckers want to blast me, and run me out of my neighborhood / And label me as a dope dealer, yo, and say that I'm no good / But I gave out jobs so niggas wouldn't have to go out / Gave up some dope on the corners so they could show out." They may have seemed the obvious antithesis of P.E.'s revolutionary archetype, but the fire of N.W.A also reflected a black political urgency peeking through the smoke screen of the Bush White House.

Anyone who thought N.W.A's means of attaining ghetto heroship destructive and too extreme needed only compare it with the righteous threat of violence—in the name of black progress—in Milwaukee. In the spring of 1991 (two months before the release of *Niggaz4life*) Michael McGee, an alderman within Milwaukee's black community, announced his resurrection of a Black Panther militia to carry out terrorist attacks. Despite losing one-third of its manufacturing jobs during the early 1980s, Milwaukee became a national symbol of urban economic rebirth and prosperity, staving off the effects of a national recession, keeping its unemployment rate below the national average, and creating, as reported by the *Los Angeles Times*, "more jobs than skilled people to work them." But the upswing hadn't reached the city's black community, whose unemployment rate topped 20 percent—five times the percentage of unemployed white Milwaukeeans and nearly five times the state's average of 4.2 percent. The city's black population was also second in the nation in the percentage of black males incarcerated. Frustrated by the economic disparity and the lack of government intervention, McGee threatened to lead his militia on violent attacks against the city government if it didn't improve conditions for Milwaukee's black citizens by 1995. McGee's wrath-filled threat of an apocalypse, though empty (no attacks were ever carried out, nor was a Black Panther militia ever proven to exist), marked a crossroads for mainstream black political leadership and its effectiveness. By 1991, there were 7,370 black elected officials (up from 1,469 in 1970), yet the percentage of black families living in poverty (now around 27 percent), according to *The Boston Globe*, hadn't really changed since 1975 despite the fact that so much emphasis had been placed, after the civil rights and black power movements, on blacks collectively advancing through one of their own holding office.

After no payoff from such a struggle, one might relate to N.W.A's sentiment of being a "nigga 4 life." In part, *Niggaz4life*, like *Straight Outta Compton*, was a soundtrack for the mounting frustrations within post–black power America, in particular the growing problem of police brutality, one of the by-products of America's War on Drugs. Whereas "Fuck tha Police" simply (and violently) addressed the issue, the song "Real Niggaz Don't Die" expanded the discussion, viewing it as a systematic means of keeping black folks down. This time, N.W.A's rant came with shocking visuals as the videotaped beating of Rodney King by five Los Angeles police officers was broadcast on news programs across the country. On March 3, 1991, King was pulled over after leading cops on a chase, the officers pursuing him because he was speeding. Having recently done a year in prison for robbery, King, driving drunk, sped off fearing he'd be sent back to prison. When footage of the traffic stop rolled, a dazed-looking King was attempting to get to his feet, surrounded by cops mercilessly beating him with batons. Along with blacks, all of America was shocked and upset. Police abuse of African Americans was real, in prime time, and drilled into the world's consciousness with replay after replay. For all the uproar over "Fuck tha

Police" and the exaggerated anger of N.W.A, here was clear evidence that their feelings were valid.

Unfortunately, though, what *Niggaz4life* ultimately revealed was that N.W.A's harangue against cops was as far as their conscious voice could stretch without the prodigious writing of Ice Cube. Their ex-homeboy was out expanding the social dialogue of gangsta rap on *AmeriKKKa's Most Wanted*, discussing topics like black dependence on government assistance ("Once upon a Time in the Projects") and racial extinction ("Endangered Species [Tales from the Darkside]"). Lacking the profundity of Cube's pen—juggling gangstaness with a politically conscious eye—N.W.A's second offering amplified its violent outlook, stalling primarily in the thematic lane of screwing women, abusing women, getting high, getting paid, and killin' niggas.

But on the production end Dre had grown immensely, concocting his own Bomb Squad–esque funk tapestry, layering phrases, unnerving sounds, and synthesized keyboard work over loops of Parliament-Funkadelic tunes. To those listening, Dre was obviously heading toward the realization of his "g funk" style, a sound developed in his later—and more celebrated—work. The lyrical potential of N.W.A, while straining under the need to up its shock value and flying an even bigger middle finger to the critics and conservative opponents, devolved even further into a tireless loop of ruthless violence and misogyny. Only now, as the leading purveyors of gangsta rap, the line separating N.W.A's badness-on-wax and real life began to blur as their open animosity toward Ice Cube led to a well-publicized display of their *real* disregard for women. Following a battle of words with their former homeboy (Ren told *USA Today* Cube had an "ass-kicking coming" while Cube called N.W.A "Slaves With Attitude"), the group became miffed after Cube's appearance on the hip-hop video show *Pump It Up*. The show's host, Dee Barnes, juxtaposed footage of Yella symbolically crushing an ice cube under his foot with footage of Cube saying he had N.W.A "one hundred miles and running." The footage so upset Dr. Dre that he assaulted not Ice Cube but Dee Barnes at an album release party, reportedly slamming her face and body against a wall and punching her in the back of the head. In the days leading to his plea of no contest to misdemeanor battery, Dre, instead of fully admitting his guilt, used the incident to enhance the outlaw image of N.W.A. "Ain't no big thing," he told a reporter. "I *just* threw her through a door . . . People talk all this shit, but you know, somebody fucks with me I'm gonna fuck with them."

No longer was N.W.A's realness just relegated to the airwaves and music video clips. Now real-life antics affirmed their gangsta cred, feeding an increasing rap listenership hunger for hip-hop heroes who were as authentic in the flesh as they were on wax. Just as Public Enemy's raptivist posturing convinced a growing hip-hop nation that hardcore rappers could be righteous racial messiahs, N.W.A convinced them that gangstafied rappers could be the street soldiers of hip-hop (and that their disregard for authority and mainstream acceptance was just as powerful and hip-hop authentic—if not more so—as their pro-black rhyming counterparts). N.W.A were indeed the spearheads of a swelling ghetto soldier movement in rap, a gangsta music industry increasing in rank, sales, and influence. There was Oakland, California's pimp-themed rhymer Too $hort, who released his double-platinum debut, *Life Is . . . Too $hort*, in 1989. Compton's Most Wanted, fronted by rapper and former Crip, MC Eiht, spiced their irreverent raps with gang lingo, entering commercial rap's airspace with 1990's *It's a Compton Thang*. The Bloods-affiliated DJ Quik, also from Compton, saw platinum sales for his 1991 LP, *Quik Is the Name*, a party-flavored mix of Compton-based gun battles and pussy-chasing. And, off the momentum of their hit "Hand on the Pump," the hardcore L.A.-based Latino-Italian outfit Cypress Hill scored platinum with their self-titled debut in 1991. By the early 1990s, the consistent gold and platinum sales of gangsta rap made it apparent: rap music's mecca had shifted from the style-conscious brand of the East Coast to the ultra ghetto badness of the West. The shift in rap's appeal, aesthetic, and commercial influence would obviously be felt by New York rappers, whose sales were consistently being outpaced by their Left Coast counterparts. (There was some backlash from the Big Apple expressed by rapper Tim Dog in the 1991 dis track "Fuck Compton.") But the gangsta revolt of N.W.A inevitably began creeping eastward as established New York rappers, such as rap's original gangsta Kool G Rap, who balanced his gritty urban gaze with unsurpassable rhyme skills, elevated the ruggedness of their image and message. For his entry onto the *Billboard* charts, G Rap upped the crime quotient on his 1992 album, *Live and*

Let Die, with songs like "Ill Street Blues" and "Crime Pays." For the album's cover art, G Rap and his partner, DJ Polo, were ski-mask-wearing assassins preparing to hang two rivals. And Long Island, New York's EPMD borrowed N.W.A's image as law enforcement's most wanted: the cover of their 1990 gold-selling LP, *Business as Usual*, illustrated the duo surrounded by rifle-wielding policemen, their ultra-screw-faced appearance (a 180-degree change from their previous releases) worn as a silent mantra for the group's burgeoning purist charge to keep rap music "underground"—a subterranean metaphor describing street-funky rap music unconcerned with mainstream approval and sales. In other words, to keep the voice of rap pure and in the hands of its core audience. EPMD's cries of "Keep it underground" were the musical equivalent of the Panthers' shouts for giving "Power to the People."

Indeed, N.W.A's gangsta revolution—speaking from the social depths of post–black power America yet posting unheard-of sales—developed into hip-hop's front line against a tidal wave of over-commercialized pop rappers. Similar to N.W.A, these unfunky, squeaky-clean rhymers were also taking advantage of the rising commercial profile of rap music, only this new breed of non-hardcore rapper was ready to embrace marketability and be nonthreatening to a larger, whiter audience. Young MC, a Los Angeles–based rap artist, saw the rewards of such a formula with the 1989 platinum single "Bust a Move." Shortly after, there was the explosion of rap's first Elvis, Vanilla Ice. From the sensation caused by his song "Ice Ice Baby," the Florida rhymester's first LP, *To the Extreme*, became one of rap's bestselling albums, moving seven million discs, momentarily turning the un-hip-hop Vanilla Ice (pompadour-like flattop and all) into the white face of rap for America. But Ice paled in comparison to the early 1990s phenomenon of MC Hammer: the Oakland rapper, frantically dancing in his signature parachute pants, infused rap with a Las Vegas–style flash, a choirboy outlook, and a pop music marketability, taking the genre to heights unimagined before. Following his double-platinum 1988 LP, *Let's Get It Started*, with the biggest-selling rap album of all time, the ten-times-platinum *Please Hammer Don't Hurt 'Em* (1990), Hammer became a pop culture tornado, snagging major endorsement deals and massive mainstream media exposure. He even became the first rap artist to get his own Saturday morning cartoon (*Hammerman*). At the height of the mania, all of America seemed to be on "Hammer Time." The sales of pop (and gangsta) rap further opened the corridors of investment from major labels into rap music and hip-hop culture. But the palatability of Hammer and the mainstream attention paid to his ilk were seen as a threat by hardcore rap artists and fans alike, who deemed such rappers as "sell-outs," rhyming shucksters who discarded brash ghetto edginess for mainstream record sales. As the antithesis of this trend, gangsta rap, with its ideological roots in the street and sales consistently on the pop charts, became the stance rap took against the watering down of its voice and perspective. Along with EPMD, another key advocate of this position was Ice Cube, who in 1991 challenged Hammer on his hit song (and in its video) to be "True to the Game."

But the precedent for making rap represent "the 'hood" had been set by N.W.A, who pushed criminal-minded rap as the *real* black CNN, an unfiltered perspective of post–black power America. And, in the process, they stumbled upon hardcore rap's new pop fan base— suburban white kids enthralled by hip-hop's beat and fascinated by the unvarnished view of black ghetto life. In N.W.A, they finally had something more than the aging sound of hard-rock music to scare the wits out of their parents. The widespread appeal of N.W.A to this audience showed that the angst hip-hop music expressed reached beyond the borders of post–black power America. Unlike white rock 'n' rollers of the 1950s, who may have wanted black music but without the black culture (and black artists) attached, this generation embraced the black rap artists, their culture (albeit a romantically gangstafied version), and their me-against-the-world attitude. Eight years after Run-D.M.C., rap music was indeed becoming America's new rock 'n' roll.

Hollywood also sensed young America's swelling interest in N.W.A-styled reports from the front lines of urban black America. So gangsta rap's highly cinematic presentation was put to celluloid in a new post-blaxploitation genre of black films called 'hood flicks— movies bringing the raw, violent, and crack-driven reality of the black ghetto to a theater near you. Films like 1988's *Colors*, about L.A. street gangs, and 1991's *New Jack City*, about a late-1980s crack kingpin in Harlem, had drawn from the crime-fighting perspective of cops. 'Hood films were from the outlook of the ghetto denizen and, like their gangsta rap soundtracks, heavily inspired by the poetic power of N.W.A and the gang-drenched landscape of black Los Angeles. Starting with *Boyz N the Hood* (1991), the gritty coming-of-age story of three friends starring Ice Cube in his acting debut, this new brand of cinema candidly presented the struggles of living in post–black power America (the epidemic of black-on-black murder, drugs, the lack of hope, and abusive police). In Hollywood fashion these thugcentric films, like *Menace II Society* (1993), always ended with the self-destruction of a promising black protagonist, swallowed by the selfish and violently nihilistic impulses of youth.

But like their N.W.A muse, these films also produced a heroic post-blaxploitation antihero in the crazed gangsta—the protagonist's wayward friend—straight from the mold of Ice Cube's archetype on "Gangsta Gangsta" ("A crazy motherfucker from around 'the way' "). Whereas the criminal-minded studs of blaxploitation movies (*Super Fly*, *The Mack*, *Dolemite*, and such) fought racial oppression by gaining wealth illegally, the violently nihilistic heroes of 'hood films—blinded by the debilitating effects of institutionalized racism—annihilated their obstacles (usually other wayward or murderous black folks) through the barrel of an automatic handgun. Their cinematic ancestors may have been rich black champions, but these gat-pulling protoypes, later to be dubbed "insane nigga heroes," were parentless, crack-age supermen: "young, black, and didn't give a fuck." No matter what their incarnation—whether Ice Cube's ruthless Doughboy shooting the gangbanging killers of his brother in *Boyz N the Hood*, or rapper Tupac's power-craving Bishop catching up to a knife-wielding bully and blowing him away (*Juice* in 1992), or actor Larenz Tate's wide-eyed O-Dog blasting a crackhead who tests his sexuality in *Menace II Society*—the commercial catalyst for the insane nigga hero and his 'hood film showcase was formed in the pop culture explosion of Niggaz With Attitude.

The Compton crew, however, like the hip-hop comets they were, didn't last long enough to bask in the brilliance of their achievement. They disintegrated shortly after the release of *Niggaz4life*, torn apart by the suspicions of Dr. Dre that Eazy and Jerry Heller were short-changing him and the rest of the group. In true gangsta fashion, Dre's departure included an infamously heavy-handed negotiation allegedly involving Suge Knight, Dre's former bodyguard and new business partner, and a group of pipe-wielding friends "persuading" Eazy to release Dre from his contract. N.W.A was over, but out of its ruin rose a stronger Dre-lead institution of gangsta rap, Death Row Records. In the end, though, no one could dispute the foundation unexpectedly laid by Niggaz With Attitude. Tapping into the painful realities of post–black power America, they unflinchingly turned hardcore rap into the pop cultural voice of "the people," black urban youth with no public voice. Whether this gangstafication of rap was positive or negative, no one knew what the future held or how long it would last. One thing was for sure: Black Los Angeles was now the cultural shot caller, as gangsta became the face of rap and L.A.'s nation of Bloods and Crips spread eastward, with kids as far away as Texas aligning themselves along the new color line—Blood red or Crip blue.

Hip-hop's sonic landscape may have started "up in the Bronx," but after the nigga riot begun by five dudes from South Central was through, it was starting to look, to quote a hit song by DJ Quik, "just like Compton."

SIX

R-E-S-P-E-C-T in PC Land
Salt-N-Pepa

A woman can bear you, break you, take you
Now it's time to rhyme, can you relate to
A sister dope enough to make you holler and scream.

—Queen Latifah, "Ladies First"

As a woman, I have no country . . . As a woman my country is the
whole world.

—Virginia Woolf

While Salt-N-Pepa's third album, 1990's *Blacks' Magic*, increased its pace toward platinum status—the LP's single "Let's Talk About Sex" becoming an AIDS-awareness anthem—Americans were being asked to take a hard look at themselves. "ARE YOU POLITICALLY CORRECT?" asked the cover of *New York* magazine on January 15, 1991. Over the headshot of a dazed-looking white woman lay a barrage of questions implying an intense internal dialogue: "Am I guilty of racism, sexism, classism? Am I guilty of ageism, ableism, lookism? . . . Do I say 'Indian' instead of 'Native American'?" At issue was an idea brewing on campuses of American colleges and universities and now creeping its way into larger society.

Political correctness, the code of conduct challenging the inherently racist, sexist, and classist notions (and language) embedded in American life, was being called the new fundamentalist movement of the left. And institutes of higher learning were becoming battlefields for initiating its enforcement: anyone caught going against the tenets of PCism (saying or doing anything deemed degrading or offensive to a marginalized group) could now be punished by the institution. The evangelical preachers of this crusade were the feminists, former hippies, gay activists, and black power figures of the late 1960s—now tenured professors and key administrators at prestigious colleges and universities. Their initial foot soldiers were the radical-thinking students filling (read: being converted in) the humanities courses taught by these professors. The philosophical crusaders of this movement were broken into three factions: the multiculturalists, the Afrocentrists, and the gender feminists, all fighting for inclusion, recognition, and respect within an America historically centered on affirming and maintaining the social superiority of white males.

Although political correctness was also pegged "the fascism of the left," one thing was abundantly clear: after ten years of a conservative White House sanctioning disregard for those on the margins, America was once again being challenged by its swelling nation of *others* (blacks, Latinos, Asians, gays, women, and so forth). And Salt-N-Pepa, the reigning godmothers of hardcore rap, were on the verge of riding this tidal wave of political correctness to challenge exclusionary forces raging both outside and within the borders of black America. For a "boys' club" such as rap music (and hip-hop culture, in general) this female outfit from Queens, New York, proved not only the commercial power of women rappers but also how the expression of womanhood within rap could expand, challenge, and enhance the music's evolving dialogue (especially within the burgeoning phenomenon of political correctness). Then again, hip-hop has always had the challenge of including outsiders, particularly females, in its hypermacho expression of black manhood.

The history has been documented time and time again: The presence of women in rap music goes back to the halcyon days of the Bronx, this pre-wax era filled with the not-so-well-documented names of female party rockers astounding crowds for their male DJs—the duo Sweet and Sour performing rhymes for Grandmixer D.ST's sound system; Little Lee skillfully wielding her mic along side DJ AJ; Lisa Lee dropping verses as a member of Afrika Bambaataa's Cosmic Force in the early 1980s, becoming one of the first female MCs featured in an otherwise all-male group. Other female soloists included Debbie B and Wanda Dee. And there were all-female groups such as Mercedes Ladies—considered the first female rap crew—and the trio Sequence. All of these female MCs rapped on the same topics as their male competition: their mic skills and abilities as the flyest individuals on earth. And when rap music leaped from the streets to the commercial airwaves, women maintained a voice—albeit minuscule—that rocked as hard as the fellows. Bringing a few of those acts to the public was rap industry pioneer (and also a woman) Sylvia Robinson, owner of Sugar Hill Records. Robinson signed Sequence, who released their 1979 disco funky classic "Funk You Up." The trio's labelmates the Funky 4 + 1 featured another female MC pioneer, Sha Rock. Her crew's groundbreaking performance on *Saturday Night Live* with Blondie was the country's first glimpse at a female MC. After the stir she caused in the burgeoning universe of rap music, though, it would be a few years before a female established any significant foothold within the genre.

That's when a fifteen-year-old Queens she-MC named Roxanne Shanté (née Lolita Shanté Gooden) decided to respond to U.T.F.O.'s hit "Roxanne, Roxanne" in 1985. In reaction to the trio's song that discussed and dismissed a female who rejected their advances, Shanté, pretending to be the girl, recorded "Roxanne's Revenge," a pubescent retort hurling sharp disses back at the crew. Never before had a female rapper spoken out against the sexist and misogynistic treatment of a woman in hip-hop—not to mention initiating a battle with male MCs. Shanté's verbal stance against U.T.F.O., while sparking a Roxanne frenzy (over one hundred Roxanne tracks, many by female rappers, were recorded), birthed the phenomenon of "dis," or response, records, an idea taken from the ideals of battle rapping. Inside a hip-hop expression that had grown overwhelmingly male-dominated, women possessed a means of expressing their ear-catching version of hardness, challenging the girl-as-target hits of male rappers. LL Cool J's 1985 tune "Dear Yvette" received a reply from the rapper E-Vette Money, "E-vette's Revenge." The Boogie Boys' song "A Fly Girl" was met with Pebblee Poo's "A Fly Guy." The popularity of the response record—a battle-of-the-sexes-put-to-wax—propelled Salt-N-Pepa into the world of rap. However, the matter was more about higher education than becoming hip-hop celebrities.

Both Salt (Cheryl James) and Pepa (Sandra Denton) were studying nursing at Queensborough Community College and working part-time at Sears on Fordham Road in the Bronx when a coworker, Hurby "Luv Bug" Azor, asked them to rap for his school project in 1985. Azor, who attended New York's Center for Media Arts, had to produce and record a song, and was inspired by the response-record craze caused by the Roxanne dis-fest. He convinced the two friends, who'd never rapped before and had no desire to MC (Sandra was a punk rocker who'd only started listening to rap two years earlier), to answer Doug E. Fresh and Slick Rick's hit rap "The Show." The result was the response tune "The Showstopper," a humorous attack with Cheryl pretending to be the girl Slick Rick raps about meeting on a subway train. Besides getting Azor an A on his project, the song, credited to Super Nature, somehow made it onto radio (the late night rap mix shows, of course) and became a minor hit, reaching number forty-six on the R&B chart. With the buzz from the song, Azor secured the group a deal with Next Plateau Records, promising the label he could produce an album for less than $5,000. Under their new name, Salt-N-Pepa (taken from a line in "The Showstopper" where they refer to themselves as the salt 'n' pepper MCs), Cheryl and Sandra were unknowingly about to lead rap's female revolution into the golden era. Completing their outfit was a new female DJ, Deirdre Roper, who assumed the title Spinderella shortly after replacing the group's original Spinderella (Pamela Greene). S-N-P were an all-female outfit, but behind the scenes Azor, as he'd done with "The Showstopper," assumed the role of Svengali, styling the duo's image and writing and producing all of the music for their debut album, 1986's *Hot, Cool & Vicious*. "We were living Hurby's dream," Pepa would later explain. Nevertheless, despite a man's touch, S-N-P's first offering thrust womanhood, alongside a bubbling Afrocentrism, into this new age of rap. If the genre's approaching golden era was retwisted funk, culture-conscious verbiage, and crack-era-fueled machismo, *Hot, Cool & Vicious* made sure it also included the undeniable power (mind, mouth, and marketability) of sistas.

Indeed, their legacy would be as Salt predicted in the liner notes for the LP: "Salt-N-Pepa will beeee the next female Run DMC's." Not just because of the group's construct (two MCs and one DJ) or their hardcore attitude, but because like their Queens predecessors, they un-abashedly presented themselves—their attitudes, battles, and perspec-tives as women—over the phat beats of hip-hop. Whereas the female MCs of yore rapped girl versions of the microphone prowess boys boasted about, S-N-P bragged and dis-fully rhymed, almost exclusively, what girls rapped (as in talked) about, especially in regard to the oppo-site sex. A burgeoning nation of hip-hoppers was introduced to the S-N-P outlook through the LP's first single, "Tramp."

Dismissing the pickup lines of men, the song "Tramp," with its sampling of Otis Redding's 1967 soul classic of the same name, was hip-hop's reconfiguration of Carla Thomas's dismissal of Otis's come-on on the original. Carla's disses were based on the soul crooner's lack of material wealth. Within the context of black America after the strug-gles of the 1960s, S-N-P's "Tramp" was a b-girl's beat-laden response to the issue of womanizing. "What would you do if a stranger said, 'Hi,' " Salt asked. "Would you dis him or would you reply / If you answer, there is a chance / That you'll become a victim of circumstance." (A powerful message, considering a 1986 "black progress" report by the Urban League stated, according to the *Chicago Tribune*, that 24.6 per-cent of all black births that year were to teenage mothers, 87 percent of those births were out of wedlock, and more than 40 percent of black families were headed by women.) The song's video, while giving the country its first glimpse at these budding queens of rap, promoted the idea of women avoiding the traps through strength and self-awareness. Set in a nightclub, the clip showed the duo—sporting the female hip-hop fashions of the day (huge doorknocker earrings and asymmetrical haircuts)—brushing off the Casanovas and their weak lines. "You ain't gettin' paid / You ain't knockin' boots / You ain't treating me like no prostitute." While warning the ladies of possible man trouble and offer-ing their own examples of self-assuredness, S-N-P confidently walk through the place showing off their voluptuous bodies. No feminist stances here, just a sobering acknowledgment of the facts according to Salt-N-Pepa: that most guys were dogs and S-N-P, as the sexiest of hip-hop damsels, could most effectively relay this to the sistas. As many writers have acknowledged, never before had female rappers (or even male rappers, for that matter) so unashamedly flaunted their sexuality, outright, before the camera. Though S-N-P's ability to balance sexiness with street-bred hubris was what broke them to a wider pop audience.

The song "Push It," the B-side of "Tramp," was a sexually suggestive dance rap that didn't garner much notice until Cameron Paul, a DJ at San Francisco's KMEL, remixed it, turning the tune into a Top 40 radio hit. After its release, the new version of "Push It" went platinum in 1988, pushing *Hot, Cool & Vicious* to platinum sales two years after its release and bestowing on S-N-P the honor of being the first female MCs to do so. The song reached number nineteen on the pop singles chart and was nominated for a Grammy, but Salt-N-Pepa joined the coalition of rap artists boycotting the ceremony that year. Nevertheless, the mainstream breakthrough of rap, thanks to the platinum success of S-N-P, now included the voice of women. Yet the genius of *Hot, Cool & Vicious* wasn't just its presentation of the female perspective, but the melding of b-girl femininity and sex appeal with the sonically hardcore beats-n-bravado usually associated with male MCs (ironic, considering a male wrote and produced the entire album).

Ditching the idea that girls had to dress and act like boys in order to get respect in hip-hop, *Hot, Cool & Vicious* skillfully packaged a pro-woman stance within rap's hardcore formula and added lipstick to the notion of hip-hop badness. Hurby's formula? If the limited perspectives of male rappers could only present women as materialistic harlots, Salt-N-Pepa, with their debut LP, returned the favor, presenting men as shallow-minded creatures who only thought with their penises. Where dudes wrote raps dissing girls who wronged or used them, Salt-N-Pepa wielded their own "man dis" record with "Chick on the Side," its title and chorus taken from the Pointer Sisters' 1975 song "How Long (Betcha Got a Chick on the Side)." The tune showcased the duo over a go-go propelled rhythm, blasting their boyfriends for cheating, letting their unworthy beaux know they'd also moved on to bigger and better, uh, things. "He fix the table for his and hers," Pepa bragged to her former lover. "And while the dinner simmers he serves the hors d'oeuvres / Then it's munch-out time, sip the wine get mellow / Clear off the table then it's, 'Hello Jell-O!' / I can't express the feeling that I get / So I just lay back and light up a cigarette." Salt-N-Pepa were equally as up front about discussing their own libidos and feminine powers.

Likewise, *Hot, Cool & Vicious* pushed the concept of female MCs extolling their own skills as hard and as confidently as the guys, all while remaining true to themselves as women. Over the simmering boom bap of "It's Alright," a tune closely resembling Run-D.M.C.'s "Together Forever," Salt-N-Pepa waxed wrathful and dominant over their male competition, though with a feminine brand of cool. "On stage I'm a terror," Salt warned. "Mascara don't smeara / Stockings don't run / And men, don't dare us / Speak out and disrespect Salt-N-Pepa / We smash MCs with one big steppa." And on the boastful "My Mic Sounds Nice," the duo, while playfully bragging about their sex appeal ("If I was a book I would sell," rapped Pepa, "'cause every curve on my body got a story to tell") and mic skills, warned sucker male MCs of an impending female MC revolution. "This is the year all men fear," rhymed Salt. "Female MCs is moving up here!" Although the line was written by a man, the words were a prophetic declaration of a gender movement within rap music. The groundbreaking achievements of Salt-N-Pepa, while presenting a solid example that women could sell rap records, sat at the center of a female MC resurgence in rap, one whose voice was as diverse as the ideas fueling the music's renaissance: Brooklyn-based MC Lyte, who, with her low, husky voice, mixed vulnerability and social messages with b-girl toughness on her 1988 debut, "I Cram to Understand U"; rapper Antoinette, wielding a delivery very similar to Rakim's, presenting unadulterated hardness on 1987's "I Got an Attitude"; and at the same time, out of Eazy-E's Ruthless camp, the Los Angeles trio J.J. Fad, who scored hip-hop's second gold-selling album by a female group with the Salt-N-Pepa–like banter of 1988's *Supersonic*. Most certainly female MCs were stepping up, increasing their numbers within rap, contributing to the music's expanding commercial profile, making sure the female voice and perspective were included in the mix. But for the most part, the ladies were still relegated to using the formula of marketing hardcore streetness—the beats, the dress, the attitude, the ultra competitiveness and aggression, even the ideas for the pop crossover—put forth (and shaped) by men.

This was especially the case when Salt-N-Pepa released their sophomore album, 1988's *A Salt with a Deadly Pepa*, because Hurby, as the Berry Gordy–style puppeteer, still held the strings of image and artistic control over the group (a third of that control maintained because he was dating Salt). Concerned with maintaining S-N-P's commercial prominence, he no doubt eyed the crossover blueprint of groups like the Beastie Boys, Public Enemy, and Run-D.M.C., blending hardcore beats-n-bravado with the popular sounds of rock, burning the candle of familiarity at both ends. So as Salt-N-Pepa's b-girl image was played up even further with colorful leather jackets and thick gold rope chains, so, too, were the b-boy elements of their sound, rhyme style, and delivery. Instead of further developing rap's feminine side, *A Salt with a Deadly Pepa*—produced at the height of rap's hardcore revolution (and innovation)—continued, by and large, to present a girl's version of what the guys were doing. There were moments that were distinctly S-N-P, such as the go-go dance hit "Shake Your Thang," a hip-hop twist on the Isley Brothers' 1969 "It's Your Thing," and the mid-tempo piano-laced push of "Get Up Everybody (Get Up)." But the rest of *A Salt with a Deadly Pepa* found S-N-P blatantly dipping, stylistically, into the formulas of the male rap hit parade. S-N-P borrowed Chuck D's authoritative choo-choo-train delivery for "Hyped on the Mic" as well as sampling the beat of P.E.'s "Night of the Living Baseheads" and the Bomb Squad's flurry-of-samples style for the title track. They crafted the storytelling cadence of "I Like It Like That" from the playful rhymes of Run-D.M.C.'s "You Be Illin' "; they did a female rendition of the Beastie Boys for the metal-inspired tune "I Gotcha"; and, sounding like every other wealth-obsessed, funk-sampling wordsmith, the duo phoned in the standard ruffian posture on "Solo Power (Let's Get Paid)."

Without a crossover hit to spur sales, Hurby's approach would send *A Salt with a Deadly Pepa* only gold. S-N-P's dilemma of finding a voice—one uniquely their own—was as crucial to their personal growth as artists as it was to their survival as a group in rap's expanding marketplace. They found it not in the hard-knock brags or crotch-grabbing rants of hardcore rap but in the self-realization movement it spurred with the likes of Public Enemy and N.W.A. Unfortunately for Hurby, S-N-P's self-realization arrived with their dissatisfaction with his omnipotence as they wrestled for input into the making of their third LP, *Blacks' Magic*. In the end, Salt produced or co-produced four tracks and Spinderella produced one. Their fight for independence was a necessary one, as other female MCs were breaking ground on hip-hop's politicized stage. While they created *Blacks' Magic*, New Jersey–born Queen Latifah was winning the respect of the hip-hop world with her 1989 debut, *All Hail the Queen*. Decked in her regal Afrocentric outfits and crown-like hats, Latifah, over a combination of hardy hip-hop dance beats and R&B-styled choruses, spouted clever battle raps, black consciousness rhymes, and pro-woman anthems like the classic "Ladies First"—cowritten by the male rapper Apache. Latifah became key to launching the female arm—some might even call it the feminist arm—of rap's consciousness movement. In the aftershock of Public Enemy and N.W.A, with the role of MCs expanded to racial spokespeople, female rappers had an even larger war to fight with their words, speaking not only against racism served up by white conservatives but against the sexism perpetuated (and condoned) by men of color within hip-hop culture. Just like the black power movement before, the burgeoning pro-black stance of hardcore rap primarily catered to the power fantasies (and chauvinism) of brothas. In the black nationalist camps—à la Public Enemy—women were, by and large, discussed as either brainwashed bourgeois strivers (as in "Sophisticated Bitch") or idealized queens in need of saving and protection. At the same time, according to the growing gangsta rap nation, women were for the most part scandalous bitches who deserved no respect or recognition. So the assertion of the female MC as strong, proud, and, most important, intelligent served not only to include women in hip-hop's growing social/racial dialogue but to remind a swelling hip-hop constituency to recognize and respect the power (and skills) of black women.

At the dawning of the 1990s, this burgeoning feminist sentiment within rap connected with a larger war—a cultural war—brewing both within and outside the borders of black America. On the one hand, the ideals of political correctness were reaching beyond the manicured campuses of American colleges. The multiculturalist fight for inclusion, recognition, and respect was moving into mainstream media as well as into the halls of the nation's capital. On the other hand, the conservative Christian right and its political cohorts, under the pretext of protecting America's family values (read: white conservative families), attempted to beat back the artistic and cultural voices now screaming within American popular culture. Rap, with its exploding popularity and hostile social outlook, had become a leading example cited for such deterioration. The subheadline for a March 1990 *Newsweek* piece titled "The Rap Attitude," while describing the music as "a new musical culture filled with self-assertion and anger" coming from the streets, also noted that some people thought the music "should have stayed there."

Amid this cultural warfare, Salt-N-Pepa released *Blacks' Magic* in

1990, catching hold of a renewed revolution in gender politics and sexuality. At colleges and universities, the women's movement was resuscitated, the cause, this time, having more to do with the violence and sexual misconduct perpetrated against women than with the career and social opportunities they were denied. On campuses nationwide, rising reports of date rape ignited an outcry from women and women's groups against sexual violence. In response to the silence both of victims, who rarely reported the crime, and of law enforcement, who wouldn't take the reports seriously, the antirape movement that had gotten its start in the 1970s regained momentum. There were rallies to fight rape and push the topic into the public dialogue—most notably, a renewed interest in the yearly national Take Back the Night march, demonstrating against sexual violence and providing a cathartic space for victims to talk about their pain and, possibly, expose their attackers. And as the issue of date rape made its way into the media in the early 1990s—the most famous case being the 1991 trial against William Kennedy Smith (nephew of Senator Edward Kennedy), who was accused of rape by a woman he met at a bar—it set off a national debate about the definition of rape. (The act usually thought of as a violent crime committed by a stranger, not as unwanted sex with a boyfriend or an acquaintance.) From this dialogue, the idea that "*no* means *no*" became the national rule of sexual engagement, and other matters of sexual misconduct and control would be broached in the future.

At the same time, the activist spirit had also rekindled in the gay and lesbian community, sparked by the AIDS crisis overwhelming the gay male population. Since discovery of the first cases in 1981, throughout most of his presidency Reagan remained silent about the disease and the epidemic. The religious right, though, used the plague as a tool to demonize homosexuals—calling it the wrath of God directed at gay men—in an attempt to beat them back into the era of closeted shame before 1969's Stonewall riots, which kicked off the gay rights and gay pride movements of the 1970s. By the late 1980s and early '90s, the gay rights movement had evolved into a struggle against the spread of AIDS, getting the federal government and the public to face this disease not as a gay sickness but as a human epidemic affecting everyone. By 1987, the year Reagan finally mentioned and acknowledged AIDS at the

Third International Conference on AIDS, over twenty thousand Americans had died from the disease. Getting the country to wake up to the crisis were organizations like ACT UP (AIDS Coalition to Unleash Power), which took inspiration from the civil rights movement. Using marches, demonstrations, boycotts, and nonviolent civil disobedience, the organization attracted massive media attention to the battle against AIDS. Another group, the NAMES Project Foundation, held yearly displays of its AIDS quilt on the National Mall in Washington, D.C., and not only drew national attention (and money) toward this health emergency but also broadened awareness about the battle against AIDS and the illness's effect on both hetero- and homosexuals.

While this gender, sexual, and cultural tug-of-war made its way toward the public's consciousness, Salt-N-Pepa waged their own personal effort against sexism (namely, the iron hand of Hurby) in the music biz with their third album. *Blacks' Magic* anchored itself in the theme of racial pride popularized by hardcore rap. But instead of resting the album's cause in activist politics (like P.E.) or ghettocentricity (like N.W.A), S-N-P chose to musically honor the spirit of black creativity, strength, and womanhood. The LP's cover was a Rockwellian portrait of Salt, Pepa, and Spinderella evoking, with the help of a *Blacks' Magic* book, the ghosts of black music legends, including Jimi Hendrix, Billie Holiday, and Louis Armstrong—artists who not only innovated American popular music but also made music that crossed all lines. The illustration, while paying homage to the pioneers of the past, also invoked S-N-P (and rap, in general) as part of the continuum of this innovation, as proof that the *soul* of African-American music still lived on.

At a time when rap's gritty, homegrown funk was experiencing both a creative/social explosion and the threat of pop washout (thanks to acts like MC Hammer), *Blacks' Magic* ingeniously melded the possibilities of both worlds to push rap even further. Within its standard hip-hop rhythms sat a distinctly melodic R&B influence, a sound that appealed to female rap fans and would eventually extend Salt-N-Pepa's message (*their* celebration of the self) to an even wider audience. Though they weren't abandoning their hardcore (read: black) audience, they were pushing the unwavering purists of hardcore rap to open their minds and tastes, to accept rap's ability to branch off in numerous directions and speak to varied non-hip-hop audiences.

They launched this challenge with "Expression," a tune produced and written by Salt, a celebration of self-expression put to a smooth, malleable R&B groove. The song's video officially unveiled a mature and artistically sophisticated Salt-N-Pepa: the trio, now decked in fashions popularized by house music devotees—vintage baggy jeans, black floppy hats, and polka-dot tops—danced and rapped and posed within an urban mosaic of black folks (b-girls, "voguing" gay men, a female vagabond) while declaring their mantra of personal liberation. "Express yourself. You've got to be you," they urged their listeners, pushing a message of self-esteem. Their assertion, their new look, even their proud embrace of sexuality, seemed to align them with another female pop star, Madonna, who also challenged America's ideas of acceptance and sexuality (and had a hit song in 1989 called "Express Yourself"). Gone were Salt-N-Pepa's own b-girl trappings; they re-emerged, well into their twenties, as women of hip-hop, "getting deep," as Pepa would explain to *Vibe* editor Mimi Valdés. The debut of "Expression," with its universal theme, palatable groove, and unconventional video sending it platinum, propelled Salt-N-Pepa from hip-hop vixens with confidence to rap stars with a mission. And that mission, throughout *Blacks' Magic*, was self-empowerment, sexual fun (and responsibility), and tolerance. The theme of "Expression," while resonating along the multilateral fronts of the cultural war, reverberated especially within the swelling right-wing assault on rap, particularly the controversy surrounding Miami's 2 Live Crew, who became the center of a national debate on censorship in June 1990 after a federal judge ruled that their raunchy 1989 LP *As Nasty as They Wanna Be* was obscene. The Florida court's decision—the first court in U.S. history to find a record album obscene—cleared the way for the album to be banned in several states. A number of record-store owners were arrested or fined for selling the record to minors. The storm over 2 Live Crew and their material was part conservative backlash (Focus on the Family, a pro-family group, sparked the campaign against the album) and part political opportunism (Florida governor Bob Martinez joined the crusade against the group to bolster his lagging reelection numbers). The case marked the steady criminalization of black popular art and culture, particularly, as phrased by a *Washington Post* reporter, "challenging forms of expressiveness." Before the ruling was overturned by a U.S. Circuit Court of Appeals in Atlanta on May 7, 1992, pundits and rap fans alike questioned the judicial strike against 2 Live Crew not only as an attack against artistic freedom but as a form of black censorship. "I don't see how people can jump into someone else's culture, with completely no knowledge of that culture," commented Henry Louis Gates, "and then decide what's obscene and what is not." Yes, many blacks (women *and* men) agreed that 2 Live's album was vulgar, sexually derogatory toward women, and not the best (or even the most authentic) that rap had to offer. But the persecution and banning of their music (*black* music), deeming its purchase a criminal act, reeked of the racist sentiment that had been rising since the early 1980s.

None of the racial tumult was lost on S-N-P. *Blacks' Magic* was laced with its own messages about racism, with Salt, over the newjack swing of "Negro Wit' an Ego," venting her frustrations about the misperceptions society has of blacks, resulting in their ill-treatment. "When I drop my 911 or 300C," she complained, "the cops are surprised to see (a minority) behind the wheel of this car / It must be narcotics / How else should she have got it / A brown skin female with 2 problems to correct / Wrong color, wrong sex." The album's title track, coproduced by Spinderella, with its tribalesque boom, decried the negative stigma attached to the word "black" throughout history (black sheep, black sleep, black lung, and so forth). But the song, ironically at the height of the nationalist craze within rap, dismissed the extremist thoughts of black nationalism, in which blacks, tired of white supremacy, might advocate painting their world *totally* black. "I want variety in my society," rapped Salt. "Where I can change if I don't like what I see."

Eschewing the nationalistic fervor prevalent among the male vanguard, *Blacks' Magic* spoke of racial pride within reason (after all, no one, especially black folks, could ignore the tension). But Salt-N-Pepa, with the social context of the culture wars, crafted their message to be more inclusive, to reflect the turbulent mix of gender and sexuality that America was being confronted with. The gold single "Do You Want Me," a song challenging the notion of loveless sex—with an ambivalent Salt demanding a hormonally charged boyfriend to wait until *she's* ready—displayed a woman aggressively dictating the terms of a *possible* sexual exchange. The song's position rang significant as the antirape movement mainstreamed the issue and debate of date rape. And the Salt-produced tune "Independent," a stern, boastful rap about female independence (as opposed to social and financial dependence on a man), found itself a semi-mantra for a renewed feminism, especially among young black women tired of the misogyny within a burgeoning gangsta rap industry.

And it was at the height of the AIDS awareness movement that the album's most risqué song, the gold-selling "Let's Talk About Sex," climbed onto the pop singles chart (number thirteen), becoming *the* social anthem promoting a healthy dialogue about the topic. Over a chugging dance track Salt-N-Pepa broached the issue, saying it was inevitable, given the prevalence of sex in pop culture ("We talk about sex on the radio and video show"). But in order for the discussion to be beneficial, especially during such tumultuous times, the duo declared honesty and open-mindedness the best route. "Let's tell it like it is and how it could be," they rhymed. "How it was and, of course, how it should be." With the joyful rhythm, their statement may have sounded like an endorsement of sexual liberation, a stance Madonna was becoming famous (and infamous) for. But its primary message was one of sexual responsibility: Sex without self-esteem or an emotional connection equals misery in the end. Although the song didn't mention AIDS or the idea of safe sex, its plea for an open dialogue became something of a rallying cry for those (gay and straight) organizing against the disease. Within black America the song's advice couldn't have been more relevant given the epidemic's spread in black urban communities nationwide, with the drug scourge and its by-products—prostitution, needle sharing, and so on—aiding its increase. As Reagan had done for most of his presidency, the black church—the spiritual and political rock for most of black America—and numerous key black organizations virtually ignored the disease, doing close to nothing to combat the spread of AIDS among black people. (At least rap had already put the word out about safe sex in the late 1980s with songs like Boogie Down Productions' "Jimmy.") For many, AIDS was still a disease of gay men and intravenous drug users, a celestial wrath brought about by an "unnatural" lifestyle. Black America most certainly received its wake-up call, along with the rest of the country, when basketball star Magic Johnson publicly announced on November 7, 1991, that he'd contracted HIV. This married legend of the macho world of sports shocked straight people, if momentarily, into taking the epidemic seriously, in a way ACT UP and the AIDS quilt had not been able to. If there was hesitancy about discussing sex before Salt-N-Pepa advised folks to do so, Johnson brought home the consequences of such denial and carelessness. But coming from a black male, his confession also spoke prophetically of an impending AIDS crisis in black America as, five years later—while declining among whites—the virus became the leading cause of death among African Americans ages twenty-five to forty-four. For a campaign to educate women about safe sex, Salt-N-Pepa rerecorded their hit song under the title "Let's Talk About AIDS," becoming the hip-hop vanguard in the ever-widening struggle for AIDS awareness and prevention.

More than helping *Blacks' Magic* go platinum, Salt-N-Pepa's courageous new direction—blending sexual, gender, and racial politics with R&B-flavored hip-hop—expanded rap's social gaze and rhythmic vocabulary, accompanying the merge of hip-hop's voice with the burgeoning multiculturalist struggle for inclusion, respect, and justice. That fight, particularly its feminist arm, would get mainstreamed in the three years leading up to the release of S-N-P's history-making disc, *Very Necessary*. The most notable inspiration came from the nomination of a black conservative, Clarence Thomas, to the U.S. Supreme Court in 1991.

Upon the retirement of Thurgood Marshall, the court's first black justice and a civil rights giant, President Bush, looking to stack the bench with conservatives while maintaining its racial makeup, named Thomas as his choice. Civil rights organizations, including the NAACP and the Urban League, opposed the nomination, fearing that Thomas's conservative views on affirmative action would reverse the gains of the civil rights struggle. Equally fearful of Bush's decision were women's groups who felt that if Thomas was appointed, he would rule against the legal right to an abortion. Despite the opposition, however, the Thomas nomination continued toward a confirmation hearing with the Senate Judiciary Committee.

Without a clear vote of confidence (split by a seven-to-seven vote between Democrats and Republicans), the nomination moved to the floor of the Senate for a final vote. But the proceedings were marred when Anita Hill, a law professor at the University of Oklahoma, brought forth allegations of sexual harassment against Thomas; her claims stemmed from the time she had worked for him when he was the head of the Equal Employment Opportunity Commission in the early 1980s. Initially, Hill's complaint had been privately dismissed by the Senate Judiciary Committee until pressure from the media and several congresswomen forced them to reopen the confirmation hearings. This time they were held live on television, with millions of Americans hearing Hill graphically describe how Thomas sexually harassed her, inappropriately discussing pornographic films and sexual acts after she had refused to date him. Her claims were backed by four people who testified that she had told them about Thomas's actions years before the hearings. If the issue of race had been absent during the first half of the hearings it was, ironically, broached in the latter half by Thomas during his testimony, in which, after denying the allegations, he called the hearings a "high-tech lynching for uppity blacks." His confirmation hanging in the balance, Thomas, feeling the pressure, desperately lashed back, pulling out the historically painful image and angrily tossing it on the floor like a grenade. But it worked. Within black America, Thomas's observation, while contradictory (given his opposition to race-based programs for educational and financial advancement), garnered sympathy. At their core, the hearings appeared to be a case of government-sanctioned black-on-black crime—in this case a black woman being used (after all, why come out *now*?) by politicians to block a black man's move upward. He also gained sympathy from whites, because in the end, with only words as evidence on both sides, the mostly white Senate confirmed Thomas's appointment to the U.S. Supreme Court by a vote of fifty-two to forty-eight.

But the immediate impact of the Thomas-Hill hearings was felt less in the highest court than it was in America's workplace and on Capitol Hill. The hearings immediately raised national awareness about sexual harassment, and the rise in cases filed over the next few years would change the social and sexual dynamics of the workplace reaching into the new millennium. Unlike Hill, who didn't get justice, victims could now be heard and even be awarded millions of dollars under federal laws.

Repercussions also came in the form of a political change in Washington, D.C. The outcome of the Thomas-Hill proceedings stung many feminists who were disturbed not only by the sexist disdain Hill received for her charge—accused by Senator Orrin G. Hatch of manufacturing her stories—but by the lack of female representation on the

Senate hearing committee (none). A major reason for this was the lack of women in the Senate and the House of Representatives. The result of this rise in consciousness came the following year, 1992, dubbed by pundits as the "Year of the Woman," as a record number of women ran for and won political offices. In all, forty-eight women were elected to the House of Representatives, twenty-four more seats than they previously held, while the number of women in the Senate rose from two to seven. Most notably, Carol Moseley Braun of Illinois became the first African-American woman elected to the Senate.

Following this historic year of women flexing their political muscle, Salt-N-Pepa captured hip-hop history with the release of *Very Necessary* in 1993. A polished, sexier continuation of *Blacks' Magic*, instead of in-your-face messages of feminism, pro-blackness, and sexuality, this disc showcased the trio looking, sounding, and wielding a well-earned attitude of full-fledged divadom. They may have started out as a school project, a rap music experiment—and an urban music anomaly—but by 1993, having been in the industry almost a decade, they were now rap music pioneers, opening—through the inspiration of their success— hip-hop's commercial space to female hopefuls, both current and future. On *Very Necessary*, the women wrote and produced more of the album, even gaining input into its sound and direction. In fact, Pepa, who had recruited producer Mark Sparks to help her and Salt produce the track "Shoop," convinced Hurby to make the sexy R&B-flavored song the LP's first single. As always, though, it was the song's video that provided the visual surprise behind the music, baring yet another S-N-P metamorphosis. The clip unveiled the trio, decked in foxy Lycra outfits and sporting newly fine-toned bodies, dancing and strolling on a beach full of well-built, handsome brothas and discussing, no-holds-barred, what kind of men turned them on sexually. "Well, I like 'em real wild," explained Salt, "b-boy style by the mile / Smooth black skin with a smile." Instead of instructing listeners to talk about sex, the trio chose to brashly discuss their own experiences. After all, the point of unleashing this new S-N-P—the svelte physiques, seductive fashion, and polished sound—was to show hip-hop's faithful they were officially women (*the* women, in fact), accomplished and with emotional and physical needs. *Very Necessary* was as much about expressing (and affirming) their sexuality as it was about grandstanding as the divas of rap.

While the gold-selling "Shoop" was a naughty confessional about their desires and "No One Does It Better" bragged on their abilities at pleasing their lovers, S-N-P attacked society's double standard with regard to female sexual freedom on "None of Your Business." (The song and its chorus of rebellion evoked the spirit of blues empress Bessie Smith, who sang a similar sentiment—the blues tune "'Tain't Nobody's Bizness If I Do"—some seventy years earlier.) The message behind their album's biggest selling single, "Whatta Man," spoke most symbolically beyond S-N-P's original intent. The song, which teamed them with the singing group En Vogue, was a slick, R&B-fueled rap celebrating their significant others. Within a genre usually utilized for criticizing the opposite sex, they rapped sober-minded praises for the great qualities of their men. "I know that ain't nobody perfect," Pepa rhymed. "I give props to those who deserve it / And believe me ya'll he's worth it." Their ode to what made their men praiseworthy (considerate, responsible, loving, great in bed, good father, and so on), while S-N-P's personal testament, unwittingly became a nationwide anthem honoring—for lack of a better description—good black men. Within black America, though, the song also seemed to speak indirectly to the troubling dilemmas of black men (prominent and otherwise) in the media.

Along with culture wars and battles of political correctness, the cameras and pages of mainstream media captured the sensational moments of black men behaving badly: the videotaped crack scandal of Marion Barry; the well-inked dismissal of Dr. Leonard Jeffries as head of the black studies department at City College for his anti-Semitic, antiwhite rhetoric; the sexual harassment charge against Clarence Thomas; the coverage of boxing champ Mike Tyson's rape trial; the rising black-on-black male murder rates; police and politicians targeting rappers for their violent and misogynistic lyrics. And there was also the escalating rate of fatherless black children. While scandalous coverage of black men being persecuted (and prosecuted) for ill behavior was nothing new, the response from black people was. Before the gains of civil rights, black-on-black criticism, especially about famous blacks "acting up," was considered a private matter, the solidarity of secrecy facilitated by segregation. Any personal feelings about the ignorant actions of another black person were expressed around dinner tables, in church, or at barbershops—away from whites who might use the intraracial discourse to negatively shade the entire race. But in post–black power America, that dialogue had begun to move outside these private spaces into arenas of mainstream media where it was reshaped.

The New York Times noted this shift in an April 5, 1992, article, citing how rising media access and the fragmentation of black America—along economic, social, and geographical lines—transformed the notion that black-on-black public criticism could be expressed without jeopardizing one's allegiance to the race. "The emergence of an expanded public dialogue in newspaper editorials, rallies and other forums," wrote reporter Lena Williams, "reflects an effort by blacks to focus the discussion from two perspectives: blacks cannot blame everything on racism, and whites cannot deny that race could be a factor." At the center of Williams's survey was how a cross section of blacks publicly felt about racism being blamed for controversies surrounding prominent blacks—particularly Barry, Tyson, and Jeffries. Does the issue of racial inequality excuse the bad behavior of black folks? A resounding no was the answer from respondents. This evolved approach to black-on-black public discourse, taking one's gripes mainstream, would play most prominently in the escalating rift between black baby boomers and black male rap artists, particularly gangsta rap artists.

But in choosing to pay homage to the noble qualities of their men, Salt-N-Pepa indirectly entered this dialogue, offering positive examples of black manhood in contrast to the ones sensationalized on the evening news. Their ode also rang prophetic in the nation's capital after Bill Clinton, the philandering Democratic governor of Arkansas, defeated George Bush in the presidential election, breaking the Republican hold on the White House (thanks, in part, to overwhelming support by the black vote). Platinum sales of "Whatta Man" proved the power of its message as the song helped Very Necessary eventually move five million units, making it one of rap's most successful albums and Salt-N-Pepa hip-hop's indisputable queens of rap. Their reign later ended with the group disbanding following the release of their platinum CD Brand New in 1997.

But without question, they had blazed a distinguished trail. Who would have dreamed that infusing hardcore rap with women's pride, sexual liberation, social awareness, and R&B would have such a profound and lasting impact on the social (and musical) dialogue of hip-hop music? In challenging the sexist machismo of rap, Salt-N-Pepa, and their subsequent phenomenon, not only helped expand the genre's social discourse but pushed its voice into a larger national discussion on women's rights, sexuality, and the correction of racist political consciousness. Their success opened doors for their contemporaries. Their outspoken pride, bold expressions of their libidos, and ingenious meld of R&B and hip-hop gave hope and inspiration to future female stars of hip-hop, from Lil' Kim to Missy "Misdemeanor" Elliott to Destiny's Child, looking to secure a space within the genre for the undeniable message of bold soul sistas.

SEVEN

Gangsta Chic
Dr. Dre and Snoop Dogg

The social treatment accorded even the most successful Negroes
proved that one needed, in order to be free, . . . a handle, a lever, a
means of inspiring fear.

—James Baldwin, *The Fire Next Time*

Whereas gangsta rap solidified hardcore rappers as black street prophets of America's ghettos, the Los Angeles riots of 1992 affirmed it. On Wednesday, April 29, a mostly white jury acquitted four white police officers accused in the videotaped beating of the black motorist Rodney King. The aftermath of the verdict was one of the largest and costliest urban rebellions in modern American history. What started in the afternoon with infuriated black men and women violently venting their rage at the intersection of Florence Boulevard and Normandie Avenue in South Central L.A. had grown, by nightfall, into a smoldering citywide explosion of civil unrest—multifaceted and multiracial—dubbed America's first multiethnic rebellion. News outlets may have spun it as a race riot—"a black thang" with Koreans and a few whites cast as victims. But the Rodney King verdict, while enraging black folks with feelings of injustice, also struck nerves of unfairness within other populations of Los Angeles. Of the nearly ten thousand arrested during the uprising, 51 percent were Latino, 36 percent were African-American, and 11 percent were white. If gangsta rap had popularized the furious spirit of the black inner city, the multihued faces of the Rodney King uprising signaled that urban frustrations now resonated beyond blackness as Latinos and Asians were fast becoming the face of urban America (the "browning of America," as it would later be called by Richard Rodriguez). Moreover, the rebellion echoed beyond Los Angeles as protest and unrest over the verdict were reported in Phoenix, Chicago, Atlanta, Seattle, and New York. By the end of the violence in Los Angeles, more than fifty people had been killed, as many as two thousand were injured, more than one thousand buildings were destroyed by fire, and between $800 million and $1 billion in material damage was done.

When journalists and TV news anchors descended upon the scorched innards of South Central looking for answers to what caused the riots, a number of them looked not to popular black political figures but to the prophetic words of rap artists. Whereas MCs like Ice-T, Ice Cube, and Chuck D had been cultural pariahs prior to the uprising, they were now viewed as messengers by the mainstream. "Rappers documented the anger of the inner city before the riots" was the headline beneath a *Los Angeles Times* piece on the uprising. "The challenge now is to examine ways to educate and heal." To make sense of the turmoil, networks like Fox and MTV turned to Ice-T, while *Billboard* magazine quoted MC Ren's thoughts on the uselessness of nonviolence in the face of injustice. "The only way you can do it is through violence," he told a reporter. "You gotta do the same thing that they doin' to you." Before America witnessed Los Angeles going up in flames, rappers— particularly L.A.'s gangsta set—were the sole means of publicly discussing the conditions and frustrations behind such an event. Now everyone understood the sentiment behind "Fuck tha Police," especially as it was being chanted by mobs of angry black, brown, and even a few white liberal types turning the City of Angels upside down.

As the L.A. riots placed the city at the epicenter of American political discourse by turning black Los Angeles into a worldwide symbol of oppression, black rage, and victimization, they also turned the gangsta and the gangbanger into emblems of strength, fearlessness, and street-level empowerment. "Mexicans & Crips & Bloods Together Tonite 4-30-92," read one piece of graffiti. From alleged gang members dishing almost-fatal retribution on the white truck driver Reginald Denny, to the most significant outcome of the rebellion—a truce between the Bloods and the Crips—to various unfounded reports that gangs were planning armed retaliations against police, the bangers were the rebellion's shadow of organized might. In the midst of the chaos, they were portrayed (at least by the media and police) as an underground force spearheading the violence and looting. If the perception of gangs was a bit overstated, one notion about them stood true: They wielded an incomparable sway over the social atmosphere of L.A.'s black community. Being the primary organizers of ghetto youth, the gangs held the clout to develop the positive *and* the negative energy of a community. No better example of this was the effect of the truce (albeit temporary) following the riots. Not a single gang-related homicide was committed in Los Angeles for weeks after the unrest. Once-war-torn black neighborhoods, divided by gang territories, started to feel like ghetto paradise as tightly held invisible borders were erased. "It feels like Heaven," a former gang member told a reporter from *Time* magazine. "I can go to places I've never been or even ridden through before . . . It's like freedom." Celebrations following the truce were brought into homes nationwide (even worldwide) via news broadcasts showing once-rival gangs throwing barbecues in local parks, tying the blue and red bandanas of their groups together as a show of unity, and partying in the name of peace. For once, in many moons, the cold war of Los Angeles seemed to melt under the warmth of the California sun.

And, as if on cue, the soundtrack for a post–L.A. riot America arrived seven months after the rebellion and the truce with the release of Dr. Dre's *The Chronic* in 1992. More specifically, it arrived with the album's debut single, "Nuthin' But a 'G' Thang," which altered the packaging and outlook of hardcore rap as American popular music. Launching Dre's masterstroke, the song was one of several that refined gangsta rap's heavy-fisted sound with tracks of laid-back, melodic funk samples and rhymes that flowed with a breezy tension. A huge part of the formula was Dre's latest discovery, newcomer Snoop Doggy Dogg, whose relaxed gangsta manner and Cali-by-way-of-Mississippi drawl perfectly served up the demeanor of a black Los Angeles enjoying a new, profound sense of freedom. His ice-cold delivery—one part pimp, two parts cool thug, while still maintaining a brash ruggedness (niggas still got smoked)—was the complete antithesis of the red-eyed hostility of preriot gangsta rap. For all the platinum sales the subgenre made below the radar, boggling the minds of the music industry, it was Snoop's appetizing delivery of street life—disarming and charismatic, yet still shocking—that pushed gangsta rap even further onto Main Street America. Under the rhythmic direction of Dr. Dre, he also helped build a black-owned music force, Death Row Records, that, while creating a headquarters for megaselling gangsta rap, would stumble over the invisible line between the violence in street rap and the violence in the street. But the collision of both, as the Death Row lore has been spun, was what brought Team Dre-Snoop together in the first place.

Like that of his predecessor Eazy-E, the main thrust behind Snoop's foray into the music biz was an exit from the dark side of ghetto life. Only the escape wasn't in Compton, but in the drug- and gang-infested streets of East Long Beach, California. Snoop's mother, Beverly Broadus, who had moved from Mississippi in the early 1960s, did all she could to cultivate the good in her son, Calvin, whom she nicknamed Snoop because of his resemblance to the cartoon character. She encouraged his singing in the church choir and playing little-league football, attempting to combat the growing lure of the block. Teenage Snoop worked within the parameters of an honest life, delivering newspapers and packing groceries at the local supermarket to help out his mother financially, until becoming attracted to the money-making endeavors of a Crip set doing business outside his building. And as with most growing boys, especially those growing up without a father, Mom's love got trumped by homie love as Snoop, now a Crip, began slinging crack rock for his set. If bullets being shot at his family's apartment by rivals weren't enough to show Snoop the error of his decision, there was another consequence that might. Just barely a month after graduating from high school he was arrested for selling crack to an undercover officer. While serving his time, Snoop honed the skills of a musical past instead of a criminal future, rhyming for inmates who encouraged him to pursue rap as a career. And with the phenomenal success of N.W.A, that was now a possibility. It didn't hurt that the loudest voice convincing Snoop, once he got out, was his best friend and Dr. Dre's half brother, Warren G. Along with gangsta crooner Nate Dogg, the three formed the rap group 213 (for their area code), with Warren performing double duty: rapping and pestering his older brother Dre to listen to their demos—which he never did. The fortress of Dre's ears was ambushed when Warren played a tape of Snoop's rhymes at a bachelor party both were attending. If Dre heard anything in Snoop's voice he definitely heard the future, a place *his* mind had been seriously pondering up until that point.

N.W.A was history, and Dre, looking for a fresh start, had formed an alliance with the six-foot-four, 315-pound former bodyguard Marion "Sugar Bear" Knight. The hulking Knight entered the music game having represented an unknown rapper/producer in a questionable "negotiation" with rap artist Vanilla Ice over royalties never received by his client for writing Ice's smash hit "Ice Ice Baby." Reportedly using the same tactic (read: intimidation) to "negotiate" Dre's exit from Ruthless Records, Suge gained a valuable asset for his plans in the music biz. The partnership the two formed afterward, along with high-powered criminal lawyer David Kenner, culminated in the creation of Death Row Records. Dre's search for the label's rap talent coincided with his commission to produce "Deep Cover," the title cut for a movie of the same name. He found his answer when Snoop's voice came wafting out of the speakers at the bachelor party. Shortly afterward, Dre debuted the lethally calm rapper on "Deep Cover" in 1991, turning both the song and the newcomer into a national sensation. Dre (or anyone) couldn't have predicted how the country would accept Snoop when prominently featured on a full album, but when "Deep Cover" received national airplay, especially in New York (a market that refused to play records by West Coast artists), Dre had to have realized folks were ready.

For all that the L.A. riots did in focusing America's attention on the anger and chaos of South Central, Dr. Dre, capitalizing on the spotlight, repackaged that widespread unease into an odyssey of pop gangstadom. Musically, Dre crafted *The Chronic* in the same vein as *Niggaz4life*, with simmering bits of electronically chopped funk, most of which were inspired by (or outright used) Parliament-Funkadelic tracks. But the studio polish on *The Chronic* was more pronounced: the eerie meticulousness of the keyboard work, the melodic arrangement of samples and live instruments, the soulful backup vocals, and the unnerving clarity of the sound. Dre's concoction, later to be dubbed "g-funk," became hip-hop's answer to George Clinton's revolution in soul music, P-Funk. Both innovations accompanied dynamic shifts in black America (George's with the rise of chocolate cities and Dre's with the explosion of Los Angeles). Both kicked stale notions of black dance music in the teeth, wrapping their narratives of black urban life in a futuristic soundscape of infectious grooves and complex rhythms. And each was fueled by his drug of choice (George's being acid and coke while Dre's crew chose, well, a strain of cannabis they affectionately called "chronic").

But unlike George, who took his cues from outer space, Dre got his new inspiration from the uneasy calm (and the false sense of street empowerment) of postriot gangstadom. Dre's innovative sound became the official pulse of Left Coast rap. The rhymes on his debut project were the party-rocking anthems that flowed from the tentative peace, the surreal sense of justice and power, and the national/global eyes on black Los Angeles, a region now at the center of American political discourse.

If *Straight Outta Compton* expressed the rage and *Niggaz4life*, following the Rodney King episode, presented reasons why, then *The Chronic* was the musical celebration of the aftermath. The album acknowledged the unrest of April 29 with "The Day the Niggaz Took Over," an ode to the momentary control folks felt in the looting, racial violence, and unity brought about by the revolt. "Sitting in my living room, calm and collective," Dre rapped, "feeling that 'Got to get mine' perspective . . . Bloods [and] Crips on the same squad / With the Ese's thumping, nigga, it's time to rob and mob (And break the white man off something lovely / I don't love dem, so they can't love me)." The woeful portrait of gang life on the cut "Lil' Ghetto Boy" indirectly asked bangers to wake up from their destructive lives. "What ya gonna do when you grow up," croons a sample of late soul singer Donny Hathaway, "and have to face responsibility."

Gruff street anthems were equally well built with g-funk musicality and danceability, turning sinister raps like "Rat-Tat-Tat-Tat," "A Nigga Witta Gun," and "Bitches Ain't Shit" into unheralded favorites. But the true force behind *The Chronic* phenomenon was the pop-crafted ingenuity of its singles. Dre, looking to *really* thrust hardcore rap into the mainstream, constructed a glamorous brand of gangsta rap with "Nuthin' But a 'G' Thang" and the ditty "Let Me Ride." Laced with memorable hooks and beats grooving on cruise control, these songs sold gangsta life not as a violent reaction to a cruel world but as a state of mind, a posture, an attitude, and a look that *anyone* wishing to act or look remotely like they have street credibility could fit into. No longer were Dre and crew dashing from the police or angrily stomping through desolate ghetto streets. Now, in videos, they were cruising L.A.'s sun-drenched boulevards in 1964 Chevy Impalas, rolling blunts at park barbecues (like gangs in a truce), coolly bouncing at a party, and dousing stuck-up chicks with malt liquor. Even the video for the single "Fuck wit Dre Day," a vitriolic response to Dre's enemies in the music biz (from Eazy-E to 2 Live Crew's Luther Campbell), put a fun, laughable spin on the verbal wrath of a "G." Whereas the threatening sounds Dre created for N.W.A were shunned by radio and television, the smoothed-out production on *The Chronic*, sounding more like R&B than hip-hop, made hardcore attractive to those outlets. As videos from Dre began to win regular airplay outside of *Yo! MTV Raps*, *The Chronic* solidified the new crossover, especially among hip-hop's growing pop audience—white youngsters whose silent majority, since the rise of P.E. and N.W.A, indirectly shaped and affirmed this direction with its monetary support. White graffiti writer/journalist William Upski Wimsatt bluntly laid this turn of events down in an essay, "We Use Words Like 'Mackadocious,'" for *The Source*. "Like it or not," Wimsatt wrote, "whites seem to be buying rap in increasing numbers . . . This has advanced rap's clout, capital, and potential to transform society. But the white audience doesn't just consume rap, it shapes it. Rappers and labels aren't stupid . . . Increasingly, rappers address their white audience, either directly, by accommodating our perceived tastes, targeting us for education/insult, or indirectly, by shunning the white audience, retreating into blacker, realer, more hardcore stances." In Dre's case, the formula proved phenomenal. To the MTV set and radio listeners nationwide (again, especially in New York), gangsta rap and the gangsta archetype were officially chic. So the focus of hip-hop music had, without a doubt, moved westward. As g-funk pushed *The Chronic* to three times platinum, it also turned its charismatic featured player, Snoop, into a household name and the undisputed king of rap. From the fading smoke of the L.A. riots, Dre and Snoop pumped new life into hardcore rap's gangsta strain—a crucial development at a time when corporations were reconsidering the political (and financial) liability of sponsoring rap's rage, especially in the wake of the uprising. The social assault on rap music was headed to the boardrooms.

But first it would manifest itself in big-league politics, toward the beginning of the 1992 presidential election. Arkansas governor Bill Clinton, on his way to officially becoming the Democratic nominee, was in search of an opportunity to appeal to disillusioned Republicans and the "swing vote," those who might have thrown their support behind the possible third-party candidate, Ross Perot. Clinton found his moment when Jesse Jackson invited him to speak before the Rainbow Coalition's leadership summit.

A month before the convention, activist/rapper Lisa Williamson was interviewed by reporter David Mills (the journalist behind the Griff dustup) for *The Washington Post*. Williamson, a prominent New York–based youth activist in the late 1980s, had joined Public Enemy in 1990 following Griff's departure and was rechristened Sister Souljah. Seeing the power of disseminating political ideas through rap, Souljah tried her hand as a solo artist, releasing an album in the summer of 1992 called *360 Degrees of Power*. The disc went nowhere. But the association with P.E. heightened her profile. She still garnered a following and some notoriety as an orator on the lecture circuit. Her interview with Mills came days after the riots in Los Angeles. On the topic of the rebellion, Mills asked for her thoughts on the violence, which she, according to Mills, interpreted as "black-on-white" retribution, "plain, simple and righteous." She was referring to the beating of Reginald Denny. "I mean, if black people kill black people every day," Souljah explained to Mills, commenting on the black-on-black violence plaguing black Los Angeles, "why not have a week and kill white people? You understand what I'm saying? In other words, white people, this government and that mayor were well aware of the fact that black people were dying every day in Los Angeles under gang violence. So if you're a gang member and you would normally be killing somebody, why not kill a white person? Do you think that somebody thinks that white people are better, or above dying, when they would kill their own kind?" "Unfortunately for white people," Mills quoted Souljah from her previous interview on the television show *Sunday Today*, "they think it's all right for our children to die, for our men to go to prison, and not theirs."

On June 13, the day after Souljah spoke at a youth forum for the Rainbow Coalition summit, Clinton turned his speaking engagement before the summit into a political opportunity, chiding the activist for her words and the organization for inviting her. Reading an edited version of Souljah's quote, Clinton told the audience: "She told *The Washington Post* a month ago, and I quote: 'If black people kill black people every day, why not have a week and kill white people? So if you're a gang member and you would normally be killing somebody, why not kill a white person?' I know she is a young person, but she has a big influence on a lot of people, and when people say that—if you took the words white and black and you reversed them, you might think David Duke was giving that speech." Aside from stunning the mostly black audience, Clinton angered Souljah, who slammed the candidate for taking what she had said out of context. "I was just telling the writer," she told a reporter for *Newsweek*, "that . . . if a person would kill their own brother, or a baby in a drive-by, or a grandmother, what would make white people think that he wouldn't kill them too?" Jesse Jackson and other black leaders also attacked Clinton, accusing him of exploiting Souljah "purely to appeal to conservative whites." Whether Clinton would admit his motives or not, his choice to distance himself from Jackson and his young, radical ally was a strategy to appeal to the much-needed white swing vote. And although Clinton's war of words with Souljah tarnished his appeal among black voters, he eventually regained their confidence and ultimately their unwavering loyalty with another well-planned opportunity. After making his famous appearance on *The Arsenio Hall Show*, donning shades and playing the saxophone for the show's black host, Clinton won the Negro vote and the election, becoming, as many blacks (and even Clinton) would later joke, America's "first black president."

But wrath over the politically acerbic views of rappers wouldn't diminish with a Democrat heading to the White House. About the same time as the Clinton-Souljah beef, the Combined Law Enforcement Associations of Texas and the Dallas Police Association made Ice-T a target. Both police organizations held a press conference on June 11 to announce a statewide campaign to have the song "Cop Killer" removed from the album *Body Count*. The LP was the self-titled debut of a new thrash metal band, Body Count, a side project of Ice-T's. They had released the controversial song in March, and it made no waves until its caustic lyrics caught the ears of Texas law enforcement. About a man driven to bloodlust by police brutality, the cut, more of a rock tune than a rap, clearly articulated the rage blacks felt over law enforcement's abuse of power. "I got my twelve-gauge sawed off," Ice-T rapped over moshing guitar riffs. "I got my headlights turned off / I'm 'bout to bust some shots off / I'm 'bout to dust some cops off." The organizations protesting the song felt it was anti law enforcement and advocated murdering police.

Calling for a boycott of Time Warner, whose Warner Bros. division distributed the Body Count disc, the campaign picked up support from police associations across the country. Then the fight went to the nation's capital. A letter signed by sixty congressmen was sent to Time Warner expressing "outrage" over those "despicable lyrics." George Bush's vice president, Dan Quayle, joined the chorus, asking the audience at a luncheon for the National Association of Radio Talk Show Hosts convention: "Why is Time Warner supporting, financing, selling a record that says it's OK to kill cops?" Quayle called the record "obscene." President Bush labeled it "sick." What didn't receive equal coverage by the media were those officers who, while refusing to join the protest, understood and supported Ice-T's articulation of a common grievance. "The song was directed at those officers that have caused havoc in the African-American community, whether they're black or white," explained Officer Greg Jhounkin, acting branch president of the Texas Peace Officers Association. Another organization, the National Black Police Association, also added its voice to the faction of Ice-T supporters. But the ball of opposition from conservatives and law enforcement, with their allies in D.C., proved stronger. Despite the backing of his label, Ice-T called a press conference on July 28 announcing his decision to pull "Cop Killer" from the *Body Count* CD. Ultimately, the rapper's choice was a move to salvage the future of his music career and celebrity, which had risen tremendously during the controversy.

Fallout from the Ice storm came as Time Warner and other major labels, afraid of another uproar over rap lyrics, began reconsidering their investment in the incendiary social outlook of rap. Lyrics that were deemed political liabilities were subject to corporate policing, and rappers on major labels were the ones most affected by the shift in policy. Tommy Boy Records, distributed by Time Warner, was forced by higher-ups to drop Oakland rapper Paris because of his song "Bush Killa," a rhyme about assassinating the president. Toward the end of the Ice-T hullabaloo, the label also dropped the Boston-based rap group the Almighty RSO after the Boston Police Patrolmen's Association threatened to sue the label for releasing "One in the Chamba," a song decrying the killing of two young black men by cops. The rap talked of "keeping one in the chamba" to stay safe from murderous police officers.

The appeal behind financing rap's unconventional views was losing its attractiveness until *The Chronic*, cultivating the gangsta party vibe, proved to the majors that investing in the ghetto or, as it was coming to be recast, "urban" attitude (minus much of the rage) was even more lucrative. Time Warner found itself back in the game of hardcore rap as its maverick sublabel, Interscope, became the distributor of Death Row Records. As music journalist Jeff Chang pointed out in *Can't Stop Won't Stop*, the massive success of *The Chronic* (and later Snoop's *Doggystyle*) was significant, "distilling this shift in corporate thinking." It was the notion that "demographic" changes (read: increase in the minority population) and the changing taste of white America fueling the rise of "urban culture" could be seen as a long-term investment, thus creating a significant doorway for generation hip-hop, particularly its post–black power population, to be incorporated into mainstream society as well (the same way black power set off "soul" chic, creating a niche for blacks, especially in film in the 1970s). "Hip-Hop offered a way," Chang wrote, "this elusive generation could be assimilated, categorized, made profitable." The beats, fashion, language, and mind-set of hip-hop culture were quickly becoming the paradigm for American popular culture. Leading this phenomenon was West Coast gangsta rap, its most commercially prevalent artist coming from the Death Row camp.

Even before Snoop's album *Doggystyle* was released in 1993, it was the most anticipated rap album in history. The disc entered the *Billboard* pop chart at number one, becoming the first debut album to achieve the honor. That same year, Snoop's face also graced the cover of another milestone in the "urban" phenomenon, the first issue of *Vibe* magazine. Also a product of Time Warner, the publication, founded by famed producer Quincy Jones, was hip-hop's answer to *Rolling Stone*.

On *Doggystyle* the g-funk party continued: tracks embedded with Parliament-Funkadelic influences and interpolations. But with Snoop poised to become the nation's hardcore darling, the LP catered more to the growing gangsta chic than it reflected ghetto ills. Social comments and cries for justice were discarded, replaced by an even bigger celebration of the "G" lifestyle, partying, having fun, and moving a crowd. Given Dre's refocus on hip-hop's funky danceability and Snoop's syrupy approach to the brag-n-boast (inspired by Slick Rick), one might argue that *Doggystyle* harked back, with a cuss-filled West Coast flavor, to hip-hop's bygone era, when rap music was simply ghetto music for rocking the parks.

Like *The Chronic*, the singles pushing *Doggystyle* were geared for maximum dance floor appeal, promoting the Long Beach rap star as the Moses of cool. The gold-selling cut, "Who Am I (What's My Name)?," while pushing the gospel and mic skills of Snoop, drove the rapper's moniker into listeners' subconscious with its irresistible chorus. The CD's other club anthem, "Gin and Juice," which followed Snoop on a hedonistic journey, driving and drinking his favorite beverage, demonstrated the power of rap artists as pop culture tastemakers. Snoop gave the liquor industry an unexpected boost when both Tanqueray and Seagram's saw significant increases in their gin sales after being mentioned in the song (more incentive for big business to consider the marketing power of rap music). The power of the songs was evident as *Doggystyle* would go on to sell four million copies, becoming an even bigger hit than *The Chronic*.

Outdoing *The Chronic* on another front, *Doggystyle* presented the dysfunctional behavior and harsh language of the black inner city as fashion statement, the unequivocal state of hipness. Snoop, in the voice of a stoic pimp, dedicated his music to a street-hardened fan base in songs like "Gz and Hustlas" and other hit gangsta ditties, and helped recast, for the rest of a growing hip-hop nation, whom rap music now represented. No longer were they the denizens of the slums looking to escape the negative conditions of their environment, but rather the rugged street (read: criminal) element basking in a destructive lifestyle. And who wouldn't want to be considered a "G" or a "Hustla" if it meant signaling your allegiance to Snoop and his brand of "authentic" rap music? The same was done on the cut "For All My Niggaz & Bitches," which turned venomous words for blacks and black women into badges of honor for *all* (including whites) to claim and wear proudly. And whereas tracks like "Bitches Ain't Shit" or N.W.A's "A Bitch Iz a Bitch" presented misogyny with an explanation, the tune "Ain't No Fun (If the Homies Can't Have None)" offered its acidic views toward women as a theme for merriment and building male camaraderie.

Though many couldn't deny the genius behind Dre and Snoop's formula, *finally* catapulting hip-hop and rap music toward the center of American popular culture, one could argue the irony of their doing so by celebrating a character—the gangsta—the subculture was originally formed to combat. But with the explosion of *The Chronic* and *Doggystyle*, gangsta rap became the face of the genre and the future of hip-hop music. The subgenre, its emphasis on being "real" and genuinely street, became the industry standard by which commercial hard-core rap was sold to the public, especially to young white music buyers. The shift was evident as more and more rap artists (no matter which coast) donned a rougher image to sell more records, and labels quickly filled their rosters with gun-happy thug MCs. Even MC Hammer, who had signed with Death Row and dropped the MC from his name, became hard-rock to stay relevant in the gangsta gold rush, releasing the hardcore flop *The Funky Headhunter* in 1994. Hip-hop was now the global face of black popular culture, and its mascot became a stone-faced nigga with a gun, a foul mouth, and a bad attitude.

The swing was also apparent in black popular culture as Afrocentric medallions, clothes, thoughts, and lyrics were replaced by the menacing glares, swagger, and jargon of wannabe gangstas. By the end of 1993, the epitome of a strong black man had become the "Ruffneck" (an archetype made popular by an MC Lyte song of the same name), while the urban symbol for a dynamic black woman had become the "Gangsta Bitch" (made popular by the rapper Apache). Not that this phenomenon was new. Black urban youth culture had always held a fascination and admiration for gangstas and "jail niggas" on the block. But with gangsta rap, this corner of black urban life gained sponsorship and a great deal of marketing from multinational corporations, giving that aspect of black culture one helluva bullhorn. Hip-hop films, once used to turn b-boys, MCs, and graffiti writers into cultural heroes, were now 'hood movies where tragic antiheroes, reflecting the nihilism of the black inner city, senselessly murdered their way to ghetto stardom, healthy box-office receipts, and adoring movie fans. Words and street jargon usually reserved for the corner or barbershops or neighborhood bars or tenement hallways—tucked in cozy spaces within black life— had a pop soundtrack and hit parade. ("All my niggaz and my bitches," rang the chorus of a Snoop song, "wave yo motherfuckin' hands in the air!") Referring to a black woman (or any woman) as a "bitch" or a "ho" became cool. And the comfort level with which blacks publicly referred to themselves as "niggas"—on the street, on CDs, in movies, on the radio, on TV—damn near created an atmosphere where the term was okay to use when addressing or referring to African Americans. ("Fo shizzle, my nizzle.")

With the waning influence of institutions like the church, schools, and even the black family—structures that used to be paramount in shaping the values of black youth—hip-hop, with its influence on music, film, television, and fashion, had become, as Bakari Kitwana wrote in his book *The Hip Hop Generation*, among the "major forces transmitting culture to this generation of black Americans." But increasing corporate control over hip-hop and rap music meant that the eyes of young black folk overwhelmingly received an escalated diet of gangsta chic, black stereotypes paraded as Negroes "keepin' it real." At a time when *The Chronic* and *Doggystyle* were being hailed as musical milestones, such a development shifted the racial makeup of the culture war against rap music, turning it from mostly white-on-black to black-on-black, this, at a time when gangsta rappers seemed to be constantly in trouble with the law. Shortly before the release of *Doggystyle*, Snoop was charged with murder. Tupac Shakur, who stayed in the news for his legal troubles, was arrested for sexual assault. These high-profile cases prompted the mainstream media to evaluate the effects gangsta rap's violent image and lyrics had on youth. Snoop's face even graced the cover of *Newsweek*, sneering above the cover line "When Is Rap 2 Violent?"

African-American baby boomers, troubled by the destructive messages being pushed by black popular culture, began their own crusade against hardcore rap. The first to gain national attention for the cause was the Reverend Calvin Butts. As the head of Harlem's Abyssinian Baptist Church, Butts came to prominence with his whitewashing of billboards advertising alcohol and cigarettes in Harlem, protesting, with a paint roller, the aggressive marketing of these substances in black communities. In the summer of 1993, he widened his cause to include vile rap lyrics. "It is not a war on rap music," Butts told a journalist, explaining that he recognized the social commentary within some of the music. "What I am opposed to is the vulgar, misogynistic lyrics that promote sex and violence and degrade black people, particularly black women." On June 5, he drove a steamroller over a pile of offensive hip-hop CDs, planning to put them in bags and dump them in front of one of the record companies. "They are the real culprits in all of this," he told a reporter for the *Amsterdam News*.

However, the figure who became synonymous with the cause—and whose motives were the most questionable—was civil rights activist and failed politician C. Delores Tucker. Prior to becoming the chairwoman of the National Political Congress of Black Women (NPCBW),

Tucker marched with Dr. Martin Luther King in the 1960s and rose to political prominence as the "highest-ranking black woman in state government" a decade later. In 1971, Governor Milton Shapp appointed her secretary of the Commonwealth of Pennsylvania, and then fired her six years later after a three-month investigation revealed she had been "running a private, profitable business at state expense," using state employees to write speeches for which she received $66,931. Following unsuccessful bids for political office, including a run for the U.S. Senate and lieutenant governor, Tucker, who had set up the NPCBW in 1984, found herself politically irrelevant until 1993, when Dionne Warwick, Melba Moore, and other prominent women suggested that she and her organization lead the fight against gangsta rap. What convinced Tucker to take action was seeing the album cover for *Doggystyle* and sifting through the album's lyrics.

Once again Tucker made headlines, staging protests in front of major music stores that sold hip-hop she deemed offensive. Although she cited her cause as a battle to protect black youth from self-destruction ("They can't call us niggers," she'd later explain to writer Kevin Powell, "but they use our kids to say it, and also use our kids to commit genocide"), her intentions came into question when she aligned herself with white right-wing conservatives William Bennett and Republican senator Bob Dole. Like, how was she trying to help by accepting support from those who oppose affirmative action and support crime laws designed to incarcerate black youth at a higher rate for a longer time for nonviolent crimes (youth like the ones she was trying to "save")?

Tucker's biggest political coup was convincing Senator Carol Moseley Braun to hold a hearing on gangsta rap's influence on criminal behavior. In February 1994, the freshman senator chaired hearings on "Shaping Our Response to Violent and Demeaning Imagery in Pop Music," calling witnesses from opposing camps to argue their positions. But when Tucker took the floor, the hearing quickly devolved into a trial to persecute Snoop Dogg, the *Doggystyle* album, and the Death Row label. She argued that gangsta rap influenced the brutal behavior of youth who were "out of control," citing murder cases involving kids who'd been listening to Snoop's music or mimicking the rap star before committing their crimes. Using the cover art of *Doggystyle* as a backdrop, Tucker pointed out the violent and sexual content of the illustrations, as well as the album's profane lyrics, as proof of her argument. In the end, though, neither she nor her ilk proved or produced anything from the hearing except a suggestion from Braun that the record industry take more responsibility for its product.

Tucker turned the senator's proposal into a tactic, purchasing stock in Time Warner and attending board meetings to protest their investment in Interscope and Death Row Records. This time her supporters included Bennett and Dole, who were also campaigning heavily against the entertainment company's ties to gangsta rap. And the push worked. Following several months of political pressure and public criticism, Time Warner, for the second time in three years, chose to divest itself of hardcore hip-hop, announcing on September 27, 1995, that it was selling its 50 percent stake in Interscope. The *real* implication was that Time Warner was severing its association with Death Row, gangsta rap, and anything remotely related to the subgenre. A year later, the company also sold off its interest in *Vibe* magazine, which covered the stars of hip-hop extensively.

For Tucker and other media watchdogs, the Time Warner decision was a victory for decency and a triumph over those who sought to corrupt the minds of America's youth. But to others, the outcome amounted to no more than a witch hunt, the fallout from an older black generation's gripe over the influence and prominence achieved by its younger counterparts, a generation with its own unique issues and modes of expressing them, and a larger platform to display them on. Writer Paul Delaney commented amid the black uproar over gangsta rap: "If playing the dozens was still on the corner; if calling women bitches and hos remained behind closed doors instead of becoming nightly offerings on cable and on CDs and blaring from loudspeakers . . . if electronic media were not so powerful and influential; if we were only back in the 1940s (as a lot of Americans wish) . . . we would not be having this debate today." There were black boomers like congresswoman Maxine Waters and NAACP chair, Benjamin Chavis, who supported the voice gangsta rap gave to the poor and disaffected, understanding that black-owned entities like Death Row (which generated during its reign more than $100 million in sales) helped employ black youth who, because of gang affiliations or jail records, would otherwise be considered unemployable. They also understood that Snoop, despite the foul lyrics and criminal past, spoke a black urban reality that needed to be challenged more than the music that expressed it. But the direction hardcore rap was taking following the aftershock of *The Chronic* and *Doggystyle*, the total embrace of gangstadom and misogyny as a selling point, further divided black America, the rift running along lines of generations (civil rights versus hip-hop), gender, political ideology (gangsta blues versus black nationalism), and class. Where was this preoccupation with all things gangsta going to take black people, black youth, and black culture?

Anyone who wanted a hint at the possibilities needed only look at g-funk's star franchise. While the Tucker-led tumult over Snoop and gangsta rap wasn't the demise of Death Row Records, the label's use of violence and intimidation as a business strategy and guiding principle was. By the middle of 1996, Dr. Dre, disillusioned by the ganglike atmosphere welling within the company, split with Suge Knight and Death Row to start another independent label, Aftermath. Then in September, Death Row's latest hip-hop icon, Tupac Shakur, was shot and killed in Las Vegas shortly after he, Suge, and an entourage beat down a gang member in a hotel lobby. A few months later, Suge would be sent to prison for a parole violation stemming from his involvement in the Las Vegas brawl the night of Shakur's murder. And Snoop, having recently been acquitted of his 1993 murder charge and released a second disc, *The Doggfather*, that got lost in the chaos, followed the herd of artists leaving Death Row. By the end of the decade, the company, in turn, would diminish behind the stone walls of prison with Suge. In the future, filling the hole left by Death Row's fall were labels like New Orleans's Cash Money, Master P's No Limit, Jay-Z's Roc-A-Fella Records, and Texas's Suave House, black-owned record companies looking to thrive off gangsta chic.

But the largest imprint Death Row left on hardcore rap was the impact of Dre and his protégé Snoop. Once again Dre proved he was a genius at rethinking the rebellious spirit (and audience) of hip-hop music, reestablishing the danceability of rap's rhythm while recasting the rap thug as American-style icon. More than any other artists, he and Snoop turned hardcore hip-hop from an underground moneymaker into the soundtrack and style of young America. Only now the criterion for a rap artist to prove him/herself a *real* MC-of-the-people wasn't prowess with the word but how insanely ghetto one's life was.

Jail time. Guns. Gang affiliations. Drug dealing prior to your big break. The new corporate hip-hop industry set a standard via marketing and massive media muscle. One now had to show, as Dre and Snoop had done in the years following the L.A. riots, how one had turned anguish, ignorance, frustration, and a dead-end life into a brand-new suit for dancing one's way out from under the concrete ruin.

EIGHT

The Myth of Thug Power

Tupac Shakur

I'm not saying I'm gonna change the world, but I guarantee that I will spark the brain that will change the world.

—Tupac Shakur

When the smoke clears from the trials, suits, allegations, and sentencing involving . . . Tupac Shakur, his budding legend will have solidified in America's ghettos—and beyond.

—Kevin Powell

In April 1993 I got a phone call from the news editor at *The Source* asking me to come to the office and report on a case of rappers caught in a state of arrested development. It had been a year since I graduated from Rutgers University with a BA in English and journalism (thanks to affirmative action courtesy of New Jersey's Educational Opportunity Fund), and this was the first breaking news item I would cover for the rapidly budding magazine. I was reporting on the arrest of two rap stars. Part of the article would cover the white rapper Everlast—then the leader of the Irishcentric rap group House of Pain—who attempted to board a plane with a gun. The rest of the piece focused on the legal troubles of rap's rebel-with-a-cause, Tupac Shakur, who had been arrested for assault the previous month in Los Angeles.

During a break from taping an appearance on *In Living Color* at Fox Studios, he and eight members of his entourage beat up their limo driver in the parking lot. According to the driver, David Deleon, and his lawyer, the problem arose when Tupac and his rowdy crew took their break in the limo and one of them sat in the driver's seat (against company policy). After Deleon informed the man he couldn't sit there, angry words were exchanged and the beat down occurred. While the driver spun his version of the story as a senseless whupping, Afeni Shakur, Tupac's mother and publicist, insisted during a phone interview that it was a matter of Tupac defending himself after the driver hurled insults at the group and went for something in the trunk of his car. Nevertheless, Tupac and an associate were collared in their dressing room by the LAPD and booked on assault with a deadly weapon—even though Shakur told officers Deleon might have had a weapon. A Los Angeles judge dismissed a civil lawsuit brought by Deleon after Deleon readied a confidential settlement.

Tupac again made headlines by adhering to the self-preservation mantra of his fledgling rap ideology, Thug Life, a ghettocentric flip of black power that turned Pac into as big a figure in the media—film, TV, and print—as he was on CD. A couple of weeks following his arrest for assaulting the limo driver, Tupac was charged with pummeling director Allen Hughes for firing him from the upcoming film *Menace II Society*. Several months after that, he was apprehended for shooting two white off-duty police officers in Atlanta after coming to the aid of a black motorist he thought was being harassed by the cops. And in November, Tupac was hit with his greatest legal dilemma, being accused of sexual assault by a female fan. All of this tumult and confusion in Tupac's life came as his second album, *Strictly 4 My N.I.G.G.A.Z.*, headed toward a million sales with the help of "Keep Ya Head Up," his ode to strong black women, and "I Get Around," a tribute to his love for sexing the hos. As it has been written ad nauseam, such contrast, contradictions, and thuggish charisma were what built up Tupac as both a hip-hop icon and, ultimately, America's mythological street warrior. Of all commercial rap idols, Tupac is considered the most successful at conflating gangsta rap's thug worship with poetry and the deferred rage of black power politics, and at translating the pain and fears of his generation on record, in films, even through his much-publicized turmoil. His command of all media, which aided in getting the essence of Tupac to the masses (more than his music), was what turned this rapper from just-another-pro-black-gangsta-MC into a legend and, in the process, created a fresh but troublesome new mold for building one's myth in commercial hardcore rap.

The seed for this changing ideal was sown just as Tupac inflamed law enforcement and conservatives with his 1991 debut, *2Pacalypse Now*, and stunned moviegoers with his acting debut in Ernest Dickerson's film of black teen angst, *Juice*, in 1992. Before the extensive rap sheet and legal entanglements, Tupac's black power pedigree promoted his relevance to a national audience (even before they got a chance to know his music). Tupac's rhymes like "Trapped" and "Brenda's Got a Baby" were songs of protest lashing out against poverty, racism, and crooked cops, but as print and television interviews made listeners understand, fueling his perspective was a genetic, albeit romanticized, link to the 1960s struggle of black nationalism.

He was the son of a Black Panther. His mother, Afeni, who'd been a member of Chicago's Gangster Disciples gang as a teen, joined the revolutionary group in 1968. In April 1969 she became part of the Panther 21 after she and twenty other Panthers were arrested and charged with conspiracy to bomb several New York City buildings. During the year or so Afeni was out on bail (the case took two years to fight), she began dating two men—Panther member Billy Garland and Legs, a Harlem hustler reportedly affiliated with the drug kingpin Nicky Barnes—and became pregnant with Tupac. Although Garland was the father, Tupac was told by Afeni that Legs was his dad. And because of the bond he developed with Legs as a child—in Garland's absence—Tupac grew up with an almost blaxploitation scenario of his conception, a tale that later fit perfectly within the rising stakes of a gangsta rap career. "My mother was a Panther. My papa was a hustler from 135th Street," he casually told Fab Five Freddy on *Yo! MTV Raps* years later. "On her trial, facing three hundred and sixty something years . . . She made love with my father, the hustler, and they had a baby." Most of his mom's pregnancy was spent in prison when her bail was revoked in early 1971. So, as Tupac would later say in another interview, "I was cultivated in prison. My embryo was in prison."

Tupac Amaru Shakur was born on June 16, 1971, a month after his mother and her Panther comrades were acquitted of all charges. His childhood and adolescent years were spent moving between the Bronx and Harlem with Afeni struggling to balance political activism and the financial responsibilities of providing for her family. Since salaries for a black revolutionary were far from lucrative, poverty—along with a sound political education—sat at the center of Tupac's upbringing. The combination of constantly moving, being poor, and bearing the pangs of loneliness (moving wasn't conducive to keeping friends) got Tupac writing—songs, poetry, diaries. He discovered his acting talents when his mother enrolled him in the 127th Street Ensemble, a Harlem-based theater group. His first acting performance was playing Travis in *A Raisin in the Sun* at the Apollo Theater. The production was part of a fund-raiser supporting Jesse Jackson's presidential run in 1984.

In his early teens he and his family moved to Baltimore. There Tupac began asserting his individuality and developing an identity, expanding his writing repertoire to include raps. He became MC New York, establishing a small name for himself, fashioning an image apart from being known solely as a Panther's son. He attended the Baltimore School for the Arts, where he further developed himself as both an artist and a person. It was there that he started to feel, as he told the writer Kevin Powell, that he "really wanted to be an artist."

But the plans went slightly askew when, at the age of seventeen, Tupac and his family moved west to Marin City, a cluster of housing projects just across the bay from Oakland. Asserting a burgeoning manhood within *this* ghetto, nicknamed "the Jungle," meant that Tupac headed toward the degenerative valley of statistics engulfing the lives of young black men. After moving out of his mother's house, Tupac was on his own, looking for his manhood in the streets. In search of a strong black male presence in his life ("I believe a mother can't give a son ways on how to be a man," he said in a *Vibe* interview. "Especially not a black man"), he befriended the pimps, crooks, and drug hustlers of the neighborhood, folks who reminded him of his first (and beloved) father figure, Legs, who had died shortly after Tupac moved to Baltimore. Tupac even tried his hand at the hustler's life, dealing drugs for a period of two weeks before his boss realized he was inept at moving product. It didn't help that Tupac discovered that his mother had become a full-blown crack addict. But from then on Tupac reset his focus back to a future in the arts, a career, he thought, of creating within his generation's loudest and most profound expression: rap. The socially righteous anger of Public Enemy and N.W.A ruled hip-hop music, and so who better to speak the soul of his peers than a child literally birthed from the black power era.

Ironically, Tupac's introduction to the commercial rap game came through more of a sex-n-party theme than a black nationalist one.

He started out as a background dancer and roadie for the George Clinton–inspired rap outfit Digital Underground, who had struck platinum in 1990 with the single "The Humpty Dance." In between performing with DU—a stage routine that consisted of dry-humping rubber sex dolls onstage—he diligently worked on his own material. Tupac's chance to introduce his rhyme skills to the public arrived with a guest appearance on DU's 1991 "Same Song." That same year, the depth of his own recordings (far from the "Now I clown around / When I hang around" verse he spoke on "Same Song") so impressed the heads of the rock-centered label Interscope Records, they signed Tupac as their first rap act.

Obviously, what label heads Jimmy Iovine and Ted Field heard in Tupac was the best of rap's biggest-selling acts: Public Enemy and N.W.A. Even in its baby steps, Tupac's music was an unconventional concoction, a noble marriage of criminality, black rage, and black nationalism. He had turned "nigga" into an acronym (Never Ignorant about Getting Goals Accomplished) and street niggas into potential revolutionaries, challenging racial oppression through self-combustion, gun violence, and passionate disclosure of the inner-city blues. Tupac's debut, *2Pacalypse Now*, more than the work of his predecessors, reflected a return of Panther ideology to black popular culture beyond just rap. In fact, the album hit the streets a year after the New York Supreme Court released Black Panther Dhoruba bin Wahad after a nineteen-year imprisonment. A month after being exonerated in the Panther 21 case, bin Wahad was arrested in June 1971 and charged with the attempted murder of two police officers. He was convicted two years later and sentenced to twenty-five years to life in prison. Following the Church Committee hearings, which uncovered COINTELPRO in 1975, bin Wahad's lawyers spent the next fifteen years compiling previously undisclosed documents, many from the FBI, involving the Panther's case and the unsavory tactics used by the FBI against the Black Panther Party. One of the primary pieces of evidence was an undisclosed phone call to police in which the prosecution's key witness, Pauline Joseph, cleared bin Wahad of the crime. Upon his release, he became the first Black Panther to overturn a conviction based on evidence released from the FBI's Counterintelligence Program.

But while bin Wahad's unjust imprisonment attested to a systematic ruin of the black revolution, *2Pacalypse* exposed the by-product of a black power dream deferred. In Black Panther fashion, the album was a gun pointed at America's containment of blacks: in ghettos (which were becoming police states during the War on Drugs), in jails, in poverty, in ignorance. "I told 'em fight back, attack on society," he rapped on the song "Violent." "If this is violence, then violent's what I gotta be / If you investigate you'll find out where it's comin' from / Look throughout history, America's the violent one." In the canon of black liberation literature, Tupac fashioned himself as James Baldwin's *The Fire Next Time*, the impending flame burning in the single "Trapped" with Tupac warning of a racial explosion a year before the L.A. riots. "One day I'm gonna bust, blow up on this society / Why did ya lie to me / I couldn't find a trace of equality / Work me like a slave while they lay back / Homey don't play that / It's time I let 'em suffer the payback."

If law enforcement and Republicans were miffed at hardcore rap's harsh position on crooked cops and racial intolerance, the Rodney King beating justified the rappers' stance. But Tupac, while adding his vengeful thoughts on abusive cops to this preriot sentiment on "I Don't Give a Fuck," also went so far as to challenge America's reliance on blacks to help fight its international wars, particularly the Persian Gulf War that broke out earlier that year. "Mama told me there'd be days like this," he shouted. "But I'm pissed 'cause it stays like this / And now they tryin' to ship me off to Kuwait / Give me a break / How much shit can a nigga take?"

But what distinguished Tupac from his radically hardcore colleagues was his mindful expression of pain from living in the inner city. He didn't just rap about the problems of the ghetto or decry the conditions; he took listeners into the lives and souls of people affected by the environment. The most heartbreaking example was the single "Brenda's Got a Baby," which told the story of a young girl who gets pregnant by her cousin. After having the baby in secret, Brenda dumps the infant in the trash, then turns to a life of selling crack, then her body, and winds up senselessly murdered by a john. But Tupac's vivid story mines the humanity of his character when he explains her background. "Now Brenda really never knew her moms," he begins. "And her dad was a junkie putting death into his arms / It's sad 'cause I bet Brenda doesn't even know / Just 'cause you're in the ghetto doesn't mean you can't grow."

His profile of a young black male is just as picturesque on "Soulja's Story," about a teenager who chooses to act out against his perceived entrapment in poverty and a virtual police state. "Is it my fault just 'cause I'm a young black male?" asks the character Soulja. "Cops sweatin' me as if my destiny is making crack sales / Only fifteen and got problems / Cops on my tail so I bail till I dodge 'em / They finally pull me over and I laugh / 'Remember Rodney King' and I blast on his punk ass." Moreover, Tupac colored these tales with sketches from his personal experiences, drawing from his own family life to show the unseen story behind ill behavior in the ghetto. "Crack done took a part of my family tree," Soulja says at one point. "My momma's on the shit / My daddy split / And momma's steady blaming me."

2pacalypse Now didn't translate into megastardom for Tupac, though the gold seller succeeded at putting his worldview on the street. He started off as a below-the-radar ghetto revolutionary. (That a couple of news articles wrongly identified him, early on, as the son of exiled Panther Assata Shakur didn't hurt, either.) What shaped and grew and sold the image of Tupac, though—his outlaw mystique and righteously ruthless attitude—were his very public run-ins with the law and with the streets. The first was an arrest in 1991 for jaywalking in Oakland. Tupac filed a $10 million lawsuit against the police, claiming they'd brutalized him during the arrest. The following year, while visiting a festival in Marin City, a six-year-old boy was shot by a stray bullet during a brawl between Tupac and two former associates. A lawsuit was filed against Tupac by the boy's family, and the case was eventually settled out of court.

But it was the controversy behind his music and a film role that brought Tupac the most notable attention in 1992. Six weeks following Ice-T's "Cop Killer" tumult, Tupac made headlines, his lyrics being blamed for the murder of a Texas state trooper. Ronald Ray Howard, a nineteen-year-old Texan, was arrested and charged with the shooting death of Officer Bill Davidson. Howard, while driving a stolen car, was pulled over by the trooper for a broken headlight. Moments after the stop, Howard shot Davidson in the neck with a 9 mm pistol, later telling authorities he was listening to "Soulja's Story" as he loaded his weapon, preparing to kill the officer. In fact, the murder played like a scene straight from the song. The sway of Tupac's music was Howard's only defense.

While a jury rejected his excuse (Howard was sentenced to death), Davidson's widow didn't, filing a multimillion-dollar civil suit against Tupac for influencing the young man to kill her husband. The unprecedented legal battle even further opened the national debate over gangsta rap's violent lyrics, over artistic expression and free speech. Moreover, it heightened Tupac's celebrity profile. Was he a gangsta rap menace preaching murder and mayhem? A mouthpiece for black urban youth under attack by society and the justice system? Or simply a rebel for the hell of it? Or all of the above? "Menace or Martyr?" asked a *USA Today* headline about Tupac. Folks were beginning to wonder about Tupac and his intentions.

No clear answer could be given. But the idea of Tupac-as-thuggish-rebel received a definite boost from his acting debut in the 1992 film *Juice*. In this tale of three black teens trying to find power (or their idea of it) on the streets of Harlem, Tupac played Bishop, a delinquent whose quest for respect drives him to become a psychopathic killer. Critics weren't overly impressed with the film, but they were enthused about Tupac's portrayal of Bishop. *The New York Times* called him "the film's most magnetic figure." Tupac played Bishop's descent into self-delusion and insanity with the skill of a natural-born actor, poignantly exposing the fine subtext of his character's fall—his loneliness, his misguided ambition, his vulnerability and childlike innocence. No doubt Tupac's training at the Baltimore School for the Arts prepared him for the role, but one couldn't help noticing that, in portraying Bishop, Tupac was really portraying himself. He, like the young character, was also a restless soul—under the delusion of gangsta theology—on a blind quest for strength, power, and love. And as Bishop found it in a .38 caliber handgun, Tupac found it in a self-made ruffian-style nationalism: Thug Life.

With the stir caused by *2pacalypse Now*, the critical acclaim garnered from *Juice*, and his growing rap sheet, Tupac found a platform to preach and give form to his new ideology. Thug Life was, as the writer Kevin Powell described it in a *Vibe* story, Tupac's "mission for the black community." According to Tupac, Thug Life was several things: "a support group, a rap act, and a philosophy." The philosophy was that black folks were the thugs of society—"thugs" meaning social underdogs as opposed to criminals. And as thugs, they would rise up to gain power over their lives and their communities. Neither the method of obtaining that control nor how such an ideology could offer support to black folks as a whole was ever clearly defined. And why was the word "thug" an identity and a definition for progress? What was clear, however, was who this movement's leader would be and how *he* would define it through rap music and lifestyle.

Tupac's second album, *Strictly 4 My N.I.G.G.A.Z.*, in 1993, could be called an announcement of the Thug Life manifesto. In lieu of outright social criticism, Tupac intensified his gangsta-revolutionary response to conservative America and law enforcement. "Oh, no, I won't turn the other cheek," he yelled on the album's first track, "Holler If Ya Hear Me." "In case ya can't see us while we burn the other week / Now we got him in a smash, blast / How long will it last: 'til the po' get mo' cash / Until then, raise up / To my young black males, blaze up!" Between *2Pacalypse Now* and *Strictly*, Tupac had evolved as commercial rap and the black political minefield had evolved. The L.A. riots rekindled and verified black outrage, while Dr. Dre turned black popular music (R&B included) into a gangsta's paradise. Sensing hip-hop's shift from nationalist fervor toward a hoodlum theology, Tupac made a calculated decision to stay within that shift, using gangsta rap as a tool of advocacy on behalf of rap's black urban audience. "He progressively became more gangsta," commented writer Cheo Hodari Coker in an interview, "because he realized that even though his political records were critically acclaimed and got him a certain amount of respect . . . he wasn't reaching the audience he wanted to reach."

Tupac's brand of gangstadom would be offered through the life of the "thug." Shortly after the disc's release, Tupac began loudly promoting his new philosophy along with the album ("Thug Life!" he would declare during news interviews), his own flesh eventually becoming its biggest advertisement (the words "Thug Life" were famously tattooed across his stomach). On *Strictly*, Tupac, as chief thug, pumped his new black archetype as the noble nigga cornered by society (and ignorant black folks) and forced to shoot or hustle his way to peace of mind. "Those who test will find a bullet in they chest," he warned on the cut "The Streetz R Deathrow." "Put to rest by a brotha who was hopeless / Grow up broke on the rope of insanity / How many pistols smokin', coming from a broken family." Taking a page from N.W.A, the violence in Pac's musical philosophy stemmed from the dramatic vein of blaxploitation with motives rooted in hardcore frustration and poverty. "Cops step off," he demanded on "Strugglin'." "They fear the ruffneck niggaz with the lunatic behavior."

Tupac's ultraviolent position was an obvious expression of leftover fury from the L.A. rebellion, his anticop sentiment validated by the very public display of cops behaving badly on Rodney King's ass. But his thuggish gallantry on disc and roguish behavior in life, captured by headlines and news cameras and film directors (he starred in John Singleton's *Poetic Justice*, receiving more acclaim), also began sculpting Tupac into something of a black knight—this as postriot fears of young colored folks fueled what many perceived as a legislative race war. Constant news coverage of the crack epidemic, mushrooming gang activity, and urban violence (especially the L.A. rebellion, with gangs of young people violently expressing their feelings) fed a national perception that crime, particularly youth crime, was on the rise, when in fact the national crime rate had been falling since 1991. Youth crime, which had peaked in 1993, was also on the decline. But that didn't stop politicians from pandering to the hysteria. Nor did it ease the fears of black and brown people that the programs, task forces, and laws created by politicians and law enforcement to combat crime were really designed to contain, lock up, and make black and brown people (folks most associated with the crime pandemic) disappear. The harshest symbol of that sentiment was the enactment of the "three strikes" laws, sentencing convicts who had committed three felonies to life imprisonment without parole.

Washington was the first state to enact such a program in 1993, though its rule only applied to violent felonies. But the following year, California passed a stricter version of the three-strikes initiative, Proposition 184, which applied to all felonies. Five years after the law was enacted, a study by UC Berkeley law professor Franklin Zimring reported that almost fifty thousand felons were sentenced to life under the three-strikes policy. According to a *Los Angeles Times* report, 70 percent of the "strikeouts" were handed down to African-American and Latino men. President Clinton even passed his own crime prevention bill, which included a federal three-strikes rule. And although opposition to such extreme laws (politicians were seen as reactive as opposed to proactive) came from black political, civil rights, and youth leadership, no one captured the reaction of young blacks feeling under attack as well as Tupac did on *Strictly*.

His most heartfelt moment on the disc was "Keep Ya Head Up," a gold-selling word of encouragement for strong black women. "I give a holler to my sisters on welfare," he offered in the tone of a soul crooner. "Tupac cares if don't nobody else care / I know they like to beat ya down a lot / And when ya come around the block brothers clown a lot." Over an ultra-sentimental loop, accompanied by a hip-hop rehash of the chorus from the Five Stairsteps' "O-o-h Child," Tupac discarded gangsta rap's code of misogyny, boldly standing on behalf of the sistas. He challenged the mistreatment of women ("I wonder why we take from our women / Why we rape our women / Do we hate our women?") and imparted his thug archetype with soul and spirituality. Along with pushing *Strictly* to platinum sales, "Keep Ya Head Up" gave future hardcore MCs the courage to express the weight of what was in their hearts, regardless of whether Tupac was sincere about the song's cause or not.

But *Strictly* also hinted at the blurring of Tupac's art with his reality, that what he rapped about was *becoming* his life, and that his turbulent life was feeding the authenticity of his music. The music and the mayhem served Tupac's wish to be perceived as a supreme outlaw. "I thought I hit rock bottom, they ban my album," he complained on "Point the Finga," referring to the suit against him in Texas. "I guess nobody loves a real nigga-slash–rap singer / I thought I'd bring a little truth to the young troops / I brought proof that the niggaz need guns too." Even if Tupac declared on the title track that "life as a celebrity ain't everything they make it," on other cuts like "Guess Who's Back" he reveled in epitomizing the black male under siege from the American justice system and the mean streets. "I struggle to be rugged and raw, duke," he rapped, "tryin' to survive in the trials and lawsuits / Everybody wants to test me / Why me / No lie, nuckas cried when they try me." Still, as the commercial success of *Strictly* pushed Tupac's Thug Life message to the masses, nothing molded the budding legend of Tupac as thug hero more than the combustible moments of his life.

One incident solidified this idea, the notion of Tupac as Thug Life personified, more than most. On October 31, 1993, he was arrested for shooting two white off-duty police officers in Atlanta. The officers, brothers Mark and Scott Whitwell, were engaged in a traffic-related argument with a black motorist when Tupac and his entourage pulled over to investigate. According to Captain Herb Carson, when the crew approached, one of the cops pointed his gun toward them. But, depending on whose lawyer was telling the story, Tupac or the officers fired first. Either way, Mark Whitwell was shot in the stomach while his brother was hit in the buttocks. Tupac, charged with two counts of aggravated assault, claimed he fired in self-defense, that he was coming to the aid of a black man whom the cops were harassing. The charges were dismissed after conflicting statements from witnesses identified one of the officers shooting first (it was also reported that the investigating detective admitted the officers' report stated: "Niggers came by and did a drive-by").

Nonetheless, the fact that Tupac had engaged in a gunfight with police (coming to the rescue of a brother being hounded by The Man, no doubt), shot the cops, and beat the case—not to mention lived to talk about it—instantly confirmed him as thug hero supreme, as bona fide freedom fighter, as a hip-hop legend. "I mean look at him," an eighteen-year-old (Lol Hayes) told a *Newsweek* reporter. "You can't take him down, and there ain't nobody like him since Malcolm [X]. He shot those white cops in Atlanta and didn't miss a step." Never before had a rap artist built hip-hop badness by making his art *and* his life inseparable. N.W.A, for all their pioneering of gangsta rap, gained fans because they *looked* and *sounded* like gangstas. Public Enemy built a following because they looked and sounded like a funky black nationalist army. All their turmoil came afterward. By merging art with reality and, simultaneously, growing a career, Tupac was raising the bar for mythmaking (and marketing) in commercial rap music. His hardcore contemporaries may have had unsavory pasts to prove their realness, but Tupac generated that realness with his life. And because of his dashing good looks and athletic physique, Tupac's rebelliousness translated well through all media—music, music videos, the evening news, and especially film. Where Snoop and Dre mainstreamed the black gangsta, Tupac, along with giving him a heart and social consciousness, made the figure into a sex symbol and a matinee idol.

That sexiness also marked an unfortunate turn in a thug's life when Tupac was charged with sexual abuse and sodomy in November 1993.

A woman whom Tupac had met at a New York City club and had consensual sex with claimed that a few days later he and members of his entourage molested her in the suite of a Manhattan luxury hotel. Tupac insisted he had been napping in another room, after being intimate with her beforehand, when the rape supposedly took place. Whether he was guilty or not, the nature of the charges, coupled with Tupac's revolutionary background and constant legal entanglements, further polarized views of the rapper. To some he was merely a careless hooligan shooting and raping his way to fame. To others he was the tortured, misguided symbol of young black manhood. But both held two thoughts in common: one, Tupac was an enigmatic ball of contradiction, confusion, and honesty that could capture the imagination (and attention) of the world; and two, as Thug Life turned Tupac into a star, it would inevitably lead to a fall.

The tipping point came the following year, when serious consequences began accompanying Tupac's gangsta fantasies. In April 1994, shortly after he played a murderous street ball recruiter in the film *Above the Rim*, Tupac was found guilty of beating up director Allen Hughes (an assault he bragged about on *Yo! MTV Raps*) and was sentenced to fifteen days in jail. After serving his time, he still had the rape trial to prepare for. As if his personal tribulations weren't damning enough, the unfortunate influence of Thug Life made the papers again. In Milwaukee, two seventeen-year-old youths were arrested for the sniper killing of a police officer. The previous week the two had discussed murdering cops and rival gang members. Officer William Robertson became their victim as one boy decided to be lookout while the other agreed to be the shooter. When explaining their motive to authorities, one of the boys said he had gotten the idea from a Tupac recording. Though the shooting didn't gain as much ink or spark as much dialogue as the Texas case, one still had to wonder what aspects of Tupac's ideology were *really* getting through to his intended audience. Even Tupac would admit about Thug Life's impact: "There's a bad part because the kids see that [violence] and they mimic it. That's the part I haven't figured out yet."

There were productive results of his gangsta-style nationalism, such as when Tupac attempted to curtail violence in black and brown communities by organizing prisoners under the "Code of Thug Life," a community-minded code of ethics, ironically, for criminals. "No slinging [drugs] in schools," read one demand. Unfortunately, those ideas were never as public as the fisticuffs and gunfire and other violent episodes that came to embody Tupac's revolution. He may have wanted folks to find hope and bravery in Thug Life, but all anyone of conscience could see was the destruction.

The day before the verdict in his rape trial was handed down Tupac was shot in the lobby of a Times Square recording studio. He'd come to the Quad Studios to record music and was approached by three men—two of them with guns—demanding his jewels. When Tupac resisted the robbers and berated them, he was shot five times. "Until it happened, I really did believe that no black person would ever shoot me," Tupac admitted some time after. "I believed I didn't have to fear my own community . . . I was like, I represent them." He seemed to forget that freedom fighters, particularly nationalists—from Malcolm to Huey—who merge the streets with the movement, have been blasted, literally, at the hands of black folks. He had also forgotten that those rebels of black power, at some point in their lives, had done time in prison.

On December 1, despite the lack of physical evidence linking him to the crime, a jury of nine women and three men found Tupac guilty of sexually abusing the twenty-one-year-old female fan. Later, he'd admit in an MTV interview: "I'm guilty of not being a smart man, of not being a good-hearted man." When asked if he could change anything about that night, he responded: "I would not have closed my eyes until she was out of the room. Until *everybody* was out of the room." He was sentenced to one-and-a-half to four-and-a-half years in prison. More than those of his pro-black predecessors, though, Tupac's ordeal read like a self-fulfilling prophecy, the end result of someone playing the role of a thug without thoroughly realizing the consequences (as thugs often don't). Then again, his ambition was to epitomize the plight—the reactionary existence—of troubled black youth for whom gangstadom was becoming the driving force of their culture. He was, after all, one himself: a twentysomething black male given money, power, and fame, trying to make a change but having no real guidance himself, using only rage and a deep-seated desire to be accepted as his guide.

The sexual trouble he'd gotten himself into, that got him sent to prison, was no different from the kind plaguing his elders. Anyone disputing the fact needed only to see the problems unfolding within

America's oldest civil rights organization before the rapper's incarceration. Eighteen months after being hired as the NAACP's executive director, Benjamin F. Chavis, Jr., was being ousted for actions "inimical to the best interests of the organization." In July 1994, reports surfaced about Chavis using NAACP funds, without the knowledge or consent of the board of directors, to pay off a former employee who had threatened to sue him for sexual harassment. Chavis, who had been hired to revitalize the group, curb its ballooning debt, and draw alienated youth back into the fold, had proven controversial soon after he took office in April 1993. He met with street gang members across the country (against the grain of his group's bourgeois image), defended rappers whose lyrics were considered offensive, and aligned the organization with radical black leaders like Louis Farrakhan. Chavis was a longtime civil rights activist who, as one of the Wilmington 10 in North Carolina, was wrongfully convicted in 1971 of firebombing a white-owned grocery store. He served four years in prison before his conviction was overturned. Under his brief leadership, the NAACP, with all its internal debates over Chavis's black power alliances and direction, seemed poised to once again lead the advancement of colored people after years of being considered irrelevant by the younger generation. That was until Chavis's mismanagement of funds—and the reasons behind it—was disclosed. Accused of sexual harassment by his former deputy Mary E. Stansel, Chavis agreed to pay the woman over $300,000 and find her a job outside the NAACP in order to keep the allegations from going public. Amid the chaos that ensued, all the potential Chavis had given the NAACP was eventually destroyed by his selfishness, deception, greed, and alleged lust.

So black leadership would continue to suffer from arrested development as rap witnessed the imprisonment of its leading thug at the start of 1995. While Tupac was incarcerated, his album *Me Against the World* was released in the spring and debuted at number one on *Billboard*'s pop and R&B charts. With production borrowing heavily from Dre's g-funk, by now the signature sound of the West Coast, Tupac's third LP was an impressive leap into artistic and philosophical maturity. Clearly Tupac recognized he was *some* kind of leader. Whereas the first two albums, musically and thematically, sounded disjointed, *Me Against the World* was a cohesive bundle of b-boy introspection and pop-star paranoia, of Panther-style commentary and Marvin

Gaye–style soul-searching. Leading the album toward two million sales was "Dear Mama," Tupac's openhearted song about his tumultuous relationship with his mother, who, by the LP's release, had kicked her drug addiction. "And even as a crack fiend, mama," he confessed, "you always was a black queen, mama / I finally understand / For a woman it ain't easy trying to raise a man." For a rapper convicted (wrongfully, many thought) of molesting a woman, "Dear Mama" seemed again to appropriately counter the negative implications of his falls from grace.

But just as pronounced on the album was Tupac's preoccupation with mortality. If fans and critics wondered if the shoot-outs, arrests, and overall drama weighed heavily on his mind, the answer was obvious. Their thuggish crusader (knowing nobody dodges bullets forever) articulated his thoughts on death through both prophecy ("And fuck the world 'cause I'm cursed," he rhymed on "So Many Tears," "I'm having visions of leaving here in a hearse") and a death wish ("Don't shed a tear for me, nigga," he demanded on "If I Die 2Nite," "I ain't happy here / I hope they bury me and send me to my rest"). The thread of death throughout the LP was Tupac talking out his fear of the inevitable as well as—let's be honest—strategically propping himself up as a hip-hop Christ figure, standing against the enemy and dying for the sins of his music and his generation. His concerns about mortality were just as much an expression of the spirituality developing inside this outlaw tempting fate. "I wonder if the Lord will forgive me," he pondered on "Lord Knows," "or bury me a G / I couldn't let my adversaries worry me."

Although exploration of Thug Life, for the most part, remained present, it was less ruthless (less "Fuck tha Police") and a bit more cautionary, speaking against those who want to be gansgtas while, as usual, exposing the hopelessness of those who are. His most ardent message went toward kids looking to become thugs on "Young Niggaz." "Them niggas that's thirteen and fourteen," he called out, "drivin' Cadillacs, Benzes, and shit . . . You could be a fuckin' accountant, not a dope dealer . . . Niggas gotta get their priorities straight." On the cut "Death Around the Corner," Tupac, portraying a ghetto desperado, fought death and the dog-eat-dog mentality of the streets: "I see death around the corner, gotta stay high / While I survive in a city where the skinny niggas die . . . I got homies in my head that done passed away, screamin', Please, young nigga, make Gs." The retooling of his hip-hop ideology, emphasizing its deadly consequences while maintaining its brave face, hinted at an artist struggling with the value (or lack thereof) of his cause. Even though Tupac proudly proclaimed in "So Many Tears," "Inside my mind couldn't find a place to rest until I got that 'Thug Life' tatted on my chest," he rethought his movement once he was *really* trapped behind bars, getting no love from those who he thought were in his corner. (His label, tired of his antics, wouldn't even put up his bail.) "Thug Life to me is dead," he declared in an interview with *Vibe*. "If it's real, then let somebody else represent it, because I'm tired of it. I represented it too much." Tupac's renouncement of his gangsta nationalism seemed prophetic, coming five months before America witnessed close to a million black men assembling on the National Mall in Washington, D.C., and pledging a spiritual revolution for black America.

The Million Man March (MMM), held on October 16, 1995, was by far the largest post-civil-rights demonstration in U.S. history. But unlike its predecessor, the 1963 March on Washington, which brought the injustices of Jim Crow to the world's attention, the MMM was a protest against the self-destructive effects of institutionalized racism. With drugs, violence, crime, and prison turning black men into what many alarmists termed an "endangered species," Louis Farrakhan and Benjamin Chavis organized the march not to ask the government to solve the problem but to get black men to shoulder the responsibility for stopping the destruction. Instead of a political remedy, Farrakhan and Chavis prescribed a spiritual one, getting hundreds of thousands of brothas—perhaps even a million—to gather in the nation's capital and promise to rebuild the black family and the black community. In doing so on a world stage (news cameras across the globe captured the event), the gathering not only countered the negative images and critical statistics of black male mortality in the news but reawakened America to the social, political, and soul power of black folks. Despite the criticism it received for not including women or having any *real* objective (writer Adolph Reed commented that it was the first time black men literally protested *themselves*), the MMM was the largest, if not the most symbolic, political statement in the age of hip-hop. Whether or not it made a difference was debatable—a future drop in crime was mostly linked to a booming economy and better policing. But undoubtedly, it had little to no effect on the corporate-sponsored nihilism of hardcore rap, or the winds of war inadvertently being stirred by an incarcerated Tupac.

As he publicly renounced Thug Life, the paranoia and mistrust Tupac developed after getting shot and overindulging in weed and alcohol made him view acquaintances and friends suspiciously. He'd expressed this sentiment in the same *Vibe* interview when, just after declaring the "addict" and "excuse maker" within him dead, he cast suspicion for his shooting on Biggie Smalls, a Brooklyn buddy and a rising rap superstar, and a slew of Smalls's East Coast rap affiliates (all of whom were in the building housing Quad) while recalling details of that night. "Nobody approached me," he commented on their response to seeing him injured. "I noticed that nobody would look at me."

Tupac's comments inflamed not only those mentioned in his interview but also many East Coast fans who felt Tupac, in implicating famed artists of their region, betrayed their unwavering love and support. (Though, before Tupac's comments, there was growing animosity between coasts given the West's rule of rap and the East's refusal, outside of Dre and Snoop, to respect their artistry or give their music radio airplay.) But as much as Tupac talked about turning toward a productive path in his career, his ego and passions guided him toward an inevitable destiny of thug living, especially after the head of Death Row—like a brawny black knight—helped him get out of prison and escape the impending jaws of irrelevance. Suge Knight, who recognized the multimedia potential of the star, signed Tupac to Death Row just before paying a $1.4 million bond to get him released from prison early in September 1995.

Unfortunately, the hip-hop landscape Tupac resurfaced in had become a hostile, divided one, a schism made official a month before Tupac's release after Suge's very public dis of Bad Boy Records's head, Sean "Puffy" Combs, at the Source Awards in New York City. Combs's record company was becoming the East Coast equivalent of Death Row. What started as a night of verbal sparring between two labels had the potential of turning into a heated rift between coasts. ("The East Coast ain't got no love for Dr. Dre and Snoop Dogg and Death Row?" Snoop angrily asked a booing crowd as he took the stage to accept an award.)

In signing with Suge, Tupac invariably chose the West's side in a rivalry that was about to split hardcore rap along the same lines as his mother's former organization: during the waning days of black power, a struggle between Panther leaders Huey Newton and Eldridge Cleaver divided the Party into two factions—East Coast (Cleaver) and West Coast (Newton). But where the internal divide in the Panthers was exploited and exacerbated by the FBI, the East versus West war in hardcore rap was given life by the print and television media, who spun a Bad Boy–Death Row feud into a Mob-style civil war engulfing the entire genre. Given the street drama within the rap industry, there were stories to feed the idea, such as the shooting death of Suge's close friend Jake Robles during an afterparty attended by both Combs and Suge. Published reports claimed witnesses fingered a member of Puffy's entourage as the shooter. Then there was the infamous disruption of a Dogg Pound video on December 16, 1995. While Snoop and Tha Dogg Pound (Death Row duo Daz and Kurupt) were in Red Hook, Brooklyn, shooting a video for the song "New York, New York," shots were fired into their trailer. No one was hurt and the gunman was never caught. Furthermore, given hip-hop's competitive spirit, dis records also fed the conflict. In response to the video for "New York, New York"—featuring Godzilla-sized members of Tha Dogg Pound crushing Manhattan—Queens rappers Mobb Deep, Tragedy, and Capone-N-Noreaga made "L.A., L.A." The song's video featured the crew kidnapping Dogg Pound look-alikes, torturing them, and throwing the two off a bridge.

Whereas legendary MC rivalries of the past (Busy Bee versus Kool Moe Dee, KRS-One versus MC Shan, LL Cool J versus every-damn-body) remained on wax or cassette—outside of popular scrutiny—the East/West battle felt as if it reached beyond the airwaves. Then again, the stakes in the rap industry were higher now, with larger sums of money and celebrity and corporate interest at risk in a duel. And with a higher premium being placed on street cred as a measure of hip-hop *realness*, hardcore rap's worshipful adoption of the gangsta played right into a skewed image of the music growing in popular culture and an escalating game of destructive one-upmanship. By the same token, the controversy, which attracted tons of free publicity, also helped sell a ton of records.

At the height of this development Tupac released *All Eyez on Me* in the spring of 1996. Rap music's first double album, Tupac's fourth LP also hit number one on *Billboard*'s Top 200. Part of its appeal was the anticipation of hearing the latest rant from hip-hop's thug revolutionary, whose life and career were an open book. But what fans ultimately received was an MC trying to fit into his new Death Row family, into its gangsta-as-lavish-lifestyle mold. Gone were the messages of resistance and painful urban blues, replaced by a postprison hedonism, materialism (thanks to the bundle of money provided by his label), and an egotistical drive to commercially crush his rap competition. No longer the urban desperado, Tupac remade himself into a flashy rap icon totally representing the West Coast. "Out on bail, fresh outta jail, California dreamin'," he declared on the Dre-produced "California Love." "Soon as I step on the scene I'm hearin' hoochies screamin' / Fiendin' for money and alcohol / The life of a west side playa where cowards die and it's all ball." Whereas Tupac's scrapes with the law fed his Christlike persona before, they were now packaged—bundled, you might say—with the infamy of other Death Row stars to affirm the label's gangsta cred and help sell units. This was obviously the case when, teaming with Snoop on "2 of Amerikaz Most Wanted," Tupac bragged: "So now they got us laced / Two multimillionaire motherfuckers catchin' cases / Bitches get ready for the throwdown, the shit's about to go down."

Also, the loving and encouraging words he'd given women on his last three discs were absent, *totally* replaced by misogyny and callousness. "It's scandalous, I never liked your backstabbin' ass, trick," he berates a fictional gold digger on "Skandalouz." "Used to watch you money grabbin', who you baggin', beeeatch?" While there had always been a few less-than-flattering words for shady women and groupies on previous discs, Tupac's views on women, under Death Row, seemed contrived, obviously shaped by his desire to blend with the camp's mantra of "Gs up, hoes down." On the cut "All About U," laced with a sample from Cameo's hit "Candy," he collaborated with rapper YGD, Snoop, and gangsta crooner Nate Dogg to cruelly discuss ladies who follow celebrities. "Every other city we go," Nate Dogg sang, "every other video / No matter where I go / I see the same ho." Tupac would even take up the label's battle with C. Delores Tucker over women being called the *b* word in rap on "Wonda Why They Call U B____."

If there were moments of Tupac the rebellious warrior, the one who spoke on behalf of the powerless, they were relegated to flashes on *All Eyez*. What remained wasn't his bold challenge to authority but his grandiose rants of victimization (songs like "Only God Can Judge Me" and the title track) and sorrow songs for the deadly lifestyle of a gangsta (like "Life Goes On" and "Shorty Wanna Be a Thug"). Otherwise, within the great divide of hardcore rap, Tupac turned to a less-conscious version of Thug Life as a means of representing his West Coast constituency. Taking up Death Row's stance against Bad Boy, Pac became the very public enemy of its superstar, Biggie Smalls (who was now known as the Notorious B.I.G.). Tupac still believed the Brooklyn MC had a hand in his getting shot, even interpreting Big's hit song "Who Shot Ya" as a taunt about the incident. After starting a rumor that he'd slept with Big's wife, Faith, Tupac responded to the song with "Hit 'Em Up," not only bragging about the rumor but verbally beating down Biggie and his entire crew.

But the irony of Tupac's Mob-style zeal at tearing down another rapper was that his own house was unraveling under the weight of violence and intimidation—the price of running a label like an actual gang. Shortly after Tupac's Death Row debut with "California Love," Dr. Dre, ironically, began making his way out of the company. The growing atmosphere of gangbangers and beat downs within the label left him uninspired and unable to work comfortably. (He had also suffered the loss of former N.W.A member Eazy-E, who died of AIDS on March 26, 1995.) Aside from "California Love," Dre hadn't produced anything for *All Eyez*, as was originally planned. Tupac, after publicly venting his frustration about Dre's lack of involvement, was able to tack together a roster of producers to assemble what would become his bestselling vision.

At five million copies sold, *All Eyez* was on its way to becoming the biggest-selling hardcore rap album in history—this despite a less-than-enthusiastic response from critics to the simple and "slapped together" feel of the music. No matter what pundits or naysayers felt about Tupac, he affirmed his power over hip-hop music. He tragically solidified his legend and myth (pushing *All Eyez* to seven times platinum) after being shot in Las Vegas on September 7, 1996, and dying six days later. As much as his murder had nothing to do with the East/West schism (regardless of how television and print media attempted to portray it), his death prompted a serious reevaluation by the hip-hop community of hardcore rap's (and black youth culture's, in general) love affair with violence. "Live by the gun, die by the gun," read one of the numerous murals painted in honor of Tupac's memory.

But beyond the bullets and mayhem, Tupac's legacy was ultimately grounded as much in his prolific musical output as it was in his sensational life in the headlines. Not long after his murder, Death Row released the posthumous album *The Don Killuminati: The 7 Day Theory*, under Pac's alias Makaveli (after the sixteenth-century political philosopher Niccolò Machiavelli). The first of many albums released posthumously, *Don Killuminati* was far from a farewell, sounding instead like Tupac was still around, affirming the belief in his indestructibility and feeding an urban myth that, like Elvis and Bruce Lee, he was still alive (living in Cuba, maybe). The LP's first single, "Hail Mary," with its biblical references ("Eat my flesh, flesh of my flesh") and dark spirituality spawned a host of Tupac-inspired street soldiers of hardcore rap. But the CD's cover articulated his legacy (and the myth of his resurrection) most clearly. Underneath a full moon and black sky, a naked Tupac hangs nailed to a cross. Instead of a crown of thorns, a bandanna, tied in his signature rabbit-ears knot, wraps around his brown head like a halo. Looking down from his suffering, Tupac gives his followers an expression of pity, not for himself but for the hard lessons they're going to experience in the days to come. All he can provide for them, at this juncture, is simply the memory and revolutionary spirit of his thug passion.

NINE

Ghetto Fab Rising
The Notorious B.I.G. and Sean "Puffy" Combs

*Every Negro boy . . . who reaches this point realizes, at once, pro-
foundly, because he wants to live, that he stands in great peril and
must find . . . a "thing," a gimmick, to lift him out, to start him on
his way.* **And it does not matter what the gimmick is.**
                                        —James Baldwin, *The Fire Next Time*

The streets is a short stop
Either you're slingin' crack rock or you got a wicked jump shot.
                        —Notorious B.I.G., "Things Done Changed"

Biggie Smalls arrives at the office of Bad Boy Records
armed with a garment bag and a shoe box. What he's wearing is a
T-shirt, shorts, and a pair of Timberland construction boots. He strolls
through the glass doors, past the company's mantra painted on the wall
(the one declaring "Life is not a game! Only the fittest and most aggressive will survive"), and into the lobby filled with a few journalists taking
advantage of this press day, a day giving urban journos a taste of this
rising New York word champ a month before the release of his inaugu-
ral LP, *Ready to Die*. Only Big doesn't stop for any quickie interviews.
He offers a friendly smile and a few pleasant hellos to the faces in the
waiting area, and then the six-foot-three, almost-three-hundred-pound
MC continues on into the office, garment bag and box in tow. "Big'll be
right out," a publicist informs us. "He's just going to get changed." But
what one knows, especially those who have followed commercial rap
since the early days, is that he wasn't merely freshening up with a new

outfit. Big, like an actor, was getting into character or, like a superhero, getting into costume. Since hardcore rap has overwhelmingly sold (and was thriving off of) the myth of the black badass, artists were like that now, always getting into character or becoming caricatures, selling us the idea of them as *the* Baddest Nigga beating the system.

And sure 'nuff, forty-five minutes later Big resurfaces looking no longer like a hood fresh off a Brooklyn corner but like a dapper, somewhat sophisticated hustler whose clothes say he's a tad higher on the illegal food chain. In a festive button-down shirt, baggy slacks, alligator shoes, and a 504 Ventair Kangol turned ever so slightly to the side, Biggie Smalls is transformed into Bad Boy's newest vision: The Notorious B.I.G. Cool, jovial, and polished, the corpulent rapper is ready to open up his former life not only as a top-notch battle MC but as a low-level crack dealer on the streets of Bedford-Stuyvesant. "I can't really say getting into the drug game was a mistake," he says matter-of-factly into my tape recorder. "I learned how money changes people, how drugs can really take over someone's body. I traveled a lot [laughs]." If silence is the code among criminals, this criminal-turned-MC was an open book, ready for the press, ready to sell us the story of *his* realness, the indistinguishable line between rough rhymes and a former rough life. "When I first got the record deal," he explained, "I was still hustling crazy because it didn't sink into my head that I had a record deal—and that things had to change. I was still the same knucklehead, and the stuff I was writing was just the real stuff that I was involved with every day."

Clearly Big isn't the man he used to be, though this has more to do with his public persona than his unsavory past. The well-draped extrovert speaking into my tape recorder is a 180-degree change from the shy and protective kid wearing army fatigues and jeans, leaning against the wall at Uptown Records a year earlier, quietly watching his future label head, Sean "Puffy" Combs, who had just recently signed him, give the interviews and work the media. Then, Puffy was the rising star: The twenty-two-year-old boy wonder who had become Uptown's new vice president of A&R (perhaps one of the youngest men to ever hold the position). The much-lauded producer responsible for the breakout careers of Mary J. Blige and Jodeci. The prodigious mind helping to pioneer R&B's latest offshoot dubbed "hip-hop soul," the meticulously rugged blend of hip-hop break beats and soulful crooning—R&B singers with the attitude and wardrobe of hardcore rappers. His golden concoction, especially Jodeci with their bad-boy ways, went slightly left of Uptown's credo of urban music with style, class, and edgy refinement (read: palatability), creating a musical milestone. But with Big, Puffy wanted to venture into the new ideal championed by Death Row and the West Coast: conceptual hardcore rap as the *new* crossover.

Only there were problems. Biggie's songs were violent, too violent for Uptown's taste, said an insider of the label's parent company, MCA. Then there was the larger issue. Puffy was becoming too big for Uptown and his mentor/father figure, the label's CEO, Andre Harrell. Reports and rumors abounded about Puffy's ego run amok: that he had a "hot temper," that he spit on a coworker, that he spent too much money on the music he produced, that he would walk around the office sometimes with his shirt off, that he had begun to openly disrespect Harrell. Either way, Puffy was no longer the polite, eager-to-please intern he'd started out as at the company. Whatever the cause or event that brought about the end, in the summer of 1993 Harrell fired Puffy, relieving him of his post with the famous line: *"There can only be one lion in the jungle."*

If it has been said that to be a great artist you must (metaphorically) kill your father, then to be a great father one should push his child out of the nest to strengthen his wings. "Go make it happen," Harrell told Combs after letting him go. "You're ready to fly." And Puffy now had to fly. Luckily, shortly after his departure, he found a sponsor for his venture when Clive Davis, the CEO of Arista Records, signed Puffy's Bad Boy label to a distribution deal. With a $1.5 million advance, the future "fudgey Thurston Howell III" was able to purchase the songs he'd already recorded for Biggie's album and negotiate the Brooklyn rapper's release from Uptown along with other artists he had signed who would later become Bad Boy superstars.

So in the summer of 1994, as a transformed Biggie spoke into tape recorder after tape recorder, answering question after question, retelling tales of his former New York state of mind over and over, he wasn't just pumping his own stardom but also sowing the seeds of Puffy's master plan. Earlier in the season, Bad Boy released the cut "Flava in Ya Ear" by Long Island rapper Craig Mack. With its pulsating rhythm track, catchy horn sample, and phonetic-heavy, fun-to-recite lyrics, "Flava in Ya Ear" was an old-fashioned "skills" record, one concerned with showcasing the MC's prowess as wordsmith as opposed to gunslinger or ruffian. And, surprisingly, the song was a hit, eventually going platinum by the fall. Released at the pinnacle of gangsta chic, "Flava in Ya Ear" was the first major hit New York had produced since the early 1990s, at least one that wholly reflected a New York City sensibility of rhyme talent over ruckus. "This bad MC with stamina like Bruce Jenner, the winner / Tasting MCs for dinner," Craig Mack declared. Finally, a label besides Def Jam and Uptown could offer promise for a metropolis trying to define itself within the redefined commercial space of hardcore rap music.

There was already a contingent of New York rap acts, including Gang Starr, Black Moon, and Main Source, attempting to sell East Coast lyricism to the masses, but which had little luck making an impact outside the tristate area. Even poetically crafted challenges to rap's gangsta fixation like Jeru the Damaja's "Come Clean" or O.C.'s "Time's Up" failed to reach beyond the ears of hip-hop purists (who'd rather tape songs off of radio mix shows than buy them). "Flava" not only gave Bad Boy its first smash but showed Puffy's talent at making the inaccessible (New York lyricism) accessible with the right packaging and marketing.

If Puffy found his start with Craig Mack (the rapper's career fizzled after the release of his *Project: Funk da World* CD), he'd find his muse, his movement, his cultural icon in the Notorious B.I.G. Upon the release of Big's *Ready to Die* LP in October 1994, Bad Boy became the undisputed industry leader in a move to place the Big Apple, once again, at the center of rap's commercial universe. While most of America's hip-hop fans weren't plunking down their dough for the city's labyrinthine poetics, they were warming to a cadre of New York poets using West Coast ideas of gangsta storytelling and rugged party anthems to create a fresh version of New York hardcore rap. These artists tinted their intricate wordplay with streetcentric meanness and vividly relayed the post-crack blight eating the lives and souls of *their* neighborhoods. Staten Island supergroup Wu-Tang Clan, after independently releasing the single "Protect Ya Neck," christened its arrival in 1993 with their debut LP, *Enter the Wu-Tang (36 Chambers)*. Seamlessly mixing kung-fu cinema thematics, dopeman blues, sword-precision rhyming technique, and atmospheric loops, the nine-member team seeped onto the national stage, their debut taking two years to go platinum.

However, most hope for a New York resurrection was placed in an MC hailing from the five boroughs' Queensbridge housing project. Inspired by the devastation the drug trade and thug mentality was having on his friends and community, Nas unleashed deft storytelling and mind-blowing street poetry on 1994's *Illmatic*. From eerie ghetto reportage on "N.Y. State of Mind," to a disheartening letter to a friend in prison on "One Love," to an introspective look at project living through the eyes of its toughest MC on "The World Is Yours," Nas was considered, by East Coast standards, the obvious voice to bring New York rap back to prominence. However, despite tremendously high acclaim from music critics ("the most anticipated ghetto griot of choice, hands down," wrote one scribe), Nas's first album only sold 200,000 the year it was released. Seven years would pass before it reached platinum.

So for Bad Boy, the job of resuscitating New York's national acclaim arrived with the same trifecta that turned Death Row into a West Coast hip-hop hit factory: an ingenious producer (Puffy), the formation of a mega-hardcore hip-hop label (Bad Boy), and an incredibly gifted and charismatic MC (Biggie Smalls). And just as *The Chronic* proved Death Row's superiority, *Ready to Die* became the album ushering in Bad Boy as a commercial rap powerhouse. That the two labels would ultimately wind up adversaries was inevitable given the pride, money, and growing regionalism pushing rap music's development. But it was ironic that in order to reclaim New York's vanguard position, Puffy (as well as his Big Apple compadres) had to gather inspiration from the competition. "We wanted to make a movie on wax," explained Puffy, detailing the motivation behind Big's first LP. "We were so impressed by the stories on Ice Cube's *AmeriKKKa's Most Wanted*, N.W.A's *Niggaz4life*, Dr. Dre's *The Chronic*. I never heard a story told like that from a New York point of view. We wanted to tell a movie *our* way." What Puffy and Big found in the West's gritty narrative was their own story of survival and dreams of wealth and power. Much like the tale behind Dre, Snoop, and Death Row, the union between Big and Puff, as well as the creation of Bad Boy Records, was born from a desire to make a change.

Puffy's seemingly innate business instincts have often been linked to his Harlem hustling lineage. He was born Sean Combs on November 4, 1969. His mother, Janice, was a fashion-catalog model, and his father, "Pretty" Melvin Combs, apart from driving a cab, was a well-known scrambler on the streets of Harlem. Gambling. Numbers.

Drugs. No one seems to pinpoint any particular vice of choice. All that remained of Melvin after his murder in Central Park on January 26, 1972, killed by a "point-blank gunshot wound," were local tales of his long fur coat and stylish Mercedes-Benz.

Following Melvin's murder, Janice, who swore that Sean and his soon-to-be-born sister, Keisha, would never know how their father died, and vowed no street life for her children, eventually moved the family out to the suburbs of Mount Vernon, north of New York City. There, a young Sean would get all that he wanted, even that huge swimming pool (bigger than his white neighbors', the ones who wouldn't invite him to swim in theirs) his mother had to work two jobs to afford. Along with material gain, Sean also developed a defiant—some say spoiled—attitude, especially when he didn't get his way. As the story goes, he'd huff and puff until he did, thus earning him his famous nickname, Puffy. But he also developed a knack for growing a dollar. Stories abound about his paper route as an adolescent when, to earn extra cash, he would hire other kids in his neighborhood to work other routes and convince them to pay him a percentage of their earnings.

It was the trips back to Harlem as a teen, though, visiting his grandmother and old friends, that gave Puffy insight into his family legacy within uptown's underworld as well as the cultural movement giving its opulence a soundtrack. Puffy deduced from stories about Pretty Melvin that his father was a hustler, eventually discovering the *New York Times* article detailing his murder (Puffy had always been told his father was a businessman who was killed in a car crash). He also witnessed hip-hop music morph into the soundscape for the illegal hustle—the crack trade—of his own generation. In the late 1980s, at Manhattan clubs like the Latin Quarter and Harlem's Roof Top, ghetto kingpins danced in furs and thick gold rope chains, drinking champagne whose bubbles mixed easily with the staccato rhyme flows and James Brown samples. Amid this blend of fashion, criminality, and street-level creativity, Puffy would get swept up not by the allure of the drug game but rather by how hip-hop music reflected ghetto youths' ability to thrive despite the obstacles—and look good doing it.

Puffy carried that über-entrepreneurial spirit and love for the sportin' life to Howard University in 1987. He majored in business, but the campus itself turned into the place where he put classroom theories to practice, first by packaging the school's moment of revolution. In

March 1989, several students, led by Ras Baraka (son of famed poet Amiri Baraka), occupied the school's administration building to protest Republican Party chair, Lee Atwater, becoming a member of Howard's board of trustees. As a strategist for Bush's presidential run, Atwater had devised the Willie Horton ad campaign. After the students padlocked themselves in the building, they drew up a list of demands and held Howard's "nerve center" hostage, effectively shutting down the university. The protest was ended when police and security guards stormed the building and forcibly removed the students. All the while, every aspect of the takeover—from the seizure of the building to students on the roof wielding chains and bats, some giving black power salutes—was being documented in photographs. Where many saw the pictures as a generation's exceptional display of principle, Puffy saw an opportunity to get paid. Even though he hadn't participated in the protest, he made a collage out of the photographs and posters out of the collage—all to be sold at $10 or $15 a pop.

By his sophomore year, Puffy, after forming his own campus crew of MCs, DJs, and beat makers (most of whom would become future Bad Boy employees), became D.C.'s biggest party promoter. His party was the main draw because his guests included the biggest names in hip-hop music from Slick Rick to Guy and Heavy D. But what Puffy ultimately wanted was to get into the music business; that opportunity arrived when Heavy D (also from Mount Vernon) introduced him to the head of Uptown Records, Andre Harrell. Puffy the future music mogul was born with an internship at the label. The biggest obstacle he had to face early on was getting money for train fare from D.C. to New York every Thursday and Friday to make it on time—a problem he overcame by hiding in the bathroom to avoid paying.

Soon school took a backseat to Uptown as Puffy steadily sought a chance to turn his unpaid internship into a full-time gig. When Kurt Woodley, Uptown's A&R director, unexpectedly quit to take a job at Columbia Records, Puffy found his chance. An impassioned plea to Harrell to give him the position ("There's nobody out there that could better serve the audience you're trying to sell music to but me," he explained to Harrell, "because I'm a part of that age group and lifestyle") not only got him the job; it instantly turned Puffy into a music executive. Proving his worth out of the gate would set Puffy off as a music star. His first assignment: producing a mainstream hit for a debuting

Uptown artist. Father MC, more of an R&B-style party rapper than a hard-rock, languished on the label's back burner until Puffy came along. The newjack A&R, with an eye on the label's underutilized R&B artists, used Father MC's music as a platform to make hits as well as introduce new talent. For the rapper's gold-selling single "I'll Do 4 U," Puffy not only had newcomer Mary J. Blige (fresh from the projects of Yonkers) sing the chorus but prominently featured her in the song's video. He did the same for Jodeci, who sang the chorus on Father MC's other hit, "Treat Them Like They Want to Be Treated." Soon after, Puffy hit a cultural milestone with Jodeci, remixing their first single, "Come and Talk to Me," with the beat of EPMD's 1988 underground hit "You're a Customer," breaking ground for the R&B subgenre later to be dubbed "hip-hop soul." And with the accomplishments (and a budding attitude and confidence) to match, Puffy blossomed into his newest incarnation: Puff Daddy.

The name reached the rest of the country in infamy before it stood for innovation. A celebrity benefit basketball game/concert in December 1991 at City College, promoted by Puffy and Heavy D, was supposed to raise funds and awareness for an AIDS charity. But instead nine people were killed in a stampede of partygoers trying to forcibly enter the oversold event. Once the debris was cleared and the images of the dead being carried out of the gymnasium's entrance were etched into the country's memory, authorities (and the media) looked for someone to blame. And that someone became Puffy. *He* had oversold the venue. *He* didn't have proper security at the door. His dealings with the charity *he* was trying to raise money for were unclear. In the news, Puffy was the symbol of all things wrong with his generation: lack of foresight, greed, selfishness, a lack of concern for human life—the same ideas being played among black youth caught in the games of the streets. The tragedy devastated Puffy, making him question whether he wanted to live with such blood on his hands—but he didn't break. The horrible publicity should have permanently held him in the box labeled "pariah." It didn't. That kind of heavy burden should have put an end to his career. It didn't, either.

Escaping his depression and feelings of despair through his work, Puffy resurfaced the following year as a musical dynamo. He ushered Jodeci to a double-platinum album with *Forever My Lady*, sculpting this North Carolina quartet into a group that appealed to the hardcore sensibilities of hip-hoppers. But with Mary J. Blige, Puffy found an R&B act whose soul, voice, and hard-knock life (growing up fatherless and with low self-esteem in Yonkers) seamlessly knit the two genres into one. Her debut album, *What's the 411?*, was released in the summer of 1992 and, besides being a hit, garnered street airplay (from cars and apartment stereo speakers) usually reserved for hot rap albums. Blige's first single, "Real Love," while (vocally) appealing to a universal desire for true romance, received heavy "Jeep rotations" because it used a familiar hip-hop drum track from Audio Two's 1988 classic "Top Billin'." But it was her hardcore (yet vulnerable) exterior, unpolished soul vocals, and fierce attitude that turned her into the R&B hero of ghetto girls across the country. Singing of love lost, found, and stolen, Blige captured the emotions of urban females the same way male rap artists tapped the starved egos of young urban males. Moreover, like those of a much-lauded hardcore MC, Blige's music and lyrics felt as *real* as the asphalt. And for that reason Blige's disc went double platinum with ease. Just as the music world heralded the Yonkers-bred vocalist as a groundbreaker, crowning her "Queen of Hip-Hop Soul," Puffy was equally celebrated as the producer/A&R guy behind Blige's stardom. Soon afterward he began gracing the pages of magazines and newspapers, covered as if he were just as big a celebrity as his artist, touted as the boy wonder of a new R&B.

But Puffy had already begun his search for the next hardcore star of rap. While he may have established his reign over hip-hop soul, the genre created in his hometown was being ruled and shaped three thousand miles away by Dre and Snoop and the Death Row camp. Puffy was on the hunt for an East Coast equivalent, a New York MC who was talented and charismatic enough to sell thuggish hip-hop to the pop world on his own terms. Puffy was well past tired of Uptown's old-school crossover tactics of selling spit-polish street music. As the motto of his future label would state, he was in search of "The Next Generation of Bad Mothafuckas." And he found it when Matty C (Matty Capoluongo), an editor of *The Source* magazine, came to his office and played the demo tape of a fat, dark-skinned Brooklyn kid who would forever change Puffy's life.

Up until the time Biggie met with Puffy at Uptown to audition he, like Snoop Dogg, had been on an uneasy mission to shift the direction of his life through hip-hop. Born Christopher Wallace on May 21, 1972, he was the biological product not of New York's mythological under-world but of the city's international offer of the American Dream. His mother, Voletta Wallace, moved to New York in the late 1950s from Kingston, Jamaica, searching out America's promise of a better tomor-row. Though she didn't find the golden paradise she had imagined, she found advancement through a college education and a special bond with a gentleman caller.

George Letore, Christopher's father, was also Jamaican, but his move to the States was from London, where he'd lived several years. He was a welder and twenty years older than Voletta. George offered her what she thought was love and companionship and familiarity, easing the grind of living in New York City. Two years into the relationship he also gave her a family, fathering Christopher, though he couldn't truly offer her and Christopher a life together because he had another family back in London. Whereas Puffy's father was taken by the cruel streets, Christopher's father disappeared through desertion three months be-fore his son's third birthday.

The early life Christopher lived with his mother in Brooklyn's Bedford-Stuyvesant was relatively quiet and middle-class, despite the crime, hopelessness, and urban blight surrounding them. Aside from showering her only child with all the love a mother could give, Voletta provided him with a solid Catholic school education. And within their spacious apartment, she attempted to create an oasis for a preadoles-cent Christopher, providing him with gadgets aplenty (boom boxes, tapes of Run-D.M.C., any video game system he desired) to keep him occupied. Anything to keep him off the troublesome streets.

While the sidewalks outside his apartment on 226 St. James Place weren't rugged and filled with chaos, trouble for a kid Christopher's age sat just a few feet away at the corner: on Fulton Street. As Christopher entered his teens, the street—a long-standing rough spot of the area—had become an open-air crack market, a wasteland for black teens looking to enter the lucrative, fast-paced arena of the drug game. Vo-letta's only remedy for keeping her boy from the life, and off those cor-ners, was to forbid him from venturing too far from the house, especially down to Fulton. Still, teenagers don't just quickly outgrow their childhood bodies (by the time Christopher was thirteen he was nearly six feet tall) and adolescent games, but also the fear of their par-ents' wrath. And so a combination of curiosity, adolescent materialism, and the aching desire to free himself from an overprotective mother, one who refused to indulge him in his desire for expensive clothes, sent a fifteen-year-old Christopher to Fulton, where he began dealing crack, first as a lucrative, part-time gig—the elaborate scheme of a hidden double life. To his mother, he was the stay-at-home son at night, adhering to her rules when she arrived home from work. To his friends and schoolmates, though, he was "Big Chris" the hustler, peddling his wares and wearing the latest expensive brand-name clothes (which he initially hid from Voletta).

Christopher's advancement in age and drug sales ultimately brought disillusionment—with school, with honest work toward a future, with hiding his business venture from his mom. So by the time Big Chris turned nineteen the crack game was no longer his job but his full-time career. In fact, by the time he turned twenty in 1992, "it was estimated that as many as 150,000 people were employed in New York City's drug trade." The only legit future for Christopher lay in a hobby—rapping—that he practiced from time to time, battling MCs on Fulton, but didn't see much promise in. A Brooklyn MC hadn't ruled hip-hop since Big Daddy Kane reigned during rap's golden era. That is, until Kane's DJ Mister Cee heard a tape of Chris (who now went by the name Biggie Smalls) rhyming and recognized the possibility of another Brooklyn star.

With Cee's help Big's voice wound up in the hands of Matty C, whose Unsigned Hype column for *The Source* featured hip-hop unknowns who would go on to become major talents: Mobb Deep, DMX, Common. Biggie became the focus of one column and sparked the interest of an A&R rep. Puffy was looking for the next big thing, and he found it literally and figuratively after Matty played him the tape of Biggie and suggested Puffy call Cee to arrange a meeting. For Puffy, sitting down to talk with the MC was a formality—what he'd heard on the tape had already sealed the deal. "He sounded like no other human being I ever heard in my life," Puffy commented. Many in the world of hip-hop would feel the same way.

With their cinematic approach to hardcore rap, L.A.'s gangsta MCs opened the world's ears to black despair and self-destruction in the age of crack, setting a new standard for popular hip-hop music. In an effort to keep up, New York's premillennial approach to hardcore became as much about discussing the hell its ghettos turned into as it was about maintaining the ideals of supreme lyricism. "Life was kicking us in the ass as young teens in the city," explained Nas about this development. "We saw a lot . . . The world needed to hear it, and the beauty of it was to put it in street poetry." The cadre of East Coast gangsta MCs adopted L.A.'s storytelling techniques, offering vivid tableaux set to hip-hop music. Only instead of merely rapping about the crisis of drugs and violence within New York, their albums exposed it through personal, almost autobiographical narratives of MCs coming of age in a neighborhood-turned-deathtrap. Big Apple decay was shown through the eyes of crack-era poets. Nas, aside from his music, relayed this idea most poignantly on the CD cover for *Illmatic*: a childhood photo of himself sporting a nappy afro and a grim expression with the projects of Queensbridge showing through his face. The Wu also acknowledged the devolution on *Enter the Wu-Tang* when they sampled Gladys Knight singing "Can it be that it was all so simple then?" Twenty years prior, "The Message" forced the reality of New York City ghettos onto the pop landscape as hip-hop offered city youth an alternative to violence. Now, as graffiti writers were increasingly using their aerosol talents to paint R.I.P. murals memorializing the growing number of New York youth killed by street violence, that cadre of MCs was going to provide the narrative for a new generation born within the crack explosion and raised in its aftermath.

Of all the albums released from New York's street poetry movement challenging what seemed an impenetrable reign of Death Row Records, *Ready to Die* marked the breakthrough moment. The biggest reason was that *Ready to Die,* more than *Illmatic* or *Enter the Wu-Tang,* was crafted for Main Street marketability without risking its much-needed street credibility. "More than any other artist," music writer Jeff Mao noted when critiquing the album, "Big was able to balance the pessimism of a harsh worldview with a craftsmanship, writer's flair, and a personable quality that established him as an utterly compelling (and ultimately sympathetic) voice." As N.W.A had done for Compton with *Straight Outta Compton,* Big tapped the despair, hopelessness, and paranoia of his Brooklyn community and delivered it with humor, disarming charisma, and ingenious narrative. Within the five boroughs of New York City, hip-hop may have turned violent gangs into crews of creativity in the late 1970s and early '80s. But progressive style wars had been replaced by destructive wars over crack sales and territory by decade's end. Having been a part of that transformation, Big siphoned the desperation from his experience as drug-pusher-cum-MC-extraordinaire and turned his debut CD into a remarkable testament of urban blues.

Clearly Big (in his calculated rhyme delivery) and Puffy (while supervising production) had Dre's formula for making albums in mind when sculpting the cohesive drama of *Ready to Die*. But instead of witnessing the birth of street knowledge, the album's intro treated listeners to the sounds of a hustler's birth: first as a baby, born to the grooves of Curtis Mayfield's blaxploitation classic "Superfly." Then as a child of hip-hop, the sounds of domestic violence intermingling with the intro to "Rapper's Delight." Then as a teenage stickup kid committing a holdup in a subway car to the beat of "Top Billin'." And finally as a prison inmate about to be released to the rhythm of Snoop Dogg's "Tha Shiznit."

But from Big's intricate cadence, clever writing, and sharp, self-conscious storytelling, it was apparent he had gathered inspiration from hometown legends of rap's golden era, like the commanding, offhanded humor of Big Daddy Kane and the crafty, bleak criminal observations of Kool G Rap. "New York's legacy of brilliant lyricists," wrote music journalist Dream Hampton, "descended on Biggie as if he were a cultural apex. Their influences were immeasurable." In his pursuit of the national music market, Big established an identity apart from L.A. chart-toppers by staying entrenched in "an unmistakably New York state of mind," observed writer Dave Bry, as if he'd stepped out of a Chester Himes or a Donald Goines novel and into a hip-hop nation. Big's character lived closer to the edge than his West Coast brethren. In contrast to Cali's sunny, open spaces, he navigated a concrete jungle filled with traffic, buildings, people, and hair-trigger tempers. The beginning of *Ready to Die* observes the evolution of this ever-changing town. If "Nuthin' But a 'G' Thang" spoke from the postriot feeling of liberation within black Los Angeles, the song "Things Done Changed" announced to hip-hop America that the nihilism destroying Left Coast communities was also in the Big Apple, turning once relatively cool neighborhoods into bloody wastelands. "Remember back in the days," Big asked listeners, "when niggas had waves / Gazelle shades and corn braids / Pitchin' pennies, honeys had the high-top jellies / Shootin' skelly, motherfuckers was all friendly." For those unaware of how things had been altered, Big reported the sobering news with the line: "Turn your pages to 1993 / Niggas is gettin' smoked, G, believe me." Considered by writer Cheo Hodari Coker as the "most powerful depictions of modern-day life in the 'hood ever recorded," "Things Done Changed" served as a gruesome report on the bloodletting crack cocaine introduced to the neighborhood and the intergenerational schism it created between young and old. "Back in the days, our parents used to take care of us / Look at 'em now. They even fuckin' scared of us / Callin' the city for help because they can't maintain / Damn, shit done changed."

For the rest of the album, Big functioned as narrator, rattling off tales of street-minded pursuits conflated with social consciousness and a disarming funny bone, all written with a brilliant lyricism. Aside from the mandatory battle fare displaying his gifted wordplay—songs like "Unbelievable" and "The What," a duet with the Wu's Method Man—Big's exceptional writing talents came through in his storytelling. Far from glorifying the criminal life, Big seamlessly blended the intoxicating highs, the life-threatening lows, and the stinging guilt brought on by the hustler lifestyle. On the cut "Warning," Big is a drug kingpin who is informed via the phone by a friend, also played by Big, of a plot to murder him for his money. "Now they heard you blowin' up like nitro," his friend tells him. "And they wanna stick the knife through your windpipe slow." But the gruesome details of his underworld are also made palatable with touches of dark humor wrapped in cultural references. Like on the stickup-kid adventures of "Gimme the Loot," where Big, again playing dual roles (this time as holdup artist and young partner), uses a bit of black history hyperbole to explain his habit of robbing. "I've been robbin' motherfuckers since the slave ship," he raps, "with the same clip and the same four-five / Two point-blank, a motherfucker sure to die."

The over-the-top violence and criminality of Big's character also shared airtime with an insightful dose of guilt-ridden introspection. The title track, besides explaining the ideals driving Big to hustle, revealed the tremendous self-loathing involved in the choice. "Fuck the world," he yells on the song. "Fuck my moms and my girl / My life is played-out like a Jheri curl, I'm ready to die." Or, more poignantly, on "Suicidal Thoughts," Big, overwhelmed with shame and self-pity ("I'm a piece of shit, it ain't hard to fuckin' tell"), having hurt family and friends because of his ill behavior, contemplates killing himself. "I swear to God," he raps, "I want to just slit my wrist and end this bullshit / Throw the Magnum to my head, threaten to pull shit / And squeeze until the bed's completely red / I'm glad I'm dead, a worthless fuckin' Buddha head."

Big equally discussed the fabulous and stressful side of his crack-running days on the song "Everyday Struggle." He may have made smart moves for quick cash, regardless of how his mother felt ("She was forced to kick me out, no doubt / Then I figured out things went for twenty down south"), but the end result was inevitably destructive. "I'm seeing body after body," he lamented. "And our Mayor Giuliani / Ain't trying to see no black man turn into John Gotti." But as L.A. gangsta rappers touted their murderous struggle for power as a form of black empowerment, Big, as supreme urban hustler, interpreted the crack game—just another form of capitalism—as a 'hood-level way of fighting for black empowerment. "I remember I was just like you," he rapped, relating to those scrambling on street corners. "Smoking blunts with my crew / Flippin' oldies '62s / 'Cause G.E.D. wasn't B.I.G., I got P-A-I-D / That's why my mom hates me." It was a black power twist—an extreme flip—on the black underworld undoubtedly influenced by Tupac. (The two had become close friends in 1993, shortly after Big's first song, "Party and Bullshit," from the soundtrack for the movie *Who's the Man?* was released.) But while messages of pride, national-ism, and revolution were fine, the Brooklyn MC's idea of power and how to obtain it was shaped by his former career as a street entrepre-neur. So he flipped the 1980s anticrack message—"crack is wack"—on its ear and began transforming the crack dealer from community pariah to hip-hop's latest folk-hero archetype.

But a song honoring hip-hop music as savior was what began pushing *Ready to Die* to double-platinum sales. Although the R&B mellowness of "Juicy" was added to soften the album's "tougher core," its lyrics were, no doubt, a reflective celebration of rap's growth both as an industry and as hope restored for a guy like Biggie. Like so many of his generation, he had made the wrong decision. But he, like a select few, was given a second chance at life and prosperity. Over a melodious loop of Mtume's 1983 hit "Juicy Fruit," Big rapped: "You never thought that hip-hop would take it this far / Now I'm in the limelight, 'cause I rhyme tight / Time to get paid, blow up like the World Trade / Born sinner, the opposite of a winner / Remember when I used to eat sardines for dinner." In building his rags-to-riches image, though, Big wasn't beyond exaggerating his humble upbringing, referring to the spacious apartment he shared with his mother as "a one-room shack." Rap may have started with MCs bragging about fictitious wealth, but now those riches, for an MC, were attainable outside the drug game. The genius behind Biggie's career was the conflation of the two: laundering the flashy lifestyle and image of the big-time drug dealer through the marketing avenues of the rap game.

This burgeoning notion was interpreted best through music video. There were hints of this vision in the clip for "Juicy," which followed Biggie from his days of slingin' rocks on Fulton to lounging with family and friends, poolside, in a mansion, celebrating his newfound fame and fortune. Pioneering video jock Ralph McDaniels would later comment on the video: "There was an instant buzz from the hustlers, drug dealers, and ghetto girls that the video captured their dreams. He gave hope to many viewers with the story and images." This merger of kingpin lifestyle, hip-hop conceit, and megapop promotion materialized, absolutely, upon the release of the video for "Big Poppa." Shot by video director Hype Williams, the clip was an innovative interpretation of Big's Mack-style rhyme about his sporting life. The scenario, at face value, was a mere club scene. But with Williams's highly stylized direction—his brilliant use of colors and tracking shots—along with Puffy's fashion influence, insisting Big and cast be clothed in the latest high-end brands, the video expanded from simply promoting an artist to marketing a new hip-hop lifestyle: ghetto fabulous. Gone was the traditional grimy wardrobe of ruffian hip-hop—hooded sweatshirt, sneakers, work boots, and oversized baggy jeans—replaced by designer suits, sweaters, slacks, and dress shoes. Instead of seeing folks struggling in the streets, viewers watched high-rolling hip-hop youth basking in the good life: dancing, drinking champagne, wooing beautiful ladies. Undoubtedly influenced by the way "Nuthin' But a 'G' Thang" reshaped America's perception of post-rebellion Los Angeles, Puffy wanted to mold Big and his New York City backdrop into the signpost for a fresh black urban culture of sophistication, opulence, and flamboyance. G-funk's impact could also be heard in the production for "Big Poppa," with its sample of the Isley Brothers' "Between the Sheets," filled with a smoothed-out Moog sound. But the song's video surpassed Dre's in technique and production, placing the clip for "Big Poppa" on par with highly stylized rock videos in heavy rotation on MTV. (Indeed, as Snoop, Tupac, and now Biggie enjoyed regular video airplay outside of hip-hop-specific shows like *Yo! MTV Raps*, hardcore rap was, without question, America's new rock 'n' roll.) G-funk rewrote the rules on how black anger and rebellion sounded for American households, making it palatable through danceable melodies. Ghetto fabulousness went for the crossover by dressing that discontent in designer name brands and expensive toys, and rationalized it with the desperation of a young black narcotics pusher, driven to the outer fringes of the American Dream by inequality.

But ghetto fab as a cultural construct made famous by a New York City rap artist also conveyed a celebratory attitude about the social and corporate growth of hip-hop. And the national constituency Big and Puffy came to represent, as children of the movement, had much to cheer. By the mid-1990s, hip-hop's popularity among blacks and non-blacks, urban and suburban (even rural), not only realigned America's racial/ethnic divide (hardcore rap bringing the country's youth and its mainstream under the banner of "urban"); it reshaped the corporate landscape, adding its own national hip-hop economy. The evidence was everywhere.

By becoming a regular presence on the pop charts and music video channels, rap had begun altering the definition of pop radio. Hiring mix show DJs, once relegated to the periphery of mainstream airwaves, stations like San Francisco's KMEL and New York's WQHT (known as Hot 97) began incorporating a predominately rap playlist, eventually giving rise to what would be known as hip-hop radio. Hip-hop's fashion sense also spawned an industry as black-owned hip-hop-inspired clothing lines like Cross Colours, which grossed over $89 million in 1992, and Karl Kani, which grossed over $97 million in 1993, spurred a new generation of fashion moguls (black and nonblack) like Marc Ecko and the black-power-tinged FUBU (For Us By Us) to start lucrative clothing lines. The trend also inspired hip-hop stars to start their own clothing lines. The Wu-Tang would be the first, with their Wu Wear line in 1995. Even the arena of print media received a jolt of urban expansion as the success of hip-hop-centered publications such as *The Source* and *Vibe* began eating at the same revenue stream as mainstream publications. These magazines also provided a valuable platform for journalists and writers of color (this writer included) who might have found it difficult breaking into predominantly white publications. As hip-hop culture settled into economic and social respectability (doing so on its own terms), its do-for-self, keep-it-real determinism steadily became the mantra of the young black America it was providing opportunities for. Hip-hop inspired a number of folks on their way to entering the country's political, economic, and cultural playing fields.

For instance, hip-hop's activist spirit and the issues its music tackled encouraged a new generation of political figures to enter the mainstream of city, state, and national politics. Traces of the shift could be felt in 1994 as a twenty-four-year-old Ras Baraka, then the head of the Panther-influenced organization Black Nia F.O.R.C.E. (Freedom Organization for Racial and Cultural Enlightenment), became the youngest candidate running in the mayoral election of Newark, New Jersey. His community-oriented "People's Platform," while inspired by Malcolm X, was undoubtedly a product of hip-hop's nationalist era. Although he lost to the incumbent, Sharpe James, Baraka's youthful gumption signaled his generation's determination to run for political office and win, as evidenced by thirty-one-year-old Detroit mayor Kwame Kilpatrick (dubbed the "hip-hop mayor" after his win in 2001) and thirty-eight-year-old Cory Booker, who in 2006 won Newark's mayoral seat. This shift would also become evident in national politics with twenty-six-year-old Harold Ford, Jr., becoming a Tennessee congressman—the youngest Congress member—in 1996, and Florida's Kendrick Meek's election to Congress in 2002.

But the seeds for America, especially black America, completely going the way of hip-hop's ghetto fabulous lay in a legislative victory by President Bill Clinton the year before *Ready to Die* was released. After the recession of 1991 helped Clinton defeat George Bush ("It's the economy, stupid" was the slogan of Clinton supporters), the newly elected president had to deliver a federal remedy for America's pocketbook. And in August 1993, without a single Republican vote, Congress passed the Omnibus Budget Reconciliation Act. Through increasing taxes on the wealthiest and decreasing them for low-income families, putting restraints on federal spending, and mandating a balanced budget over the next few years, the act, in part, set the U.S. economy on a course of historic growth. The financial windfall from this boom would significantly characterize African-American advancement during the latter half of the 1990s.

Until the arrival of such blessed fortunes (or at least the perception of them), rap music, with the unstoppable rise of Death Row and Bad Boy Records, was the watershed symbol of social and economic progress—or lack thereof, depending on which side of the "bitch, nigga, violence" gangsta rap debate you chose to stand on. Nevertheless, no matter how the media or Congress wanted to argue the pros and cons of hardcore rap, the heart of their arguments ultimately acknowledged the inevitable: that hip-hop, to borrow a phrase from rap's dance hall reggae cousin, was "runnin' tings." And two years after Dre, Snoop, and Death Row had commandeered the airwaves and video waves and cultural runways for gangsta chic hip-hop, their rule was being upset by the ascendance of Biggie, Puffy, and the redefined cool of Bad Boy Records. By polishing the crude, rough, and lyrically complicated edges of New York street poetry, the Bad Boy crew swayed America's taste, once again, back toward the East. Aside from Biggie's immediate record sales, the results were noticeable over the next couple of years as, increasingly, New York and East Coast artists rang up chart hits as well as gold and platinum sales: Queensbridge's Mobb Deep, rapping their gruesome thug noir, pushed a half a million units of their 1995 disc, *The Infamous*, while solo projects from Wu members Raekwon (1995's *Only Built 4 Cuban Linx*) and Method Man (1994's *Tical*) saw quick gold and platinum status, respectively. New Jersey–based alterna-rap trio the Fugees became a global phenomenon in 1996 with their six-times-platinum sophomore disc, *The Score*. Even the critically acclaimed but underappreciated Nas, obviously moved by Bad Boy's blueprint of R&B-looped thuggery and colorful, flashy Hype Williams–produced videos, saw double-platinum sales for his second album, 1996's *It Was Written*. Judging from the fine cars and fly clothes he sported in the videos promoting the album, especially the one for "If I Ruled the World," Nas was clear proof that the ideals of ghetto fabulous were catching hold. But its future and fulfillment, unbeknownst to hip-hop nation, would rest with another Brooklyn MC, Jay-Z, who, while being featured on Biggie's second and (unfortunately) final album, would see a gold plaque (and the buzz of hip-hop's underground) for the sales of his first CD, *Reasonable Doubt*.

The tremendous irony of this regional shift was that while it meant expansion and development for rap music, it also marked its most toxic period. First between friends (Tupac and Biggie). Then between labels (Death Row and Bad Boy). Then between coasts. And finally, in the blurring of the line between violence committed on records and the murderous results that can manifest themselves in real life. Shortly after Tupac was killed, Biggie began work on his second LP. The atmosphere in which he created *Life After Death* was similar to the one in which Tupac had created *Me Against the World*, one of legal troubles and constant conflict and adversity. More so than in his former life as a crack hustler, Biggie was caught up in trouble with the law: an aggravated assault and robbery charge in 1995 after the limo driver for a concert promoter accused Big of beating and robbing him when the promoter refused to pay Biggie the other half of his performance fee. Another assault charge followed the next year for breaking the windows of a New York City cab with a baseball bat, trying to get at the two fans inside who'd insulted him. Another bust for smoking weed in downtown Brooklyn. Then another arrest for disorderly conduct in Teaneck, New Jersey, after police came to Biggie's house about a parking violation, smelled weed burning, returned with a search warrant, and found marijuana, guns, and ammunition. But, most notably, there was his contentious relationship with Tupac, a situation that wouldn't rest even after Tupac's death or the incarceration of Suge Knight. Making matters worse were the far-fetched rumors, no doubt fed in part by Tupac's infamous *Vibe* interview (implicating Big in the Quad shooting), that he'd been responsible for Pac's murder. Another factor fueling such a belief was the resentment many Tupac fans, mostly on the West Coast, felt because their beloved soldier lay in a grave while his perceived adversary still lived and basked in national acclaim. This toxic sentiment was at its most public when Biggie was a presenter at the eleventh annual Soul Train Awards. His appearance onstage to present R&B singer Toni Braxton with an award was met with a venomous round of boos from the "cheap seats" in the balcony where the fans sat.

It was during such external duress as well as being enveloped in an overwhelming sense of accomplishment (after all, Big didn't have to hustle on corners anymore) that *Life After Death* was conceived and molded. While the album still possessed a tough center, its hardened perspective had to come from one who'd matured with fame and fortune but could still communicate the sentiment of the streets. "When I was writing stuff like 'Fuck the world, fuck my moms and my girl,'" Big explained in an interview, "there was nothing but anger coming out about everything: about having to go out and sell crack, to hustle for a living . . . People know Biggie ain't on the corner selling drugs no more . . . I got other problems now." In fact, the harrowing bubble of celebrity, with its notions of limited trust, fleeting power, and a constant need to be on the defensive, could be easily translated through the lyrical (and literal) underworld of gangsta rap. And the convergence of the two worlds, once again, revisited the world of hip-hop in the tragic loss of yet another leading voice. Six months after Tupac was shot and killed in Las Vegas, rap music suffered the murder of Biggie Smalls on March 9, 1997, shot in Los Angeles following an afterparty for the Soul Train Awards (a gathering that also doubled as the unofficial release party for *Life After Death*). Eerily similar to Tupac's, Biggie's death was also the result of a drive-by shooting, the chain of events in the murders almost identical, with a mysterious car pulling alongside the rappers' vehicles and ending their lives in a hail of bullets.

The commercial impact of *Life After Death* was immediate, selling 690,000 in its first week and eventually going ten times platinum. Although grief may have pushed the album's profile and initial sales, it was the hip-pop craftsmanship that helped its impact grow. Whereas *Ready to Die* was a youthful lament on the woe-filled money chase of the crack game, *Life After Death*—coincidentally a double album like Pac's last disc—was an exploration of "betrayal, notoriety, excess, and greed" from the perspective of a Mafia-style MC don. Rhymes about scrambling on Brooklyn corners were replaced with the macabre bluntness of a drug boss enjoying wealth while at the same time defending himself against jealous enemies. The criminal universe Biggie wrote about had become a metaphor for the criminal-driven celebrity within hardcore rap. Biggie not only battled with the hostility coming from out west; he also dealt with lyrical and verbal attacks from MCs on his own coast (such as Wu-Tang's Raekwon and Ghostface Killah, who, on Rae's 1995 solo disc, *Only Built 4 Cuban Linx*, accused Big of biting off—that is, copying—Nas). *Life After Death*, as with any sophomore offering from a pop music superstar, was Biggie's fight to stay on top.

"Pardon my French," he rapped on the cut "What's Beef?," indirectly responding to criticism, in part, from Ghostface. "But, ahh, sometimes I get kind of peeved at these weak MCs (don't stop) / With the supreme-baller like, lyrics I call 'em like I see 'em, G / Y'all niggas sound like me (yeah)." While there was no blatant mention of Tupac, many interpreted the track "Long Kiss Goodnight" as Big's response to Pac's blatant disrespect. Some even thought, after hearing lines like "Now you rest eternally sleepy / You burn when you creep me / Rest where the worms and the weak be," that Big was publicly gloating over Pac's death.

Aside from responses to real adversaries, Big further explored ambition and treachery through extending the ingenious storytelling and narratives he'd displayed in "Warning," setting the bulk of his battles in Mob-type scenarios, with him defending his life and affluence or taking someone else's—those moments when his drug-hustling archetype could play out his struggles most heroically. No matter if he was a kingpin avenging the murder of his partner-in-crime on "Somebody's Gotta Die" or a ruthless henchman robbing a dealer for a huge score on "Niggas Bleed" or "Playa Hater," Big's cold-blooded quest for cash and respect was underscored by a perception of himself as a victim. "You know, we *need* this money," he informed his victim on "Playa Hater." But his character could also offer guidance and inspiration (though highly misguided) to those slum entrepreneurs seeking their fortune by any means necessary. On the darkly humorous cut "Ten Crack Commandments," Big doled out keen advice on how to win in the crack industry. "I been in this game for years," he began his yarn of wisdom. "It made me an animal / It's rules to this shit, I wrote me a manual / A step-by-step booklet for you to get / Your game on track not your wig pushed back." The fact that the song samples P.E.'s "Shut Em Down," with Chuck D defiantly counting down the song's intro, further twisted the concept of black empowerment to fit the commercial needs of gangstafied rap music. Whether anyone thought it progressive or not (an offended Chuck D sued for the track's unauthorized use of his music and eventually settled out of court), Big's hit song was a clear statement that hardcore rappers, from West to East, were the voice of the corners, places they weren't necessarily trying to change (like the old guard) but rather to articulate, no matter how destructive or unprogressive, the point of view of folks who hung out there. "To my hustlin' niggas," he says, dedicating his rhyme to the street dealers. "Niggas on the corner, I ain't forget you . . . My triple-beam niggas."

On *Life After Death*, Big more than anything advanced the image of the black inner-city baller. In the same way he and Puffy sold *Ready to Die*, pushing its popularity with R&B-backed songs about desperation mixed with 'hood opulence, *Life After Death* packaged its condensed salute to being rich and famous in the danceable licks of rhythm and blues. He and Jay-Z honored their passion for the almighty dollar with "I Love the Dough," sampling Angela Winbush's 1981 classic "I Love You More." While on "Mo Money Mo Problems," Big, Puffy, and Bad Boy newcomer Mase lyrically flaunted their jewels, cars, and yachts over the tune of Diana Ross's 1980 disco smash "I'm Coming Out." The video for "Mo Money," also directed by Hype Williams, further elevated the visual interpretation of ghetto fab, increasing its appeal with candy-colored sets and backdrops and artists dressed in shiny, metallic suits. Hardcore rap was definitely headed for—to borrow a phrase from the diamond-obsessed rappers to follow in Big's footsteps—an "ice age." The track indicating this evolution in hip-hop's video marketing was the album's single "Hypnotize." The year before, Tupac's video for "California Love," a *Mad Max*–themed clip with Pac, Snoop, and Dre as doomsday road warriors wreaking havoc across a desert, pushed rap's visual envelope. Within a similar action movie vein, video director Paul Hunter edged his vision for "Hypnotize" toward an even larger, unheard-of production. At a mammoth cost of $700,000 (one of the biggest budgets for a rap video at the time), the song's video resembled a blockbuster mini adventure movie. As Big, accompanied by Puffy, boasted about refining the taste of ghetto denizens nationwide ("I put hoes in N.Y. on to DKNY / Miami, D.C. prefer Versace"), he was being pursued by mysterious bad men. Big's speedboat is chased by black helicopters, his luxury car is chased by a fleet of cars with tinted windows. Dodging their foes, Big and Puff escape to a hideout filled with beautiful dancing women. More than telling a James Bond–type story, the video blatantly announced that hip-hop music, via Biggie and Puffy, was playing in the same league as other hugely popular (read: white) genres.

What made *Life After Death* such a groundbreaking LP was that, like *The Chronic*, it unrepentantly aimed for maximum appeal, flawlessly matching hip-hop's troubled worldview with a polished urban pop sound. In fact, it was later written that "sonically [*Life After Death*] was less a 'hip-hop' album in the classical sense than an urban pop album." That's because, on the one hand, Puffy and his production collective, known as the Hitmen, refined the disc's rhythms—even ones from outside producers—altering them so they stayed within a cohesive, malleable sound; more than *Ready to Die*, this project was crafted to appeal to the tastes of as many markets as possible. On the other, Big, as a master of rhyme styles, was able to switch his cadence to complement any track blatantly aimed at a particular region. The example cited most often is "Notorious Thugs," Big's collaboration with the Cleveland foursome, Bone Thugs-N-Harmony, where Big rocks their staccato syllabic style as well as they do. The song most hauntingly and prophetically referenced by journalists and critics is "Going Back to Cali." Produced by Easy Mo Bee, the track, with its loop of Zapp's 1980 funk hit "More Bounce to the Ounce" (commonly used by West Coast gangsta MCs), was a rhythmic peace offering by Mo Bee to quell hip-hop's coastal conflict. "I wanted L.A.'s attention," Mo Bee said in an interview with *XXL* magazine. "That was always the L.A. anthem . . . I felt that maybe through music or a beat, anything that gets everybody in harmony." Emphatically, the tune fit within the semiautobiographical narrative of *Life After Death* as Big wanted to clarify his feelings about that region and its people. "Smoke some nice sess in the West," he playfully commented. "Y'all niggas is a mess / Thinkin' I'm gonna stop givin' L.A. props / All I got is beef with those that violate me / I annihilate thee / Case closed / Suitcase filled with clothes." Regrettably, the actual trip Big took to Cali—partly to promote *Life After Death* and partly to make amends with the West—didn't end as happily as the one he'd taken on his album. As if Biggie were destined to fulfill some morbid prophecy of hip-hop-age martyrdom with Tupac (a pseudo Martin and Malcolm), his life was taken as he, his music, and his message were at a crossroads. No doubt, commercial rap music came to a crossroads following his murder—so soon after folks were coming to terms with Pac's murder. All signs pointed to the obvious: that hardcore rap, at the threshold of its commercial apex, had become no different from the deadly streets it proudly represented, that, as Ras Baraka stated in a 1997 address titled "Black Youth Black Art Black Faces": "We have carved out a place where we have become comfortable with death and self-destruction." Not that this was rap's first experience with a rap star getting murdered (BDP Posse's DJ Scott La Rock was shot and killed in 1987), but never before had the music seemed so synonymous with the gruesome images and dangerous statistics of black urban communities. Aside from news footage of Tupac's and Biggie's bullet-riddled cars, other images communicated this sobering reality. The most obvious was coverage of the funeral procession transporting Biggie's body back to Brooklyn for one last goodbye to his old neighborhood, first down St. James and then on to Fulton Street, where hundreds of people lined the sidewalks to send off another brotha who'd left way too soon. The atmosphere surrounding rap music had become a lot like the sad, frustrated, and darkened mood on Fulton that cold March day. But events that followed the procession immediately afterward also became a metaphor for hip-hop's days in the latter half of the twentieth century.

Just as quickly as Biggie's hearse arrived, it passed through and was gone, leaving an overwhelming gloom that overtook the throngs of fans lining the street, weighing down the air heavy with sadness . . . until a Bad Boy anthem, in this case Big's "Hypnotize," unexpectedly erupted from someone's speakers, instantly lifting the crowd's mournful load and sending them into a state of raucous jubilation. Shouts of celebration went into the air as many a mourner danced—on the sidewalks and in the street. Some danced on Dumpsters; some, who assembled near the speakers, danced on top of cars. Not only was the music a way of rejoicing over the incredible talents of a hometown hero; it was a blaring affirmation of one's own existence—through the expression of that hero—in a world that constantly wants to render you invisible or at least silent. In that instance, the metaphorical oppression came in the form of New York City police officers dressed in full riot gear, moving in to break up the disruptive crowd boogying atop the car roofs and Dumpsters, macing some and arresting several. Only they couldn't, as one writer noted, totally stop the joy or that music still blaring in the background and growing louder as folks questioned and resisted the police who met them with a repressive force as old as America itself.

A few months later, as a hip-hop nation once again healed, Puff Daddy, Bad Boy's last hope, released his own solo album, *No Way Out*. Part Biggie tribute, part affirmation of Puff's unstoppability (having, once again, overcome a tragedy involving his business ambitions), the album, which would eventually go seven times platinum, brilliantly bridged the gap between Big's demise and the explosion of ghetto fabulousness by decade's end. While Puff wasn't impressive as an MC ("his voice is often slow and choppy," commented Touré in a *Village Voice* review), he had a gift for gauging the nation's dance floor and giving the people what they wanted. And what they wanted, in light of their loss, was to dance and to be happy and, like their rap stars, to be rich and in control. And so Puffy led that parade—appropriately with the anthem "It's All About the Benjamins." Making people dance to forget their troubles, he brought the worlds of rich and poor together, creating the illusion that, at least in rap music videos and in magazines, pennies (or, in this case, dollars) were indeed falling from heaven.

TEN

The Ice Age
Jay-Z

If the joyous equivalent of Christmas had ever come to hip-hop and its flourishing economy, it was in the year 1998, when everything about the music, the culture, and its industry—components sitting just below the radar, confounding corporate marketing paradigms and conservative ideals of the status quo—officially *became* the mainstream, when the Recording Industry Association of America stated hands down, "Rap music was the biggest story of the year in the music industry."

And the people associated with the various aspects of hip-hop music—fashion, film, TV, publishing, and so on—were suddenly recognized and praised as the new kids in America's capitalist playground with the most—if not the biggest—marbles. Especially at the offices of *The Source*, where I worked as an editor in September 1998. Moving 475,000 copies every month, this "magazine of hip-hop music, culture and politics," as it calls itself, began receiving recognition for having the highest newsstand circulation of any U.S. magazine on the market. Its main competitor, *Vibe*, whose rate base had swelled to 600,000 in just five years, had become "the fastest growing magazine ever." If anything else proved that, by all accounts, hip-hop ruled, it was the October 17, 1998, issue of *Billboard* that arrived at my office. The magazine's cover made no grand announcement, but its Top 200 chart clearly spoke the watershed moment. Not only were four of the six new albums in the Top 10 rap LPs, but those four discs simultaneously sat at the top of the chart. Along with the solo project of ex-Fugees member Lauryn Hill, *The Miseducation of Lauryn Hill*, which had been in the Top 5 for six weeks and had gone double platinum, there were three new hip-hop albums: *The Love Movement* by A Tribe Called Quest; *Aquemini* by Atlanta duo OutKast; and *Vol. 2 . . . Hard Knock Life* by Jay-Z. Of the new entries, none seemed to embody rap's momentous legitimacy as well as Jay-Z's album, which held the top slot.

For five weeks his album stayed at number one, gaining the bulk of its thrust from the title track, "Hard Knock Life (Ghetto Anthem)," a catchy but skillful rhyme affirming the "get paid by any means necessary" ethos of the 'hood. But where other MCs used the ethereal melodies of R&B to move their urban blues up the pop charts, Jay, with the aid of producer Mark "The 45 King" James, sampled a scrappy snippet from the musical *Annie* over a towering rhythm. What better way to capture the universal social struggles of black, white, and everybody than to enlist America's classic tale of a kid's struggle against tyranny, finding wealth and acceptance in the process? Not many epitomize the rise of America's street poetry from sidewalk bragging to urban legend to becoming the darling of American society quite like Jay-Z. His is the story of hip-hop's explosion—its acceptance into the halls of American high society—at the dawn of the new millennium.

While the ever-growing cliché of hardcore MCs finding solace in rap from the unforgiving stakes of the drug biz became hip-hop's latest version of the American Dream, Jay-Z's story inverted the myth. The narrative of Jay-Z's ascendance had as much to do with the cruel lessons he'd learned in the music business as it did with the narcotics game that provided an outlet (and a ghetto fortune) for his frustration and disillusionment with it. Born in Brooklyn—just across the bridge from the mecca of the hip-hop industry—and growing up in the Marcy projects, Jay (born Shawn Carter on December 4, 1969) had teenage dreams of becoming a rap superstar, and had the stylistic chops to confirm it. After all, the proof of attaining such a goal boomed all around him—from the street spirituality of Rakim to the pop universality of Jazzy Jeff and the Fresh Prince. His chance, or so he thought, might have resided in rapper and fellow Marcy resident Jaz-O, who brought a then-nineteen-year-old Jay-Z on as hype man and de facto rhyme partner after signing with EMI. But then Jay learned of the career-damaging conflicts between the aspirations of a project-roughened MC and a hit-driven record company. Instead of making his public debut on a certifiable street jam, Jay appeared on Jaz's 1989 single "Hawaiian Sophie," EMI's attempt at marketing Jaz as the next Fresh Prince. Needless to say, it didn't work out.

Witnessing the deterioration of his benefactor's deal, the underhanded manipulation of music companies, and the fact that his industry connection couldn't land him his own deal, Jay dropped out of rap to focus on elevating his drug-dealing exploits. From mere street peddling, something he'd done since high school, Jay-Z became a part of the lucrative business of cocaine distribution, joining the legion of New York dealers moving product down south. But, as with all tales of the promising-MC-gone-bad, the voice of reason and belief directed the desperate artist back to his true calling. For Jay that was DJ Clark Kent, an A&R man at Atlantic Records who promised to secure Jay-Z a deal (if not with Atlantic, then somewhere else). But, as the famous DJ found out, there was a gap in this budding business of hip-pop between Jay-Z's tremendous talents (a dizzying meld of meter and hustler narrative) and the labels' desire to buy into them. New York may have been back on top, but its verbal dexterity (of which Jay had an abundance) was still a hard sell. With no offers (and no promises of one) Kent introduced Jay to Damon Dash, the manager for the rap group Original Flavor. But even Dash would soon find out that selling Jay-Z's vision to record companies was as difficult as hustling kryptonite on Planet Krypton. So the typical manager/artist relationship was reconfigured to that of coconspirators and business partners in 1995, when Jay, Dash, and Dash's friend Kareem "Biggs" Burke decided, in response to the industry's refusal to accept Jay-Z, to form their own label, Roc-A-Fella Records, and sell Jay-Z themselves.

They used their own money—to make videos, to press up vinyl and CDs, to promote the image of Jay-Z and his business partners as the flashy hustlers of the industry. Without major financing from a big label (Priority Records, which agreed to handle manufacturing, refused to put any money behind marketing and promotion), they produced videos of MTV quality, showcasing Jay-Z on a boat in the Caribbean, profiling in luxury cars, reenacting tales of major drug scores. For his hip-hop persona, Jay chose the nonchalant kingpin who possessed a poetic precision and a smirk that acknowledged the question coming off the tongues of the curious: Where in the hell did they get the money to do all of this? Part of the answer might have been suggested on Jay's 1996 single "Dead Presidents II" as he playfully bragged: "I dabbled in crazy weight / Without rap I was crazy straight / Partner, I'm still spending money from '88." For Jay, there were no redemptive messages of hip-hop as savior or verses of a criminal pushed to the edge, just the unscrupulous drive of a young black player circumventing the square life to stay rich and in luxury, parlaying the scenes from one lucrative and illegal game to position oneself as an independent player in the legal (but just as cutthroat) corporate game of hip-hop music. Jay ultimately displayed his winning hand in 1996 with the gold-selling cut "Ain't No Nigga," the B-side to "Dead Presidents." This duet with female newcomer Foxy Brown, with its chorus taken from the Four Tops' 1973 "Ain't No Woman (Like the One I Got)," was a back-and-forth rhyme of ghetto fab banter ("You get the keys to the Lexus, with no driver," says Jay) between a street hustler and his main squeeze. Winding up on the soundtrack for the comedy *The Nutty Professor*, the song not only became a hit but turned Jay-Z, whose swagger was the rap music version of a Rat Packer, into a national figure. The moment was set for the launch of his own epic vision, interpreting the struggles of inner-city black America.

Jay's first disc, 1996's *Reasonable Doubt*, debuted just a week after the release of "Ain't No Nigga." To the undiscerning ear, Jay's highly stylized rhymes detailing the life of a narcotics king—with the utmost reverence for all the luxuries accompanying it (cars, women, jewelry)—made him just another purveyor of ghetto fabulousness. And he was. No doubt, the doors opened by the Notorious B.I.G., Nas, and the Wu-Tang Clan provided commercial and aesthetic space for his message, an undeniable piece of work that went gold in three months. His duet with Big on "Brooklyn's Finest" is seen by many as Big passing his ghetto fab torch to the Brooklyn newcomer. But with his predecessors occupying the upper stratosphere of popular music, Jay-Z filled hip-hop's ever-present need for a grassroots hero, one with the hunger of escaping poverty still fresh in his lyrics. "At my arraignment," he vowed on "Can't Knock the Hustle," "screamin': All us blacks got is sports and entertainment / Until we even, [I'm] thievin' / As long as I'm breathin' / Can't knock the way a nigga's eatin' / Fuck you, even." Compared to Biggie's wild crack-dealing/stickup desperado on *Ready to Die*, Jay-Z was the focused, calculating Big Willie, more Michael Corleone (or even Priest in *Super Fly*) than a Michael Myers of the underworld. In fact, like that of the protagonists of *The Godfather* and *Super Fly*, Jay-Z's motivation for his criminally enterprising ways was disillusionment with the American economic system, with the axiom that the road to wealth is hard, legal labor. "Nine to five is how you survive," Jay-Z rhymed, recounting the unfortunate destruction of a friendship on "D'evils." "I ain't trying to survive / I'm tryin' to live it to the limit and love it a lot / Life ills poison my body / I used to say, 'Fuck mic skills,' I never prayed to God, I prayed to Gotti." Though, like the tale of the slick mobster, whether fiction or fact, the ideals Jay-Z pushed on *Reasonable Doubt*—gutsy entrepreneurship (the song "Can't Knock the Hustle"), extravagant living ("Feelin' It"), protecting one's interest ("Friend or Foe"), and learning to live with remorse ("Regrets")— were, ironically, steeped in the American Dream of freedom and independence. And, through rhymes laced with sharp-witted narratives, brain-tickling cross-references, and acute introspection (all delivered with icy assuredness), Jay hit upon the capitalist desires and dreams (the "Americanist," so to speak) of young black America, a sentiment that shouted, "U.S.A.!" as loudly as any patriotic rally.

The same could also be said for Jay's sophomore album, *In My Lifetime, Vol. 1*. Similar to Biggie's *Life After Death*, it spoke from the vantage point of an embattled don grappling with the hardships of his once-unfathomable success. Once again criminal exploits are the metaphor for the greed and lack of trustworthiness within the business of rap. And the production, like that on *Life After Death*, is a refined mix of hardy hip-hop rhythms and R&B danceability. Only instead of having to deal just with rumors or industry beefs or fans questioning his street authenticity ("A lot of speculation on the monies I've made," he acknowledged on "A Million and One Questions/Rhyme No More"), Jay crafted his second LP under the black hole left by Biggie's death. *In My Lifetime* was released eight months after Big's murder. And although it marked a new beginning for Roc-A-Fella (which signed to a partnership with Def Jam), the album showcased a Jay-Z saddened by both a friend's departure and the pressure to fill his shoes as the "king of New York." "What the deal, playboy, just rest your soul," he says to a fallen Biggie on "The City Is Mine," which sampled Glenn Frey's 1985 "You Belong to the City." "I be holdin' it down, yo, still love the dough . . . Don't worry about Brooklyn, I'll continue to flame / Therefore a world with amnesia won't forget your name." While Jay's commitment to Biggie's legacy may have inspired his usual fare of exceptional hardcore rhymes with a baller's flair, following the marketing blueprint of Big's benefactor Puffy could have proven career suicide, particularly the video for the R&B-bopped single "(Always Be My)

Sunshine." Shot by Hype Williams in his signature fish-eye lens, the clip shows Jay-Z dressed in a colorful suit, turning in a very "Puffy-esque performance": dancing in front of flashy, brilliantly colored backdrops and mugging it up for the camera. (A clear departure for someone trying to speak for the ghetto and court credibility.) But taking up Big and Puffy's (and Death Row's) crossover ideal of the hardcore rapper as ghetto advocate also proved a moment of artistic transition for Jay-Z, of positioning himself as the conductor through which the joys, fears, and capitalistic pleasures of black popular culture flowed. Those moments went the opposite of "Sunshine," onto the front lines of sober ghetto reportage, like the menacingly clearheaded depiction of his old Marcy neighborhood on "Where I'm From." "I'm from the place where the church is the flakiest," he explains. "And niggas been praying to God so long that they atheist." The commentary talked bluntly not only about the edgy lifestyle of his former neighborhood but also about his ranking among the hip-hop elite who are revered in the 'hood. "I'm from where niggas pull ya card," he indifferently raps. "And argue all day about who's the best MCs: Biggie, Jay-Z, or Nas?" Most crucial, though, to Jay's rise as ghetto ambassador—regaining his street cred following the "Sunshine" video misstep—was "Streets Is Watching," a song that wasn't necessarily a hit but whose content and title inspired another media venture. The 1998 straight-to-video film *Streets Is Watching* was a semi-autobiographical look at Jay's life as a Brooklyn drug dealer. As a vehicle to further market Jay-Z (who portrayed himself), the movie was shot not just to sell videos—of which Roc-A-Fella Films reportedly sold over 100,000 copies—but to remind fans of the MC's "struggle" and to reestablish his credibility. The ingenious move, while reaffirming Jay-Z's authenticity as an MC-of-the-people, shortly preceded his ascendance to pop music stardom with the September 1998 release of *Vol. 2 . . . Hard Knock Life*. The disc's lead single, "Hard Knock Life (Ghetto Anthem)," set the class struggles of poor, urban black folks to the chorus of the *Annie* tune. But while it exclusively referred to the 'hood, the anthem also sounded as if it were a well-timed response to the deterioration of black advancement taking place in America's courts and voting booths.

The year before the release of *Vol. 2*, affirmative action, which had been limited in the past, seemed on the verge of total elimination. One of the key moments was the Supreme Court's refusal to block California's Proposition 209, which banned affirmative action in state-run employment, contracting, and education programs. The initiative's main proponent was the black Republican businessman Ward Connerly, who likened affirmative action to "stealing from someone." He began his campaign against affirmative action in 1994 within the University of California system, where he was a regent. His Proposition 209, which expanded UC's ban on affirmative action to all government programs, was passed by 54 percent of the state's voters the following year. Anyone who doubted its deleterious results needed only consider the fall in black and Latino college admissions after the ban took effect in 1998. Aside from the 10 percent drop in the overall system, UC Berkeley's admission of minority students fell by 55 percent. Affirmative action was also challenged in Texas, where, after a 1996 court ruling banned race-based admissions at the University of Texas, the state replaced it with a "Ten Percent Program." Students who ranked in the top 10 percent of their high-school class were automatically admitted to the state's public universities. But the most significant challenge loomed as the Supreme Court prepared to hear the case of a white schoolteacher who was suing the school board of Piscataway, New Jersey, for reverse discrimination. In 1989, Sharon Taxman, the plaintiff, was laid off by the board in order to keep Debra Williams, a black teacher. The decision, the board admitted, was based on race, an effort to maintain diversity. Although she later won back her job—having prevailed in the lower courts—Taxman's discrimination case continued on to the Supreme Court. If the judges ruled in her favor, their decision, setting the precedent for the country, could have struck down programs that benefited minorities altogether. The possibilities conjured horrors of the 1896 Supreme Court ruling in *Plessy v. Ferguson*, which decided "separate but equal" was a reasonable solution to preventing races from mingling, making Jim Crow legal. Fearing the outcome and its repercussions, the NAACP and other civil rights organizations halted the proceedings by financing an out-of-court settlement, agreeing to pay Taxman $433,500 for her back salary and legal bills. Where passionate protests had gotten affirmative action on the books during civil rights and black power, in the age of hip-hop money became the key to protecting what was left.

This notion wasn't lost on an MC like Jay-Z who'd understood having tons of funds—and the hard scramble to obtain them—as the crucial means of advancement. "I flow for chicks wishin' they ain't have to strip to pay tuition," he says on "Hard Knock Life (Ghetto Anthem)." "I see your vision, mama / I put my money on the long shots / All my ballers that's born to clock." Told from the standpoint of a former hustler who'd beaten the system and dismal statistics to find wealth, Jay-Z's anthem, in the absence of rap's iconic revolutionary (Tupac) and criminal capitalist (Biggie), turned boom-bap advocacy for the hardened streets, once again, into pop success. "Hard Knock Life," with its towering drum and *Annie*-inspired chorus exclaiming, "Instead of treated, we get tricked / Instead of kisses we get kicked," both transformed Jay into a household name and answered the question of who would fill the void left by Biggie Smalls. If the song's catapult of *Vol. 2* to the top of the pop chart didn't confirm this, the LP's cover stated the obvious. Staying within the playeristic theme of his first two CD covers, Jay-Z upped the display of hustler materialism. Dressed in a black designer suit, he leans on the side of a brand-new Bentley, the hand he props himself on the car with sporting a pinkie ring flooded with diamonds. Rap's leadership was definitely in flux, but its new vanguard was planning a trip to the top with the finest of toys.

Whereas *Vol. 1* found Jay coping with Big's murder and getting acquainted with the legacy he'd inherited, *Vol. 2* revealed a clear-minded Jay-Z, focused on synthesizing the rhythms, sounds, and commercial outlook that made his deceased predecessors (Biggie and Tupac) great. *Vol. 2* continued Jay's celebration of beating the black class struggle with criminal wisdom, but its overwhelming success stemmed from its seamless meld of regional sounds, interests, and styles. When listening to Big's *Life After Death*, which Puffy and the Hitmen produced for maximum appeal, one could easily mark the album's musical stabs at attracting a specific market. (All one had to do was point out loops and samples as well as the disc's smooth and rough edges.) But *Vol. 2*, produced by a patchwork of new-breed, synth-funky producers like Timbaland, Irv Gotti, and Swizz Beatz, drew its mass market from an indistinguishable mixture of rhythms (regional and otherwise) that proved just as inviting to a pop audience as an R&B groove. For instance, Timbaland's spastic beat for the single "Jigga What, Jigga Who" (titled "Nigga What, Nigga Who" on the album), fusing New York's big beat aesthetic with the electric drum-line sound popular in southern hip-hop music, could appeal to folks above and below the Mason-

Dixon Line. And Jay's syllabically swift rhyme on the cut, its style some-what resembling the cadence of Midwestern rappers, its cutthroat wit indicative of New York, could turn a wider audience on to his mastery of verse. Likewise, Swizz Beatz's hyper production on "Money, Cash, Hoes," with its booming kettledrum punctuated by a keyboard's rain-ing notes, pumped Jay's celebration of the sporting life from urban boulevards to the most exclusive dance floors of America. And ditto for the cut "Money Ain't a Thang," produced by (and cofeaturing) Atlanta beatsmith/record mogul Jermaine Dupri.

But also woven into the winning ingredients of *Vol. 2* was an MC's awareness of his consequential rise in the aftermath of hip-hop's dead-liest battle. The murders of Big and Pac made many a rap star ponder his mortality in song the way Tupac did. Jay-Z did so with the track "If I Should Die," featuring a group called Da Ranjahz. "Don't cry my nig-gas," he consoled. "It's been one hell of a ride my niggas / In the middle of the trial I flip pies my niggas / I did joints with Mary J. Blige my nig-gas." Aside from borrowing Pac's fearless outlook on death, Jay indi-rectly paid homage to the thug warrior, resurrecting the West Coast mantra for street loyalty Tupac made famous with the cut "Ride or Die." But what loomed even larger throughout *Vol. 2* was Jay-Z's con-sciousness, which had risen in the wake of Biggie's fall. "I'm platinum like American Express," he lamented on "It's Alright." "My boy died, and all I did was inherit his stress to make every jam tougher." Of all his influences Jay now had to count the Notorious B.I.G. as his biggest, not as MC (they had bonded over their shared ability to create complex rhymes purely from memory) but as a star, as an emerging hip-hop icon, and as the ultimate symbol of ghetto fabulousness. "Let's take the dough and stay real jiggy," he rapped on "Hard Knock Life." "And sip the Cris and get pissy pissy / Flow infinitely like the memory of my nigga Biggie, baby." At the zenith of hip-hop's commercial and cultural dominance in 1998, Big's legacy was carried on as much through Jay's references to him as it was through Jay's celebration of the flashy lifestyle Big championed in the halcyon years before his death. The subtext of this new, garish materialism was celebration, paying homage to hip-hop as a generation's ticket to social, cultural, and economic le-gitimacy (even if only as an emblem for those who couldn't benefit). By the end of *Super Fly*, the life journey of the film's former coke-dealing hero is uncertain after giving up the biz (like much of black America after its fight for social justice). But Jay-Z had transferred his capitalist dreams to hip-hop, which had crossed over far enough to become the face not only of black popular culture but of American popular culture.

By the time *Vol. 2* made its debut at number one, eventually selling five million copies, hip-hop was being hailed as the culture that changed U.S. business, social, and cultural aesthetics. With eighty-one million CDs, tapes, and albums sold in 1998, rap outstripped America's top-selling format, country. Up from its seventy-two million sales mark the previous year, rap music had increased its sales by 31 percent, more than rock, which saw only a 6 percent increase, and more than country, which experienced a 2 percent gain. In fact, if the South gained any momentum in the music industry in 1998, it was through rap. The rising southern hip-hop music movement, led by rap acts like Atlanta's OutKast and Goodie Mob and labels like Houston's Rap-A-Lot, garnered its biggest story in New Orleans rapper and No Limit label CEO, Master P. A product of Nawlins's Calliope projects, Master P (born Percy Miller) grew a $10,000 family settlement check from the death of his grandfather into rap's most significant label deal since Death Row, with albums to match. After selling thousands of albums independently, P negotiated a partnership deal with Priority Records for his No Limit label that gave him not only eighty-five cents on each dollar generated (Priority, which only distributed product, received fifteen cents plus marketing expenses) but also ownership of his masters, his publishing, *and* his company. The deal was emblematic of just how powerful hip-hop had become, and how much power it allowed some of its movers to wield. Of the twenty-three albums produced by No Limit in 1998, fifteen went either gold or platinum, earning the label $200 million in sales. As with *Vol. 2,* Master P's *MP Da Last Don* was a chart-topping mystery as it jumped from number 112 on *Billboard*'s Top 200 to number 1 in just one week. Like Jay, Master P rode into hip-hop's history on a dream deferred: his promising future as a basketball player (at the University of Houston) dashed when he blew out his knee. That loss of hope sent him home and, with the murder of his brother by a drug addict, searching for an alternative to the streets. And like the marriage of pain, joy, and creativity giving birth to artists like Master P and Jay-Z, the chic of *realness* that rap now monopolized helped icons like these to begin recoloring the face of American high society.

Indeed, as hip-hop had become big business, its social stock gave rap's power players enough leverage to merge black street culture with the traditionally unhip world of the white rich and powerful. One figure being celebrated for such a phenomenon was Puff Daddy, who, after his LP *No Way Out* went seven times platinum, became synonymous with rap music for the celebrity and corporate classes. (After all, he made the March 22, 1999, cover of *Forbes*.) His parties, most notably his twenty-ninth-birthday bash and his famous "white" parties in the Hamptons, got him as much notice in the press as his scrapes with the law because his guest lists included everyone from "the Duchess of York to rapper Heavy D." The arrival of ghetto fab in the insulated circles of WASP society extended beyond Puffy's throwdowns. "It was Foxy Brown . . . who performed at the Whitney's Brite Nite fund-raiser this year," read a story in the May 10, 1999, issue of *New York* magazine, "not the Peter Duchin Orchestra in their tuxedos." The story, about "who rules hip-hop"—Puffy or Russell Simmons—described John and Caroline Kennedy asking Brown if she was going to perform "Hot Spot." Of course Puffy, and anyone bringing these worlds together, was obviously following the blueprint set by Russell Simmons, who had initiated this type of commingling when he thrust rap music into the halls of corporate America, put guitars in the music of Run-D.M.C., and sold it to white boys, ultimately creating the mold of the "hip-hop mogul." Simmons's business moves—his clothing line, his record label, his magazine (*One World*), even the development of himself into a brand—inspired much of the social and hypercapitalist ambitions of rap's megastars. The genre's top figures had gained so much cultural cachet that, for the first time, *Time* magazine featured one (Lauryn Hill) on its cover with the cover line "Hip-Hop Nation: After 20 Years—How It's Changed America."

The grand prosperity enjoyed by hip-hop was also being enjoyed by blacks across the country. Five months after the piece in *Time* ran, *Newsweek* published its cover story titled "The Good News About Black America." Economic stimulation, in part due to Clinton's Omnibus Budget Reconciliation Act, had finally kicked in, with the wealth gains extending to all of America, including black folks. Against "the backdrop of a superheated economy," fueled by the technology boom, the *Newsweek* story reported on the historic upswing of black economic and social advancement. The percentage of black employed and home owners was up, while murders and violent crimes within black communities were down. Median weekly earnings were up slightly, along with life expectancy. And at around 25 percent, the number of black families living below the poverty line was at the lowest it had been "since the Census began keeping separate black poverty statistics in 1967." Despite problems that included more black men languishing in prisons than ever, black academic achievement still falling behind whites, and the ever-invisible presence of inequality, black America, along with every race in the country, increasingly found progress, especially in the upward tide of Clinton-era prosperity. In fact, of the factors considered most important to improving the conditions for black America, 37 percent of blacks polled credited the policies of the Clinton administration. Overall, the economic upturn during the Clinton years pulled 4.1 million of the working poor out of poverty, while Reagan's boom in the 1980s had done the same for only 50,000.

If any statement from hip-hop captured the optimism of such a hopeful report, it was Jay-Z's "Big Pimpin'," the lead single from his 1999 disc, *Vol. 3 . . . Life and Times of S. Carter*. This collaboration with Texas rap duo UGK was Jay's brash, upbeat ode to ghetto fabulousness set to an infectious Caribbean-tinged rhythm. "I'm still big pimpin', spendin' cheese," Jay bragged to listeners, "with Bun B, Pimp C, and Timothy / We got bitches in the back of the truck laughin' it up / Jigga Man, that's what's up." Most powerful was the song's visual display of Jay and his Houston cohorts enjoying the lives of the rich and famous: Jay and Damon Dash entertaining a bevy of beautiful women at a mansion in the Caribbean and on their yacht while Bun B lounges outside his luxury car as a video vixen dances around him and Pimp C pursues beauties on the beach. By the end of the video, Jay is one of a crowd of revelers enjoying Trinidad's famous Carnival, celebrating the spiritual liberation of the flesh. So between the Brooklyn MC, his Texas collaborators, and the Trinidadians partying under the warm West Indian sun, the perception was that ghetto fabulousness was indeed worldwide.

But *Vol. 3* was less a promotion of the sporting life and drug-game metaphors than it was Jay's affirmation of his hip-hop greatness, his 'hood relevance, and his identity outside of Biggie's kingly shadow. Not the least was the nickname of omnipotence Jay had given himself: Jay Hova (like the god Jehovah). With a firm grip on both the pop and urban markets, he was building a legacy and a legend of his own: winning a 1999 Grammy for Best Rap Album for *Vol. 2 . . . Hard Knock Life* (accepting the award but boycotting the ceremony); being arrested for stabbing Lance "Un" Rivera at a New York club (a charge he pleaded guilty to and was sentenced to three years of probation for); setting box-office records with his *Hard Knock Life* tour, selling out most of its fifty-two dates, earning $18 million, and experiencing no incidents of violence; launching his Rocawear clothing line in the summer of 1999 and in three years reaping $500 million in retail sales; earning his own record company millions as the best artist on the Roc-A-Fella label and the best (and possibly the most influential) lyricist in rap.

Vol. 3 . . . Life and Times of S. Carter was Jay's platform to establish and acknowledge such notions. "Radio's gotta play me though I cuss too much," he rapped on the cut "So Ghetto." "Magazine said I'm shallow, I never learned to swim / Still they put me on they cover 'cause I earn for them." Jay keenly put forth a politicized self-perception (exdealer-as-capitalist-revolutionary) on the song "Dopeman," where, on trial for pushing his dope (slang for "good") music similar to the way he pushed coke in the past, he explains to the judge and jury: "I try to tell them I'm where hope floats, man. A ghetto spokesman," going so far as to invoke the image of imprisoned Black Panther Mumia Abu-Jamal to describe his mission among black folks. "Your honor, I no longer kill my people," he rapped to the court. "I raise mine / The soul of Mumia in these modern day times." (Though his mission on disc was hardly that of a compassionate revolutionary.) But Jay definitely asserted his leadership of the spoken word on tracks like "It's Hot (Some Like It Hot)," on which he verbally chastised 50 Cent for a shot the newcomer took at him on the single "How to Rob." ("I'm about a dollar," Jay rapped. "What the fuck is 50 Cent?") He continued the creative exchange between the North and South ("Big Pimpin'" and "Snoopy Track" featuring New Orleans's Juvenile) as well as East and West ("Watch Me" featuring Dr. Dre). Still, most important was Jay's affirmation of his worth to his young ghetto constituency, whose respect was of the most value to his status as hip-hop power player. "Product of Reaganomics, you know that motherfuckin' stoop raised me," he rapped on "Things That U Do." "Ringin' in the hoops, but I was too lazy / School made me sick, teachers said I was too crazy." His most vehement reminder, though, was recited on the song "Come and Get Me," with Jay rapping to his old neighborhood: "I made it so you could say Marcy, and it was all good / I ain't crossover, I brought the suburbs to the 'hood / Made 'em relate to your struggle / Told 'em about your hustle / Went on MTV with do-rags, I made them love you."

To his credit, Jay, like numerous rap stars before him, certainly possessed the power of persuasion that, while sending his fourth LP platinum in two months, made him a major tastemaker, altering (if not completely changing) what was desired by and rapped about within hip-hop. He changed the ghetto fab standard from drinking Moët to the über-expensive champagne Cristal, which Jay constantly referenced in song. From wanting to drive Benzes to Bentleys, which he rapped about driving. And, most profoundly, from the banality of gold to higher-grade metals and stones like platinum and diamonds, which Jay meticulously bragged about sporting. (Though New Orleans turned that "shine" Jay bragged about into pop culture terminology when rapper B.G. released the massive hip-hop hit "Bling Bling.") Jay's infectious sway was enough to push two million more units of *Vol. 3* by the time he released his less notable—yet double-platinum—album *The Dynasty: Roc la Familia* in 2000.

Most certainly, by the arrival of the new millennium Jay in many ways epitomized the might hip-hop wielded and the changing face of the corporate/cultural paradigm. For one, as a record label owner: his Roc-A-Fella Records became an audacious symbol of black ownership taking root within the record industry as other black-owned labels like Cash Money, Bad Boy, So So Def, No Limit, and Ruff Ryders—all in joint ventures with major labels—became music industry leaders, putting a larger share of the wealth in black hands, more so than in previous generations. Next, as a mogul: Jay's entrepreneurial ventures (his clothing line, film production company, and, later, his vodka company and Manhattan nightclub) were the centerpiece, along with Master P and Puffy's growing empires, of an enterprising movement among hip-hop artists to expand their bottom line by diversifying their brand. Furthermore, as a benchmark of innovation: Jay's flossy-hustler-as-ghetto-mouthpiece archetype became the pattern that numerous future rap stars—from Miami's Rick Ross to Atlanta's Young Jeezy—used to shape their careers. But also, Jay's overall influence and artistic contribution to rap music in general inspired the theme of his sixth LP, 2001's *The Blueprint*.

From the standpoint of a veteran offering his soul, wrath, and wisdom to a core audience who either loved him, were growing tired of his materialism, or flat out wanted to be in his position of wealth (or close to it), Jay crafted his most expressive album. The disc's soulful edge, with its soul-music-inspired choruses and epic production using samples (the technique having waned in the last few years), was due, in large part, to innovative, newjack producers like Just Blaze and Kanye West. Their uncanny ability to explicitly impart emotion through hip-hop music allowed Jay to powerfully communicate strength, vulnerability, and the signature steel confidence of a great MC. "I sell ice in the winter," he exclaimed on the Blaze-produced "U Don't Know," a song explaining the street enterprising instincts that got him here. "I sell fire in hell / I am a hustler, baby, I'll sell water to a well / I was born to get cake / Move on and switch states." In a retrospective mood, he articulated love and appreciation for the blood/extended family that raised him to manhood ("Blueprint [Momma Loves Me]") as much as he would for a crime family that helped build his former cocaine empire ("Never Change"). And after exploring the topic of friendships destroyed by the drug game five years prior on "D'evils," he revisited a romance lost to his celebrity as a philandering coke dealer on "Song Cry." "I'm a man with pride," he rapped to a former girlfriend. "You don't do shit like that . . . You don't throw away what we had just like that . . . I'll mourn forever / Shit, I gotta live with the fact I did you wrong forever." But the most forceful expression on *Blueprint* was Jay's aggravation with "haters," those who criticized him for his ghetto fab flamboyance, obsession with wealth, and bragging about having sold drugs, feeling that his music lacked substance. "Motherfuckers say that I'm foolish, I only talk about jewels," Jay quipped on "Renegade," a duet with the great white hope of rap, Eminem. "Do you fools listen to music or do you just skim through it?" For those who had forgotten his intent, being a "voice of the young people" and "mouthpiece for hustlers," as he called himself on the Bink-produced "The Ruler's Back," Jay announced: "I'm representing for the seat where Rosa Parks sat, where Malcolm X was shot / Where Martin Luther was popped." His venomous response also came in the form of the legendary battle song "Takeover," Jay's skewering of Nas and Mobb Deep's Prodigy over Kanye West's interpolation of the Doors' "Five to One." Though what set *Blueprint* off to double-platinum sales was his radio-friendly response to critics of his former occupation on "Izzo (H.O.V.A.)." "Hov is back," Jay announced. "Life stories told through rap / Niggas actin' like I sold you crack / Like I told you, 'Sell drugs' . . . No, Hov did that / So hopefully you won't have to go through that."

Over shots of the Jackson 5's classic "I Want You Back," Jay defended his rough-n-tumble beginnings as a narcotics player, discussing his extravagance and greed as a means of teaching his core audience the benefits of being business savvy, particularly in an industry that has historically underpaid rap artists. "I do this for my culture," he explained. "To let 'em know what a nigga look like when a nigga in a roadster / Show 'em how to move in a room full of vultures / Industry is shady, it need to be taken over / Label owners hate me, I'm raising the status quo up / I'm overchargin' niggas for what they did to the Cold Crush / Pay us like you owe us for all the years that you hold us / We can talk, but money talks so talk mo' bucks."

On the one hand, Jay interpreting his industry rip-off as a collection of hip-hop reparations articulated the revival of an even wider national movement within black America to collect reparations for slavery. Led by groups like the Reparations Coordinating Committee, whose members included such prominent figures as attorney Johnnie Cochran and activist Randall Robinson (whose 2000 book, *The Debt: What America Owes to Blacks*, popularized the idea—and debate—of reparations), the slavery reparations movement, which had existed in one form or another since Reconstruction, was black folks' attempt at getting America to compensate them for building her wealth and power off their 246 years of free labor. Inspired by the legal and monetary victories of Japanese Americans who were stripped of their property and relocated to internment camps after Pearl Harbor and of Jewish victims of the Holocaust (after Germany paid billions in reparations to Jews in Europe, they also paid Jewish Americans who suffered in concentration camps), African Americans attempted to win compensation for their suffering through the courts. On behalf of the thirty-five million descendants of slaves, lawyers filed nine landmark class-action lawsuits between 2000 and 2002 against eighteen corporations, including Aetna and Bank of America, that had unfairly profited from the slave trade before the end of the Civil War. In 2002 those lawsuits were consolidated into one and brought before a federal court in Chicago for a significant legal battle. But unable to prove these companies harmed the plaintiffs directly, the case was dismissed in 2005, winning no more than an apology from companies like Aetna and J. P. Morgan. Seven years earlier, President Clinton seemed to be setting the stage for such expressions of regret when, on a trip to Africa in 1998, he came close to apologizing for slavery on behalf of America.

On the other hand, Jay's insistence on cash also reflected a seismic shift in the focus of the post–black power generation on what the struggle for empowerment should currently emphasize. Journalist Todd S. Burroughs noted the swing in a 2001 piece, "Revised Revolution," for *The Source*. Reporting from the Urban League's annual convention, Burroughs discussed the results of the civil rights organization's survey of the "hip-hop generation" called "The State of Black America 2001: Black Americans Under 35." The poll showed that 60 percent of blacks surveyed believed that economic opportunity should be the focus of civil rights groups. Sixty-seven percent of those polled wanted to own their own business, and 87 percent believed in a "need for affirmative action and more educational and employment opportunity." Noticing the overwhelming entrepreneurial spirit of the young crowd at the convention, Burroughs noted: "The goals of African Americans under thirty-five are collectively less radical and more individualistic." Whereas the goal of this generation's parents was to challenge the system, then work from "within or outside" it to change society, the aim of young black America—disillusioned by the old belief that political power would solve everything—was to *work* the system (looking past its faults) for their own personal advantage. "After all," wrote Burroughs, "why attack America's contradictions when you can make them work for you?" Writer Bakari Kitwana also noted the generational change when he wrote in *The Hip Hop Generation*, "This desire to achieve not only financial security but millionaire status is the driving force of our generation's work ethic." When it came to former notions of a "black revolution" (fighting white supremacy with protests and outcry), Burroughs wrote that blacks weren't scared to initiate one, but that "they're just over it."

Nowhere was this attitude more widespread than in rap music, with act after act—from the Bronx's Fat Joe to the entire roster of Cash Money Records—adopting the hypermaterialistic theme of ghetto fabulousness. With a reduced concern for shouting down (or at least giving a cursory mention to) social injustice, the primary focus of rap stars was reciting the laundry list of possessions (*my* car, *my* jewels, *my* clothes, *my* women, and, most important, nigga, *my* money). Even less of a concern (much less than when every rapper wanted to be a "gangsta") was rap's former emphasis on originality and pride in craft as artists. Now under pressure from major record companies to produce hits, rappers had no problem "biting," or copying, the style and themes of other rappers to launch their careers. That Master P and a slew of rap stars sounded like Tupac or other MCs, and referenced drugs and jewels the way Jay-Z did, was of no consequence to their bottom line. Nor was the fact that valuing mindless, catchy, simplistic rap styles over prodigious (or even semi-prodigious) rhyme skills in order to consistently sell hip-hop music to a mass audience signaled the downslide of hip-hop's legitimizing strides in the late 1990s. Having become the urban face of pop music, rap, like other popular genres before it, had turned into merely a product of large corporations and independents to be bought and sold. Rap became less of a means to honestly and holistically express the social range of its core audience than a way for hungry newcomers to get rich selling dumbed-down versions of black criminal stereotypes. Jay-Z, while having insightfully pioneered the benevolent-hustler prototype fueling hip-hop's new school, was also guilty of contributing to the factory treatment of rap music, even cranking out a not-so-fantastic—yet still multiplatinum— sequel to *Blueprint* (the double CD *The Blueprint²: The Gift & The Curse*).

Then again, as one of the architects of rap's corporate formatting (following Big's hit formula of including "club bangers" and "chick singles" on LPs in a blatant, uninspired effort to go pop), Jay couldn't help but become a hostage of the spoon-fed tastes of hip-hop's cross-cultural audience. After all, 70 percent of those who purchase rap, especially when an album goes multiplatinum, are white and nonblack, and if rappers want to continue selling at high volume, they have to keep their projects simple, familiar, thuggish, and somewhat socially neutral (a mandate numerous rappers after Jay's crown and record sales had no problem following). Though it would eventually leave a competitive Jay-Z feeling unfulfilled as an artist. "I can honestly say I'm bored with hip-hop," Jay confessed in a 2003 essay for *Vibe* as he prepared to release his (supposedly) final LP, *The Black Album*. "I spend a lot of time feeling uninspired . . . It's not about music anymore. It's about numbers." More expressive than *Blueprint*, 2003's *The Black Album* was Jay's redemption as an MC of the people, an artistic catharsis before slipping, as he had so often promised since *Reasonable Doubt*, into retirement.

Having already exposed, explored, and examined his unsavory past ad nauseam, Jay, conjuring the confessional spirit of Tupac, delved even deeper behind his curtain of coolness. While recollecting life in Marcy on the autobiographical cut "December 4th," Jay traced the roots of his foul choices and devious attitude, most movingly, to the breakup of his mother and father. "Now all the teachers couldn't reach me," he acknowledged, "and my momma couldn't beat me / Hard enough to match the pain of my pop not seeing me / With that disdain in my membrane / Got on my pimp game / 'Fuck the world,' my defense came." Likewise, his thoughts were just as forthcoming, more so than on *Vol. 3*, about the hip-hop industry, which he had so often expressed contempt for. Before spinning the true-life tales of "99 Problems"—one story being nearly getting busted for cocaine possession in 1994—Jay bluntly vented about his business relationship with magazines and radio. "Got beef with radio," he said. "If I don't play they show / They don't play my hits, well I don't give a shit, so / Rap mags try and use my black ass / So advertisers can give them more cash for ads." His response to critics and rap purists on "Moment of Clarity" spoke, with as much jaw-dropping honesty, about the conflict between his artistic desires—to flex his skills like the best, though struggling, lyricists—and the realities of pop stardom. "The music I be makin', I dumb down for my audience," rapped Jay. "And double my dollars . . . If skills sold, truth be told / I'd probably be, lyrically, Talib Kweli / Truthfully, I wanna rhyme like Common Sense / (But I did five mil) I ain't been rhyming like Common Sense / When your sense got that much in common / And you been hustlin' since your inception / Fuck perception, go with what makes cents."

Of course, what moved units of *The Black Album*, about three million of them, were superfluous commercial hits like "Change Clothes," the standard ode to Jay's affluence, and "Encore," the standard brag on his mic skills. The moment offering an official goodbye, though—one that would only last three years before his return in 2006—was on the video for the gold single "Dirt off Your Shoulder." After taking over a radio station to dispense his message—the chorus of his tune advising listeners, when confronted with obstacles, to "brush ya shoulders off"—he joins a throng of bejeweled black folks dancing in a parking lot amid pimped-out cars, celebrating the retirement of hip-hop's ultimate hustler. At the sign of a dawning sun, Jay leaves the crowd and the rap game, though not without tipping his Yankees baseball cap in thanks before getting back in his Bentley ("the best rapper alive," a sample of his voice utters in the background). But Jay's retirement wasn't so much a break from rapping and the grind of the business as it was proof, further, that hip-hop, no matter what one thought of it, was running the airwaves and the boardroom. And Jay, being a major player, had become its most tangible symbol, whether as the first rapper to have a signature sneaker line (for Reebok)—his S. Carter shoe becoming the fastest-selling sneaker in the company's history, providing opportunities for other MCs like 50 Cent to procure deals—or becoming the president of Def Jam, or the co-owner of the New Jersey Nets, or even the co–brand director of Budweiser Select, his celebrity used to hawk beer to his multiethnic fan base. Whether one frowned or rejoiced at a former-drug-peddler-cum-street-representative (a phenom that would give rise to a future rap subgenre called cocaine rap) reaching the pinnacle of corporate leadership and influence, or at a ghetto music and culture of young black and brown folks rising to ultimately become a valid piece of Americana, one couldn't help but marvel at the achievement. Whether this was a gift or a curse remained to be seen.

ELEVEN

Dog Eat Dog
DMX

Most people would describe DMX's arrival at rap stardom the same way comedian Jamie Foxx described encountering a hostile Mike Tyson at a nightclub: like someone letting a pit bull loose at a party to roam among the guests. But unlike Mike's rise to fame, not many saw DMX coming. Plus no one could imagine the breadth of his impact on rap music and post–black power America, especially if all you had to go on was an exceptional cameo on an LL Cool J single. And that was about all he had when I sat down to interview him in February 1998. The interview was scheduled at the original offices of Ruff Ryders on West Fifty-third Street in Manhattan. I had been assigned by *The Source* to write a 2,100-word profile on the newcomer—the first feature the magazine published on him—and it was an assignment I approached with the utmost apprehension and suspicion.

When I was given the story to write, I initially contested my editor's decision to give the emerging rap star a three-page spread instead of *The Source*'s usual one-and-a-quarter-page Q&A. My primary reason was DMX didn't have an album finished yet for me to hear, and the buzz for his debut single, "Get at Me Dog," the first cut from his to-be-released CD, *It's Dark and Hell Is Hot*, hadn't caught on nationally. In other words, he hadn't proven himself. Like many hip-hop heads, I was impressed with DMX's breakout verse on LL Cool J's "4, 3, 2, 1." The dramatic inflections of his gruff vocals. His gruesomely imaginative lyrics ("Don't make me put you somewhere where nobody'll smell ya"). And the sincerity in his delivery, which undoubtedly screamed, "I'm a real nigga!" But every commercial rap artist, by this time, was a real nigga. I still saw no reason to give that much ink to an MC on the verge, especially since hardcore rap was overrun with rap stars claiming street cred.

But I also had no illusions about the music journalism industry in which I worked. I was now a mercenary being used to systematically push this newcomer on the masses (I know, I know: Isn't most music journalism about systematic promotion?). Having my doubts about the rapper's importance, I vehemently argued my points to the editor, but he wouldn't budge. To my point about DMX not being a star yet or having a hit record, my editor smirked and calmly replied, "This guy's a little different. Trust me, he's going to be huge when he does come out. You just write the story and get it in." End of discussion.

With that reply I wound up at Ruff Ryders to interview DMX. Like its burgeoning star, the label's office—literally a one-room affair—was unfinished: painted white, sparsely furnished with two desks sitting at one end and two folding chairs at the other. The only things hanging on the walls were a map of the United States and a small poster of DMX advertising "Get at Me Dog," which had been released weeks prior to this interview. Before DMX arrived, Chivon Dean, the CEO of Ruff Ryders, gave me the preliminaries on what to expect from the Yonkers MC, telling me simply, "X is off the hook" and "very animated." DMX arrived shortly afterward, letting out a signature bark as he came through the door. Animated, indeed.

But upon meeting him, surprisingly, I immediately sensed that the vibrancy wasn't just hip-hop shtick (like, say, the rap group Onyx) but who he was. "Honest" was a word that came to mind upon seeing him. Honesty in the sense of unabashedly speaking his mind, and how he presented himself. Dressed in a worn woolen jacket, baggy jeans, and untied Timberland boots, holding a plastic cup of Hennessy, DMX wasn't caught up in hip-hop's jiggy-nistics or the age of bling. The metal choker around his neck, literally a dog's chain, was a mild contrast to the volumes of platinum and diamonds now adorning the necks of numerous commercial MCs—established and emerging—like Bad Boy's Mase or any number of artists on Cash Money Records.

If DMX wasn't trying to make any declaration with his clothes, he definitely made some during the interview. "This isn't hip-hop," he said, commenting on the current state of the music, his voice moving with the spirit and rumble of a fiery preacher. "This is rap going down. If it were hip-hop, niggas would be real with it. They would communicate with the essence of the culture, which is the streets. They wouldn't just take it to make sales . . . sayin', 'I want to dance like this. I want to shine like this.' You can't take money with you to heaven, baby. You can only take love." He sure *sounded* sincere.

Apparently, love's benevolent embrace was the key factor missing from DMX's life. During the course of the interview I learned about the hard-knock tale of his upbringing, a story that has now been well documented. Born Earl Simmons, he was the only son in a family of four girls and raised by his mother in Yonkers, New York's School Street Housing project. His father, an out-of-work artist, a painter, who barely saw X as a child, eventually disappeared from his life altogether. There was also the physical abuse DMX received from his mother, who had no patience for her son's animated personality or his healthy appetite. Growing up without a stable male figure in his life or family and feeling isolated, X became a loner. Then disruptive: in the house, on the street, especially in school, which led to his being put in a group home. Crimes followed, mostly robbery and eventually car theft, and jail. Then came a bout with drug addiction—to crack—that would fuel more robberies.

In between the muggings and incarcerations, DMX's emotional and social development would be guided by two factors: dogs and hip-hop. The canine love was sparked in his preteen years after he found a stray dog in downtown Yonkers. For the lonely, impoverished kid, dogs became a way to fight the pangs of loneliness and feelings of inadequacy. "I've always been the outcast," he told me. "I didn't blend in with anybody else because I didn't have all the shit that everyone else had." So dogs became the supreme symbol of family and loyalty. "My dog was my friend," he continued. "He ain't give a damn if I had on hand-me-downs or not. He ain't care if I drank sugar water instead of Kool-Aid or if I ate eggs all day. The dog was just there because he loved me."

Dogs may have been DMX's panacea for companionship and honest familial ties, but hip-hop, as for so many of his generation, opened a path to self-expression and social acceptance and, eventually, fame. Whereas antics as a stickup kid fueled X's infamy and his comfort within feelings of isolation on the street, hip-hop music would turn him into a local star as a human beatbox for a Brooklyn MC named Ready Ron in the mid-1980s—until he discovered that being a human percussionist didn't get him what he needed.

"I'd be beatboxin'," X said, "and he's getting all the attention, all the love. I'm makin' him look good. I know where to throw the pauses in and how to come back in with the beat. Keep it persistent and not have it drag. Why am I not getting the love that he getting? I have nothin' but a hand full of spit. Then I figured it out—you've got to be the rapper. You must be the rapper." Initially, rhyme writing and reciting would be a personal thing, a secret, a soulful expression done while grappling with the wild side of life. "If I was in the streets robbin' niggas, I was rhyming. If I was locked down for robbin' niggas, I was rhymin'. If I was stealin' cars to go rob niggas, I was rhymin'." It was while doing a two-year bid at the age of fifteen in McCormick Juvenile Institution that DMX's personal hobby became his mission, a talent that would both build self-esteem and become his calling card. "In jail you hear other niggas rhyme," X explained. "But I kept my rhymes to myself, but I kept doin' it. Then I decided, I'm like, well, let me let other niggas hear my rhymes. Then I started believing I was the nicest I could be. I ain't want to believe that at first, because no one heard my shit. But when they did, niggas started giving me my props. And after a while, I was holding down the whole jail." Even back then, X's rhymes were touched with a dramatic edge and imagery to match, as evidenced in his first rhyme, where he wrote: "One night while I was sleeping an image appeared / It was an old man with a long gray beard / He said so brother DMX of you I've heard so much / It's about time I bless you with the MC touch / Then the room began shaking and it shook like a rattle / That's when I knew I would have my first MC battle."

From a teenager rhyming in jail to a young man rhyming in the street, DMX used his skills to eventually gain a short-lived management deal with Jack MacNasty, followed by one with Ruff Ryders, a fledgling production company/record label in Yonkers, in the early 1990s. The union produced a few singles, one called "Born Loser" put out by Ruffhouse Records in 1995, but nothing substantial materialized. Then on to more work, doing live shows and working the mixtape circuit in a hip-hop landscape being critically reshaped by the deaths of Biggie and Tupac. Next, on to guest spots on records, and while helping reestablish a veteran rapper's street credibility—which was what LL's "4, 3, 2, 1" was all about—DMX caught the ever-elusive "street buzz." Only now in hip-hop music, which had managed to become *the* driving force behind pop music and American popular culture, street buzz meant industry buzz, which translated into mainstream buzz, which meant a star was about to be born—which is what ultimately led DMX and me to this interview.

But with all the hype beginning to swirl around DMX, he seemed prepared to handle it, as if he studied rap's current climate and knew exactly how to ride its ever-changing currents. If life's answers were blowin' in the wind for Bob Dylan, for DMX they were blowin' in the streets. "If I keep my ear to the streets, I will hear the entire world," X contended. "But only if I keep my ears to the ground. If I lift up and try to hear what these other niggas are sayin', to see what the party is all about, then I'll be lost. Fuck the party! Ear to the street." It was midway through these salvos when, for me, the anticipation surrounding DMX, this musical hunch I was assigned to cover, became clear. DMX marked the return of hip-hop's Thug Messiah, its messenger of rage and advocate of the streets, rejuvenating rap's ability to express post–black power America's angst and frustrations in the years ahead.

When Ruff Ryders released DMX's "Get at Me Dog," commercial rap music and America were waist-deep in the ice age. Rap's proverbial dark cloud—the murders of Tupac and Biggie and the so-called East/West rap war—lifted at the mixed sounds of hip-hop's new hedonistic danceability, self-indulgence, self-absorption, and rampant materialism. And who could blame the artists or the music? Through all of its peaks and valleys, rap music was now at its apex of mainstream acceptance, being, as producer Stevie J. told *Vibe* magazine, "made safe for the Republican Party to party [to it]." Even though rap music is black music, two-thirds of it was purchased by whites and other non–African Americans, helping to turn hip-hop into a $2 billion business. But hip-hop music wasn't just celebrating its hard-won acclaim. It was also a reflection of America's record-breaking economy, driven mostly by technology stocks and the dot-com boom. African Americans saw unemployment and poverty rates drop to an all-time low. And many a folk could floss like a Jay-Z or a Mannie Fresh, or at least pretend to be showing off. (After all, rappers were the quintessential playas of "the system," badass niggas getting over on a system designed to keep most of them out.)

But to another segment of black America, the folks still feeling the sting or at least aware of America's ever-existing double standard, rap music had also become the wealthy, detached uncle who constantly reminded you how rich he was and how much of a broke-ass nigga you were. For Jay-Z and Jermaine Dupri, it was "Money Ain't a Thang." With Puffy (who now went by "P. Diddy") and his Bad Boy Records empire, black life was "All About the Benjamins." And, according to New Orleans's Cash Money Records, "Bling Bling" was the gospel. Furthermore, when it came to responding to black folks' social ills and anger (and even with a prosperous economy, there was plenty), rap simply became the dumb monkey in denial: seeing no evil, hearing no evil, and purposely speaking no evil. Even Cash Money producer/rap artist Mannie Fresh would admit to a *Vibe* magazine reporter in 2003: "The Bling Bling era wasn't the message-important era, like how Marvin Gaye and them went through their save-the-world mission. We didn't do that. Hopefully, the next era will be more serious and focus on regular stuff like that."

As any significant voice emerges out of mass need, the star of DMX rose because folks needed a mouthpiece fearlessly representing them in rap's pop prominence. With all its wealth and possessions and posturing, commercial rap had all but disconnected from the collective "blues" of young black people. Yes, chasing the dollar and hustling the system were ways of fighting the power. But greed, individuality, and selfishness don't overtly challenge the status quo. The sentiment of DMX's "Get at Me Dog" barked in the artistic tradition of getting back-to-basics, putting heart and soul—rap's core audience's heart and soul—back into the music. Like a refreshing blast of heat for a genre growing cold from too much ice (and the platinum it was set on), the song spoke directly to the spiritual deficit of rap and its followers in post–black power America.

In his universe, DMX was Robin Hood robbing rich hoodlums with the backing of his "dogs": his niggas, real friends, and extended family from the streets. For anyone paying attention, this family also included listeners and future fans (poor or otherwise) hungry for a message of loyalty over wealth who were fed up with emotionless rappers overcrowding the music with a laundry list of their riches. DMX zeroed in on this sentiment with verses like: "You know what I mean, I'm just robbin' to eat / And there's at least a thousand of us, like, we mobbin' the street / When we starvin' we eat whatever's there / Come on, you know the code in the street: 'Whatever's fair.' "

The video for "Get at Me Dog" launched as a sharp visual accompaniment to this assault. In contrast to the Technicolor rap videos, with rappers in shiny suits, surrounded by expensive cars, mansions, and half-dressed women—all shot through a distorted fish-eye lens—"Get at Me Dog" stripped away the gimmicks and illusions. Shot in grainy black and white, the video—a frenetic live performance—showed a bare-chested, crazy-eyed, soulful DMX, accompanied by a heavily thugged-out constituency, putting a hip-hop club into a frenzy. Although simple, the energy with which DMX's audience received him and the heartfelt energy with which he delivered his message visually broke down an invisible wall between MC and the angry heart of the post–black power generation. It definitely set DMX in motion toward becoming *the* voice for a segment of hip-hop and black America that needed a symbol to shout down the illusions and to speak to the hell folks were still catching.

Rap music's tragic thug angel, Tupac Shakur, had been dead for two years. And even though several posthumous Tupac albums (bootleg and otherwise) had been released since his murder, a void had developed in hardcore rap. There was a need for a rebel, a larger-than-life street nigga to make commercial rap speak for black folks (the ones losing to the system) in the streets again. Before DMX, there were only glimmers of hope. Master P tried, enlisting Pac's throaty sing-along delivery on rhymes about desperate ghetto living (hustling to make it for you and your homies). But P was hailed more for his prowess as an entrepreneur—again becoming an ultimate player of "the system"—than for his artistry, which was neither original nor inspiring. Other hardcore acts either couldn't make the national scene or were on their way out. For instance, Brooklyn's M.O.P. (Mash Out Posse) had promise, but were too underground and—sounding like slum-dwelling drill sergeants who'd rob you in a heartbeat—never succeeded at appealing to a wider audience. And the Wu-Tang Clan, while still cranking out hardcore commercial rap, by now were sounding directionless, played out, preachy, and *too* grimy.

By comparison, DMX, with his shaved head, thugged-out persona, and singsong lyrics of street life, was poised to be Tupac's heir apparent—many a hip-hop head could see this. There were also similarities in their brushes with the law: Pac was imprisoned for rape and X was charged with rape (though the charge was later thrown out). But DMX didn't emerge just to be a substitute for a missed prophet. He emerged to firmly reestablish Thug Life, Tupac's ruffian reinterpretation of the black power movement as the vanguard voice in popular rap music. The ice age of rap, with its recognizable pop samples and Cristal-drenched lyrics, was an appropriate barometer for those getting along with their premillennial affluence. But black America also had another reality, an institutionalized racial reality, underneath the influx of cash, flowing champagne, rising stock prices, and illusions of massive black progress. Racial injustice—as old as America itself—was again making its presence known, a sore contradiction in these prosperous times.

Those too blinded by rap's bling to acknowledge racism (or who thought that hip-hop's reign mysteriously erased America's aversion to black social progress) were reminded of this country's ugly social problems eight months before the release of DMX's *It's Dark and Hell Is Hot*. That's when Geronimo Pratt, a former Black Panther leader and Tupac Shakur's godfather, was released after spending twenty-seven years in a Santa Ana, California, prison following a judge's ruling that Pratt had been falsely convicted of murder. Like Dhoruba bin Wahad, he had been a victim of J. Edgar Hoover's Counterintelligence Program.

As head of the Southern California chapter of the Black Panthers, Pratt was arrested in 1969 for the robbery and murder of a twenty-seven-year-old schoolteacher, Caroline Olsen. Following a heavily politicized trial, at which Pratt's political beliefs and Panther association were tried more than the murder, Pratt was found guilty. (The only key evidence against him being the testimonies of Panther turned police informant Julius C. Butler, who testified that Pratt confessed the crime to him, and Kenneth Olsen, the murdered woman's husband, who identified Pratt as the killer.) On May 29, 1997, Pratt's murder conviction was overturned by Orange County Superior Court judge Everett Dickey after it was discovered that prosecutors purposely concealed evidence that could have led to Pratt's acquittal in the first trial.

Amid hip-hop's celebration of America's embrace (even old white ladies were "gettin' jiggy wit' it"), Pratt's release, and the shady circumstances surrounding his incarceration, were a prophetic (even historic) reminder to many within black America. There were people—foot soldiers of a pre-hip-hop movement, in fact—still suffering, paying a government-sanctioned price, for the social advancement of black folks. Also, America, even at the highest level, was willing to lock up people, especially black people, in order to systematically suppress the truth.

Along with the bittersweetness of Pratt's release from prison, the release of DMX's album *It's Dark and Hell Is Hot* was a subconcious jolt to the selfish and ultramaterialistic dance of hip-hop America. DMX, on this sinister and criminally macabre debut, didn't portray himself as the cocksure playa of "the game." Like Tupac, he was on the losing end of it, somewhat confused, violently struggling to win. In a rap game full of flossin' house niggas, X positioned himself as the anti-jiggy field nigga, constantly fighting—actually, robbing and murdering—stingy individuals out to disrupt his hustle or those who value money over loyalty to friends. If "Get at Me Dog" was a boastful call to reality-thirsty listeners—"real niggas"—to check out X, the greed-decrying anthem "Stop Being Greedy" was at the base of what he would shout on their behalf. "Y'all been eatin' long enough now, stop bein' greedy / Just keep it real, partner, give to the needy / Ribs is touchin', so don't make me wait / Fuck around, and I'm gonna bite you and snatch the plate."

And for all the illegal riches X snatched on his debut, he gave back to his growing audience in cathartic, passionate music: his growling voice, delivering sermons of ghetto life and desperate criminality with the cascading inflections of a holy man; his honesty about himself, openly struggling with his spiritual weakness of the flesh and mind, candidly talking to and thanking God on "The Convo" and tussling with the devil's influence on "Damien"; his benevolent thuginess, smiting tightfisted hooligans and constantly talking of loyalty to his partners. All of which was infused with the truthful candor that sprang from his performance.

In contrast to the cool vocals and passionless rhymes and styles of other commercial rappers, DMX roared. Surely, with all his brutal frankness and personal struggles and pop-ready looks, DMX was Tupac's heir. Only unlike Pac, whose criminal and jail experience hadn't come until after the fame, DMX built his criminal fantasies on an actual illicit past, on his own lack of love, on his own time in the streets robbing and stealing, and having spent half his early life in and out of penal institutions. As writer Heidi Siegmund Cuda would later write about him, "Where Tupac is the rose that grew from the concrete, DMX was the concrete."

The authenticity of X's struggle and his conviction were his ticket to reaching the people. Searching for the social commentary within DMX's music, you have to, as he implores listeners on the song, "Look Thru My Eyes": "See what I see. Do as I do. Be what I be. Walk in my shoes and hurt your feet." For his core audience, it was about speaking for the 'hood by showing how dark and hellish and disheartening ghetto life (and life, in general) could be. University of Southern California professor Todd Boyd later wrote in his book *The New H.N.I.C.* that "you might get a better read of what's going on in the world of black people today by listening to DMX on *It's Dark and Hell Is Hot* than by listening to repeated broadcasts of Martin Luther King speeches."

But whereas Tupac's Black Panther upbringing fueled the political nature of his rhymes and his aura as a leader of his generation, DMX compensated for his lack of political astuteness by creating a sentimentality for the confusion in his criminal savagery, his struggle to win at the game. For the new age of rap, DMX was that new by-any-means-necessary nigga tussling with his inner demons and getting his audience to tussle with theirs. Only X didn't call out the real enemies pulling the strings to the demons of his life (the police, the justice system, institutionalized racism, politicians). In the confusion of life, he couldn't see them. In the world of his album, other thugs—jealous and loathsome—were his enemies. He didn't ask the relevant social questions Pac asked, but his emotions spoke just the same. Whereas people responded to Tupac's insight and political compassion, the post–black power generation responded to DMX's nerve and fervor as well as his search for truth and love.

His place in pop music's commercial space was another case of hip-hop insurrection. In May 1998, *It's Dark and Hell Is Hot* debuted at number one on *Billboard*'s Top 200 Albums chart, all with no MTV rotation (they refused to play "Get at Me Dog" because X refused to edit out the curses) or pop radio play. He was hailed critically as *the* return of the hardcore MC, the new James Dean of hip-hop, putting angst and emotion and street reality and the voice of the unspoken-for back into commercial rap music. Hip-hop and the post–black power generation would now have a new hero, a delegate to represent the perspective of those angry niggas at the bottom of the world stage of American pop culture. The apathy and nonchalance behind the rhymes needed to be challenged.

For a generation with no collective political agenda—socially maneuvering in a black leadership vacuum—hardcore rap music was now the voice and guiding principle, *the* de facto leader, so to speak. It was the only vehicle capable of reflecting a black reality, albeit crudely, that wasn't being addressed, bluntly or soberly, on the stage of mainstream politics or within the agendas of established black leaders and organizations. That is, until civil rights leaders attempted to galvanize the post–black power generation's growing cultural influence and social ills under the banner of the Million Youth Movement in 1998.

As a little-league version of the Million Man March, this was an attempt, though halfhearted, by old and new civil rights/black nationalist figures to get the post–black power generation politically active en masse to deal with serious issues like insufficient education, joblessness, self-destruction, and lack of empowerment. Only it became a fiasco, in part turning into a contest between competing rallies: the Million Youth Movement in Atlanta and the Million Youth March in Harlem.

The Atlanta event was organized by Nation of Islam leader Louis Farrakhan, the NAACP, and a host of civil rights activists, including Jesse Jackson. Held on Auburn Avenue, the street where Dr. Martin Luther King, Jr., was born and is entombed, the September 7 march was less an edifying event than its MMM predecessor, consisting of an endless succession of political speeches with musical acts sprinkled in to break the monotony. The "Million March" franchise Farrakhan founded, a concept that shot him to mainstream recognition as a prominent black leader, proved stale and less effective in Atlanta, only attracting 500 to 700 attendees and, in the end, becoming nothing more than a brief report on the evening news.

In contrast to Atlanta's rally, Harlem's Million Youth March became a youth movement powder keg, its volatility a consequence of its organizer, former Nation of Islam minister Khallid Abdul Muhammad. An ominous cloud hung over the September 5 march from its inception. Between Mayor Rudolph Giuliani's promise to use police to enforce a strict cutoff time and Khallid's racially incendiary remarks, fears of a riot kept the number of attendees down to six thousand. And the fear of violence became real when police in riot gear moved in aggressively to shut down the march, causing clashes between marchers and the police. In the end, the great experiment by the elders of civil rights and black power had failed. Not because of apathy on the part of the post–black power generation, but because of the egotistical media grandstanding that had and has become part of established black leadership—a solipsism not dissimilar to what had plagued rap during its commercial and popular ascendance.

While the MYM failed to constructively harness the post–black power generation under a high-profile movement, DMX, within the context of hip-hop music, rose even further in his station as premier truthsayer of the streets. DMX again defied the boundaries of commercial rap—quickly proving his impact—nine months after dropping his debut CD. In December of the same year, X released his second disc, *Flesh of My Flesh, Blood of My Blood*, again debuting at number one on *Billboard*'s album charts. He became the first rap artist and the second pop artist (the other being pop legend Elton John) to release two number one albums in the same year.

The album proved another success for DMX, going triple platinum and further establishing his star within hardcore rap's dominance of American pop music. But, as if further channeling his artistic gaze into the underbelly of America's prosperity, X heightened the emotional intensity of his second offering. First, within the murderous image of the CD cover: against a stark white background, DMX glares sternly into the camera, his naked torso and outstretched hands covered in blood and pieces of flesh. As gruesome as the image looked, it was merely an expression of how deeply DMX was about to delve into his personal pain in order for the post–black power generation to see their own. Like his debut CD, *Flesh* extolled camaraderie and loyalty to ya dawgs over greed. Unlike it, *Flesh* didn't emphasize the Robin Hood theory as much. Rather, it was more a portrait of DMX examining himself, his society, his spirituality, and his street constituency. While themes of loyalty were pronounced in songs like "My Niggas," "Dogs for Life," and the title track and battles against greedy MCs (and hustlers) continued on "Ain't No Way" and "Bring Your Whole Crew," X widened the scope of his work by openly exploring himself and his tumultuous upbringing. On the CD's first single, "Slippin'," an autobiographical cut, X raps his story, surveying not only the events shaping his life but also the emotional consequences of such hard living. "First, came (Whoow!) the drama with my momma / She got on some fly shit so I split and said that I'm a be that seed that doesn't need much to succeed / Strapped with mad greed, a heart that doesn't bleed."

The blues within X's autobiographical songs weren't simply woe tales about himself but glimpses into the confusing and violent journey many young people have to navigate, not only in life but within themselves. On "Coming From," a song whose swaying chorus takes its cues from Negro spirituals, X examines the violent, loveless, and unpredictable nature of his life. Wondering if it's "love or a slug" that he's going to get first, X morbidly reflects: "My journey's been a rough one, I'm not sure when it began / But from the way it looks I know when it's gonna end." Ultimately, though, it's while reflecting on the roots of his own volatile nature ("I can be a beast or I can be a gentleman") that DMX taps into the collective blues and social neurosis of post–black power America, cracking open the pain and obstacles of his life, offering a voice and symbol to theirs: "When I was bad I was forgotten like I was dead rotten / Should have been getting love but instead was plottin'." Starting at the loveless relationship between his mother and his father (after all, doesn't all psychosis start there?), X examines his life, giving listeners his soul and story and, eventually, the ingredients of his salvation, ingredients that could also save his people. One being hip-hop: "Didn't know I was special 'til this rap shit came to be / Gave me a way out / Showed it was better to teach / Than to bust niggas with the .44 and leave them dead in the street." The other, love and truth: "What's the sense in hatin' when I could show love / What's the sense of fakin' when I can show blood." But, in the end, what X wanted his listeners to understand was the influence their past, especially their personal past, has on their present and that only by going over and understanding the past—no matter how ugly—will their vision of a future be clear.

A poignant message—especially considering that six months before *Flesh*'s release, the post–black power generation was abruptly reacquainted with racial hatred and butchery thought to be buried with the tattered, blood-caked overalls of Jim Crow. James Byrd, a forty-nine-year-old black man, was brutally murdered by three white supremacists in Jasper, Texas, a killing reminiscent of an old southern lynching. To gain attention for a new white power group the three men were trying to form, they took Byrd, who had hitched a ride with them, to a clearing, beat him, chained him by his feet to the back of their pickup truck, and dragged him for miles until his body tore to pieces, his torso and head littering the road. Aside from the clear racial motivation of the crime, it was the viciousness of the murder, the callousness of the killers, and the location of the crime (the Deep South) that were the most disturbing. It harked back to a time—in the not-too-distant past—when white men could commit any unthinkable act against a black man without consequence. This historical memory weighed heavily, prompting outcries against the crime and the need for justice.

Even though the murderers—Shawn Allen Berry, Lawrence Russell Brewer, and John William King—were convicted of the killing (Brewer and King received the death penalty while Berry was sentenced to life), one couldn't help but interpret the murder in Jasper as a sign of rising resentment not just against African Americans but against the cultural influence and power the post–black power generation exerted on mainstream America during the late 1990s. Just check the aftershock: A month after Lauryn Hill swept the Grammys, winning five awards, Washington, D.C., shock jock Doug "The Greaseman" Tracht commented, "No wonder people drag them from trucks" after playing a portion of Hill's hit single "That Thing." There was also the infamous 1998 Labor Day parade in the Howard Beach section of Queens, where New York City police and firefighters, dressed in afro wigs, blackface, and hip-hop-style clothing, appeared on a racist float whose title, "Black to the Future," expressed mockery as well as fear of black advancement. While most participants rode the float making exaggerated hand gestures aping those done by rappers, one participant followed behind with a noose around his neck that was tied to the back of the float, mimicking the murder in Jasper. (Three of the parade's participants—two firefighters and a police officer—were fired.) Both occurrences were jarring reminders to the post–black power generation that the rise of their cultural movement didn't erase the resentment (or flat-out hatred) many whites expressed (or secretly felt) toward black sociocultural advancement. Compared to diamonds and platinum, racism was still the harder stone to crack.

In addition to the self-examination, the drastic emotionalism and imagery of X's sophomore release played perfectly alongside national exposure of racial profiling—that unspoken practice within the parameters of institutional racism. Young African Americans, for eons, had known the hazards of "driving while black" and that blacks, more than any other American ethnic group, are overwhelmingly targeted for stops by police. In fact, a limited study revealed that while African Americans made up 15 percent of the driving population, 72 percent of all routine traffic stops occurred with African Americans.

The infamous videotape of the Rodney King beating, although exposing the brutal results of the issue, didn't prove the existence of racial profiling as would an April 1998 shooting on the New Jersey Turnpike. Four young unarmed men—students on their way to a basketball clinic—were stopped by New Jersey state troopers allegedly for speeding. The traffic stop turned near deadly when the two officers, claiming the van carrying the men lurched forward, began shooting into the vehicle, wounding three of the occupants.

Protests by civil rights advocates ensued, and a minor victory was won when racial profiling was proven to have been behind the incident. The troopers ultimately admitted to stopping the van because of the men's skin color, revealing they were trained by supervisors to single out dark-skinned drivers as the most likely to be carrying drugs. An investigation would reveal the officers' "special" training was encouraged as far up as the federal government, which, during its War on Drugs, alleged ethnic minorities were the main drug dealers. In connection with the investigation, the state's attorney general, Peter Verniero, released an official study, which found that minority drivers had "been treated differently than non-minority motorists during the course of traffic stops on the New Jersey Turnpike." According to the report, 77.2 percent of searches were of black and Latino drivers, and only 21.4 percent were of whites. Now there was proof that the problem of unequal treatment of black drivers was "real, not imagined." But for years government and law enforcement denied the practice. Even more peculiar was when former New Jersey governor Christine Todd Whitman, who had condemned the troopers' actions, became ensnared in the issue after a photo surfaced of her—accompanied by a couple of Camden, New Jersey, police—smiling while frisking a young black man. It was later revealed that the individual who was stopped and frisked hadn't done anything but fit the "profile" for a photo op with the governor to promote her tough stance on crime. And after all, hasn't the post–black power generation always epitomized rampant crime in America—at least according to the six o'clock news in most American cities?

But just as the young men shot on the turnpike exposed America's War on Drugs as really a war on young black people (innocent or otherwise), DMX, within the parameters of commercial hardcore rap, came to also embody the criminalization of the post–black power generation. Unlike Tupac, DMX was run through the penal system during the emerging crack epidemic of the 1980s, before he even picked up a mic. His status as former "jail nigga" worked twofold. On the one hand, his experience spoke directly to millions of young men and woman incarcerated under crime policies such as mandatory minimums and three-strikes laws, crack era laws that, since drugs were such a problem in black and brown communities, overwhelmingly handed longer prison time to young blacks and Latinos. On the other hand, the notion of DMX's jail niggadom was also extended to the nonincarcerated and non-ex-cons as simply a symbol for being trapped within the parameters society places on them, an unspoken reality the post–black power generation is all too aware of. With that in mind, DMX's struggle to beat the odds could be embraced by all, whether it's a brotha locked down, a college student trying to find his way in the world, or a corporate brotha struggling to crack the glass ceiling. And within the families of those mentioned, there's always someone like DMX.

By the time X released his third CD, . . . And Then There Was X, in December 1999 (again debuting at number one on Billboard's Top 200), he was well situated in the pop landscape—a bona fide rap superstar balancing fame and celebrity while carefully maintaining his role as 'hood spokesperson and voice of rage. By now he was "the realest nigga up in this game." And, appropriately, none of this awareness was lost on the album. The song "Fame," with its dramatic percussive buildup and candid lyrics about the dark and bright sides of celebrity, was X's attempt at shaping and defining his own musical legacy despite how the media played up the violence in his lyrics: "No second guessing on what I stood for / I was good for . . . Stopping niggas from killing each other in the hood or . . . Comin' through showing love."

But for X's arrival as a mainstream juggernaut, Then There Was X primarily served to connect his street ministry to a wider audience, repackaging X with a slightly pronounced rock music edge. The album's single "What's My Name?," which helped the disc go five times platinum, was an apocalyptic roar against fake rappers, strategically placed over an epic rhythm accentuated by blasts of synth-horns and piano. Even the song's video, inspired by Lenny Kravitz's 1993 "Are You Gonna Go My Way," was a rock-style version of X's "Get at Me Dog." Only instead of holding court bare-chested in a sweaty, dimly lit club, X does so at the base of a brightly lit space-age observatory—his subjects cheering and shouting in circular rows above him. In the tradition of hardcore rappers before him (Run-D.M.C., Public Enemy, N.W.A), X skillfully merged his angst with rock's palatable bad-boy packaging to advance his agenda. And now was as perfect a time as any, with new rock stars like Korn, Limp Bizkit, and Kid Rock merging their thrashing guitars with hip-hop's rapping and turntable scratches, creating a budding rock subgenre called nu metal.

X made his anti-jigginess plain on cuts like "More 2 a Song," which, unlike the encoded thrust of other songs, spoke unfiltered to rap's rampant materialism ("It's more 2 a song than jewelry and clothes"). At a time when *Newsweek* magazine trumpeted the advancement of blacks during the economic windfall, X held the vision for those not benefiting from "The Good News About Black America." Moreover, X's growing exposure allowed his expression of frustration and anger to resonate beyond his faithful fan base to an older, non-hip-hop audience. It was this exposure that turned the CD's follow-up single, "Party Up," with its chorus of "Y'all gonna make me lose my mind up in here—up in here!" into a universal anthem for anyone young or old who was fed up with ignorance or ill-treatment.

The sentiment behind the chorus seemed especially relevant in the wake of the shooting death of Liberian immigrant Amadou Diallo in 1999. Diallo was shot nineteen times (out of forty-one rounds fired) by officers of NYPD's Street Crime Unit, and his killing became the nation's most brutal example of insensitive and inhumane policing within the black community. Approached by officers who thought he might be a rape suspect or a lookout for a robbery, Diallo was riddled with bullets when he attempted to retrieve a wallet from his coat pocket. To black America, and blacks of the Diaspora, it was a case of profiling turned execution. The scholars Henry Louis Gates, Jr., and Charles J. Ogletree, Jr., wrote in the *Los Angeles Times*: "We share the somber view that had Diallo been a European immigrant in a white neighborhood, he would be alive and unharmed." The senseless killing and subsequent trial (all four officers were acquitted) undoubtedly confirmed black America's fear that, regardless of class and social status, their lives were worthless to the police and the American justice system. "America killed Amadou Diallo," wrote Derrick Z. Jackson in *The Boston Globe*, "with a barrage of our perceptions that led the officers to assume that a hardworking, black street merchant could be a hardened black criminal." Amid the protests demanding justice for the killing, the only sentiment that could be heard nationally, in the realms of rap's bling fascination, was X's stir of frustration. Though "Party Up" was specifically written with sucker MCs in mind, the chorus was an indirect expression of rising intolerance.

If *Then There Was X* was a sounding board for young black America's premillennial jitters, DMX's next CD, 2001's *The Great Depression*, was a repository of new-millennium turmoil. In the two years preceding the disc, America had experienced a jarring political and economic shift. The presidential election of 2000 played as much in the arena of civil rights as it did in the piles of hanging chads declaring George W. Bush's unpopular win over Al Gore. In Florida, conspiracy overshadowed coincidence after reports of voter suppression and irregularities in predominately black districts (12.4 percent of the ballots in Gadsden County were invalidated due to faulty counting machines) revealed unbelievable disparities between white and black voting districts. Overwhelmingly, black districts were at a disadvantage to handle their roster of registered voters with antiquated or broken voting booths and a lack of computers at voting sites. That the fiasco took place in Florida—the pivotal state coincidentally governed by George W.'s brother Jeb—instantly defined Bush's election as an undermining of both black voting power (90 percent of blacks voted for Gore) and the will of the American populace (Bush lost the popular vote).

Even more coincidental, as if America had become snagged in a 1980s soundloop, the Bush in the White House again was accompanied by the quieting of an economic boom. The dot-com revolution crumbled in the deafening wake of American consumers' failure to make a massive lifestyle exodus to the Internet combined with the brutal reality of many of the start-ups' hollow business models. And fallout from corporate scandals like the Enron debacle further shook the stock market into instability.

In April 2001, mounting rage over police brutality exploded into three days of rioting in Cincinnati after an officer killed nineteen-year-old Timothy Thomas. The teenager was shot after fleeing from police who had attempted to stop him for outstanding warrants, mostly traffic violations. But instead of a wallet triggering the suspicious movement, it was Thomas's attempt to pull up his baggy jeans, a hip-hop fashion staple, that triggered the shooting—making Thomas the fifteenth black person to die at the hands of the Cincinnati police since 1995.

But DMX's *The Great Depression* rang most significantly in the wake of September 11, 2001. The CD was released a month after the tragic attacks on the World Trade Center and the Pentagon, and its cover art seemed to prophesy, or at least coincide with, the economic and spiritual devastation the terrorist attacks brought to the country. Against the backdrop of an ominously clouded sky, X's large, sad eyes stare straight ahead while a deteriorating pier—crumbling, deserted, and littered—stretches out into dark waters. On the inside flap, an introspective DMX sits on the other end of the pier in front of the battered shell of a Rolls-Royce—a useless remnant of the bling era quickly slipping away as the terrorist attacks sent America's economy into a recession. Even the world of rap didn't go untouched as music sales declined by 5 percent with many a commercial rap star failing to post his former numbers. Although *The Great Depression* was a message to material-obsessed rappers that they were about to experience hard days, the timing of the release was perfect for X's wholehearted expression of his role as *the* hip-pop representative of the streets.

Now with his status as thug angel and hip-hop icon firmly established, X bluntly spoke his intentions in between bluesy biographies and encoded crime tales of hungry versus greedy. The album was both X's celebration of his success and his chance to offer some direction to the game—to dictate and speak directly to rap music's shallowness. "The difference between right and wrong is me," X raps on "Trina Moe." "Niggas talk shit but you can't MC / We already know how much your watch is worth / Talk about helpin' the hurt, savin' a church / Why don't you brag about helpin' out where you come from or givin' brothers a job that really want one."

With hardcore rap music lacking a firm voice of black advocacy, X's decision to take the position was especially needed as Washington's "War on Terrorism" steadily drowned out a momentous, global dialogue on bigotry. (Just a week prior to the 9/11 attacks, the World Conference Against Racism, held in Durban, South Africa, was in the midst of addressing the racism that affects black, brown, and Middle Eastern people worldwide.) On the brash, rocked-out cut "I'ma Bang," X boldly states who his constituency is, rapping: "I speak for the meek and the lonely, weak and the hungry / Speak for the part of the street that keep it ugly." Ultimately, though, X executed this best on the CD's song "Who We Be," an electrifying anthem of America's ignorance about the suffering of black folks. Released shortly before 9/11, the song took on a whole new meaning in the face of racial issues drowned out by the drums of war. "It represents all the drama we go through as a people," X told MTV's *Diary of DMX, Part II*. "It's a reality-based song—something hip-hop is in desperate need of right now." The cut became an affirmation of the daily terrors many young blacks face, as if it were a rapped version of former Clinton adviser Vernon Jordan's words during a speech at Howard University after 9/11. "Slavery was terrorism," he proclaimed. "Segregation was terrorism, the bombing of the four little girls in Sunday school in Birmingham was terrorism."

"What they don't know is the bullshit, the drama, the guns, the armor / The city, the farmer, the babies, the mama," X began "Who We Be." "The projects, the drugs, the children, the thugs / The tears, the hugs, the love, the slugs." The song gave voice to the collective consciousness of black America. In the face of the country's lockstep against terrorism—Middle Eastern terrorism—"Who We Be" revealed what was already clear to many in post–black power America: racism is terrorism—the oldest form of terrorism—which America has known and has freely committed.

Further pushing X's profile as leader was the song's video, a rousing visual of X chanting his lyrics while turning angrily toward historical footage of battles for racial and social justice. Shot by director Joseph Kahn, the video was the first time that DMX blatantly positioned himself as a leader of the streets on camera and in a pop context. But in the arena of hardcore rap music, the streets had now grown to include a global community of hip-hop fans, a point that wasn't missed at the video's conclusion. Borrowing from the end of Spike Lee's film *Malcolm X*, individual children (all from different ethnic groups) shout, "I am DMX!"

Their declarations showed not only the now massive appeal of DMX but how the appeal of hip-hop culture and rap music had linked the struggles and fears of black folk with other oppressed and depressed peoples. The multiculti montage presented the broadening appeal of X and the emotional impact rap and hip-hop culture were having on the globe. Rooted in the emotions of post–black power America—the main artery of the music's appeal—rap music, especially the hardcore MC, was now the chief export of the post–black power generation. Although *The Great Depression* wasn't X's biggest-selling album, only going platinum, it marked the fruition of his mission. He had reestablished the hardcore ghetto-conscious MC as the premier figure of popular rap music, speaking uncompromisingly for the streets and to the angst of the people.

Without question, X's stardom was anchored in an audience not quite over the phenomenon of Tupac Shakur. With Shakur's death, the post–black power generation lost a warrior, a Huey Newton of the hip-pop world, a fiery, frustrated voice with Hollywood looks. But to his credit, X's impact on hip-hop music, unlike that of his predecessor, was more spiritual than sociopolitical. With commercial rap at a creative crossroads, torn between selling its soul to a lucrative mainstream and speaking the suffering heart of its core audience, DMX emerged not only as Thug Life but as Thug Christ, refocusing hip-hop music's gaze on healing the people. He boldly laid open the dark crevices of his heart, mind, and life as a means of giving hip-hop music and its audience a new, honest energy. And in the process, X—the menacing growl, the anger, the unflinching candor, the self-examination, and the Christian gaze (which could also be seen as a Tupac influence, given Pac's numerous references to God and Christ)—would ultimately become the thrust of hardcore rap at the start of the twenty-first century.

But the phenomenon of DMX and his rage against the pop machine eventually dwindled. X ultimately became a caricature of himself (the growling-dog thing just got old), and Queens-born rapper Ja Rule, with his gravelly sing-along voice, thuggish sensitivity, and scripture-influenced album titles like 2000's *Rule 3:36* and 2001's *Pain Is Love*, stepped into his spotlight, garnering multiplatinum sales but giving listeners a less convincing, R&B'ed version of DMX. Ja's reign, too, would crumble in the wake of another Queens-raised Thug Messiah, 50 Cent, whose phenomenal debut CD, *Get Rich or Die Tryin'*, would defy slumping music sales by infusing DMX's street-corner cred and Tupac's hardcore introspection with the hustler-like charisma of Biggie Smalls.

Nevertheless, within the unbalanced relationship between America and its post–black power youth, rap music—through reestablishing the hard-rock MC—had once again managed to recharge its social relevance. And most important, after twenty-five years, the music—despite critics, naysayers, and other obstacles—had finally (and firmly) rooted itself in the lexicon of mainstream American culture. But, through the rise of its influence, it had ultimately become something greater than music: it overwhelmingly became *the* vehicle for expression and philosophical exchange within the post–black power generation. Moreover, whether rap's nihilism was believed to contribute to or merely report the self-destruction, pain, and joys of post–black power America, at the dawn of a new millennium it would have to begin facing *some* responsibility for the long-standing issues within (and outside of) its borders.

TWELVE

Vanilla Nice

Eminem

I walked with every muscle aching . . . wishing I were a Negro,
feeling that the best the white world had offered was not enough
ecstasy for me, not enough life, joy, kicks, darkness, music, not
enough night . . . I wished I were . . . anything but what I was so
drearily, a "white man" disillusioned.

—Jack Kerouac, *On the Road*

So there was a new breed of adventurers . . . who drifted out at
night looking for action with a black man's code to fit their facts.
The hipster had absorbed the existentialist synapses of the Negro,
and for practical purposes could be considered a white Negro.

—Norman Mailer, "The White Negro"

A venture to the movies on the weekend of November 8, 2002, meant, more than likely, a trip to see *8 Mile*, starring hip-hop's white mic wonder, Eminem. No doubt you weathered crowded lobbies and long lines filled with teens and young adults (most of them white) dressed in hip-hop or simply hip gear, amped to partake in an American pop capitalist tradition: the cinematic mega-marketing of a music icon. After selling twelve million Eminem albums (his second disc, 2000's *The Marshall Mathers LP*, sold 1.7 million units in a week), Universal, the parent company of Interscope, wanted to "expand the demographic of its hottest music property." Enlisting the screenwriter Scott Silver to craft a story that "could reach an audience with reservations about Eminem," that could, as the *Village Voice* writer Richard

Goldstein wrote, act as a "stump speech" for the rapper, Universal created a *Rocky*-esque tale of a young white guy whose struggle with poverty coincides with his aching desire to earn respect in a black man's sport. (Instead of boxing, it's freestyle battle rapping.) With comparisons to how Elvis's career had been given a major boost by film—and, indeed, comparisons between Eminem and the "King of Rock 'n' Roll" were plenty—the media and the country were abuzz with Eminem's cinematic debut.

Though I wasn't particularly a fan, curiosity had gotten the best of me. And there I was in a packed theater in Manhattan's Union Square witnessing this phenomenon, a quasi-biographical vehicle designed to mine my sympathy for this MC who was vilified by a few (gay activists, feminists, and conservatives) and loved by millions. (Apparently, looking at his sales, loved a lot more than the bestselling black rapper.)

Named after the stretch of road separating poor black Detroit from its poor white suburbs, *8 Mile* is the story of Jimmy Smith, Jr. (played by Eminem), nicknamed B-Rabbit. He's an aspiring rapper who has moved back in with his alcoholic mother (they live in a trailer) in order to save money to make a demo. He works a dead-end job at an auto plant. And worst of all he has embarrassingly choked in a verse-for-verse rap competition and lost, sending his confidence plummeting. The loss is the biggest obstacle standing in the way of Rabbit achieving stardom within Detroit's underground rap scene and possibly beyond . . . That, and the fact that rap is *black* poetry ("the only legitimate profession in America," wrote writer S. Craig Watkins, "where being white is a liability") and the local scene is ruled by Rabbit's nemesis—the crew he lost the battle to—an all-black posse called Leaders of the Free World, whose leader's name is Papa Doc. While Rabbit doesn't play the race card in battle, his enemies do, referring to him as "Elvis," "Beaver Cleaver," and "Nazi," the names playing particularly well for the all-black crowd attending the contest. Out of Rabbit's multiculti crew, his black best friend, Future (these names could only come from a Hollywood daydream), believes in his abilities the most, and spends most of the film convincing Rabbit to return to the stage and slay his adversaries. After gathering enough courage to do so (a huge chunk of that process coming from Future inspiring our hero to embrace his identity as "white trash"), Rabbit gives it one last try.

At the film's climax, as Rabbit's rival Papa Doc appears on the verge of winning, Rabbit turns the tables on him, not only "acknowledging his own whiteness" and lower-income status (removing Doc's power over him) but exposing the upper-middle-class and privileged background of his opponent. With the overall hip-hop message of *8 Mile* being that class trumps race and "keeping it real" means "keeping it poor and impoverished," the Leaders of the Free World are leaders no more, and the new rhyme king who wins the crowd and the crown is a white boy (a story that is as American as a cross-burning rally). While the film's tale of struggle and perseverance was no doubt endearing— enough so that it opened number one and made $51 million its first weekend—the ending, as much as it borrowed from old westerns, was a chilling one. Having built Rabbit's self-assurance and given him the tools to become a champion, Future offers Rabbit a partnership in running the venue, called the Shelter, which holds these battles. He also offers Rabbit a chance to use the space to promote himself. Instead of gladly accepting the offer, or at least expressing some appreciation, Rabbit, with a stoic look, his eyes staring off into the night, refuses, saying he wants to do his own thing. After coolly stating his goal, our hero walks exhaustedly away from his rainbow coalition down an alley into the dark, like the Lone Ranger. The film ends.

While the image by itself meant nothing, its implications went deep. The vision of a white boy leaving his black bud hanging, moseying off with the crown and the potential to reap untold fortunes, inevitably stirred me and a number of folks to imagine rap music, after Eminem's enormous success, slipping from the creative hands of blacks and becoming totally white. One could see this on the horizon as white writers and cultural pundits started tossing the title "King of Rap" Eminem's way. Greg Tate articulated the concern best when he wrote in an essay: "Black people have good reason to fear expropriation of their cultural property. A certain anxiety about one's expiration date creeps in: What's going to happen to me now that there are white boys out there doing me better than I do me?" Unfortunately, public dialogue about Eminem would be broached not constructively by MCs of any relevance, such as DMX or Jay-Z, but only destructively by a rapper steeped in infamy, first as a member of Boston's Almighty RSO, then as the co-head of *The Source*, using the magazine to attempt to build his career and air his grievances with Eminem. (That battle will be discussed later.) But unease over the larger implications of the superstar-

dom of Eminem—an incredibly gifted MC, at that—was a valid emotion, especially given the history of black music in America: one example after another of stolen property. Blacks build it and whites, while
earning most of the money, take the credit. The most noted example is
rock 'n' roll. Although the genre was created from black rhythm and
blues, its most famed architects being Little Richard and Chuck Berry,
the "King" is Elvis, and the genre, without much debate, is considered
"white music," the emblematic channel for American white teen angst.

Even though rap has primarily been a channel for black machismo,
following the phenomenon of Run-D.M.C. white boys were inspired to
flex their inflated sense of manhood through the music, whether the
retro-rap punk stylings of the Beastie Boys, the ultra-I'm-down-for-
hip-hop-and-black-folk rhymes of 3rd Bass, the mall-packaged coolness of Vanilla Ice, or the Irish-pride gangsta rants of House of Pain.
But as much as rappers and rap fans have fought dilution of the music,
either by decrying non-hardcore rappers for selling out ("Pop goes the
weasel," famously—and ironically—rapped 3rd Bass) or by claiming
appropriation of the music by whites (especially with Vanilla Ice), there
isn't much public discussion among MCs about how rap's large white
audience—that two-thirds who buy rap and send it multiplatinum—
dictates the sound and attitude of the music. While rap speaks for the
streets of black ghetto U.S.A., it does so at the cost of peddling stereotypes as "realness." (After the revolution of N.W.A, any rapper who desired huge sales had to be a "nigga" . . . with an attitude representing
niggas without a voice.) While there isn't much debate or constant acknowledgment of the whites who buy rap or how they're affected by
the music, the rise of Eminem is most profound because not only is he
a member of this demographic, having gotten into rap around the time
P.E. released *Nation of Millions* and N.W.A released *Straight Outta
Compton*, but because he was able to channel the discontent that
turned his rap heroes into icons of the disaffected and make rap *really*
speak for a white audience. Instead of being among the legions of
middle-class suburban white kids fascinated with looking at black urban angst through a hip-hop lens, Eminem was a product of America's
other invisible nation, the white underclass, unable to shake the contradictions of race and class (America screws white folks, too) and coming
of age in close proximity to black folks. A lot like Elvis.

As fans and the curious have often read or heard, Eminem was the offspring of a teenage bride, Debbie Mathers-Briggs, who was fifteen when she married and around seventeen when she gave birth to Eminem, born Marshall Mathers III on October 17, 1972, in St. Joseph, Missouri. The family moved to North Dakota, where his father, Marshall Mathers, Jr., was supposed to work as an assistant manager at a hotel. But after the marriage deteriorated, reportedly because of Pop's erratic behavior, Debbie left with her son, first moving around Missouri. Then, when Marshall was a few years older, they headed to Warren, Michigan, a section just north of Detroit described by Hilton Als as a "blue-collar suburb . . . populated by white laborers from the South." As one of Detroit's few white suburban neighborhoods—the city on its way to becoming over 80 percent black—Warren saw its population explode after the city's civil unrest in 1967, almost exclusively as a result of white flight from Detroit. Although Warren's manufacturing and economic base declined over the years, its heavily southern population didn't. And so the sight of Confederate flags hanging in windows mixed easily with calls of "nigger" to any black person bold enough to venture there.

But when Marshall and his mother moved to Roseville, another blue-collar white enclave surrounded by the black underclass, he received a fiery baptism in black rage while a student at Dort Elementary School. In 1981, at around nine years old, Marshall was given the first in a series of alleged beatings from a black student, D'Angelo Bailey, that, according to a 1982 lawsuit filed by his mother, left him suffering headaches, nausea, post-concussion syndrome, intermittent loss of vision and hearing, and nightmares. Though the lawsuit his mother filed against the school was dismissed in 1983—the judge ruled that schools were immune from lawsuits—Marshall exacted his revenge on Bailey several years later. Most acerbically, he settled the score through rap music, which his uncle Ronnie, who wasn't much older than Marshall, introduced him to as Marshall entered high school. Ronnie later died from a gunshot wound—his death was ruled a suicide by police—but the streetcentric genre he'd bonded with his nephew over gave Marshall an outlet: for being accepted as, entering Warren's predominantly black Lincoln High School, his circle of friends became mostly African Americans; for his lack of academic abilities, dropping out of school at seventeen after failing ninth grade three times; for a dismal future staring him in the face as he took a $5.50-an-hour job as a cook/

dishwasher for the restaurant Gilbert's Lounge; and, eventually, for his turbulent life with his mom, a woman who loved her son but whose dysfunctional behavior (a social worker suggested she suffered from Munchausen syndrome, saying she exhibited "a very suspicious, almost paranoid personality") made home life, well, a bit dramatic.

Though Marshall was proficient with the *word*, rap, as he'd so often be reminded, was still black music, its language intrinsically connected to a population of young folk who were vehement about not wanting their soul to go the way of rock 'n' roll. By 1990 Marshall had become M&M—a play on his name that he later modified to Eminem—recording music with a partner at a neighborhood studio and developing an intricate rhyme style his friends dubbed "insider," rhyming many words within a line as opposed to rhyming words at the end of each sentence. (He was hardly the originator, though; Rakim had developed the concept in rap four years before Em added his own cadence.) But outside of the studio or his crew of fellow hip-hop enthusiasts, as M. L. Elrick wrote in "Eminem's Dirty Secrets," black folks "just weren't willing to listen to a skinny white dude rhyming—regardless of his talent." Unlike in other black genres of yore, which were heisted and given a racial makeover (never considering how the black audience felt), respect in hip-hop comes through earning validation from rap's core black audience and black icons (something that would later help Eminem in his rise to superstardom). And so if Eminem wanted to build the name and career he so desired, he'd have to earn it on hip-hop's field of competition, going head-to-head with other (mostly black) MCs in Detroit's underground battle scene. Becoming a battle MC proved more rewarding for Eminem as—with each contest won—his skills overshadowed the fact that he was an outsider, a "wigger" fascinated with black culture. His ability to freestyle (recite impromptu raps) landed him a recording agreement with local producer Marky Bass. The result was Eminem's first LP, *Infinite*, a low-budget disc "with tracks about love, unity and trying to get on in spite of hard times." But, just as Eminem learned when he decided to choose rap as his artistic expression, no one *really* listened. Then again, Eminem, sounding like so many other rappers, wasn't really listening to himself, to what made him angry: the resentment, joy, and fury inside that expressed who *he* really was—poor white trash, America's other Frankenstein produced in trailer parks across the country. His answer to releasing that rage through rap was adopting an alter ego, Slim Shady, the white version of black criminal kookiness. If Eminem couldn't pull off being a pill-popping, crack-smoking, 'shroom-gulping, murdering rapist on disc, then maybe Slim Shady could. And if there weren't many label execs out there who would get a white MC with such dark humor, there was a black exec who might.

When Jimmy Iovine played Dr. Dre a few songs off Eminem's independently produced *Slim Shady EP* in 1997, Dre must have felt like he had been struck by lightning. In his third incarnation as the owner of the Interscope-distributed Aftermath, Dre was looking for his next big bang theory, another revolution in hip-hop that would shake and scare folks. He had already opened the white youth market to rage, gangsta cool, and nihilism in blackface, turning hardcore rap into hard-rock Americana (co-ventures with black folks—Eazy and Suge—that got him screwed royally, he alleged in a pending lawsuit). Upon hearing Eminem, he got his most brilliant and lucrative idea: Why not sell those millions of white fans a white MC who, through his own experience and fantasies, articulated, in the age of hip-hop, *their* rage against the machine?

By the time Aftermath released Eminem's commercial debut, *The Slim Shady LP*, in 1999, not only was rap outselling rock music, but rock was starting to look and sound a lot like rap. The 1994 death of rock's tortured god Kurt Cobain ended both pop culture's grunge-mania and rock's reign as the pacesetter of American alternative music. The death of grunge also ended rock's role as primary outlet for white teen angst. Save for Marilyn Manson, not many rock stars were doing their job of scaring the shiznit out of society in general and the parents of their young audience. But a new crop of rockers developed in the mid-1990s—artists influenced as much by Rakim as they were by Metallica and Suicidal Tendencies—and began moving units of the genre's latest pop incarnation known variously as nu metal, rapcore, and rap-metal. Acts like Limp Bizkit, Korn, Rage Against the Machine, and Kid Rock were the platinum-selling vanguard of this rap/heavy metal/hardcore punk hybrid—in which the raps and turntable scratches were as loud and confrontational as the blaring guitar riffs. Moreover, rap's influence didn't stop at hard rock, but stretched further to include American alternative rock, particularly the artist Beck, who was dubbed the Bob Dylan of Generation X while rapping and beat-sampling his way onto the pop charts with the song "Loser." These artists may have awed fans and critics alike with their offshoots of hip-hop, but none stirred both hip-hop's creative/racial consciousness and society's fear/tolerance of rap music as pop quite like Eminem.

The Slim Shady LP, with its rhymes about rape, drug taking, and murder, its expressions of white poverty, and its punch lines that beat white popular culture with a maniacally humorous bat, offered hard-core rap packaged in a rock tradition, specifically, the use of the alter ego—onstage personas like Screamin' Jay Hawkins or Alice Cooper or David Bowie's space-glamorous Ziggy Stardust or George Clinton's Dr. Funkenstein—which allowed artists a way of becoming cooler, crazier, and larger than themselves, giving listeners more for their imaginations. In the case of Eminem, Slim Shady—the name for his "attitude"—was both his way to become as raw and raunchy as his black counterparts (without coming off as a wannabe) and a means to challenge all that white America—its moral and cultural ideals, and its glorious notions of "whiteness"—held dear. "Hi Kids! Do you like violence? (Yeah! Yeah! Yeah!)," he asked on the song's debut single, "My Name Is," introducing Slim to the world. "Do you wanna see me stick Nine Inch Nails through each one of my eyelids? (Uh-huh!) / Wanna copy me and do exactly like I did? (Yeah! Yeah!) / Try 'cid and get fucked up worse than my life is? (Huh?)."

With Slim Shady, Eminem possessed a means—an excuse, some might say—of unleashing his own ill inner thoughts and behavior. The character could be translated through numerous personas and princi-ples conveying the attitude, bravado, and style of hip-hop while solidly maintaining Eminem's identity as a crazyass white dude, the product of an "All-American" environment. He could wryly delve into Em's life as the warped product of the quintessentially dysfunctional American family ("ninety-nine percent of my life I was lied to," he rapped. "I just found out my mom does more dope than I do"). He could personify violent impulses, as he does for several individuals driven to their breaking point on the follow-up single, "Guilty Conscience." Playing the voice of the men's rage, Slim battles with their guilt (played by Dr. Dre), finally winning over their conscience by hilariously calling Dre to task for his own real-life transgressions. "You gonna take advice from somebody who slapped Dee Barnes!" he yelled. "Mr. Dre, Mr. N.W.A / Mr. AK comin' straight outta Compton, y'all better make way." On the cut "Brain Damage," he's a rebellious white grade-school student asserting that he was beaten senseless by a black student, D'Angelo Bailey, and gets his revenge through rhyme. "This is for every time you took my orange juice," Em says before returning the brutal favor, "or stole my seat in the lunchroom and drank my chocolate milk . . . I cocked the broomstick back and swung hard as I could / And beat him over the head with it until I broke the wood." Slim would also hand out fantastical retribution to the mother of his daughter on "'97 Bonnie & Clyde," using a day at the beach as a way to dump the body of his baby's mother after murdering her.

On the lighter side, there was Slim's over-the-top mischief, as a "raver" who introduces a girl to hallucinogenic mushrooms on "My Fault"; as an outrageous rap star clowning celebrities (and having a fantasy orgy with Nicole Brown Simpson) on "Role Model"; or as an MC badman flexing his middle finger to the world (and other white rappers) on "Just Don't Give a Fuck." "I'm nicer than Pete, but I'm on a Serch to crush a Miilkbone," he signified to members of 3rd Bass and white Jersey rapper Miilkbone. "I'm Everlast-ing, I melt Vanilla Ice like silicone."

But the profundity of Slim rang loudest in his role as the voice of white America's poor, as a guy who's so down on his luck, his funds, and his hope that—like many of his impoverished black compadres— he's got to rap his blues away. "I'm tired of being white trash, broke and always poor," Eminem reflected on "If I Had." "Tired of taking pop bottles back to the party store . . . Tired of not driving a BM / Tired of not working at GM . . . Tired of not sleeping without a Tylenol PM." To anyone with even a cursory knowledge of commercial hardcore rap, it was apparent that Eminem—besides mining his own life—drew inspiration from the pages of Tupac's Thug Life, communicating the dissatisfaction of an existence at the bottom of America's socioeconomic heap. "My life is full of empty promises and broken dreams," Eminem laments on "Rock Bottom." "I'm hoping things look up but there ain't no job openings / I feel discouraged, hungry, and malnourished / Living in this house with no furnace . . . I'm sick of working dead-end jobs for lame pay / And I'm tired of being hired and fired the same day." In exposing his own hardships, Eminem exposed, for those who still refused to acknowledge a population of white poor and dispossessed, another shade of rage and frustration that could be just as desperate as a black gangsta's. Driven to violence and crime by his dire situation, Eminem, comparing his discontent to Tupac's, threatens society: "Holdin' two Glocks, I hope your door's got new locks on 'em / My daughter's feet ain't got no shoes or socks on 'em."

A week before the LP's release, *Rolling Stone* writer Matt Diehl declared, "When the world finds out what Eminem is talking about, it may not feel so enlightened." But for all of its graphic lyrics and twisted humor, the biggest stir caused by *Slim Shady* was the instant sensation it and its creator became. Before going on to sell three million copies by the end of the year, Eminem's national debut was on its way to becoming the breakout album of the year. (Even garnering—thanks to his association with Dre—the respect of black hip-hop fans.) With the videos for "My Name Is" and "Guilty Conscience" in heavy rotation, Eminem, as the white MC with major rhyme skills, became the newest hardcore darling of MTV (more so than any of its rap-metal stars). And at the 2000 Grammy Awards, *Slim Shady* captured two wins: Best Rap Album and Best Rap Solo Performance for "My Name Is." Finally, the face and perspective of the young white hip-hop fan were here in the flesh.

Though for all of his rage and resentment, Eminem, while given his props as a gifted wordsmith, was viewed by the larger public as quirky and quaint, a white rapper with a "skewed, bratty humor" (as one *Washington Post* critic wrote). If most of America wasn't paying much attention to Eminem or his Slim Shady attitude, they would the week after his album went double platinum, when the Columbine High School massacre brought senseless violence—usually experienced by black and brown urban youth (though on a smaller scale)—to a quiet, predominantly white Colorado town. On Tuesday, April 20, 1999, two Columbine students, Dylan Klebold and Eric Harris, went to their high school armed with shotguns, pistols, and pipe bombs and opened fire. Aside from shooting students at random, they specifically targeted jocks and girls. (Their hate also extended to race, as one black student athlete was reportedly called a "nigger" before he was shot to death.) By the end of the attack, Klebold and Harris had killed twelve students and a teacher and wounded twenty-four others before committing suicide. Footage of terrified students trying to escape the slaughter, running across campus and jumping out of broken windows, made the news worldwide. Furthermore, the school shooting was dubbed the "deadliest" in U.S. history, turning the word "Columbine" into a catch-phrase for future murderous rampages where a student shoots (or threatens to shoot) classmates and faculty. But once the shock of Columbine subsided, and the grown-ups went looking for the cause of this rampage (read: white kids acting like they "Just Don't Give a Fuck"), scrutiny—or, rather, blame—went everywhere: on lack of school safety, prompting many schools to adopt zero-tolerance policies on weapons and threatening behavior; on bullying in schools (because numerous Columbine students stated bullying was rampant on campus), causing schools across the country to implement anti-bullying rules; and in the specific case of Klebold and Harris, blame was primarily focused on violence in the media and its influence on youth. Many of the victims' families alleged that the killers were merely imitating the violence they had witnessed in a number of video games they played and films they watched, especially the 1995 movie *The Basketball Diaries*, which had a school shooting scene similar to Columbine's. (A lawsuit was filed against a number of entertainment companies, citing their products as an influence, but it was dismissed.) The most recognizable scapegoat became shock-rock superstar Marilyn Manson, who, in all the hysteria, was wrongly reported as being idolized by the killers. Since America had never experienced such a cold-blooded, hate-filled killing spree of this magnitude by, of all people, white teenagers, folks refused to examine the obvious—flimsy gun laws and easy access to guns, or better yet, the deranged and bigoted hearts and minds of the killers themselves. Instead, important people of conscience, once again, began focusing on the violent and misogynistic (and even homophobic) language in popular music. And so, along with protests and attacks against the devilish influence of films, video games, and Marilyn Manson, who became the most vocal critic of such misdirected concerns, public outcry found its most fascinating target in Eminem following the release of his third disc, 2000's *The Marshall Mathers LP*.

Given the overall message of the last album, it wasn't as if Eminem was trying to avoid provocation ("God sent me to piss the world off," he uttered on "My Name Is"). *The Marshall Mathers LP*, while spouting the usual pressures of hip-hop stardom (overzealous fans and greedy record labels), deepened its perverted expressions of anger, frustration, and dissatisfaction, turning them into critiques of society's hypocrisy. On this disc filled with his gripes, Eminem gave more musical space to Slim Shady, who this go-round was stretched into a zany, Jeffrey Dahmer–like caricature ("Well, some of us cannibals . . . cut other people open like cantaloupes"). But as hip-hop's latest poet laureate, one who, being Caucasian, felt he could challenge white society in a way black rappers couldn't, Eminem added another layer to rap music's effectiveness at getting under people's skin. "Y'all act like you never seen a white person before," he scolded on the first single, "The Real Slim Shady." "Jaws all on the floor like Pam, like Tommy just burst in the door / And started whupping her ass worse than before."

As the lone white MC, now sharing the pop charts with other white music acts famous for performing black music forms—Britney Spears and "boy bands" like *NSYNC and the Backstreet Boys—Eminem, wishing to separate his intentions from this pack of interlopers, positioned himself as the white pop antihero of dissatisfaction. "I'm sick of you little girl and boy groups," he rapped. "All you do is annoy me / So I have been sent here to destroy you." He sustained such verbal assaults on pop music with the cut "Marshall Mathers," saying: "I'm anti-Backstreet and Ricky Martin / With instincts to kill NSYNC, don't get me started / These fuckin' brats can't sing, and Britney's garbage / What's this bitch retarded?"

But aside from lampooning celebrities (or grossing you out with talk of raping his own mother), Eminem aimed most of his vitriol at the hysteria white America was in over artistic expressions of anger and violence. Communicating how annoyed he was with his own celebrity on the single "The Way I Am," rhyming he's "so sick and tired of being admired," Eminem compared his fury to that of the killers who shot up Columbine. "When you won't just put up with the bullshit they pull," he rapped. " 'Cause they full of shit, too / When a dude's getting bullied and shoots up his school / And they blame it on Marilyn . . . and the heroin / Where were the parents at / And look where it's at / Middle America, now it's a tragedy." To confront the witch hunt on pop culture, he also unmasked the contradictions of society on songs like "I'm Back" and "Who Knew," telling delusional parents: "Told me that my tape taught 'em to swear / What about the makeup you allow your twelve-year-old daughter to wear / So tell me that your son doesn't know any cuss words / When his bus driver's screamin' at him, fuckin' him up worse ('Go sit the fuck down, you little fuckin' prick!')."

Most effectively, though, he provoked through what some felt was the language of hate. At one end, there were his misogynistic rants—as Slim Shady, of course—about female fans, such as "Kill You," where he tells a girl: "Bitch I'ma kill you / Like a murder weapon, I'ma conceal you in a closet with mildew, sheets, pillows, and film you." Or the second installment to Eminem's horrific fantasy about killing the mother of his daughter on "Kim." "Don't you get it, bitch, no one can hear you," he screams over a titanic drumbeat before murdering her. "Now shut the fuck up and get what's coming to you." While at the other end, there was his venomous language about gays—his use of the words "fag" and "faggot"—which was hotly expressed on the song "Criminal." "My words are like a dagger with a jagged edge," Eminem explained. "That'll stab you in the head whether you a fag or lez / or a homosex, hermaph, or a trans-a-vest / Pants or dress, hate fags? The answer's yes."

But to antagonize white America's grown-ups into a confrontation, Eminem, who'd joked on *Slim Shady* about persuading white kids to act out ("do exactly what the song says: smoke weed, take pills, drop outta school, kill people, and drink"), now bragged about the sway he held over the youth. "I take each individual degenerate's head," he explained over the wobbly rhythm of "I'm Back," "just to see if he's influenced by me, if he listens to music / And if he feeds into the shit he's an innocent victim / And becomes a puppet on the string of my tennis shoe." Most movingly, he turned this adoration and influence into elaborate and eye-opening hip-hop theater on the hit song "Stan." Through a series of letters, listeners heard an obsessed Eminem fan degenerate into lunacy and murder when his notes to the star go unanswered. Infuriated at his idol, the deranged fan attempts to show Eminem how crushed he is, recording a tape while driving around with his own pregnant girlfriend tied up in the trunk of his car (similar to "'97 Bonnie & Clyde"). "Hey Slim," he says into the tape recorder, "that's my girlfriend screaming in the trunk / But I didn't slit her throat, I just tied her up / See, I ain't like you / 'Cause if she suffocates, she'll suffer more, and then she'll die too." Before he could get the tape to Eminem, though, the fan, along with the kidnapped girl, is killed driving off a bridge.

Whereas ideas of such influence didn't raise much concern before *Slim Shady*, they did around the time Eminem's second album was released. Particularly when the larger white non-hip-hop public learned how much of a phenomenon Eminem had become. In a mind-boggling leap, on its way to selling nine million albums overall, *The Marshall Mathers LP* moved 1.7 million units in just six days. MTV, already a fond supporter, not only dedicated an entire weekend of programming, called "Em-TV," to promote his new disc but gave Eminem six Video Music Award nominations. And, for the 2001 Grammy Awards, *Marshall Mathers* received four nominations, including Best Album of the Year. The arrival of each milestone was accompanied by a growing furor surrounding the album and the high-powered cultural platform given to this poor white rap star from Michigan. Besides the legal wrath Eminem incurred from his mother (in 1999 she filed a $10 million defamation suit against him, which was subsequently settled, claiming he slandered her in several interviews and the song "My Name Is"), Eminem found himself becoming, for a number of groups, the repulsive face of hatred and violence.

The first was among gay activists who were still reeling from the murder of gay college student Matthew Shepard. On October 7, 1998, the twenty-one-year-old University of Wyoming student was beaten, robbed, tied to a fence, and left to die by two men, Aaron McKinney and Russell Henderson, with whom he'd caught a ride from a local bar. (It was later revealed by a news report that Shepard knew McKinney.) Shepard died a week later from his injuries. The subsequent trial—with Shepard described as an openly gay man and the defendants' lawyers using the "gay panic defense" (that they defended themselves from Shepard's sexual advances)—turned its focus more on the issue of *why* the murder happened than on prosecution of the murder itself. Since Shepard's family and friends (and a number of gay rights groups) believed the savage beating occurred because of Shepard's homosexuality, the case, overall, became a cause for gay rights. Although the men were found guilty of murder, they weren't charged with committing a hate crime, because under U.S. federal law and Wyoming state law crimes committed on the basis of sexual orientation are not prosecutable as hate crimes. (Not long after Shepard's murder, President Clinton attempted to get Congress to include sexual orientation under the hate crimes law, but his proposal was defeated.) Left with no legislative support against "gay bashing," gay rights activists began pushing for a public dialogue about the promotion of antigay behavior in American culture. In May 1999 the Gay and Lesbian Alliance Against Defamation (GLAAD), an organization dedicated to fighting homophobia through ensuring fair and accurate representation of gay people in the media, began a campaign against "hate lyrics and the continued glorification of violence against lesbian, gay, bisexual and transgender people." When the group had a listen to lyrics from the upcoming *Marshall Mathers*, Eminem became public enemy number one. One of GLAAD's stops was MTV, where they protested the network's heavy promotion of the album. They also contacted several of the country's top music retailers, calling on them to curtail their promotion of Eminem's album. GLAAD's gripe, though, stopped short of calling for censorship, instead asking Interscope Records to be more "responsible" by not putting out material with such hate-filled lyrics.

Others, mostly from the conservative right, such as James Dobson's right-wing family values group, Focus on the Family, and Lynne Cheney, former chairperson of the National Endowment for the Humanities and wife of vice presidential nominee Dick Cheney, also called for corporate restrictions on Eminem's art. Similar to the way C. Delores Tucker used Senator Carol Moseley Braun's 1994 hearing to single out Snoop's *Doggystyle*, Cheney singled out Eminem's *Marshall Mathers* during a September 2000 Senate hearing on violence and entertainment. (The hearing was sparked by a Federal Trade Commission report asserting that the entertainment industry was marketing violent, adult-oriented music, video games, and films to underage kids.) After citing lyrics from the song "Kill You," Cheney commented that the lyrics "could not be more despicable. They could not be more hateful in their attitudes toward women in particular." But what concerned those opposed to Eminem more than what he said about women or gays was his influence over the youth, about what his music said was okay for kids to do. "This is especially negligent," one of GLAAD's press releases read, "when considering the market for this music has been shown to be adolescent males, the very group that statistically commits the most hate crimes."

Of all the groups gunning for Eminem, GLAAD dominated the headlines, meeting with MTV's CEO, Judy McGrath, to make several demands, including that the network run a public service announcement featuring Eminem discussing antigay violence and that they not permit him to perform at the 2000 MTV Video Music Awards. (The most they received from MTV was a PSA on hate speech *after* Eminem's performance at the show and a day's worth of programming focused almost entirely on hate crimes.) Following the announcement of Eminem's Grammy nomination by the National Academy of Recording Arts and Sciences (NARAS), GLAAD, joined by various gay and women's groups, publicized its plans for a "Rally Against Hate," to be held outside the Grammy Awards on February 21, 2001. Heightening the tension surrounding the ceremony was NARAS's announcement that Eminem would perform at the show and an announcement from openly gay rocker Elton John that he would be performing *with* Eminem. (Elton was one of several music artists, including Madonna and Stevie Wonder, defending the artistic integrity of Eminem's music.) In fact, the entire brouhaha over Eminem as hatemonger, particularly among gays, was quieted on Grammy night when Eminem and Elton John, following their performance of "Stan" together, hugged each other onstage and then, in a show of solidarity, held their interlocked hands in the air. In the face of all the demonstrations, and in large part because of them, the gesture symbolically advanced, on a global stage, the cause of tolerance.

But, more than anything, the turmoil caused by *The Marshall Mathers LP*—and Eminem's very public response—helped advance the cause of Eminem. With eight million albums sold in eight months and a 2001 Grammy win for Best Album of the Year, he hadn't just become a music icon and a youthful symbol of free speech; he damn near became the American face of rap music. And there wasn't much to doubt about the idea: similar to the most skilled black MCs, Eminem was indeed a gifted poet and wordsmith, and, like a number of black hip-hop moguls (especially his mentor, Dre), Eminem had business acumen, parlaying his own label deal, Shady Records, through Interscope. Though anyone witnessing the overwhelming response to Eminem—the astounding sales, the red-carpet treatment from MTV and NARAS, even the very public defense he received from a rock legend—knew it was because of his color, the white-skin privilege Eminem made a point of humorously acknowledging in his music. "Became a commodity," he teased on "I'm Back," "because I'm W-H-I-T-E / Cuz MTV was so friendly to me."

This was especially obvious in 2002 as Interscope Records and Universal Pictures, realizing their commodity had grown beyond the "wigger" hip-hop set, prepared for a multimedia sale of Eminem, first with the summer 2002 release of his fourth LP, *The Eminem Show*. For this disc, the Detroit bad boy quieted his demented humor, whipping out his Slim Shady character only for the first single, "Without Me." "Though I'm not the first king of controversy," Slim explained with a wink, "I am the worst thing since Elvis Presley, to do black music so selfishly / And use it to get myself wealthy." Now hip-hop's poster boy of white youth angst (smelling like teen spirit), Eminem, handling more of the production, sought to fuse hip-hop's rhythmic badness with the on-edge feel of rock. *The Eminem Show*, with its power ballad strings, funky guitar riffs, and haunting piano work, displayed a sober Eminem taking himself, his position, and his message a lot more seriously than he previously had. In the absence of popular guitar gods or white punk rock deities articulating the trouble with lil' Johnny and Jane, Eminem represented the new look and sound of rock 'n' roll rebelliousness. "Kids flipped when they knew I was produced by Dre," he proclaimed over the stomping rhythm of "White America." "That's all it took / And they were instantly hooked / Right in, and they connected with me, too, because I look like them / That's why they put my lyrics up under this microscope / Searching with a fine tooth comb, it's like this rope waiting to choke." But instead of provoking thought through gross imagery or offensive rants, Eminem, as a former member of the white underclass, bluntly communicated the function his music (and rap music, in general) plays in the lives of the youth. Rhyming over a sample of Aerosmith's classic "Dream On," he said: "It's fucked up ain't it, how we come from practically nothing / To being able to have any fuckin' thing that we wanted / That's why we sing for these kids, who don't have a thing / Except for a dream and a fuckin' rap magazine." Though, while speaking the boastful cause of hip-hop music, as he'd done on "Business" and "'Till I Collapse," Eminem also expressed his dissatisfaction with the politically powerful. "With a plan to ambush this Bush administration," he announced on "Square Dance." "Mush the Senate's face in, and push this generation / Of kids to stand and fight for the right / To say something you might not like."

And whereas Em had painted portraits of his family and relationships in exaggerated and grotesque strokes before, on *The Eminem Show* he rapped candidly about all that was already being discussed in the news. About the turbulence of his on-and-off marriage to Kim, the mother of his daughter, on "Say Goodbye Hollywood." About how much his daughter meant to him on "Hailie's Song." About the details of his dysfunctional upbringing on the hit single "Cleanin Out My Closet." "Now I would never dis my own mama just to get recognition," he confided. ". . . But put yourself in my position / Just try to envision witnessin' your mama poppin' prescription pills in the kitchen."

If anyone knew the value of opening an icon's life for public scrutiny, it was Eminem's corporate sponsors, who followed up *The Eminem Show* with the fall release of his film debut in *8 Mile*, Em's *Love Me Tender*. Also released was the movie's soundtrack, which, although featuring the film's star on less than half of the tracks, was primarily sold as an Eminem album. Its gold-selling single "Lose Yourself" pushed the disc and the movie to the top of the charts in *Billboard* and *Variety*, respectively. And in the end, the moneymaking instincts of Interscope/Universal were correct. By the close of 2002, *The Eminem Show* had sold seven million records, and the *8 Mile* soundtrack had gone double platinum (on its way to selling four million), while the film grossed over $242 million worldwide. Topping off the trifecta was Eminem's 2003 Oscar nomination and win for the song "Lose Yourself," the first rap song ever to win the award.

Furthermore, Shady Records became a lucrative venture in February 2003, when it released the album *Get Rich or Die Tryin'* by black Queens rapper (and former crack dealer) 50 Cent. Despite the slumping sales of the music industry in general, the LP, besides selling 872,000 copies in its first week, moved six million units by the end of the year. (Thanks, in part, to the label marketing the fact that 50 survived being shot nine times. Talk about street cred getting out of hand.) This at a time when a number of black producers, like Timbaland, began chasing Dre's formula by pushing their own version of Eminem. (Tim would only find minor success with the white southern rap artist Bubba Sparxxx.) But no other Caucasian rapper—Wu-Tang's Remedy or underground luminaries like R.A. the Rugged Man and Non Phixion—could top the phenomenal success of Eminem: the recognition, the sales, the high praise from white America, the eager support from mainstream media, the personal freedom to say what *he* wanted how *he* wanted to say it. The only problem was . . . neither could many of the best—or worst—selling black rappers. Aside from the obvious reason (being white in a country run by whites), Eminem outsold and out-shined them. Being a part of America's majority, he was allowed access and freedom by the corporate powers to say whatever he wanted on disc while black MCs were strongly encouraged by labels to rap about niggas, bitches, and riches. Such double standards brought the tensions of race to Eminem, though not from critics or any well-known rap star, but from the hardly recognized rap artist and "Chief Brand Executive" of *The Source*, Raymond "Benzino" Scott.

Feeling Eminem was part of a racist corporate "machine" out to destroy or possibly whitewash hip-hop music, Benzino started verbally attacking Em publicly. On the dis track "Die Another Day," released in 2003, he referred to Eminem as "a culture stealer" and a "rap Hitler." In interviews Benzino pointed to Eminem when griping about what was wrong with rap music. "Certain media outlets . . . look at him as the savior of hip-hop," he told *MTV News*. "Eminem is just a hood ornament for the machine . . . You think I could grab my crotch and put my ass in people's faces the way he does? No way." Another grievance Benzino expressed was what he saw as a double standard: Eminem being allowed to rap about deeply personal issues while black rappers like himself had "to talk about the bling bling (materialistic things) because that's all the people who control the images want to hear" from black artists. And, having taken less of a "silent" role in running *The Source* not long before the beef (until then, he had primarily focused on his floundering rap career, which was managed by *Source* co-owner David Mays), he even used the magazine to air his grievances with Eminem. (At one point the mag featured an illustration of a superhero-like Benzino holding the severed head of Eminem.) In response, Em released his own dis records, "The Sauce" and "Nail in the Coffin," which, while responding to his adversary's issue of race ("Comin' up, it never mattered what color you was / If you could spit, then you could spit / That's it; that's what it was"), viciously articulated what most hip-hoppers—black and white—thought about Benzino's beef: that it was a publicity stunt to bolster his rap profile and that he was unethically using *The Source* to promote his feud *and* himself. (In one issue he not only graced the magazine's cover but planted several stories featuring himself and his personal views on the rap industry—all without having released even a semi-hit album.) Despite Benzino's attempting to portray himself as the "rap Huey," trying to make himself out to be another Tupac—with the help of his white *Source* business partner, David Mays—hardly anyone believed his sincerity or his intent.

However, he and Mays did grab America's ear after November 17,

2003, when they held a press conference—a "listening session" they called it—for the media. There, Mays and Benzino played pieces of two recordings of what sounded like someone's old freestyle or improvised rap. Only the rhymes of this MC, who identified himself as "the funky Eminem," descended into a juvenile, racist tirade about black women. "Black girls are stupid," he rapped. "White girls are cool." And using the n word ("All the girls I like to bone have big butts / No they don't, 'cause I don't like that nigger shit"). "The tape contains what is clearly identifiable as Eminem's voice," read a statement released during the press conference, "reciting racial slurs targeted at black women, and it proves Benzino right after a year of being vilified . . . for bringing such questions surrounding Eminem to the fore . . . Bringing this tape to the public is the latest chapter in *The Source* magazine's ongoing effort to expose influences corrupting hip-hop, including racism." The tape, which was recorded in the late 1980s or early '90s, had been given to Benzino and Mays by former Eminem associates.

As news of the recording began raising eyebrows, particularly in black America, Eminem immediately issued an apology. After admitting it was his voice on the tape, he added that the song "was made out of anger, stupidity, and frustration when I was a teenager," having just broken up with a girlfriend who was African American. "I hope people will take it for the foolishness that it was," read his statement, "not for what somebody is trying to make it into today." Eminem knew, as S. Craig Watkins wrote, that the allegations against him were "potentially far more damaging than the previous accusations of homophobia and misogyny," especially given his prominence in a music and culture so intimately connected with black and Latino communities. Ultimately, what kept the incident from becoming detrimental to Em's image and career was that once again, an industry legend—in this case, Russell Simmons—came to his defense. "These lyrics are disgusting," said Simmons in a statement, "but the oneness of hip-hop culture has transformed many young people in trailer parks around the country away from their parents' old mind-set of white supremacy. We believe Eminem's apology is sincere and forthright. He continues to not only be an icon of hip-hop but . . . gives back money, time and energy to the community." In the end, not much of an uproar was raised within or outside the rap industry following the support Eminem received from Simmons. (Part of the reason could have been that no black rapper wanted to disrupt a chance to increase his or her bottom line by working with him in the future.) In the end, the most *The Source* gained from the feud was grave damage to its journalistic credibility and a loss of ad revenues over the next three years. (In protest of Benzino's use of *The Source* for unjustly airing his vendetta, Interscope, along with other major record labels, pulled all their advertisements from the magazine.) In 2006 Mays and Benzino eventually lost their stake in *The Source* when Black Enterprise/Greenwich Street Corporate Growth Partners, which had bought an 18 percent interest in the magazine in 2002, ousted them for mismanaging the company and its finances.

Eminem, who by now was the bestselling MC in the history of commercial rap music, had dodged yet another plot to scapegoat him for the ills of American culture. Though in the year leading up to the release of his 2004 CD, *Encore*, a swelling national divide—between those who were for and those against the reelection of President George W. Bush—would bring Eminem to the fore (at least in pop music) of an electorate civil war. The tragedy of 9/11 brought the country together in shock, in grief, and in anger, turning terrorism into a prime issue for the Bush administration. But its policies, particularly its decision to go to war with Iraq on March 20, 2003, caused many to question the direction America was headed in. (After all, weren't we supposedly looking for Osama bin Laden—the man responsible for 9/11—in Afghanistan?) This was especially pertinent when, after almost a year of waging war in Iraq, the U.S. forces still had found no weapons of mass destruction—the "imminent threat" that ultimately provoked the invasion. Nor were there found any links between Iraq's president, Saddam Hussein, and the attacks on September 11. As the United States headed into the 2004 presidential election, aside from people's dissatisfaction with the heavy-handed governing style of the current administration (anyone who criticized Bush was roundly dubbed unpatriotic or un-American), the Iraq War, like the Vietnam War some thirty years earlier, was growing into *the* point of contention among voters.

As a result, the 2004 presidential election became one of the most spirited political contests in American history. Passions among those who opposed Bush stirred an avalanche of activism in the form of massive voter registration drives, with the primary target being the youth vote, seen as crucial to the election's outcome. (Over the previous four years the percentage of young people voting had declined considerably.) Among young black and Latino voters, there was a massive campaign to cultivate what many were calling the "hip-hop vote," enlivening a group who, more than most, weren't convinced of the power of the ballot. There was the National Hip-Hop Political Convention, held in Newark, New Jersey, in June 2004, which attempted, albeit fruitlessly, to construct a political agenda for this bloc to unite around. The Hip-Hop Summit Action Network, co-chaired by Russell Simmons and Benjamin Chavis, held massive rallies and panel discussions across the country to register voters. The draw for these events was the numerous celebrities—hip-hop and otherwise—whom Simmons convinced to come out in support. Even Puffy got political: Citizen Change, a hip-hop vote initiative created by Puffy, also encouraged and registered young voters using the pull of celebrity (backing Diddy were Mary J. Blige, 50 Cent, and pop diva Mariah Carey). Diddy even returned to his undergrad roots of marketing political revolution, turning his "Vote or Die" T-shirts into the fashion sensation leading up to the November 2 election. Six years after hip-hop became America's cultural revolution, the hip-hop nation, with the ear of the country and the world, was now convinced it could equally leverage its political power. And if there was a rap artist convinced of this notion, it was Eminem. In an effort to persuade young voters whom they shouldn't vote for, he released a video for his anti-Bush song, "Mosh," a week before the election. Circumventing mainstream media outlets, which feared a backlash from Bush supporters or the administration for airing scathing indictments of the president, the clip was leaked to the Internet before making its way onto MTV.

In this angst-filled animation video, directed by Ian Inaba, Eminem, parodying the president, sits in front of an elementary-school class reading *My Pet Goat* as the sound of a plane flying overhead ends with a crash. Once he leaves the students to launch his own "War on Terror," though, it's not against Al-Qaeda or bin Laden; it's against what he and many others feel is America's warmongering, hungry-for-oil president. "Strap him with an AK-47," Eminem yells to a youth-filled, multiethnic crowd before leading them in a takeover of Capitol Hill. "Let him impress Daddy that way / No more blood for oil / We got our own battles to fight on our own soil / No more psychological warfare to trick us to thinkin' we ain't loyal." Throughout the clip are messages against the war and the political deception of the Bush administration, including a cut-n-pasted image of Vice President Cheney snickering behind video footage of bin Laden. (Given Cheney's business ties to Halliburton—which won billions in no-bid government contracts to repair oil pipelines in Iraq, among other duties—many could see who was *possibly* benefiting from this war.) But of all the efforts to get youth to vote and to steer them *which way* to vote, Eminem's message, many pundits felt, had the most potential of influencing the presidential race. "It could have unprecedented cultural and political impact," wrote Sam Graham-Felsen in *The Nation*. "Even if the song's late arrival gives it a limited impact on the vote, Eminem's pronounced political shift should send shivers through the largely unchecked right-wing establishment." Unfortunately, neither Eminem's efforts nor Russell Simmons's nor Diddy's nor those of the numerous other celebrities who energized America's young voters would sway the presidential race. Bush was reelected—this time with a majority of the vote. But the rallies and registration efforts, overall, did help increase the number of young folks at the polls (4.4 million more than voted in 2000). And among the age-group of eighteen- to twenty-four-year-olds, Bush's Democratic opponent, John Kerry, won more votes (54 percent to 44 percent).

Whether "Mosh" was one of the factors handing Kerry the youth vote is debatable, though it can be definitely said that the song and its video, at a time when many feared to speak out, were a wake-up call for their young audience to defend *real* democracy. And once again, Eminem's beat-driven defiance, along with his blues-laden confessionals and the usual comedic fare, was enough to push his fourth album to multiplatinum sales (four million, to be exact).

Released toward the end of 2004, *Encore* was a self-conscious and, at times, heartfelt recap of a turbulent career that turned Eminem into hip-hop's biggest star and, at one point, its largest whipping boy. While doling out the usual celebrity-clowning material on singles like "Just Lose It" and "Ass Like That," a tired and somewhat shell-shocked Eminem, in between decrying his ex-wife ("Puke") and family ("Evil Deeds"), delivered epic thoughts on matters that touched his fame the most. At times they were humorous quips, like his tease of the gay issue on "Rain Man." "Is it gay to play putt-putt golf with a friend," he asks, "and watch his butt-butt when he tees off?" But, most notably, they were rap confessionals around the issue of hip-hop and race, which especially loomed over his career within the last year. On the song "Like Toy Soldiers," to the beat of a slow, processional drum cadence, Eminem revisited his rap feuds, particularly with Benzino, discussing what drove him to finally respond (Benzino rapping he would hurt Em's daughter) and admitting the internal conflict he had with responding. "He's fucked the game up," he rhymed about his adversary, "'cause one of the ways I came up was through that publication, the same one that made me famous." Moreover, he addressed the infamous issue of the recordings that momentarily painted Slim in the shady tones of racism. After telling the story of his rap life as a white boy totally enthralled by and immersed in hip-hop's version of black popular culture, he detailed his brief relationship with the black girl who dumped him and once again apologized for his remarks. Though as always with Eminem, it came with a twist of irony. "I've heard people say they heard the tape, and it ain't that bad," he rapped on the cut "Yellow Brick Road." "But it was: I singled out a whole race / And, for that, I apologize / I was wrong / 'Cause no matter what color a girl is she's still a . . ." If Eminem had become anything for rap music and hip-hop culture—besides its Elvis—he was (and still is) a symbol of how profoundly the voice of post–black power America has become a voice for twenty-first-century America, one that's an increasingly multiracial, multiethnic, and technologically connected America, one where *every* kid has a democratic means to air his feelings without selling himself or his audience short. And if he or she has skills enough to move the crowd, then he or she can become that somebody—that anybody—who grabs the mic and screams.

THIRTEEN

Keep On . . . To the Break of Dawn

I see the best minds of my generation trying to get it together, collect themselves, and move hip-hop beyond song, dance, art, and poetry—to make hip-hop a force of progressive politics, beyond its present role as high commerce. It's June 19, 2004, and I'm sitting in the bleachers of the Essex County College gymnasium on the final day of the National Hip-Hop Political Convention (NHHPC) in Newark, New Jersey. On a stage set up in front of the gym, the radical rap duo Dead Prez chant, "It's bigger than hip-hop." As thousands of attendees take their seats, delegates from all over the country gather on the convention floor to adopt and endorse an agenda reflecting the needs, interests, and experience of a post–black power generation, now dubbed by the writer Bakari Kitwana, one of the convention's cofounders, "the hip-hop generation." The convention's opening date was June 16, Tupac's birthday, while its final day marked the 139th anniversary of Juneteenth, commemorating the abolishment of slavery.

It's thirty years since black power's demise, and the generation afterward, some people in their own positions of power, is attempting to unite itself into a cohesive political movement. The issues that shaped their lives and their communities over the past thirty years—education, economic justice, health, criminal justice, and human rights—are what have brought them together. That and a cultural movement, born in the Bronx, that has shaped and defined much of their lives. And like hip-hop, this gathering is an extension of the black power model that inspired it, specifically the 1972 National Black Political Convention in Gary, Indiana. Considered the zenith of the black power movement, the Gary convention brought together a variety of black groups—prominent politicians, nationalists, civil rights figures—to nail down and write a "Black agenda" that would mark a new phase of the struggle. Amiri Baraka, the father of the NHHPC's chairperson, Ras Baraka, played a central role in the 1972 event. But while that conference and its agenda signified the high point of black unity and struggle going into the 1970s, their cohesion eventually faded as civil rights leaders and the newly emerging black political leadership neither embraced nor followed the program. "Continuation of the Gary confab," wrote one journalist, "faded by the coming of the late Ray-Gun [Reagan], followed by the now-irrelevant Jesse."

So at the NHHPC, which also signals a new chapter in the movement of hip-hop, the same concerns are floating inside this college gym as delegates begin intensely deliberating over proposed amendments to the agenda (a process that will go long into the night and not yield much of a follow-through after the convention is done). But in the few years leading up to this day, there was a swelling combination of hope, frustration, and apprehension about the future of hip-hop, particularly its music, and the generation it claims to speak for. Once again, a Republican administration roused the political consciousness of hip-hop, a phenomenon going back to Bambaataa organizing the culture under the Zulu Nation, attempting to save Bronx youth from street violence and self-destruction at a time when the New York *Daily News* ran the famous headline "Ford to City: Drop Dead."

And, once again, the power players of the scene have become the organizing force behind the movement's next step. Outside the NHHPC, Diddy's Citizen Change is doing its part, driving home the urgency of young people voting with his "Vote or Die" campaign (primarily a scare tactic playing on the possibility of a military draft sweeping the youth into the Iraq War). Russell Simmons, who founded his Hip-Hop Summit Action Network in 2001, uses the power of celebrity, publicity, and economics to confront the social and legislative issues affecting black and brown people, as can be seen in his involvement with the fight to modify New York's Rockefeller drug laws in 2003. Many felt the laws, enacted in 1973, were unfair because by requiring harsh mandatory sentences for possession of even small amounts of drugs—regardless of a person's role in the crime—the system overwhelmingly handed out long prison sentences to blacks and Latinos. Where previous rallies to raise awareness on the issue would only attract a few people, once Simmons joined, bringing along famous friends like Diddy and Jay-Z, attendance at demonstrations reached twenty thousand. Simmons's clout also got him into the seven-hour session with key New York politicians, including Governor George Pataki, trying to carve out reform legislation. But Simmons and hip-hop soon learned the difference between "star power" and *real* power when the session, resulting in the Drug Law Reform Act of 2004 (which increased the quantity of narcotics triggering long sentences), only freed a small number of prisoners locked up due to the draconian law. Well-informed noncelebrity organizers who were kept out of the meeting realized that politicians had no intentions of *really* reforming the Rockefeller laws. If Simmons or any hip-hop figure trying to translate pop culture power into political power learned anything from this, it was that celebrity only gets you access. It doesn't necessarily translate into substantial change.

But as organizations like the Hip-Hop Summit Action Network and Citizen Change try to harness the cultural might of rap and hip-hop music as a vehicle to promote issues that empower their core audience, one key issue—the music itself—has to be seriously addressed along with other topics. Specifically, commercial rap's longtime use of gangsta (or thug or pimp or drug hustler) culture as a marketing tool, the role of multinational corporations in promoting and encouraging it among their artists, and how hip-hop culture is affected by it. Without a doubt, hip-hop music, rap in particular, has been the miracle of post–black power America, going from the burned-out streets of the Bronx to impact the farthest corners of American (and global) society, helping a generation turn its pain, joy, swagger, and bravado into major cultural, social, and economic currency. More than any other outlet—politics especially—rap music is the most substantial means poor black and brown folks, who would usually be locked out of the democratic process, can use to publicly speak their minds. But with commercial rap having become, as one writer put it, less of a buyer's market, in "which we, the elite hip-hop audience, decided what was street legit," and more of a seller's market, "in which what does or does not get sold as hip-hop to the masses is whatever the boardroom approves," what price is paid for rap gaining the world's dollar with violent and demeaning stereotypes—all under the guise of "keeping it real" or "keeping it street"—and losing its soul?

Rap artists have felt some of the repercussions. Particularly in 2004, when, after the arrests of several rap stars in New York fueled suspicions of profiling, it was revealed that the New York City Police Department had formed a "Hip-Hop Task Force," an intelligence operation designed to keep an eye on rap artists. Former New York detective Derrick Parker, who claimed to have founded the unit, told *The Village Voice* that ideas for such a task force began to take shape following the murder of Biggie Smalls. "It wasn't until after Biggie Smalls that everybody's eyes became open," he said, explaining how police departments across the country were getting concerned with what was perceived as increasing violence in the rap music industry. After Parker made a presentation on hip-hop and its connection to gang violence at a police convention in 1999, he was given the task of heading the intelligence unit. He not only observed rap stars and their entourages but kept files on them. He even aided the police in other U.S. cities such as Miami where violent incidents involving hardcore MCs had occurred. News of the task force, especially combined with several arrest scenarios (mostly after traffic stops) where police seemed to be targeting MCs, fueled comparisons to COINTELPRO. But, as many observers might ask, would there have been this much scrutiny by law enforcement if the line between bloodshed on disc and bloodshed in real life had not become the selling point for commercial rap music?

And the growing degradation and exploitation of black and brown women in hip-hop music, especially in music videos, have provoked powerful responses from hip-hop's female core. One of the first to spark major public discourse was writer Joan Morgan when she published her seminal book of essays, *When Chickenheads Come Home to Roost: My Life as a Hip-Hop Feminist*, in 1999. In the essay "From Fly-Girls to Bitches and Hos," Morgan, despite her great love for rap music, decried its blatant misogyny. "Props given to rap music's artistic merits," she wrote, "its irrefutable impact on pop culture, its ability to be alternately beautiful, poignant, powerful, strong and mesmerizing . . . But in between the beats, booty shaking, and hedonistic abandon, I have to wonder if there isn't something inherently unfeminist in supporting a music that repeatedly reduces me to tits and ass and encourages pimping on the regular."

Reactions from women have also come in the form of direct confrontation, such as in 2003 when a scheduled appearance by St. Louis rapper Nelly at Spelman, a historically black women's college, was canceled due to protest from students over his demeaning portrayal of women in his videos. (They were specifically incensed by his video for the song "Tip Drill," featuring barely dressed women dancing around and simulating sexual acts with each other while men threw money at them.) A most significant blow was dealt to misogyny within the industry itself when Kim Osorio, former editor in chief of *The Source*, filed a lawsuit against the magazine and its former heads David Mays and Benzino for sexual harassment, defamation of character, and retaliatory discharge. After filing a complaint with the Equal Employment Opportunity Commission in 2005, citing discrimination and harassment from her male bosses, including Benzino, Osorio was suddenly fired. (Both Mays and Benzino were quoted in the media saying Osorio had slept with several rap stars and was merely extorting *The Source* for having been let go.) While Osorio didn't prove her case of sexual harassment, she did win on her charges of defamation and retaliatory discharge, and in October 2006 she was awarded several million dollars in compensatory damages. The victory, a triumph in the first legal battle against sexual discrimination in the hip-hop industry, wasn't just historic; it turned Osorio into a major figure in the struggle against ill-treatment of women in rap. "I didn't ask to be a spokeswoman for female dignity in hip-hop," she wrote in an opinion piece in the New York *Daily News*. "But now that my lawsuit against *The Source* has thrust me into the spotlight, I'm not going to back down."

Despite the unsavory developments that have accompanied rap music's rise to fortune and prominence, there are moments when rap artists show they can still be *the* progressive voice for those who can't speak for themselves, as after Hurricane Katrina touched down in the Gulf Coast region on August 29, 2005. The storm devastated cities like Biloxi and Gulfport, Mississippi, and Mobile, Alabama, but it hit the city of New Orleans the hardest. Massive flooding occurred after the levees holding back Lake Pontchartrain broke, and America watched thousands (some estimated over 250,000) of New Orleans residents, most of them poor, black, and without transportation, wait almost a week on rooftops and at the city's Superdome, surrounded by water and destruction and extreme heat, before the Bush administration sent help and aid. Even though class was a major factor in the disaster— many couldn't escape, because they had no vehicle to escape in nor money to pay for a place to escape to—black America couldn't help but see race as a glaring factor in Bush's extremely slow response. Race also played heavily in the media coverage, as an infamous caption for an Associated Press photo described the actions of whites who broke into a store as "finding" food and supplies, while a black person who did the same was looting. And the predominantly African-American crowd waiting to be evacuated from the Superdome was referred to as "refugees," as if they were immigrants from a third-world country.

When it came time for folks to respond to the tragedy, rap artists were among those offering their help. Not so much with their music as with their money, celebrity, and hip-hop-style sense of honesty. As several MCs such as Mississippi's David Banner used their wealth and prominence to help raise funds for the predominantly African-American victims, one artist, Chicago's Kanye West, took to the airwaves the frustration black America felt watching the federal government disregard black people once again. Using his appearance on an NBC telethon to criticize the media for its racist coverage and to express the pain he felt watching folks who looked like him blatantly neglected, West, also the son of a former Black Panther, uttered his famous words to the world: "George Bush doesn't care about black people." His statement, like the culture he represented, wasn't the most elegant or eloquent or cohesive, but through his emotions and the sentiment of his words—even the color of his skin—his message, as well as the power rap music had acquired, was loud and clear.

Unfortunately, even after such a catastrophic moment in American history, there are still areas where rap, too caught up in the corporate money gang bang, misses the boat. While Hurricane Katrina put the topic of racism back in the media, the storm—its winds tearing down shacks as well as mansions, its waters washing away the lives of those too poor to get away—exposed one of America's most underdiscussed problems, poverty: most notably, as much of New Orleans's underclass consists of African Americans, the topic of race and poverty. This is especially the case not only in the northern ghettos but, more prominently, in southern ones, as black (and white) southerners languish in cities like New Orleans that have some of the most poverty-stricken and crime-ridden communities in the country.

And statistics for African Americans, particularly young urban males, get worse and worse: in education (Gary Orfield, an education expert at Harvard, said more than 50 percent drop out of high school), incarceration rates (*The New York Times* reported that 21 percent of black males in their twenties who did not attend college have been locked up), and joblessness (even with a high-school diploma, half the population of black males in their twenties lacking a college education, according to the same *New York Times* report, is unemployed). Indeed, the gains won forty years ago seem to recede further and further for those left behind in the progressive march forward, this at a time when southern hip-hop music has become the current face of rap. Like most commercial rap music produced by artists across the country, southern hip-hop was extremely preoccupied with making folks dance and chant and bling and consume and pimp and hustle and worship at the altar of cocaine-rap Robin Hoods like T.I. and Young Jeezy and anyone else who wants to be hip-hop's head nigga, and more concerned with chasing that green paper and pleasing investors than really telling us which way the wind blows.

But as the overall message of commercial rap has been so unwilling to bend with the times, the winds have shifted, threateningly, away from rap music. On the one hand, the genre has diminished in its pop appeal—most notably its sales. From 2005 to 2006, sales of rap music fell a whopping 21 percent, and in 2007 sales were down 33 percent from the previous year. Although the rise of downloadable music may be partially to blame (hurting music sales across the board), the fact that listeners may be becoming tired of rap's banality could, ultimately, be the reason for the downturn. In a survey conducted by the Black Youth Project, under the direction of Dr. Cathy Cohen of the University of Chicago, the majority of youths surveyed (black, white, and Hispanic) agreed that "rap music videos portray both black women and men in bad and offensive ways." Moreover, 41 percent of black youth said rap music videos should be more political.

Within black America there's a swelling national furor over commercial rap's crass language, glorification of all things gangsta, and ill-treatment of black women. All of this came to a head when the white shock jock Don Imus called the Rutgers women's basketball team "some nappy-headed hos" in April 2007. Imus defended his casual on-air use of the term by pointing out that rap artists "routinely defame and demean black women" and call them "worse names than I ever did." Once again, battle lines were drawn, mostly along generational lines, about the positive and negative effects the music has on black America's image and treatment within larger, mainstream society. Was the music creating an environment where use of disrespectful and demeaning language (and actions) toward blacks was okay? Rappers may not be able to solve the ills around them, but with so many of the world's eyes on them, true consciousness-raising could be more quickly forthcoming with their vocal protest and call to arms added to the mix. Or will hip-hop music, like rock before it, simply run its course as a relevant agent for social change?

Whether it lives or gradually fades from the larger commercial space remains to be seen, but rap has most definitely established itself as one of the most important art forms leading into the twenty-first century, anchoring itself as the heartbeat of an American story that continues to turbulently keep on . . . to the break of dawn.

Notes

Bibliography

Acknowledgments

Index

Notes

31 "conspiring to violate the constitutional rights of Americans": Robert Pear, "President Reagan Pardons 2 Ex-F.B.I. Officials in 1970's Break-ins."
31 "end the terrorism": Ibid.
36 "the most detailed and devastating report": Kurt Loder, "Album Reviews."

3: Black Pop in a B-Boy Stance: Run-D.M.C.

41 "Man, y'all come just like y'all come off the street": Ronin Ro, *Raising Hell*, 79.
43 "I think I passed on that kind of controlled anger": Bill Adler, *Tougher Than Leather*, 19.
43 "a ghetto in the suburbs": Ibid., 16.
44 "The Funky 4 was the aggressive niggas": Ibid., 54.
45 "shows that black youth have always been ready": Norman Kelley, *Head Negro in Charge Syndrome*, 60.
45 "easily the canniest and most formally sustained": Bill Adler, *Tougher Than Leather*, 94.
47 "They've got the headlines and the street news flashing": Ibid.
48 "Rap is black outlaw music": Ibid., 91.
48 "A million people wouldn't know us": Omoronke Idowu, "MTV Wants Their R-A-P!"
48 "In today's pop landscape of megastars": Bill Adler, *Tougher Than Leather*, 94.
49 "black talk": Milton Coleman, "A Reporter's Story."
50 "alienating their core audience of black teens": Bill Adler, *Tougher Than Leather*, 121.
50 "These guys are no mere pretenders": Ibid., 120.
53 "Since 1980 black families have lost ground": "Black Power, Foul and Fragrant."
53 "I feel strong because under my arms": Patrice Gaines-Carter, "Farrakhan Speech."
55 "increasingly nihilistic and materialistic": Nelson George, *Buppies, B-Boys, Baps & Bohos*, 27.
57 "the first true rap album, a complete work of art": Chuck D, "48 Run-DMC."
60 "The curses are like punctuation marks": Bill Adler, *Tougher Than Leather*, 173.
60 "Angry, disillusioned, unloved kids": Ibid., 176.
60 "Instead of attacking rap": Ibid.
60 "nothing in the lyrics that [was] really explicit": Ibid.
61 "The problems that people have with rap concerts": Ibid., 178.
61 "the modern hip-hop music business": Harry Allen, "Rhythmic Heart."
62 "profound anger festering and smoldering": Lawrence W. Levine, *Black Culture and Black Consciousness*, 418.

4: Stumbling Through Black Power Revisted: Public Enemy

63 "This project, here, has been an internal and external hell": Interview with the author, February 1998.
64 "I've been waiting around since six-thirty this morning": Interview with the author, February 1998.
64 "I paid for it, and am still paying for it": Ibid.
65 "you're talking about individuals": Interview with the author, February 1998.

66 "A sampler is basically a sonic copy machine": Harry Allen, "Hip-Hop Hi-Tech."

67 "onto streets and highways and freight trains": Jeff Chang, *Can't Stop Won't Stop*, 228.

69 "That's when I decided to get involved in this": "Rap—the Power and the Controversy."

70 "It didn't turn out the way we wanted it": Interview with author, February 1998.

70 "No more music by the suckers!": Ronin Ro, *Raising Hell*, 191.

73 "Run-D.M.C. . . . enjoyed unprecedented popularity": Bruce Britt, "Hackle Raisers."

75 "I set traps for [the media]": "Rap—the Power and the Controversy."

75 "One must wonder just how much the group's confrontational approach": Steve Hochman, "Rap-Meets-Rock Concert Marred by Violence."

78 "We use samples like an artist would use paint": Alan Light, "Public Enemy," in *Vibe History of Hip Hop*, 168.

78 "Compare Brown's case to the separate but unequal treatment": Dave Marsh, "Rocking Racism."

80 "The Grammys should give more of a fuck": Bill Adler, *And You Don't Stop*.

80 "What [P.E.] are doing is trying to uplift the black youth": Ibid.

80 "Every generation needs a Chuck D": *Black in the 80's*.

81 "What struck me, we saw these guys": Jeff Chang, *Can't Stop Won't Stop*, 270.

81 "the majority of wickedness": David Mills, "Professor Griff: The Jews Are Wicked."

82 "Here's the sad part": Jeff Chang, *Can't Stop Won't Stop*, 291.

82 "I remember around the period": Interview with the author, March 1998.

84 "young people are out of touch with history": Kirk Johnson, "A New Generation of Racism."

89 "We exist in a time": Rob Marriott, "Resurrection of the Jester King."

90 "A strong case could be made": Nelson George, "They Stand Accused."

5: Niggas Selling Attitude: N.W.A

93 "One day Dre and Eric picked me up in the van": Cheo Hodari Coker, "N.W.A," in Alan Light, *Vibe History of Hip Hop*, 257.

95 "as contemptuous of opposing belief systems": Nelson George, "Goin' Off in Cali."

95 "eliminating unionized manufacturing jobs": Jeff Chang, *Can't Stop Won't Stop*, 314.

96 "steal cars and all kinds of shit": Carter Harris, "Eazy Street."

99 "The rap game wasn't looking too solid": Jeff Chang, *Can't Stop Won't Stop*, 303.

100 "We knew the value of language": Terry McDermott, "Parent Advisory."

102 "was akin to being wired into a sensory camera": Cheo Hodari Coker, "N.W.A," 258.

102 "malt liquor, bitches and ultraviolence": Ibid., 258.

102 "weaned on racism and Reaganism": Jeff Chang, *Can't Stop Won't Stop*, 320.

104 "violence against and disrespect for": Cheo Hodari Coker, "N.W.A," 258.

104 "L.A. gang members using their tour": Jeff Chang, *Can't Stop Won't Stop*, 325.

105 "The FBI should stay out of the business of censorship": Steve Hochman, "Compton Rappers."

105 "That's how we sold two million": Jeff Chang, *Can't Stop Won't Stop*, 320.

106 "I'm Huey P. motherfuckin' Newton!": Hugh Pearson, *The Shadow of the Panther*, 310.

107 "The bitch set me up": Kathleen McHugh, "Videotape Shows Barry Smoking Crack."

108 "more jobs than skilled people to work them": Anthony Shadid, "Urban Decay Is Brewing Trouble."

109 7,370 black elected officials: Michael K. Frisby, "The New Black Politics."

110 "ass-kicking coming": Cheo Hodari Coker, "N.W.A," 261.

111 "Ain't no big thing": Ibid.

114 "young, black, and didn't give a fuck": *Menace II Society*.

6: R-E-S-P-E-C-T in PC Land: Salt-N-Pepa

117 "Am I guilty of racism, sexism, classism?": John Taylor, "Are You Politically Correct?" cover.

118 "the fascism of the left": Ibid., 35.

120 "We were living Hurby's dream": Mimi Valdés, "Salt-N-Pepa," 210.

121 "black progress": George E. Curry, "Boom No Boon to Blacks."

125 "a new musical culture filled with self-assertion and anger": Jerry Adler and Jennifer Foote, "The Rap Attitude."

128 "getting deep": Mimi Valdés, "Salt-N-Pepa," 213.

128 "challenging forms of expressiveness": David Mills, "Rap on 2 Live Crew."

129 "I don't see how people can jump": Ibid.

132 "high-tech lynching for uppity blacks": Reuters, "The Thomas Nomination."

135 "The emergence of an expanded public dialogue": Lena Williams, "Growing Debate on Racism."

7: Gangsta Chic: Dr. Dre and Snoop Dogg

138 "Rappers documented the anger": Robert Hilburn, "Beyond the Rage."

138 "The only way you can do it": Chris Morris, "TV a Platform."

138 "Mexicans & Crips & Bloods": Jeff Chang, *Can't Stop Won't Stop*, 371.

139 "It feels like Heaven": Sylvester Monroe, "Life in the Hood."

143 "Like it or not, whites seem": William Upski Wimsatt, *Bomb the Suburbs*, 23.

144 "I mean, if black people kill black people": David Mills, "Sister Souljah's Call to Arms."

144 "Unfortunately for white people": Ibid.

144 "She told *The Washington Post*": Thomas B. Edsall, "Clinton Stuns Rainbow Coalition."

145 "I was just telling the writer": John Leland and Farai Chideya, "Rap and Race."

146 "despicable lyrics": Chris Morris et al., "Quayle, Congressmen, L.A. Pols."

146 "Why is Time Warner supporting": Ibid.

146 "The song was directed": Thom Duffy and Charlene Orr, "Texas Police Protest."

147 "distilling this shift in corporate thinking": Jeff Chang, *Can't Stop Won't Stop*, 420.

147 "Hip-Hop offered a way": Ibid.

150 "major forces transmitting culture": Bakari Kitwana, *The Hip Hop Generation*, 7.

150 "It is not a war on rap music": Herb Boyd, "Butts Steps Up."

150 "They are the real culprits": Ibid.

151 "running a private, profitable business": John Connolly, "The Minister's Daughter," 94.

151 "They can't call us niggers": Kevin Powell, "Mama Said Knock U Out," 93.
152 "If playing the dozens was still on the corner": Paul Delaney, "Gangsta Rap vs. the Mainstream."

8: The Myth of Thug Power: Tupac Shakur
157 "My mother was a Panther": Lauren Lazin, *Tupac: Resurrection.*
157 "I was cultivated in prison": Ibid.
158 "really wanted to be an artist": Editors of *Vibe, Tupac Shakur,* 31.
158 "I believe a mother can't give a son": Lauren Lazin, *Tupac: Resurrection.*
162 "Menace or Martyr?": James T. Jones IV, "Menace or Martyr?"
162 "the film's most magnetic figure": Editors of *Vibe, Tupac Shakur,* 29.
162 "mission for the black community": Ibid.
163 "He progressively became more gangsta": Bill Adler, *And You Don't Stop.*
166 "Niggers came by and did a drive-by": *Tupac Shakur,* 31.
166 "You can't take him down": Kendall Hamilton et al., "Double Trouble for 2Pac."
167 "There's a bad part because the kids see": Lauren Lazin, *Tupac: Resurrection.*
167 "No slinging [drugs] in schools": Ibid.
168 "Until it happened, I really did believe": Ibid.
168 "I'm guilty of not being a smart man": Ibid.
169 "inimical to the best interests": Steven A. Holmes, "N.A.A.C.P. Board."
171 "Thug Life to me is dead": Editors of *Vibe, Tupac Shakur,* 51.
172 "addict" and "excuse maker": Ibid., 46.
172 "Nobody approached me": Ibid., 47.
172 "The East Coast ain't got no love": *Welcome to Death Row.*
175 "slapped together": Editors of *Vibe, Tupac Shakur,* 80.
175 "Live by the gun": Ibid., 127.

9: Ghetto Fab Rising: The Notorious B.I.G. and Sean "Puffy" Combs
177 "Life is not a game!": Marcus Reeves, "Bad Boy Entertainment," 17.
178 "I can't really say": Ibid., 19.
178 "When I first got the record deal": Ibid., 20.
179 "*There can only be one lion in the jungle*": Cheo Hodari Coker, *Unbelievable,* 85.
179 "Go make it happen. You're ready to fly": Ibid.
181 "the most anticipated ghetto griot": David Bry, "New York State of Mind," 330.
181 "We wanted to make a movie on wax": Mark Ford, *Behind the Music.*
182 "point-blank gunshot wound": Cheo Hodari Coker, *Unbelievable,* 58.
183 "There's nobody out there": Marcus Reeves, "Sean 'Puffy' Combs," 23.
187 "it was estimated that as many": Nelson George, *Hip Hop America,* 40.
187 "He sounded like no other human being": Mark Ford, *Behind the Music.*
188 "Life was kicking us in the ass": Bill Adler, *And You Don't Stop.*
188 "More than any other artist": Cheo Hodari Coker, *Unbelievable,* 309.
189 "New York's legacy of brilliant lyricists": Dream Hampton, "Bad Boy," 343.
189 "an unmistakably New York state of mind": David Bry, "New York State of Mind," 331.
190 "most powerful depictions": Cheo Hodari Coker, *Unbelievable,* 104.
192 "There was an instant buzz from the hustlers": Ibid., 334.

196 "When I was writing stuff like": Ibid., 213.
197 "betrayal, notoriety, excess, and greed": Dream Hampton, "Bad Boy," 348.
199 "sonically [*Life After Death*] was less a 'hip-hop' album": Jeff Mao's discography in Cheo Hodari Coker, *Unbelievable*, 319.
200 "I wanted L.A.'s attention": Ibid., 214.
200 "We have carved out a place": Kevin Powell, *Step into a World*, 372.
201 Only they couldn't, as one writer noted: Cheo Hodari Coker, *Unbelievable*, 257.
201 "his voice is often slow and choppy": Touré, "Best Rapper Alive."

10: The Ice Age: Jay-Z

203 "Rap music was the biggest story": S. Craig Watkins, *Hip Hop Matters*, 62.
203 "the fastest growing magazine ever": Ibid., 56.
208 "Puffy-esque performance": *Vibe*, January 2004, 77.
209 "stealing from someone": Tamala Edwards, "Bad to Worse," 90.
213 "the Duchess of York to rapper Heavy D": Nancy Jo Sales, "The Mix Master," 20.
213 "It was Foxy Brown": Ibid., 24.
213 "Hip-Hop Nation: After 20 Years": Christopher John Farley, "Hip-Hop Nation."
213 "the backdrop of a superheated economy": Ellis Cose, "The Good News," 31.
214 "since the Census began keeping": Ibid., 30.
219 "need for affirmative action": Todd S. Burroughs, "Revised Revolution," 113.
219 "The goals of African Americans": Ibid.
219 "After all, why attack America's contradictions": Ibid., 114.
219 "This desire to achieve": Bakari Kitwana, *The Hip Hop Generation*, 46.
219 "they're just over it": Todd S. Burroughs, "Revised Revolution," 114.
220 "I can honestly say": Shawn Carter, "Hova and Out," 75.

11: Dog Eat Dog: DMX

224 "This isn't hip-hop": Interview with the author, March 1998.
225 "I've always been the outcast": Ibid.
225 "I'd be beatboxin' ": Ibid.
226 "If I was in the streets robbin' ": Ibid.
226 "In jail you hear other niggas rhyme": Ibid.
226 "One night while I was sleeping": Ibid.
227 "If I keep my ear to the streets": Ibid.
228 "The Bling Bling era": Mimi Valdés, "The Sound of Music," 208.
232 "you might get a better read": Todd Boyd, *The New H.N.I.C.*, 12.
236 "No wonder people drag them": Csar G. Soriano, "The Greaseman Tries."
236 "Black to the Future": Jim Yardley, "An Island Sees No Racism."
237 "been treated differently than non-minority motorists": Alan Jenkins, "See No Evil."
239 "We share the somber view": Charles Ogletree, Jr., and Henry Louis Gates, Jr., "Would a European Diallo Be Dead?"
240 "America killed Amadou Diallo": Derrick Z. Jackson, "Injustice, American-Style."
242 "It represents all the drama": *The Diary of DMX, Part II*.
242 "Slavery was terrorism": Vivian B. Martin, "Sept. 11 in Black and White."

12: Vanilla Nice: Eminem

245 "expand the demographic" and "stump speech": In Hilton Als and Darryl A. Turner, *White Noise*, 130.

246 "the only legitimate profession in America": S. Craig Watkins, *Hip Hop Matters*, 99.

247 "Black people have good reason": Greg Tate, "Hip Hop Nightmare," 62.

249 "blue-collar suburb": In Hilton Als and Darryl A. Turner, *White Noise*, x.

250 "a very suspicious, almost paranoid personality": Ibid., 7.

250 "just weren't willing to listen": Ibid., 10.

250 "with tracks about love, unity and trying": Ibid.

254 "When the world finds out": Matt Diehl, "Pretty Fly," 34.

254 "skewed, bratty humor": Richard Harrington, "No Sugar Coating."

259 "hate lyrics and the continued glorification": Gay and Lesbian Alliance Against Defamation, "GLAAD Puts Hate Lyrics Debate Center Stage."

259 "could not be more despicable": Tom Brokaw, "Senate Hearings Attack Entertainment Industry's Practices."

259 "This is especially negligent": Gay and Lesbian Alliance Against Defamation, "Musical Gay Bashing Doesn't Sound So Good."

263 "Certain media outlets": Rahman Dukes, "Benzino Ignites Beef."

264 "The tape contains what is clearly identifiable": S. Craig Watkins, *Hip Hop Matters*, 86.

264 "was made out of anger, stupidity, and frustration": Ibid., 87.

264 "potentially far more damaging": Ibid.

264 "These lyrics are disgusting": Hip-Hop Summit Action Network Press Release.

267 "It could have unprecedented cultural and political impact": Sam Graham-Felsen, "Eminem Aims at Bush."

13: Keep On . . . To the Break of Dawn

270 "Continuation of the Gary confab": Todd S. Burroughs, "Upturning the Children's Table."

270 "Ford to City: Drop Dead": Peter Goldman et al., "Birth of an Issue."

271 "which we, the elite hip-hop audience": Greg Tate, "Hip Hop Turns 30," 35.

272 "It wasn't until after": Dasun Allah, "The Hip Hop Cop," 31.

272 "Props given to rap music's artistic merits": Joan Morgan, *When Chickenheads Come Home to Roost*, 66.

273 "I didn't ask to be a spokeswoman": Kim Osorio, "Break the Chains," 37.

274 "George Bush doesn't care about black people": Steve Hochman, "Pop Eye: Riffing on the Grammy."

274 50 percent drop out of high school: Erik Eckholm, "Plight Deepens for Black Men."

274 21 percent of black males in their twenties . . . half the population: Ibid.

275 From 2005 to 2006, sales of rap music: Steve Jones, "Can Rap Regain Its Crown?"

275 "rap music videos portray": Black Youth Project, "Largest Ever National Youth Survey Illuminates the Attitudes, Experiences, Hopes, and Expectations of Young African Americans," press release, February 1, 2007.

275 "some nappy-headed hos" and "routinely defame and demean black women": Marcus Franklin, "After Host Don Imus Fired for Sexist Remarks, Is Rap Next?"

Bibliography

Adler, Bill, producer and writer. *And You Don't Stop: 30 Years of Hip-Hop*. 2004.
———. *Tougher Than Leather: The Rise of Run-DMC (The Authorized Biography)* (Los Angeles: Consafos Press, 2002).
Adler, Jerry, and Jennifer Foote. "The Rap Attitude." *Newsweek*, March 19, 1990.
Allah, Dasun. "The Hip Hop Cop: A Tale of NYPD's Rap Intelligence Unit." *The Village Voice*, April 7–13, 2004.
———. "NYPD Admits to Rap Intelligence Unit." *The Village Voice*, March 23, 2004.
Allen, Harry. "Hip-Hop Hi-Tech." *The Village Voice*, 1988.
———. "Rhythmic Heart of the Kings of Rock: Jam Master Jay, 1965–2002." *The Village Voice*, November 6–12, 2002.
Als, Hilton, and Darryl A. Turner, eds. *White Noise: The Eminem Collection* (New York: Thunder's Mouth Press, 2003).
Associated Press. "Cincinnati Officer Is Acquitted in Killing That Ignited Unrest." *The New York Times*, September 27, 2001.
Associated Press and Reuters. "Murder Charges Planned in Beating Death of Gay Student." CNN.com, October 12, 1998.
Ayres, B. Drummond. "Gathering in Virginia Turns Violent." *The New York Times*, September 4, 1989.
Baker, Soren. "All Eyes on DMX." *Los Angeles Times*, December 5, 1999.
Baldwin, James. *The Fire Next Time* (New York: Penguin, 1964).
———. "Notes on the House of Bondage." *The Nation*, November 1, 1980.
Barrett, Ted, and Associated Press. "President Clinton Urges Congress to Pass Hate Crime Bill." CNN.com, September 13, 2000.
Barry, Dan, David M. Halbfinger, and Kit R. Roane. "Misunderstandings Led to Melee at Rally in Harlem." *The New York Times*, September 13, 1998.
Beaird, Joe. "The Trials and Tribulations of S. Carter." *Vibe*, December 2000.
Benjamin, Playthell. "The Attitude Is the Message: Louis Farrakhan Pursues the Middle Class." *The Village Voice*, August 15, 1989.
Berke, Richard L. "The Thomas Nomination: Thomas Backers Attack Hill." *The New York Times*, October 13, 1991.
"Black College Women Take Aim at Rappers." *USA Today*, April 23, 2003.
"Black Power, Foul and Fragrant." *The Economist*, October 12, 1985.
Blum, Howard. Quoted in Steve Hager, *Adventures in the Counterculture: From Hip Hop to High Times*, 36.

Blumenthal, Ralph. "Black Youth Is Killed by Whites; Brooklyn Attack Is Called Racial." *The New York Times*, August, 25, 1989.

Boven, Sarah Van, and Anne Belli Gesalman. "A Texas Man Is Dragged to Death Behind a Truck." *Newsweek*, June 22, 1998.

Boyd, Herb. "Butts Steps Up to Fight Against Vile Rap." *Amsterdam News*, May 29, 1993.

Boyd, Todd. *The New H.N.I.C.: The Death of Civil Rights and the Reign of Hip Hop* (New York: New York University Press, 2002).

———. "A Trip Down Soul Train's Memory Lane." *Los Angeles Times*, November 22, 1995.

Boyer, Edward J. "The Killing That Keeps Spawning Mysteries: Did Geronimo Pratt Kill Caroline Olsen in 1968?" *Los Angeles Times*, December 15, 1998.

———. "Prosecutors Defend Case Against Ex–Black Panther." *Los Angeles Times*, December 16, 1998.

Britt, Bruce. "Hackle Raisers: Public Enemy Remains Rap's Most Controversial Group." *Chicago Tribune*, September 6, 1990.

Brokaw, Tom. "Senate Hearings Attack Entertainment Industry's Practices." NBC News Transcripts, September 13, 2000.

Brown, H. Rap. *Die Nigger Die!* (New York: Dial Press, 1969).

Bry, David. "New York State of Mind." In *The Vibe History of Hip Hop*, ed. Alan Light.

Buder, Leonard. "Police Kill Woman Being Evicted: Officers Say She Wielded a Knife." *The New York Times*, October 30, 1984.

Burroughs, Todd S. "Revised Revolution." *The Source*, October 2001.

———. "Upturning the Children's Table: Hip Hop Generation Attempts to Claim Leadership." *Organized C.O.U.P. News*, June 21, 2004.

Butterfield, Greg. "NJ Admits Police Target Black, Latino Drivers." Workers World News Service, May 13, 1999.

"Can Bush Mend His Party's Rift with Black America?" *The New York Times*, December 17, 2000.

Carter, Shawn. "Hova and Out." *Vibe*, January 2004.

Caruso, Michelle. "Judge Springs Ex-Panther." *Daily News*, June 11, 1997.

Chambers, Veronica, with Alisha Davis. "With a Bite as Big as His Signature Bark, Rapper DMX Debuts at the Top of Charts." *Newsweek*, June 15, 1998.

Chang, Jeff. *Can't Stop Won't Stop: A History of the Hip-Hop Generation* (New York: St. Martin's Press, 2005).

———. "Stakes Is High." *The Nation*, January 13, 2003.

———. "This Ain't No Party." *AlterNet*, June 25, 2004.

Chideya, Farai. "Begging for Crumbs." *Vibe*, 1997.

Chuck D. "48 Run-DMC." *Rolling Stone*, April 15, 2004.

Churchill, Ward, and Jim Vander Wall. *The COINTELPRO Papers: Documents from the FBI's Secret Wars Against Domestic Dissent* (Boston: South End Press, 1990).

Clary, Mike, and Chuck Phillips. "Verdict Is Guilty in 2 Live Crew's Rap Album Sale." *Los Angeles Times*, October 4, 1990.

Coates, Ta-Nehisi. "Compassionate Capitalism: Russell Simmons Wants to Fatten the Hip Hop Vote—and Maybe His Wallet." *The Village Voice*, January 7–13, 2004.

Coker, Cheo Hodari. *Unbelievable: The Life, Death, and Afterlife of The Notorious B.I.G.* (New York: Three Rivers Press, 2003).

Coleman, Milton. "A Reporter's Story." *The Washington Post*, April 8, 1984.

"Columbine Families Sue Game Maker." *BBC News*, May 1, 2001.

Connolly, John. "The Minister's Daughter." *Vibe*, September 1995.

Cook, Rhonda. "Youth Rally Measured in Spirit." *The Atlanta Journal-Constitution*, September 8, 1998.

Cooper, Nancy. "Keeping His Eyes on the Next Prize." *Newsweek*, November 21, 1988.

Cose, Ellis. "The Good News About Black America." *Newsweek*, July 7, 1999.

Cowan, Tom, and Jack Maguire. *Timelines of African-American History: 500 Years of Black Achievement* (New York: Roundtable Press, 1994).

Cuda, Heidi Siegmund. "God and Monsters." *Vibe*, October 2001.

Curry, George E. "Boom No Boon to Blacks: Income Gap Widens." *Chicago Tribune*, June 24, 1986.

Daley, Suzanne. "New Study Faults Police in '83 Death." *The New York Times*, January 24, 1987.

DeHart, Greg, writer. *Street Gangs: A Secret History.* The History Channel, 2001.

Delaney, Paul. "Gangsta Rap vs. the Mainstream Black Community." *USA Today*, January, 1995.

Diary of DMX, Part II. MTV, 2001.

Diehl, Matt. "Pretty Fly." *Rolling Stone*, February 18, 1999.

DMX and Smokey D. Fontaine. *E.A.R.L.: The Autobiography of DMX* (New York: HarperCollins, 2003).

Duffy, Thom, and Charlene Orr. "Texas Police Protest Ice-T Song." *Billboard*, June 20, 1992.

Dukes, Rahman. "Benzino Ignites Beef by Calling Eminem '2003 Vanilla Ice.' " *MTV News*, November 22, 2002.

Dyer, Ervin, and Dennis B. Roddy. "Election 2001: Black Voters' Abiding Aversion to Bush Not Easily Explained." *Post-Gazette* (Pittsburgh), February 4, 2001.

Eckholm, Erik. "Plight Deepens for Black Men, Studies Warn." *The New York Times*, March 20, 2006.

Editors of *Vibe*. *Tupac Shakur* (New York: Crown, 1997).

Edsall, Thomas B. "Clinton Stuns Rainbow Coalition." *The Washington Post*, June 14, 1992.

Edwards, Tamala. "Bad to Worse: Ward Connerly Says Affirmative Action Is Morally Wrong. Can He Get a Witness." *Vibe*, 1997.

Espar, David, writer and director. *Rock & Roll*, PBS, 1995.

Farley, Christopher John. "Hip-Hop Nation." *Time*, February 8, 1999.

Fenner, Austin. "A Hip-Hopping Mad Rally Over '70s Drug Laws." *Daily News*, June 4, 2003.

Fletcher, Michael A. "How New York Fell for a Demagogue Rap." *The Washington Post*, September 13, 1998.

"Florida Judge Finds 2 Live Crew Album Legally Obscene." *The Entertainment Litigation Reporter*, July 9, 1990.

Ford, Mark, producer and director. *Behind the Music: The Notorious B.I.G.* VH1. July 8, 2001.

Franklin, Marcus. "After Host Don Imus Fired for Sexist Remarks, Is Rap Next?" Associated Press and Local Wire, April 13, 2007.

Fricke, Jim, and Charlie Ahearn. *Yes Yes Y'all: Oral History of Hip-Hop's First Decade* (Cambridge, Mass.: Da Capo, 2002).

Fried, Joseph P. "Man Struck in Howard Beach Recalls Start of Confrontation." *The New York Times*, October 16, 1987.

Frisby, K. Michael. "The New Black Politics." *The Boston Globe*, July 14, 1991.

Fritsch, Jane. "The Diallo Verdict: The Overview; 4 Officers in Diallo Shooting Are Acquitted of All Charges." *The New York Times*, February 26, 2000.

Gaines-Carter, Patrice. "Farrakhan Speech Draws a Large Crowd." *The Washington Post*, July 23, 1985.

Gay and Lesbian Alliance Against Defamation (GLAAD). "GLAAD Puts Hate Lyrics Debate Center Stage at the Grammys," press release, February 22, 2001.

———. "Musical Gay Bashing Doesn't Sound So Good," press release, May 25, 2000.

Geist, William E. "Residents Give a Bronx Cheer to Decal Plan." *The New York Times*, November 12, 1983.

Gelman, David. "Black and White in America." *Newsweek*, March 7, 1988.

George, Nelson. *Buppies, B-Boys, Baps & Bohos: Notes on Post-Soul Black Culture* (New York: HarperCollins, 1992).

———. *The Death of Rhythm & Blues* (New York: Penguin, 1988).

———. "Goin' Off in Cali." *The Village Voice*, August 15, 1989.

———. *Hip Hop America* (New York: Penguin, 1998).

———. "Hip-Hop's Founding Fathers Speak the Truth." *The Source*, November 1993.

———. "They Stand Accused." *The Village Voice*, August 9, 1994.

Goldman, Peter, with Thomas M. DeFrank and Hal Bruno. "Birth of an Issue." *Newsweek*, November 10, 1975.

Gonzalez, Juan. "Hip Hop's Elite Join Pol's Drug Law Rally." *Daily News*, June 5, 2003.

Gourevitch, Philip. "Mr. Brown." *The New Yorker*, July 29, 2002.

Graham-Felsen, Sam. "Eminem Aims at Bush." *The Nation*, October 26, 2004.

Hager, Steve. *Adventures in the Counterculture: From Hip Hop to High Times* (New York: High Times Books, 2002).

Halbfinger, David M. "Maynard H. Jackson Jr., First Black Mayor of Atlanta, Dies at 65." *The New York Times*, June 24, 2003.

———. "New Jersey Troopers Again Face Charges in Turnpike Shooting." *The New York Times*, January 6, 2001.

Hamill, Pete. "The Gangs." *New York Post*, quoted in Jeff Chang, *Can't Stop Won't Stop*.

Hamilton, Kendall, with Allison Samuels and Pam O'Donnell. "Double Trouble for 2Pac." *Newsweek*, December 12, 1994.

Hampton, Dream. "Bad Boy." In *The Vibe History of Hip Hop*, ed. Alan Light.

Harrington, Richard. "No Sugar Coating: This Rapper Makes His Witty Lyrics Sting." *The Washington Post*, February 24, 1999.

———. "Public Enemy's Assault on the Airwaves." *The Washington Post*, July 31, 1988.

———. "Public Enemy's Rap Record Stirs Jewish Protest." *The Washington Post*, December 29, 1989.

Harris, Carter. "Eazy Street." *The Source*, July 1994.

Hentoff, Nat. "Unleashing the FBI." *The Village Voice*, May 31, 2002.

Hepburn, Bob. "The Reagan Years." *The Toronto Star*, January 7, 1989.

Hilburn, Robert. "Beyond the Rage." *Los Angeles Times*, May 24, 1992.

Hinds, Lennox S. *Illusions of Justice* (Iowa City: University of Iowa, 1979)

Hip-Hop Summit Action Network. "Statement from the Hip-Hop Summit Action Network in Regard to Eminem," press release.

Hochman, Steve. "Compton Rappers Versus the Letter of the Law." *Los Angeles Times*, October 5, 1989.

———. "Pop Eye: Riffing on the Grammy." *Los Angeles Times*, October 2, 2005.

———. "Pop Review: Rap-Meets-Rock Concert Marred by Violence." *Los Angeles Times*, December 19, 1988.

Holmes, Steven A. "N.A.A.C.P. Board Dismisses Group's Executive Board." *The New York Times*, August 21, 1994.

Hot, Cool & Vicious, liner notes. Next Plateau Records, 1986.

Idowu, Omoronke. "MTV Wants Their R-A-P!" *The Source*, December 1998.

Isikoff, Michael, and Tracy Thompson. "Getting Too Tough on Drugs." *The Washington Post*, November 4, 1990.

Jackson, Derrick Z. "Injustice, American-Style." *The Boston Globe*, March 1, 2000.

Jackson, Jesse L., Jr. "George Bush's Democrats." *The Nation*, January 22, 2001.

Jenkins, Alan. "See No Evil: Bans on Racial Data Collection Are Thwarting Anti-discrimination Efforts." *The Nation*, June 28, 1999.

Jenkins, Sacha. "Family Matters." *Vibe*, September 2000.

Johnson, Kirk. "A New Generation of Racism Is Seen." *The New York Times*, August 27, 1989.

Jones, Charles E., ed. *The Black Panther (Reconsidered)* (Baltimore: Black Classic Press, 1998).

Jones, James T., IV. "Menace or Martyr? Shakur Says He Gets Bad Rap for Society Ills." *USA Today*, March 29, 1994.

Jones, LeRoi. *Blues People: Negro Music in White America* (New York: William Morrow, 1963).

Jones, Steve. "Can Rap Regain Its Crown?" *USA Today*, June 14, 2007.

Jones, Syl. "Cincinnati: Confederate to the Core." *Star Tribune* (Minneapolis), April 7, 2002.

Kelley, Norman. *The Head Negro in Charge Syndrome: The Dead End of Black Politics* (New York: Nation Books, 2004).

Kenner, Rob. "13 Ways of Looking at a Whiteboy." *Vibe*, July 1999.

Kitwana, Bakari. *The Hip Hop Generation: Young Blacks and the Crisis in African American Culture* (New York: Basic Civitas Books, 2002).

Kopano, Baruti A. "Rap Music as an Extension of the Black Rhetorical Tradition: 'Keepin' It Real.' " *The Western Journal of Black Studies*, December 22, 2002.

Lacayo, Richard. "In Search of a Good Name." *Time*, March 6, 1989.

———. "The New Gay Struggle." *Time*, October 26, 1998.

Lazin, Lauren, writer and director. *Tupac: Resurrection*. Paramount, 2003.

Leland, John, and Farai Chideya. "Rap and Race." *Newsweek*, June 29, 1992.

Lemann, Nicholas. "The Origins of the Underclass, Part 2." *The Atlantic*, July 1986.

Levine, Lawrence W. *Black Culture and Black Consciousness: Afro-American Folk Thought from Slavery to Freedom* (New York: Oxford University Press, 1977).

Levine, Richard. "Charge Against Officer in Stewart Case Is Dropped." *The New York Times*, October 28, 1987.

Light, Alan, ed. *The Vibe History of Hip Hop* (New York: Three Rivers Press, 1999).

Loder, Kurt. "Album Reviews." *Rolling Stone*, September 16, 1982.

Lowery, Mark. "The Rise of the Black Professional Class." *Black Enterprise*, August 1995.

Mackey, Catherine. *Red Wall* (painting), 2005. catherinemackey.com.

Manson, Marilyn. "Columbine: Whose Fault Is It?" *Rolling Stone*, March 28, 1999.

Marriott, Robert. "Resurrection of the Jester King." *The Source*, August 1994.

Marsh, Dave. "Rocking Racism." *Playboy*, March 1990.

Martin, Vivian B. "Sept. 11 in Black and White." *The Hartford Courant*, September 12, 2002.

May, Lee. "See Heavy Losses and Few Gains; Blacks Look Back with Anger at the Reagan Years." *Los Angeles Times*, January 20, 1989.

McAlpin, John P. "Step by Step Papers Show Profiling Grew." Associated Press & Local Wire, December 3, 2000.

McDermott, Terry. "Parent Advisory: Explicit Lyrics; No One Was Ready for N.W.A's 'Straight Outta Compton.' " *Los Angeles Times*, April 14, 2002.

McFadden, Robert D. "3 Youths Are Held on Murder Counts in Queens Attack." *The New York Times*, December 23, 1987.

McHugh, Kathleen. "Videotape Shows Barry Smoking Crack." United Press International, June 28, 1990.

McWhorter, John. "Profiling and Black Victimhood." *Los Angeles Times*, December 2, 2001.

Milloy, Marilyn. "What Jackson Achieved." *Newsday*, July 20, 1988.

Mills, David. "Professor Griff: The Jews Are Wicked." *The Washington Times*, May 22, 1989.

———."Rap on 2 Live Crew; The Obscenity Case: Criminalizing Black Culture." *The Washington Post*, June 17, 1990.

———. "Sister Souljah's Call to Arms." *The Washington Post*, May 13, 1992.

Monroe, Sylvester. "Life in the Hood." *Time*, June 15, 1992.

Moon, Tom. "Sampling or Stealing." *St. Louis Post-Dispatch*, January 24, 1988.

Morgan, Joan. *When Chickenheads Come Home to Roost: My Life as a Hip-Hop Feminist* (New York: Simon & Schuster, 1999).

Morley, Jefferson. "Barry and His City: Crack in the Washington Culture." *The Nation*, February 19, 1990.

Morris, Chris. "TV a Platform for Rappers' Reactions to Riot." *Billboard*, May 16, 1992.

Morris, Chris, Bill Holland, Charlene Orr, Paul Verna, and Ed Christman. "Quayle, Congressmen, L.A. Pols Join 'Cop Killer' Posse." *Billboard*, July 4, 1992.

Muwakkil, Salim. "Racial Profiling Is Bad Policing." *Chicago Tribune*, January 21, 2002.

Neal, Mark Anthony. "Sold Out on Soul." *Popular Music and Society*, September 22, 1997.

"Newspaper: NYPD Training Other Cities How to Spy on Rapper." *MTV News*, March 9, 2004.

"New York Hails Arrival of Mandela." *The Philadelphia Inquirer*, June 21, 1990.

"New York's Prescription for Urban Blight: Hide It Behind a Wall of Decals." *People*, December 12, 1983.

"No to Minority Scholars?" *St. Petersburg Times*, December 17, 1990.

O'Dair, Barbara, ed. *Trouble Girls: The Rolling Stone Book of Women in Rock* (New York: Random House, 1997).

Ogletree, Charles, Jr., and Henry Louis Gates, Jr. "Would a European Diallo Be Dead?" *Los Angeles Times*, March 26, 2000.

Ogunnaike, Lola. "Jay-Z, from Superstar to Suit." *The New York Times*, August 28, 2005.

Osorio, Kim. "Break the Chains: Women Must Free Themselves from Shackles of Hip Hop's Sexism." *Daily News*, November 19, 2006.

Overbea, Luix. "Farrakhan's Dual Message Draws Cheers and Sharp Criticism." *The Christian Science Monitor*, October 9, 1985.

Pablo, Juan. "Bum Rap's." *The Village Voice*, December 17–23, 2003.

———. "Rappers Lament." *The Village Voice*, December 17–23, 2003

Page, Clarence. "My, Oh, My, Look Who's Profiling Now." *Chicago Tribune*, October 3, 2001.

Pear, Robert. "Number of People Living in Poverty Increases in U.S." *The New York Times*, September 25, 2002.

———. "President Reagan Pardons 2 Ex-F.B.I. Officials in 1970's Break-ins." *The New York Times*, April 16, 1981.

Pearson, Hugh. *The Shadow of the Panther: Huey Newton and the Price of Black Power in America* (Reading, Mass.: Addison-Wesley, 1994).

Pike, David F. "Rage in Miami a Warning?" *U.S. News & World Report*, June 2, 1980.

Powell, Kevin. "Enemy Territory." *Vibe*, September 1994.

———. "Mama Said Knock U Out." *Vibe*, September 1995.

———, ed. *Step into a World: A Global Anthology of the New Black Literature* (New York: Wiley and Sons, 2000).

Puente, Teresa. "Latinos Battle for Their Place in History." *Chicago Tribune*, June 5, 1996.

Raab, Selwyn. "Autopsy Finds Bumpurs Was Hit by Two Blasts." *The New York Times*, November 27, 1984.

———. "State Judge Dismisses Indictment of Officer in the Bumpurs Killing." *The New York Times*, April 13, 1985.

"Race and the Florida Vote." *The New York Times*, December 26, 2000.

"Rap—the Power and the Controversy; Chuck D.—the Interview." *Los Angeles Times*, February 4, 1990.

Reed, Adolph, Jr. "The Rise of Louis Farrakhan." *The Nation*, January 21, 1991.

Reeves, Marcus. "Arrested Predicaments." *The Source*, June 1993.

———. "Bad Boy Entertainment: Kickin' Flava in Ya Ear." *The College Entertainment Revue*, September/October 1994.

———. "Barakas: Father and Son Team Up to Unseat Newark Mayor James." *Amsterdam News*, March 26, 1994.

———. "B-Boy Stance: The Old-School Posse Symbolized Fearlessness, Style and an Effortlessly Cool Attitude." *Vibe*, March 2004.

———. "Dogstar Rising." *The Source*, May 1998.

———. "The Fire This Time: Ras Baraka and Angela Brown Make Waves—and Make Moves." *Vibe*, April 1996.

———. "Insane in the Membrane: The Black Movie Anti-hero of the '90s." *The Source*, May 1997.

———. "The Million Man March: A Monumental Event That Sought to Open the Eyes of a Nation." *Vibe*, October 2005.

———. "Sean 'Puffy' Combs: Certified Hitmaker." *The College Entertainment Revue*, March/April 1993.

Reuters. "The Thomas Nomination; Excerpts from Senate's Hearings on the Thomas Nomination." *The New York Times*, October 12, 1991.

Rhea, Shawn E. "The Voice of a Generation." *Black Enterprise*, August 2002.

Richardson, Clem. "Rap's Golden Oldie: It's All 'Breaks' Right for Kurtis Blow." *Daily News*, November 10, 2003.

Ro, Ronin. *Raising Hell: The Reign, Ruin, and Redemption of Run-D.M.C and Jam Master Jay* (New York: Amistad, 2005).

Rodriguez, Luis J. "Turning Youth Gangs Around: Throwaway Kids." *The Nation*, November 21, 1994.

Rodriguez, Richard. "America Discovers AIDS Is Real." *Los Angeles Times*, November 10, 1991.

Romanowski, Patricia, and Holly George-Warren, eds. *Rolling Stone Encyclopedia of Rock & Roll* (New York: Simon & Schuster, 1995).

Rosemary, Bray L. "The Way We Live: An African American Life." *The New York Times*, April 23, 1989.

Rowland, Mark, producer and director. *American Gangster*. Asylum Entertainment, 2006.

Rubin, Mike. "Profits of Rage." *The Village Voice*, July 20, 1999.

Sack, Kevin. "Atlanta Rally Unburdened by Ills of Harlem's." *The New York Times*, September 8, 1998.

Safire, William. "Let's Talk Black Talk." *The New York Times*, April 9, 1984.

Sales, Nancy Jo. "The Mix Master." *New York*, May 10, 1999.

Schruers, Fred. "Survival of the Illest: New Orleans' Master P Builds an Empire from the Underground Up." *Rolling Stone*, November 27, 1999.

Scott, Vernon. "Only Black Show for Blacks." United Press International, March 9, 1994.

Shadid, Anthony. "Urban Decay Is Brewing Trouble in Milwaukee." *Los Angeles Times*, March 10, 1991.

Shakur, Assata. *Assata: An Autobiography* (Westport, Conn.: Lawrence Hill & Company, 1987).

Shapiro, Peter. *Turn the Beat Around: The Secret History of Disco* (New York: Faber and Faber, 2005).

Sheler, Jeffery L. "Budget War; Jobs: It'll 'Be Like Custer's Last Battle.' " *U.S. News & World Report*, March 16, 1981.

Shenon, Philip. "Beat Cuffed Man, Inquiry on Death Finds." *The New York Times*, August 24, 1984.

Simmons, Russell, with Nelson George. *Life and Def: Sex, Drugs, Money, and God* (New York: Random House, 2001).

Simon, Stephanie, and Eric Slater. "Cincinnati Imposes Curfew After 3 Nights of Racial Violence." *Los Angeles Times*, April 13, 2001.

Simpson, Janice C. "Yo! Rap Gets on the Map." *Time*, February 5, 1990.

Sleeper, Jim. "The End of the Rainbow: America's Changing Urban Politics." *The New Republic*, November 1, 1993.

Smith, Vern E., and Matt Bai. "Evil to the End." *Newsweek*, March 8, 1999.

Smith, Vern E., and Sarah Van Boven. "The Itinerant Incendiary." *Newsweek*, September 14, 1998.

Soriano, Cesar G. "The Greaseman Tries to Clear Air." *USA Today*, March 4, 1999.

Spurrier, Jeff. "A Hoofer's Place in History; Before Popping, Posing, Breaking, Hip-Hop, and Even Disco, There Was Locking." *Los Angeles Times*, July 23, 1995.

Sudo, Phill. "A Source of Pride and History; Afro-Centrism." *Scholastic Update*, March 23, 1990.

Swarns, Rachel L. "After Race Conference: Relief, and Doubt Over Whether It Will Matter." *The New York Times*, September 10, 2001.

Tate, Greg. "Hip Hop Nightmare." *Vibe*, October 2001.

———. "Hip Hop Turns 30: Watcha Celebratin' For?" *The Village Voice*, January 5–11, 2005.

————. "A 20-Year Journey: TV's 'Soul Train' Musically Follows the Tracks of Black Cultural Progress." *Chicago Tribune*, June 19, 1994.

Taylor, John. "Are You Politically Correct?" *New York*, January 21, 1991.

Thigpen, David E. *Jam Master Jay: The Heart of Hip-Hop* (New York: Pocket Books, 2003).

Toop, David. *The Rap Attack: African Jive to New York Hip-Hop* (Boston: South End Press, 1984).

"Top Billboard 200." *Billboard*, October 17, 1998.

Touré. "Best Rapper Alive." *The Village Voice*, August 5, 1997.

Valdés, Mimi. "Salt-N-Pepa." In *The Vibe History of Hip Hop*, ed. Alan Light.

————. "The Sound of the Music." *Vibe*, September 2003.

"The Voice of a Generation." *Black Enterprise*, August 2002.

Walters, Ron. "The First Generation of Black Mayors." *Washington Informer*, November 26, 1997.

Watkins, S. Craig. *Hip Hop Matters: Politics, Pop Culture, and the Struggle for the Soul of a Movement* (Boston: Beacon Press, 2005).

Weaver, Maurice. " 'Soul Train' Awards Are a 1st for Black Music." *Chicago Tribune*, March 23, 1987.

Weingarten, Marc. "Large and in Charge; Rap Hasn't Merely Survived the Shocking Deaths of Hip-Hop Leaders Tupac Shakur and Notorious B.I.G. It's Thriving Now, Thanks to Fresh Infusion from Today's Masterminds." *Los Angeles Times*, July 26, 1998.

Welcome to Death Row. Directed by S. Leigh Savidge and Jeff Scheftel. Written by Jeff Scheftel. Produced by Jeff Scheftel and Stephen A. Housden. Xenon Pictures, 2001.

White, Allen. "Reagan's AIDS Legacy." *San Francisco Chronicle*, June 8, 2004.

White, Nicole, and Evelyn McDonnell. "Police Secretly Watching Hip-Hop Artists." *The Miami Herald*, March 9, 2004.

Williams, Lena. "Growing Debate on Racism: When Is It Real, When an Excuse?" *The New York Times*, April 5, 1992.

Wimsatt, William Upski. *Bomb the Suburbs* (New York: Soft Skull Press, 1994).

Wolfe, Tom. *Radical Chic & Mau-Mauing the Flak Catchers* (New York: Farrar, Straus and Giroux, 1970).

Woodard, Komizi. *A Nation Within a Nation: Amiri Baraka (LeRoi Jones) & Black Power Politics* (Chapel Hill: The University of North Carolina Press, 1999).

Yardley, Jim. "An Island Sees No Racism." *The New York Times*, September 14, 1998.

Zeleny, Michael J., Michael J. Berens, and Geoff Dougherty. "Still Too Close to Call." *Chicago Tribune*, November 12, 2001.

Interviews

Conducted by Toni Judkins (from VH1): Big Bank Hank for *Classic Soul*, 2004.

Conducted by Toni Judkins (from VH1): Run-D.M.C. for *All Star Jams*, 2004.

Conducted by Marcus Reeves: Public Enemy, DMX, Christopher "Notorious B.I.G." Wallace, Sean Combs, Afeni Shakur, Bill Adler.

Acknowledgments

First, I have to thank the legends whose visions were the foundation for this work: the Godfather, James Brown, whose bold spirit, music, and leadership were the muse and inspiration for this book. Also, George Clinton and Parliament-Funkadelic for showing me my place in the galaxy at a time when I was searching in all the wrong places.

To the hip-hop pioneers: DJ Kool Herc, Afrika Bambaataa, Grandmaster Flash & the Furious Five, the Rock Steady Crew, and Run-D.M.C. (thanks for answering those e-mails).

To my family and my family of friends whose love and support got me over the humps: my brother Kyle Reeves, my sister, Rhonda Reeves, my brother-in-law, Salah Ismail, and my aunt Beatrice Belous. To my brother from another mother, Turhan Ali Welch, and the Welch family (Mom and Pop Welch, Girard, Regina, and Vincent). My Rutgers family: James Austin Jones, Esq., and Karenga Arifu. And a special thanks to my spiritual mother: Leonora Brazell-Rafua.

To my family who go beyond the term "in-law" with their love and support: Joyce Idowu, Derin Young, Tunde Idowu, and Joy Idowu.

To the DJs who've mattered greatly to this and other work: Toriono "RPGeez" Gandy, DJ Kaleem, and Bobbito Garcia (Cucumber Slice).

A huge shout-out to the publications that gave me the freedom and the platform to say something: *The Source, The College Entertainment Revue, Vibe*, and *The Village Voice*.

Thanks to those editors, writers, and others who helped me along that journey: Tricia Rose, Deborah Smith, Edward Riley, Matty C (Matt Life), Reginald C. Dennis, Selwyn Seyfu Hinds, Todd S. Burroughs, Herb Boyd, Sheena Lester, Lisa Kennedy, Evette Porter, Natasha Stovall, Angela Ards, Nathan Brackett, Anthony Bozza, Ann Powers, Joe Wood (R.I.P.), Leroy Wilson (R.I.P.), Jabari Asim, Oscar Villalon, OJ Lima,

Alan Light, Rob Kenner, Laura Checkoway, Dave Cohen, Bill Adler, Kevin Powell, Nia-Malika Henderson, Candace Sandy, Dawn Marie Daniels, Dimitry Leger, Nelson George, Eric Weisbard, and Jeanine Amber.

And a huge thanks to the folks who helped take this book from idea to reality: Cheo Hodari Coker; Ayesha Pande; my agent, Manie Barron; and my editor, Denise Oswald.

Index

Cheney, Lynne, 259
Chicago, 5, 14, 42, 48, 93, 138, 157
Chicago Tribune, 5, 121
"Chick on the Side" (Salt-N-Pepa), 122
Chief Rocker Busy Bee, 18
Chisholm, Shirley, 48
"Chocolate City" (Parliament), 12
Christgau, Robert, 45
Chronic, The (Dr. Dre), 139–43, 146–47,
    148, 150, 153, 181, 199
Chuck D, 57, 63–65, 68–91, 101, 103,
    124, 138, 198
church, black, 130, 149, 150
CIA (Criminals in Action), 98
Cincinnati, 241
Citizen Change, 266, 270
City College concert stampede (1991),
    184
"City Is Mine, The" (Jay-Z), 207
Civil Rights Act (1964), 4, 43
Civil Rights Act (1990), 85–86
civil rights movement, 4–5, 8, 10, 13, 28,
    45, 49, 131, 219, 233; white conserva-
    tive backlash against, 23, 31–33, 42,
    43, 73, 84, 86
Clark, Dick, 51
Clash, 34
"Cleanin Out My Closet" (Eminem),
    262
Cleaver, Eldridge, 172
Clinton, Bill, 135, 143–45, 164, 194, 213–
    14, 219, 251, 258; 1992 presidential
    campaign, 143–45, 194; -Souljah feud,
    144–45
Clinton, George, 12, 18, 34, 35, 41, 141–
    42, 159
clothes, *see* fashion
Cobain, Kurt, 251
Cochran, Johnnie, 218
COINTELPRO, 10–12, 14, 23, 31, 32,
    159, 272
Coker, Cheo Hodari, 163, 190; *The Vibe
    History of Hip Hop*, 101–102
Cold Crush Brothers, 18, 22, 44
"Cold Lampin' with Flavor" (P.E.), 77
Colors (film), 113
Columbine High School massacre, 254–
    55

Combs, Janice, 181, 182
Combs, "Pretty" Melvin, 181–82
Combs, Sean "Puffy," *see* Puff Daddy
"Come and Get Me" (Jay-Z), 215–16
"Come and Talk to Me" (Jodeci), 184
"Coming From" (DMX), 235
Common, 187
Compton, California, 96–115, 188
Compton's Most Wanted, 111
computerized music, 33–34
Congress, 43, 105, 194, 195, 258; 1994
    gangsta rap hearings, 151–52;
    Thomas-Hill hearings, 131–32; 2000
    hearings on violence and entertain-
    ment, 259
Connerly, Ward, 209
conservatism, 118, 151, 259; of 1980s, 28,
    31–33, 42, 48–49, 68, 73, 84, 126
Conservative Vice Lords, 8
"Convo, The" (DMX), 231
Cooper, Alice, 252
"Cop Killer" (Ice-T), 145–46, 161
copyright infringement, 78
Cornelius, Don, 5
corporate control of rap, 149–53, 173,
    203–204, 213, 216, 220, 222, 262
country music, 211
crack, 32, 54–55, 68, 87, 89, 94, 95, 97,
    103, 106–107, 158, 164, 182, 187, 188,
    190, 191, 198, 205, 225, 238
crime, *see* violence and crime
"Criminal" (Eminem), 257
Crips, 15, 95, 111, 115, 138, 140
Cristal, 216
Cross Colours, 193
Crown Heights riot (1991), 88–89
Cuda, Heidi Siegmund, 231
culture wars, 125–26, 128, 129, 134, 150,
    153
cutting, 29
Cypress Hill, 111

Dallas, 145–46
"Damien" (DMX), 231
dance styles, 6–8, 17, 147; boogaloo, 7–8;
    breaking, 17, 44, 60, 67; disco, 24–25;
    late 1980s, 67; locking, 7; popping, 7;

Dynamic Breakers, 53
Dynasty: Roc la Familia, The (Jay-Z), 216

Earth, Wind & Fire, 25
East/West rap war, 94–96, 105, 111, 141, 172–75, 180–81, 187–88, 195–201, 211, 215, 227
East Long Beach, California, 140
Easy Mo Bee, 200
Eazy-Duz-It (Eazy-E), 100–101, 107
Eazy-E, 93, 94–115, 123, 143, 175, 251
Ecko, Marc, 193
Economist, The, 53
economy, 240; Clinton-era upturn, 213–14, 219, 239; dot-com bust, 241; post-9/11, 242
education, 12, 16, 68, 105–106, 149, 219, 233, 269, 274; Bakke decision, 23; ban on affirmative action, 209; of early 1980s, 32; racial and sexual incidents of college campuses, 84, 126
"8 Ball" (Eazy-E), 102
8 Mile (film), 245–47, 262
Eiht, MC, 111
Electric Boogaloo, 7–8
electrofunk rap, 33–35
Elijah, Muhammad, 71, 74
Elliott, Missy "Misdemeanor," 136
Elrick, M. L., "Eminem's Dirty Secrets," 250
EMI, 204
Eminem, 217, 245–68; acting career, 245–47, 262; anti-Bush politics, 266–67; celebrity of, 255, 256; childhood of, 249–50; Dre and, 251, 252, 254, 260, 261; *The Eminem Show*, 260–62; *Encore*, 265, 267; homophobia and censorship issues, 258–60; image of, 250–51, 252, 260–61; *Infinite*, 250; *Love Me Tender*, 262; *The Marshall Mathers LP*, 245, 255–60; Slim Shady attitude, 251–54, 256, 261, 268; *Slim Shady LP*, 251–54, 257; *Source* feud, 263–65, 268; views on women, 257–58
Eminem Show, The, 260–62
"Encore" (Jay-Z), 221
Encore (Eminem), 265, 267

Enjoy Records, 28, 29
Enron, 240
Enter the Wu-Tang (Wu-Tang Clan), 188
En Vogue, 134
EPMD, 112, 113, 184
"Eric B. Is President" (Eric. B and Rakim), 56, 67
escapism, 24, 25, 30, 33, 35, 58, 106
Europe, 21; New Wave, 34
Everlast, 155
"Everyday Struggle" (Notorious B.I.G.), 191
"E-Vette's Revenge" (E-Vette Money), 119
"Expression" (Salt-N-Pepa), 128
"Express Yourself" (Madonna), 106, 128

Fab Five Freddy, 34, 80, 105, 157
Fad, J. J., 123
"Fame" (DMX), 238
family, black, 149
Fantastic Five, 18, 39
Farrakhan, Louis, 49, 53, 72, 74–76, 87, 169, 171, 233
fashion, 6, 182; DMX, 224; drugs and, 55, 87; early-to-mid-1970s, 6; early-to-mid-1980s, 34, 41, 55; gangsta, 149–50; ghetto fab, 192–93, 215; hip-hop clothing lines, 193, 215; Jay-Z, 208, 210, 215, 216, 222; of 1990s, 87, 149, 192–93; Notorious B.I.G., 177, 178, 192–93; Public Enemy, 71; Puff Daddy, 192–93; ruffian hip-hop, 192; Run-D.M.C., 41, 45, 46, 47, 50, 55, 56, 59; Salt-N-Pepa, 121, 124, 128
Fat Albert and the Cosby Kids (TV show), 6
Fatback Band, 21–22
Fat Boys, 53, 58
fatherless black children, 134, 186
Father MC, 184
Fat Joe, 219
Fear of a Black Planet (P.E.), 64, 81, 85
Federal Bureau of Investigation (FBI), 10–12, 31, 104–107; COINTELPRO operations, 10–12, 14, 23, 31, 32, 159, 272

Mays, David, 80, 263–65, 273

MC, 18, 30, 62; Bad Nigga archetype, 62; of early-to-mid-1980s, 29–31, 33, 34–36, 40, 45, 52, 62; female, 117–36; of mid-late 1990s, 149, 153, 173, 178, 180–81, 187–88, 208; of twenty-first century, 224, 234, 243, 246, 247; white, 245–48; *see also specific MCs*

McDaniels, Ralph, 192

McDuffie, Arthur, 27

McGee, Michael, 108–109

McGrath, Judy, 259

McKinney, Aaron, 258

Me Against the World (Tupac), 169–70, 196

medallions, 87

media, 6–8, 33, 125, 147, 234; on black men behaving badly, 134–35; on DMX, 223–24, 227, 232, 238; on Dre-Snoop team, 143, 147, 150–53; on Eminem, 245–46, 247, 254, 263–65, 267; gays represented in, 258–60; hip-hop, 48, 80, 147, 158, 187, 193–94, 203, 223–24, 247, 263–65, 273; on Hurricane Katrina, 274; on Jay-Z, 220; on late 1990s black prosperity, 213–14; on N.W.A, 101–102, 104–107, 110–11; on Notorious B.I.G., 177, 188, 189, 200; on Public Enemy, 64, 75–76, 80, 81, 82, 88, 90; on Puff Daddy, 178, 185, 201, 213; on Run-D.M.C., 45, 47, 48, 57–61, 73; *Soul Train*, 5–8; on Tupac, 155, 156, 158, 162, 171, 172, 175, 196; *Vibe* debut, 147; violence in, 255; *see also* radio; *specific publications*; television

Meek, Kendrick, 194

Melle Mel, 36

Memphis, 24, 79

Menace II Society (film), 114, 156

Mercedes Ladies, 119

Mercury Records, 26

"Message, The" (Grandmaster Flash & the Furious Five), 27, 36–37, 39, 188

Metallica, 251

Method Man, 190, 195

Miami, 27, 128, 216, 272

Michigan, 246–47, 249–50

"Mickey" (Toni Basil), 7

middle class, black, 13, 24, 27, 75

Miller, Edward S., 31

Million Man March (1995), 171, 233

Million Youth Movement (1998), 233–34

Mills, David, 144

Milwaukee, 108–109, 167

Miseducation of Lauryn Hill, The, 203

misogyny in hip-hop, 77, 85, 88, 103, 110–11, 119, 125–26, 127–28, 148–53, 165–68, 174, 255–57, 272–73, 275

Mobb Deep, 173, 187, 195, 217

"Moment of Clarity" (Jay-Z), 221

"Mo Money Mo Problems" (Notorious B.I.G.), 199

"Money, Cash, Hoes" (Jay-Z), 211

Money, E-Vette, 119

"Money Ain't a Thang" (Jay-Z), 211, 228

moonwalking, 7, 8

Moore, Melba, 151

M.O.P. (Mash Out Posse), 229

"More 2 a Song" (DMX), 239

Morgan, Joan, 272

Moseley Braun, Carol, 133, 151–52, 259

"Mosh" (Eminem), 266–67

Motown, 44

Mount Vernon, New York, 182

MOVE, 54

movies, 7, 44, 67, 94, 203; black stereotypes in, 85, 94, 114; blaxploitation, 52, 77, 114, 189; Eminem in, 245–47, 262; hip-hop, 44, 51–52; 'hood, 113–14, 149; of 1980s, 44, 51–52, 63–64, 81, 85; of 1990s, 113–14; Spike Lee Joints, 63–64, 81, 85; Tupac in, 156, 157, 158, 162, 164; of twenty-first century, 245–47

MP Da Last Don, 212

Mr. Magic, 70, 76, 85

Mr. T, 42

Mtume, James, 78, 191

MTV, 43, 138, 242; censorship issues, 105, 259–60; early racial policies, 48; Eminem controversy, 254, 259–60; rap on, 48, 50, 80, 104, 143, 193, 259–60; 2000 Video Music Awards, 259–60; *see also* videos, music

Murphy, Eddie, 42, 49